OUR WAR

Christopher Somerville is a well-known journalist and broadcaster, and a prolific author. His grandfather was wartime leader Admiral of the Fleet Sir James Somerville, and both his parents served with the Royal Navy during the Second World War.

OUR WAR

How the British Commonwealth Fought the Second World War

CHRISTOPHER SOMERVILLE

CASSELL

Cassell Military Paperbacks

Cassell
Wellington House, 125 Strand
London WC2R 0BB

1 3 5 7 9 10 8 6 4 2

Copyright © 1998 Christopher Somerville

First published in 1998
by Weidenfeld & Nicolson
This Cassell Military Paperbacks edition 2005

British Library Cataloguing-in-Publication Data.
A catalogue record for this book is available
from the British Library.

ISBN 0 304 36717 6

Printed and bound in Great Britain by
Clays Ltd, St Ives plc

www.orionbooks.co.uk

To the staff of the British Commonwealth
Ex-Services League in London, and to the
officials of welfare organisations all
over the world, who care for the
ex-servicemen and women of the
Commonwealth with such dedication
and good humour.

CONTENTS

ILLUSTRATIONS

Section two

Indians unloading truck[1]
Nila Kantan today[2]
Indians laying rail[1]
Two Tobruk Aussies[1]
Vernon Northwood then and now[2]
Two New Guinea Aussies[1]
Phil Rhoden then and now[2]
Australian troops in New Guinea[1]
2nd Lt. S. K. Anthony[1]
Frank Sexwale
Frank Seswale today
West African soldiers in the Kaladan Valley, north-west Burma[1]
Cassino, Italy[1]
Paul Gobine today[2]
Indian stretcher bearers at Cassino[1]
New Zealand gunners fire on Cassino[1]
Connie Macdonald with bike[1]
Connie Mark today
Sheila Parkinson with jeep
Sheila Parkinson today[2]

Section three

Tom Somerville, New Zealand –
– in the British War Cemetery in Alexandria
– at the summit of the Great Pyramid, Egypt, 1941
– after Anzac Day parade, 1997
'Dusky' Sinyinde, a South African balloon operator, amuses RAF
    colleagues[1]
West Indian ATS volunteers taking tea and biscuits[1]
A V1 explodes near Drury Lane[1]
British prisoners-of-war sweep the streets of Singapore, February 1942[1]
Allied prisoners-of-war are liberated, Fallingbostel, Germany, April 1945[1]
At Belsen[1]
Krishen Tewari and Salim Yazdani, Kuala Lumpur, 1945
Krishen Tewari today, Aurobille in south-east India[2]

Balwant Singh Bahia
Balwant Singh Bahia today[2]
Al-Haji Abdul Aziz Brimah[2]
Nana Kofi Genfi II[2]
John Mumo[2]
Mutili Musoma[2]
VE day in London, 8 May 1945[1]

Sources

[1] © The Imperial War Museum
[2] © Author's Collection

MAPS

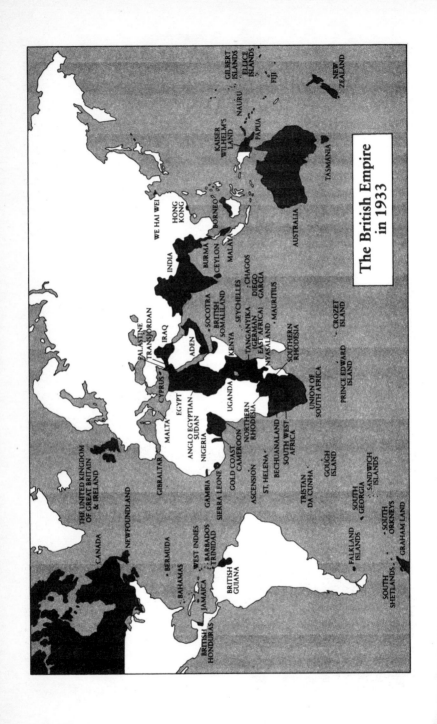

The British Empire
in 1933

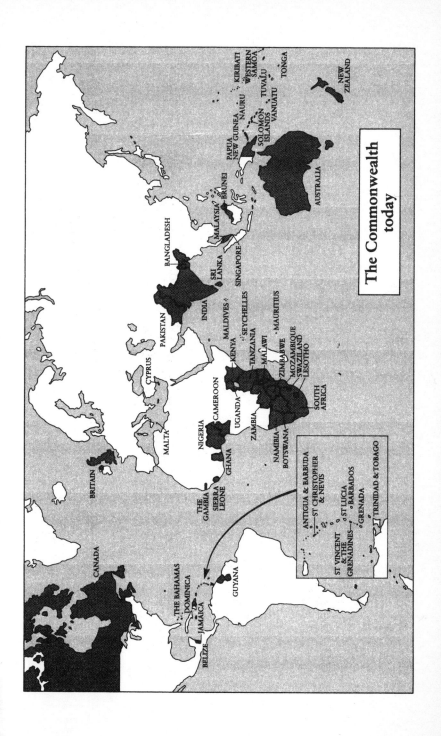

The Commonwealth today

INTRODUCTION

'Antigua ... Barbados ... Cameroon ... Dominica ...' Dozens of square white placards, bobbing under the trees along Birdcage Walk. 'Fiji ... Ghana ... Kenya ... Lesotho ...' A roll-call of Empire in the heart of London, to the thump and blare of military bands. 'Mauritius ... St Lucia ... Trinidad and Tobago ... Turks and Caicos ...'

Under the placards the sun winked on cap badges and medals, and on brass cuff buttons, carefully shined, rising and falling as their owners marched past towards Buckingham Palace. Some marched with chests out and heads up, keeping step; others shuffled along, limping and puffing, or were trundled by in wheelchairs. On this hot August morning in 1995, under berets and regimental headgear, hundreds of elderly faces trickled with sweat, and with tears.

The onlookers stood five and six deep along the roadway. Fifty years ago there had been crowds here in London, at the centre of the great British web of Commonwealth, applauding some of these same marchers. Back then, on VJ Day 1945, they had cheered the young men and women in their chaotic flush of celebration of victory over Japan, and the final slamming of the door on the war they had all been fighting. Now the crowds, stimulated by enormous newspaper, radio and television coverage of these never-to-be-repeated events, were cheering the wrinkled faces and stepping out into the roadway to shake the thin-skinned hands of these grandfathers and grandmothers in their kaftans and blazers, berets and head-dresses, flown in from the five continents and the scattered ocean communities of the world for one last gathering in the little island off north-west Europe that had once mothered them all.

What lay behind the tear-streaked cheeks, the surprisingly unsmiling faces of the marchers, few of the onlookers could guess. The veterans had kept their own counsel all too well. Very few had ever sat down with their children and told them what had really happened, what they had actually seen and done in the jungles of Burma or the prison camps of Poland and Borneo, in the wadis of the Western Desert, in the night sky over Berlin, out among the Mediterranean islands or in the North Atlantic Ocean. The old taboo on 'being a bore about the war' forbade it. Those who were there would know. As for those who were not, they'd never understand. They'd be bored, or pruriently greedy for horrors that were better left with the trapdoor shut on them. A generation – the veterans' own children – had grown up and grown middle-aged with only a shadowy notion, at best, of the world-shaking events that had shaken their parents' lives to the very roots. Few schools in the post-war years had bothered with the Second World War – such recent history – as a serious subject for study.

One veteran, a former bomber pilot with the RAF, died shortly after being interviewed for this book. At his funeral service it came out that he had never spoken a word about his war experiences to his own family. The tape-recording of his interview – a perceptive, bulldog account of seventy operations over Germany – had been his first and last testimony of war.

There has never been a mobilisation of peoples, in the history of the world, comparable to that during the Second World War. About five million men and women from the countries of the British Commonwealth saw wartime service; about six million from Great Britain itself. One hundred and seventy thousand Commonwealth servicemen and women died or went missing; 260,000 Britons. Eleven million people came together under the same flag. Not necessarily for the glory, the honour or even the survival of the Union Jack: many did join up for reasons of the purest patriotism, but more gave their services with motives that were mixed. Most of them were volunteers, ordinary people, joining in as and when they could during the six years that the war lasted. Some had to overcome, or disregard, family disapproval; some wrestled with their consciences, wondering if this was their war or Britain's, a global response to a deadly threat or a white man's colonialist exercise. Many disapproved greatly of British policies or presence in their countries; their disapproval would take sharp political shape after the war and lead very rapidly to the flight from the colonial nest of all but a few of the old Empire's dependencies. The war shook the lives of individuals; it also shook the British Commonwealth to pieces, or rather, it blew the fragments of the disintegrated Empire into a modern Commonwealth shape, an organism that newly forming countries would become eager to join, rather than to leave.

Part of the story of the British Commonwealth in the Second World War took place in a climate of stark racial prejudice. In one quarter at least, black men were not even permitted to lie as corpses alongside the white corpses of their fellow men, let alone to receive equal levels of pay or promotion while still alive. Some were issued with spears and clubs, rather than rifles and grenades. Some volunteers plotted to be free of the men they fought alongside; others were received with wonder and admiration in homes ten thousand miles from their own, or were inspected furtively on Indian river banks to see if they had tails, or were paraded on freezing English barrack squares until sullen and mutinous. Some won medals and found glory; others were sacrificed, they felt, as 'foreign fodder' in hopeless ventures. Many now hold strong opinions, on both sides of the fence, about the British as former colonial rulers and as contemporary Commonwealth 'equal partners'. Very few made a full disclosure to their families or friends of what the war had done to them, or how they felt about having survived it. Very few came wholly unscathed out of the war.

They would not want to be acclaimed as heroes, or as anything more than ordinary people who did their best under extraordinary circumstances. Here, brought together for the first time and told largely in their own words, is the story of these now elderly adventurers – their very ordinary and very extraordinary story.

PART ONE
BEFORE THE GUN

ONE

Belonging

British? Yes! Why not? We felt proud of being in with the
British – we felt British!   Kofi Genfi II, Gold Coast

On 30 January 1933 Adolf Hitler became Chancellor of Germany . . .

Kofi ('Born-on-a-Friday') Genfi was eighteen years old, a skinny African youth about to finish his schooling at Primary Standard 7. There were few opportunities for secondary education in Kumasi, the capital of the Asante kingdom at the heart of Britain's West African colony of the Gold Coast. The houses of Kumasi were mud-brick, with thatched roofs: you could walk from one end of the city to the other in half an hour. The Asante and the British had fought six more or less bloody wars during the nineteenth century, ending when the British razed Kumasi and sent Prempeh, the young Asante king, into exile in the Seychelles. In 1924 Kofi Genfi had been in the crowd on the streets of Kumasi to welcome home the newly restored king. The following year he was out again to greet Edward, Prince of Wales, when his royal tour came through the town: 'Oh yes, everyone came on the street to see the Prince of Wales. Chief

Commissioner, all the paramount chiefs with their retinues – all should be in Kumasi. A very high welcome. Kumasi was completely full; people were sleeping on the pavement. I hadn't then attended school – I was a very young boy of ten–eleven, waving my flag at the Prince.'

In Accra, capital of the Gold Coast, nine-year-old Aziz Brimah was growing up. His father, Chief Brimah III, was a prosperous cola-nut trader, and a chief of the long-established Muslim community in Accra and the surrounding region.

I grew up in a society of chieftaincy, of very serious traders. We were rather born with a golden spoon in our mouths. We practised the British habit of eating with a knife and fork, although in other ways it was a strict Muslim upbringing. Almost all of us were sent to school, girls included – there was no purdah in our house. At home, let us say, I was taught the Islamic tradition – at school we were taught the British tradition and a wider education to fit us to communicate with the outside world.

After all this we felt we were British, that we were safe under the British administration. That is why, when they requested help for the British in Abyssinia, in Burma, we surrendered ourselves and went.

The British first settled in the Gold Coast in the late sixteenth century. Gold and slaves were their main preoccupation until the nineteenth century. Then, parallel with attempts to quell the self-assertive Asante with whom they had never been able to come to terms, the British tried to place local people from the more docile coastal tribes into administration positions – chiefly, it seems, because whites could not stay alive on the fever-ridden Coast long enough to do the job themselves. In the 1880s most such posts were held by locals. By the time young Kofi Genfi was waving his Union Jack at the Prince of Wales, half a century on, medical science had leaped forward sufficiently for whites not only to survive, but to prosper. Now they held twenty times as many senior posts as did blacks. Increased 'Africanisation' was an issue, but only a nascent one as yet. It would take a world war to turn that situation on its head, once and for all.

The Gold Coast had a fundamental connection with another British colony – Jamaica. Many Jamaicans could trace their ancestry back to slaves brought to the West Indies plantations from the Gold Coast. By 1933 plenty of Jamaicans were dissatisfied with their lot: universal suffrage was still a decade away, and there were widespread economic problems linked to the great world trade depression. But for the majority of the islanders, Jamaica's status as a British colony was still a source of pride and satisfaction.

Dudley Thompson was sixteen years old in January 1933 – a bright boy being raised in a rural part of the island. Both his parents were teachers, keen for their son to get a good start and make something of himself. Soon young Dudley would be off to teacher training college; by 1940, with hard work and a bit of luck, he might hope to have his foot on the ladder of promotion.

Colonial days – few people are old enough now to remember what it was like, but I remember quite clearly. Living as a colony we were quite happy. We had very little knowledge of the outside world; we felt very secure, in an international way, though we knew nothing about it. We were very well looked after – we lived in a sort of ignorance, but happy. We had a peace of mind.

England was the mother country. You felt that you had protection. We were *proud* of being part of the Commonwealth, or Empire as it was – we were very proud of it. We felt proud to look on the map and see all these places painted red: big Australia, big India, rich Burma – little Jamaica! We felt proud to have the same colour, to be a family of nations. We felt proud that we had huge battleships like the *Hood*, which was the best in the world. We accepted all of the British traditions. We felt *safe*.

The hierarchy went something like this. The Governor lived at King's House. From King's House the next step would be Buckingham Palace; and the next step above Buckingham Palace was the gates of Heaven itself!

Connie Macdonald was growing up in Kingston, Jamaica's capital, and had just celebrated her ninth birthday. Her grandfather had been a Macdonald from Scotland, her grandmother a black Jamaican and descendant of slaves. Her father worked for the railways, and was giving Connie a decent middle-class Methodist upbringing, with piano lessons and a good school to which she was taken by her nurse. A maid did the housework and there was a man to look after the garden.

We were *British*! We were proud to be British. We didn't want to be anything *but* British. England was our mother country. We were brought up to respect the Royal Family. I used to collect pictures of Margaret and Elizabeth, you know? I adored them.

It was the British influence – what other influence have I had? We didn't grow up with any Jamaican thing – we grew up as British.

Canada was Britain's oldest self-governing colony – the term 'Dominion' had been in use since 1907. During the nineteenth century Canada, with its Celtic climate and topography as well as its geographical position, had been a natural magnet for Scottish and Irish people emigrating from their own poverty-stricken, famine-blighted lands.

Out on the Pacific coast, thirteen-year-old Glen Niven was at boarding-school on Vancouver Island in January 1933. Glen's father had been an adventurer, who in his youth had 'wandered around the Arctic with a dog sled, probably selling whisky to the Indians!' Now, pursuing a more conventional army career, he had been posted to the island with his family, a comfortable life in a big house. Glen's mother, born in Scotland, had been one of those British brides who were taken out to the Dominions and colonies by returning First World War servicemen. She was deter-mined, says Glen, to keep her family firmly in touch with the Old Country.

We were very Scottish in our upbringing. We learned Scottish country dancing, that sort of thing. At the Highland Games in Victoria we saw Highland regiments wearing kilts. There was Burns Night – it was all terribly Scots, terribly British. Everyone said, 'I'm going home for the holidays. I'm writing home, I've heard from home.' It was *home*. You saluted the flag and sang 'God Save The King' at the drop of a hat. We were more patriotic, I think, than half of Britain.

Other Canadians whose origins lay in the Celtic fringe of Britain felt differently. Frank O'Donnell was just seven years old, a bright, restless child, son of a bank manager from Pipestone, Manitoba. Frank would go on to enter High School aged ten – 'extraordinarily young. I was a little too big for my britches' – and would eventually run away from home at sixteen to join the Army.

As a family we didn't celebrate a lot of Irish tradition; we might do in passing, but we really thought of ourselves as more Canadian. I don't know that we had a particularly British or Irish connection, because by that time my mother's family had been in the country for, I think, two generations, and my Dad's family was deeply rooted here. I suppose that our name itself was the biggest Irish tradition we had.

We didn't follow Irish politics; we did follow British politics, more so, through the newspapers and the radio. I suppose we knew who de Valera was. At school, of course, we were taught mainly British history. We'd sing songs like 'The Days of Yore for Britain', or 'Wolfe the Dauntless Hero Came'.

Geraldine Turcotte, a sixteen-year-old with flame-red Irish hair and a temperament to match, spent her childhood in the Ontario logging town of Sturgeon Falls, not far from the north shore of Georgian Bay on Lake Huron, where her father worked on an 'alligator' towing logs to the planing mills. 'Turcotte sounds French, doesn't it? But my grandfather rode the white horse on 12 July every year, to celebrate King Billy and the Battle of the Boyne, so he surely wasn't French! His family was from Belfast. But we were Canadians, there was no doubt about that. We were just surrounded by Canadians. I wouldn't say that we felt at all British.'

There was no question of feeling British, either, for Wilmer Nadjiwon, five years Geraldine's junior, who was growing up on the Cape Croker Indian reservation on the far side of Georgian Bay. Members of his tribe, the Ojibwe, had concluded a peace treaty with the Canadian government in 1854 which had seen them concentrated into reservations and persuaded to give up their traditional hunting and fishing.

> The religious denominations started to come in – one of them was the Wesleyan faith – and they used to teach that a good farmer is a good Christian. So this is how they sold us the idea and we all got to be farmers. Then the Methodists came in, the Catholics came in. In no time at all there were three religions operating; and then there was the Indians' own faith, the Great Spirit. Orangemen came in – I don't know where in the hell they came from; part Irishmen or something. It tore the people apart. A tribe is a unit, not a split faction. The people in a tribe stay within a unit, operate by the same rules. As soon as religion comes in it divides them.
>
> My mother, I think she was the daughter of a British immigrant. Her name was Penn. I don't know how she ever got on the reservation, where she met my dad, but they raised a big family – there was eleven of us. My dad was native Indian; he was a counsellor for many, many years and he was Chief for one term.
>
> The tribe never wanted to be British – they never wanted to be white. They wanted to be tribe. Even the mixed-blood, like myself – I want to be Indian, I don't want to be identified outside that.

Across the world in New Zealand there were plenty of Scots too. The two New Zealand islands, remote at the southern end of the world between the Pacific Ocean and the Tasman Sea, had taken their share of Celts from nineteenth-century Britain. Jim Tait's parents were both New Zealand born, but his father came of a line of Shetland Islanders, while his mother was a Highlander of the Gordon clan. Jim, at fourteen, was getting a very

British schooling: 'I felt very much a New Zealander, but it was part of the way we were brought up and educated that all the history taught to us at school was English history. I mean, I can still just about recite the dates of the kings and queens from 1066 on – I might get mixed up a bit with the Henrys around about the 1300s! We did learn a bit of basic New Zealand history, but not a great deal.'

In a bush area of the Upper Hutt valley north of Wellington, Tom Somerville had just turned seventeen. Tom's father worked in a sawmill there; his grandfather had come out to New Zealand from Somerset in England during the late nineteenth century, in order to repair the family's dented fortunes. Tom and his brothers and sisters had been brought up simply enough, as self-reliant Kiwi bush children; but on their minds, too, the Old Country threw a powerful image. 'Oh, England was always the mother country to us. I remember in the little country school that we went to, with about five kids in it, I sang a song in a concert: "You Gentlemen of England". We always had a great respect for the Old Country, though it was always a far-off place to me.'

Before another ten years were up, all these young people would be plunged into war. Kofi Genfi and Aziz Brimah joined the Gold Coast Regiment and suffered the miseries of the Burmese jungle while fighting the Japanese. Dudley Thompson found himself belly-down in a Lancaster of 49 Squadron, unloading bombs on German cities. Connie Macdonald was to spend her days working in Kingston's military hospital and some of her nights down at the pier receiving wounded men from the troopships. Glen Niven would pilot a Spitfire in the tail-end of the Battle of Britain and later over occupied France. Geraldine Turcotte was to serve overseas with the air forces too, experiencing the horrors of the V1 and V2 rocket bombardment of London. Wilmer Nadjiwon, as an artilleryman in the Perth Regiment, fought his way up through the Italian peninsula. Tom Somerville would be in Italy with the artillery too, having served his gun in the retreat through Greece and in the North African desert at El Alamein. And Jim Tait, as a destroyer officer and then a submariner, would serve in, on and under the Mediterranean and North Atlantic seas.

In 1933 the British Empire and Commonwealth comprised about a quarter of the world's population and nearly a quarter of its land surface. 'Empire', with its overtones of domination and submission, was by now becoming a less than acceptable term, especially to the already largely autonomous 'white Dominions' of Australia, New Zealand, Canada and Newfoundland, South Africa and the Irish Free State. 'Empire and Commonwealth' was a rather cumbersome mouthful, but it did point neatly to a distinction between the Commonwealth of the Dominions and the Empire of the other dependencies – which, crucially for the future of this agglomeration of British-influenced and British-flavoured countries, included India.

India, the jewel in the crown, was the paramount symbol of the power and pride of Imperial Britain. At the same time, in 1933, it stood for everything that was uncertain, shaky and unresolved about the future of the British Empire and Commonwealth. How the British had managed to hold it all together for so long is hard to explain. Hindus and Muslims despised and distrusted each other; the caste system separated men from men more rigorously even than the British class system; maharajahs, rajahs and nawabs exerted their own authority to a greater or lesser degree over their dozens of princedoms; 222 separate languages were each spoken by more than a million people. Since the First World War, a figure had emerged round whom the growing nationalist and independence movements could coalesce their aims: the rake-thin, ascetic, bespectacled Mahatma Gandhi. Gandhi's *satyagraha* or Force of Truth campaign of non-violent protest and civil disobedience had developed a rapier point, digging away at both the conscience and the pragmatism of British politicians.

If the British had been slow to wake up, they were becoming keen to get on with 'Indianisation' – the taking over by Indians, from the European expatriates, of the upper echelons of the Indian Civil Service and the Indian Army. A half-Indian Civil Service was envisaged by 1939, a half-Indian police force by 1949, a half-Indian Army officer class by 1952 – a pace of change too slow for most Indian nationalists, and one that the war would in any case soon make redundant. As for self-rule: an Act of Parliament passed in 1919 had enshrined the principle of parliamentary self-government for India. The reality in the 1930s was a dual rule by Indian ministers with 'soft' portfolios – health, agriculture, education – and British ministers with 'hard' responsibilities – defence, police, treasury, justice. All their decisions, of course, were subject to approval by the Viceroy, the King of India in all but name.

India had become the running sore in the side of British imperial self-satisfaction. The situation was potentially explosive; sometimes actually so, as in the notorious incident in Amritsar on 13 April 1919 when, after a series of attacks by Indians on British people, Brigadier-General R. E. H. Dyer ordered his Gurkha and Baluchi riflemen to open fire on a banned meeting of 10,000 Punjabis. Four hundred were killed, 1100 wounded. Afterwards General Dyer issued an order that any man going down a certain street, in which a British woman had been beaten and left for dead, must do so crawling on hands and knees. These echoes of the brutal punitive measures carried out after the Indian Mutiny, sixty years before, were condemned on all sides; Dyer was censured and retired home on half pay. Since then, British politicians had been very attentive to what was going on in India. A mirror was being held up to the imperial system, in which it could see its own future. In 1926 Lord Irwin, the newly appointed Viceroy, released Gandhi from one of his periodic jailings; and Winston Churchill, growling and lashing his tail over Indian nationalism, articulated what plenty of British politicians – and soldiers and civil servants – felt, when he deplored 'the nauseating and humiliating spectacle of this one-time Inner Temple lawyer, now seditious fakir, striding half-naked up the steps of the Viceroy's palace, there to negotiate and parley on equal terms with the representative of the King Emperor'. The seeds of Indian change were bitter on Churchill's tongue. Yet 2,500,000 Indians, of every shade in the political, social, religious and cultural spectrum, were to serve alongside Britain during the Second World War.

When Adolf Hitler came to power on 30 January 1933, Nila Kantan was about to have his twelfth birthday. The family had recently moved to Tamil Nadu in southern India; Nila's father, an irrigation engineer with the Public Works Department (PWD), had been posted there from Nila's birthplace in Andra Pradesh. Ten years from now Nila would be part of a Transport Supply Unit, joining in the 8th Army's great desert battles with the Afrika Korps – a far cry from his peaceful upbringing.

I am a Brahmin – though I don't believe in caste. I hate talking about caste. I lost my mother very early; I don't even remember her face. My father married a second time and she was not like the proverbial stepmother – she brought us up very well. God has been extremely good to me.

Where I grew up in Andra Pradesh it was rather hilly and forest area. There was no road or railway. If you want to come to Rajahmundry, you had to come by the boat on the Godavari river. We were living in a small village on the banks of the Godavari. Mud house and thatched roof. It was a sort of camp for the PWD workers; it was not pukka building.

I never came across any high-class society people. It was just a rural atmosphere at that time. I never came across an Englishman; I had no chance to meet the British. I was a young fellow, going to school, and there was no Britishers there. I have seen, of course, the British Superintendent of Police – but from a distance, that's all.

The upbringing of Danny Misra, also a Brahmin, could hardly have been more different. On 30 January 1933 young Danny – he would win a Military Cross in Burma and eventually become a major-general – had been at the Indian Military Academy at Dehra Dun, in the Himalayan foothills, for a month. By keeping his temper, seventeen-year-old Cadet Misra had ridden out a nasty storm of *Tom Brown's Schooldays*-style bullying and ragging; a terrible shock for a green youth, who'd come straight from a privileged upbringing in which Indian and British traditions mingled to produce a civilised atmosphere of cultured comfort:

My father was a magistrate, a top-caste Brahmin. My mother was from the same caste – these were the intellectual aristocracy. One of my ancestors had been treasurer to the East India Company.

Those early days were days of comfort and ease. About every three years my father was moved, always to a large house, with lots of people in it – we lived in joint families. So you had cousins, and cousins' cousins, and so on. Any number of servants, and always a big compound.

Father believed in the so-called missionary schools, run by Catholics and Protestants. All our teachers were British, so from the word go our contact with the British was strong. Father always had British friends, mostly in the Indian Civil Service. His best friend was Mr Hobart, a kind of godfather to me, who discussed with my father which school we should go to. These men were outstanding civil officers. They didn't go on leave for three or four years; they spoke the language. They treated my brothers and me as their own children. And we learned from them. You would say to your English friend, 'Oh, what a *lovely* day!' He would reply, 'Not bad.' The beauty of understatement – that we learned.

We spoke English and Hindi at home, though the ladies generally spoke Hindi. At home with my mother and the ladies the Indian culture was very much passed on to us, and we grew up as Indians. We had to learn our scriptures; we had to learn our languages, Sanskrit and Hindi. The emphasis was always on culture, with manners. We never spoke loudly to elders and seniors; we only spoke when we were spoken to. If someone came into the room, no question of sitting down: we stood up. A tremendous emphasis was put upon good manners – a decent upbringing. One of my teachers, a Muslim, told me when I was about to go to the Indian Military Academy: 'If you are guilty of misconduct I shall forgive you; but if you are guilty of bad manners I shall commit suicide.'

In spite of the cordial relations between the British and the Indians at this exalted social level, Danny Misra was aware even as a teenager of the political surges eroding the imperial sea-wall under the calm surface of good breeding and good manners:

> A consciousness about our being independent was there. The anti-British feeling surfaced after those horrible incidents like General Dyer's massacre at Amritsar, or after lathi charges by the police. That created the anti-British feeling. Some of the British administrators did not understand what I find the most beautiful thing in the British culture – the liberal view. There were some – I call them enemies of Empire, not anti-Indian – who thought that the only way to run the country is with the lathi and the boot. They had their own rules and regulations: admission to the club, for example. Now, if they wanted to be together, away from Indians, that's their business. They didn't want to come inside and sit in *our* gatherings. It was a sort of arrogance. Some of them, I regret to say, the narrow-minded ones, made it their business to show who was the ruler and who was the ruled.

No country in the British Commonwealth more clearly demonstrated ruler and ruled than South Africa. The rulers here were not expatriate Britons, however, but white South Africans of both British and Dutch stock. The flag of antagonism between these two groups had been nailed to the mast during the Boer War and still fluttered there thirty years on. Bob Gaunt was ten years old in January 1933 and, far unhappier at his boarding-school in the Orange Free State than Cadet Misra amid the bullyragging of Dehra Dun. Both on his father's and mother's side, Bob was descended from Britons. His maternal family had been in South Africa for a hundred years and were highly critical of many British policies. But this cut no ice for Bob in the dormitory kangaroo courts at his school in Bloemfontein. For his last two years of schooling before he joined the navy he went to Selborne College in East London, which was run on the lines of an English public school, and enjoyed every minute of it. But at the Bloemfontein school most of the boarders were Afrikaners of Dutch extraction, and they lost no time in picking on the little boy – two years younger than them – with his 'British' background, and beating seven shades of hell out of him in revenge for what the 'Rooineks' had done to their families in the concentration camps of the Boer War. Near the school there was a large memorial to the 26,000 Afrikaner women and children who had died in the camps, so Bob was unlikely to be allowed to forget it.

Strange though it may seem, I understood why I was being beaten up. I felt very strongly about such cruel and degrading British action. But I was also terribly proud of my English background, because my family had fought in the Zulu wars, the Boer wars, at the Western Front, at Ypres and the Somme and Passchendaele.

However, I was also taught that the Zulus were great people and had to be respected. My great-uncle, who must have been in his late seventies, lived at home with us. Most of his time was spent driving off in his ox waggon or donkey cart into Kwa Zulu to visit many different Zulu kraals and tribes, and to hunt. He had many Zulu friends; some were those he'd fought against during the Zulu wars and some had fought with him against the Boers.

On rare occasions my uncle would take me hunting and on some of his short visits to Kwa Zulu. My memories of these visits are still very clear: the smell of the wood fires around the large black cooking pots early in the mornings, the children playing, their laughter and singing. Above all, watching the Zulus perform their war dances. At times these could be frightening. The noise was terrific, with the banging of knobkerries and assegais against their hide shields. At times the ground felt as if it was going to open up with the stamping of the warriors' feet. They all wore traditional dress, shouting their war cries while others blew horns or whistles.

There was also the dance of the maidens; they would dance wearing only a string of beads and plenty of fresh air. As a child I didn't give it a second thought; this was the way they dressed when they came into town or when they were visiting the trading stations.

One of my greatest pleasures was to hear stories about the great Zulu kings, Shaka Dingane and Cetshawayo, told by the Zulu elders who had fought in their great wars. Looking back, this really was a very wonderful experience for a young boy. My lasting impressions were that the Zulu were a very brave, proud and kind people who were members of a great nation. Even at this early age I could never understand why they were treated so badly by the white people. It was drummed into me that they had to be respected; that if South Africa was going to achieve anything in the future, you had to learn to live together.

Four hundred miles north of Grey College in the wide open country of Northern Transvaal, not far from the northern border of the Union of South Africa, Frank Sexwale was two weeks short of his fifteenth birthday.

13

He, too, was going to school: one of the lucky ones, in terms of the black South African culture into which he had been born.

> Pietersburg, where I grew up, was a rural area like any other place in South Africa. My father was just an ordinary man – he was not a farmer in a sophisticated manner, but he did some ploughing and reared cattle.
>
> My parents, in this rural area, never went to school. In the place where I was born there was no school, there was absolutely nothing. So my father decided to take me to live with my aunt, his sister, about 100 kilometres away, so that I would be nearer to a school. If I had stayed in the place where my father was I would never have gone.
>
> My parents did not even know what Britain was. They knew absolutely nothing except the place in which they were living. I had never heard about Britain until I went to school and we learned history and geography.

In 1933 things were bad for South African blacks. General J. B. Hertzog had succeeded Jan Smuts as Prime Minister of the Union of South Africa in 1926. Both men were brave and competent soldiers who had led the British by the nose during the Boer War of 1899–1902. But while Smuts had since transformed himself into one of Britain's strongest supporters, Hertzog retained an iron-hard Afrikaner nationalism and a white-supremacist agenda that he allowed full play once in office. By 1933 blacks had lost the right to strike; a 'glass ceiling' had been positioned between blacks and Indians and all management positions in the all-powerful mining industry; the 'pass laws' denied freedom of movement to blacks. In the Cape they had the right to vote, but only for white parliamentary representatives; everywhere else the black man had no say at all in the policies that affected his everyday life. In the House of Assembly three Europeans represented the entire black population of South Africa. Things were bad; and they would get worse before the outbreak of the Second World War. The Native Trust and Lands Act of 1936 would point blacks firmly towards the black 'homelands' or Bantustans, enclaves not yet self-governing, in which blacks had rights of franchise and free movement – but not outside in the wider, whiter South Africa. The Native Laws Amendment Act of the following year would tighten the pass laws even further. Land ownership was out of the question for most South African blacks. As for education, that key to self-advancement, prized so highly throughout the rest of the Commonwealth, was only on offer in its most basic form to all but a lucky few black children; entirely unavailable in rural areas such as the agricultural lands of Northern Transvaal. Frank Sexwale entered teacher training college in 1935; when he graduated in 1939 as a fully qualified teacher he was a rarity among his race.

The Coloured community of the Cape Province, at the southern tip of the Union, was also racially disadvantaged. In spite of a technically open-to-all franchise, qualification based on property ownership meant that many Cape Coloureds could not vote. They had drifted into a no man's land where glass ceilings were applied to job promotion and education. The Cape Coloureds had originated three hundred years before, when Dutch settlers first came to the Cape and took local sexual partners – as did the Malay and Indian workers who followed them. In eleven-year-old Charles Adams's case English, Irish and German genes added to the mix.

> I grew up in Kensington – that was a quiet area of Capetown, all the roads around our house were sand roads. My father was a saddle and harness maker, not a bad job, and he was also a musician; he played the violin.
>
> On his side, I know, there were certainly English and Irish forebears. My mother's father was a German from South West Africa. But I looked to England. England was the special country to me. In fact, I always said that England was my second home.

The wartime fortunes of these three South Africans were to mirror the fortunes of their respective races. For Bob Gaunt, the white, a dashing and successful war overseas in the Royal Navy's motor torpedo boats; for Charles Adams, the Cape Coloured, a war spent driving supply trucks in the North African desert and instructing young Coloured soldiers at a training school back home; for Frank Sexwale, the black, a war of lowly fetching-and-carrying jobs and of clerking, breeding disillusion and resentment.

On 30 January 1933 there were other young men and women, other young boys and girls all over the world growing up under the wing of the British Empire and Commonwealth – in the Seychelles and the Solomon Islands, in The Gambia and Burma and Nigeria, in Malaya and Malta, the Falkland Islands and the Fiji Islands, North Borneo and Kenya and Southern Rhodesia, Hong Kong and Togoland, St Helena and Tristan da Cunha. All these lives the war would engulf and change. Of all the countries in the Empire–Commonwealth, none more strikingly mingled a proud 'damn-your-eyes-Jack' independence of spirit and a half-cynical, half-sentimental affection for Britain than Australia. What the Australians said about the 'bloody Poms' and what they actually felt about the Old Country, where almost all of them had their roots, were two sides of the same coin.

Eleven-year-old Pierre Austin was a Melbourne city boy. His grandfather had been a Herefordshire man, who had served in the Indian Army and arrived in Australia after the rebellion of 1857. Pierre's father had served in France during the Great War; he had been wounded at Passchendaele in 1917 and met his future wife there – she was a French girl who nursed him back to health.

I don't think one greatly separated the notion of being Australian and British. Australia was part of the Empire, very much so. One felt Australian, specifically, but very much within the Empire. The family was very pro-British. Britain was best. Empire Day was celebrated with, 'You're going to see that film about Trafalgar', or 'How the Empire was Won' – that kind of thing. Flag-waving ... And of course, in my case, I had this obvious liking for France, through my mother.

There was very much a sense of pride in my father's service in the First World War. If there was another lad, whose father hadn't fought, one thought, 'Poor chap.' Australia found itself, at Gallipoli. My father wasn't there, but an uncle was, with the Light Horse. One was immensely proud of it: this was where we grew up.

Rod Wells was thirteen years old when Hitler came to power in Germany. The kind of tough farming life that the Wells family led in the state of Victoria could stand for all those pioneering family lives that had shaped the outback of Australia over the past century and a half:

Dad bought a block of land at Dhuringile, that's a tiny place outside Murchison. Really outback Australia at that time. When he took the place over, it was 160 acres of scrub and thistle. So my early recollections are of a dusty backyard and of Dad working really hard to turn the land into something we could make a go of. He'd milk the cows at 7.30 in the morning – but he'd have put in three or four hours' work before that.

Dad was a pretty strict disciplinarian; a man who hadn't had a great deal of education, but he wanted his children to have it. From the age of eight I'd be put in charge of a pony and jinker, and take my sister to school in the town three or four miles away. It was a hard, outback kind of life, but a good one.

Dad's family had come over from Wells in Somerset, some time in the last century. During the First World War he'd been a transport officer with the 24th Infantry Battalion in France and went across to England on leave, to

Brighton – that's where he met my mother. She was a Brighton girl, English *ad infinitum* – we can trace her family back in Sussex to about 1820. So my family background was one of absolute, implicit loyalty and love of country.

That sense of loyalty and love of country was to lead Rod Wells, ten years later, to a prison camp in Borneo and to sessions of torture at the hands of his Japanese captors that would still affect him fifty years afterwards. It was the same love and loyalty that had led so many of the preceding generation, in every corner of the British Empire, to join up and offer their service during the first of the century's two great global conflicts – their own Great War to end all wars.

In 1914 Britain had declared war on Germany on behalf of the whole Empire, without consulting any of its component members. The Dominions were self-governing colonies, it was true, but they would not officially become fully autonomous communities within the Empire until 1931's Statute of Westminster. As for considering the wishes of the people of Trinidad, or the Gold Coast, or Mauritius, on the matter – that would have been, and was, literally unthinkable. It still was unthinkable five years later, when the Treaty of Versailles was being negotiated and signed; but by then, at least, the Dominions and India had impressed the mother country sufficiently by their service during the war to ensure themselves the right not only to sign the Treaty individually, but to join the emerging League of Nations as individual members.

The Great War produced a strong feeling of unity and common sense of purpose among its Empire participants. At the same time, powerful self-interest was also at work, a forcing of the imperial parent to recognise that some at least of her children were now adult enough to want to leave home and set up on their own. They might choose of their own accord to remain attached to the wider family, if given proper recognition. In fact, back in the practical post-Great War world, the Empire was to be rep-resented on the Council of the League of Nations by a single spokesman – from Britain. And the League's Covenant obliged the whole Empire, as one entity, to fight any war declared on behalf of the League.

The wider post-war politics of the Empire and Commonwealth did not ring much of a bell with the younger generation in 1933. They were listening to tales their own parents had to tell of the war they had fought between 1914 and 1918, and of the pride that they took in what the bloody episodes of the war had done to foster their own countries' emerging sense of nationhood.

Keith Rossi, Australia:

The Anzac legend, as it's called, is a very important part of Australian culture. If you're going to understand us, you must learn about Gallipoli. A few years ago historians began to decide that we'd been looking at those heroes of the First World War through rose-tinted glasses. And they were largely right, in some ways. For example, we had a syphilis rate, and a desertion rate, miles higher than any other bloody nation fighting in France. Probably because we didn't introduce conscription, so our regiments were down to half strength and full of old lags. But Gallipoli – the effect it had on the Australian public back then was enormous.

You have to remember that within two weeks of the First World War starting we'd already sent two battalions round to occupy Rabaul, mostly sailors. They'd recruited them, they'd equipped them and within a couple of weeks they were on their bloody way! I think the Australian public liked that: a real contribution. And then, of course, on the first convoy on its way to Egypt, *Sydney* breaks off and wrecks the *Emden*. Beached and done for! Oh, what an effect that must have had in Australia: we're really contributing to this war.

And then, a long silence. All this fighting in France, all the taxis rushing soldiers out from Paris to defend the Marne – and the Australians had disappeared into Egypt. Stuff in the newspapers, talking about the deeds of both sides, but about the Australians there's a silence. Then, all of a sudden – Gallipoli! The great landing – glowing reports – the first landing since the Dardanelles were crossed by Xerxes! The much larger role played by the British and French was conveniently ignored, I suppose. The idea of the soldiers crossing that narrow beach and going up those slopes – and, Jesus, they're steep – galloping up like young antelopes, hard fit from route marches through sand ... something – something seized their imagination.

The retreat – well, again, it's a powerful legend, but I reckon it's a myth. I reckon the Turks knew we were going and let us go. Snow had fallen, and both sides were going to be in trouble if they wintered on the peninsula – and what did it matter to the Turks if we went?

Now, it's all right for historians to talk like this. But I'd say to them: don't destroy the Anzac legend. We all fought better in World War Two, trying to emulate the supposed deeds of our fathers.

Glen Niven, Canada:

My father joined Princess Patricia's Canadian Light Infantry in 1914. They got 1000 men in two weeks. The whole of the Police Pipe Band of Edmonton joined as a body. My father joined as a private, but he shot up to lieutenant-colonel. He got wounded several times; he got two DSOs, an MC and three Mentioned in Despatches. In the First Battle of Ypres in 1915 all the officers except him were wounded or killed. A hundred and fifty out of 500 men survived. He heroically stuck the regimental colours in the ground and said, 'We stay here. We defend the colours' – which they bloody did. One officer – Father – plus about sixty men marched out. He was a very brave man – did extremely well in France – and expected me to do the same.

Bob Gaunt, South Africa:

In World War One my father and uncles enlisted in the South African Army, and saw action in South West Africa and France, including the Somme and Ypres. I have vivid recollections of stories told of the horror of the trenches, the mud, going over the top, guns, bayonet charges, heavy shelling at Passchendaele. I particularly remember the description of the battle of Delville Wood, when 6000 South Africans went into battle and only about 750 men, many of them wounded, answered the roll-call at the end of the day. I don't think any of those who took part in those awful battles, on both sides, were ever free from the nightmare of it all.

My family were closely involved in the erection of the Delville Wood Memorial in Pietermaritzburg. The timber used to make the cross came from the actual trees of Delville Wood. I was very proud to stand in the front row when the memorial was being consecrated. My more personal trophies from the war included a tin hat with bullet holes, a gas mask, a German bayonet and a Mills bomb.

I think that the experience of their involvement in the war by my relations made them very proud to be South African, although they continued to refer to England as home. They admired enormously the bravery and courage of the British troops who'd fought alongside them in France. Many were the nights when I was woken by the singing of 'Land of Hope and Glory', 'Rule Britannia', 'Soldiers of the King' and other patriotic war songs by members of my family and their war veteran friends.

Not everyone, of course, felt quite the same about it ...

Thomas Scoon, Trinidad:

My father Thomas fought in the 1914–18 war. Eventually he got a piece of shrapnel in his hand, and when he got home it started to wither. Now when I joined the Army, and I got into the contingent to go away, I went to spend the last week of embarkation leave with him. He told me, 'Don't go.' I said, 'Why?' He said: 'The British people – you fight for them, and they give you a lime to suck!'

Jan Smuts, the 'Boer rebel' who had been transformed into an indispensable ally, was the only Dominion statesman to gain a place in the British War Cabinet during the First World War. Smuts had painted for the British a tremendous and flattering picture of their own Empire on the broadest of canvases: 'We are a system of nations, a community of states and of nations far greater than any Empire that has ever existed. All the nations that we have known in the past and that exist today are founded on the idea of assimilation, of trying to force human material through one mould so as to form one nation. Your whole idea and basis is entirely different. You want to develop them into greater nationhood ... The successful launching of her former Colonies among the nations of the world, while they remain members of an inner Britannic circle, will ever rank as one of the most outstanding achievements of British political genius.'

Smuts was referring exclusively to the 'white Dominions'. Both in those self-governing former colonies, and in the dependent colonies more firmly under British rule, antennae were still tuned to the little island in the North Sea. What happened in Britain, what British politicians and royal persons, socialites and sportsmen said and did, really mattered to hundreds of millions of people who would never set foot in the island. As for the British themselves, it is doubtful if many in 1933 were aware of the enormous emotional pull their island exerted around the world, though most were proud enough of their country's international prestige and influence. Having had the Empire for such a long time, they took it more or less for granted.

Echoes of Empire, however, sounded strongly in the childhoods of some of those Britons who would soon be embroiled in the war. Alec Dennis, three weeks short of his fifteenth birthday when Adolf Hitler became Chancellor of Germany, had barely recognised his own parents when he met them after a four-year separation – they had been away living and working in India. His father had served in the Boer War as a medical officer and had been captured by the Boers, 'who treated him like a gentleman, but took his horse'. Now Dennis was in his second year as a cadet at the Royal Naval College at Dartmouth, and beginning to find his feet in his chosen profession.

We were all brought up to admire the Empire, I think with good reason, really. The globe was covered in pink; the feats of arms of our forebears in Quebec and India and all over the world were really rather remarkable. I think we were brought up to feel that fellows went out to 'administer the natives' and did the best job they could. Now, there was a bunch who made lots of money out of it, especially in the eighteenth century; but I think in our time the whole lot had turned rather sort of do-gooders and did the best they could, really.

You felt proud of the Empire, no doubt about it. When I went to sea, you knew that the Navy stood between the Empire and dissolution of one kind or another. During combined fleet manoeuvres at Gibraltar, Admiral William Wordsworth Fisher – a forbidding figure – sent for all the gunlayers of all the fifteen-inch guns of about twelve battleships, got 'em all up there and said, 'Now you people with your fingers on the trigger – *you* stand between the British Empire and its enemies.'

Sheila Kershaw was just nineteen, newly returned to Britain from Jerusalem where she had been enjoying an interlude as part of the 'fishing fleet' – young girls of good family sent out to the colonies to trawl for a suitable husband. Palestine, mandated into British trusteeship at the Treaty of Versailles, was already a hot potato in 1933, as the irresistible force of homeland-seeking Jews met the immovable object of the Palestinian Arabs. For Sheila Kershaw, however, Jerusalem had been a whirl of tennis parties and of dances on the black-and-white-tiled floor of the King David Hotel, twirling to a Scots pipe band in the arms of the young Adonises of the 51st Highlanders. Soon she would be out in Kenya, another corner of the Empire, running the household of coffee farmer Gerry Easton and his wife, Olwen, playing more tennis, learning how to spot and cut dead the sex-and-booze-addled reprobates of white settlers who dwelt in Happy Valley, gaining and losing boyfriends, taking part in the summer camps of FANY, the First Aid Nursing Yeomanry – and admiring the work of the youthful British administrators.

It was taken for granted that you'd got an Empire. One of the things that reinforced this was that Kenya was such a quiet, ordered land. All these different tribes who'd been at each other's throats, murdering each other since time began, were looked after by District Commissioners. Now these were the second or third sons of British families who'd had a public-school education and nobody could quite think what to do with them. So out they went. They learned the local dialect, and they lived in great solitude and they dispensed justice. Most of them were around twenty-five. And they did this in a way which kept quiet on the land.

Derek Watson in 1933 was in many ways a typical young subaltern of his day – twenty-two years old, overspending his allowance, without a thought to spare outside hunting and rugger.

When I joined the Leicesters in 1929 I went to see the CO.

'Morning, m'boy.'

'Morning, Sir.'

'What d'you want?'

'I want to join your regiment, Sir.'

'Hmm. What was your father?'

'7th Dragoon Guards, Sir.'

'Why don't you join his regiment?'

'Can't afford to, Sir.'

'Why don't you go for Sandhurst?'

'Failed the exam, Sir.'

'Why can't you stand straight?'

'Buggered up my leg, Sir.'

'Christ Almighty!' he said. 'I've never heard so much bloody cheek in my life. Here we have a pauper, a half-wit and a bloody cripple into the bargain, asking to join my regiment! Go down and see the MO. If he passes you fit for active service I'll take you.'

The MO was an Irishman, who'd obviously been lifting his elbow a bit. All he did was held my balls and said, 'Cough' – and passed me fit. And that's how I got into the Leicesters.

In 1933 Watson was posted to Londonderry in Ireland:

Ran a pack of draghounds in winter. Mondays I walked the line, approximately twenty miles. Hunted it Tuesday. Wednesday, I hunted with the harriers. Thursday, walked the line. Friday, hunted it. Saturdays I played rugger. In summer I got put on courses so I could play cricket.

I used to take the hounds through the Bogside, and people would clap and cheer. No question of jeering or throwing bottles. Some farmers would have 'Up the Pope! Down the King!' written up, but that was all they did in those days. I suppose we took being British for granted. You just showed your passport and said 'British', and you expected first-class treatment – which one got.

I was running a motor car and two horses on £100 a year, so after three years I was broke. Had to go out to Nyasaland in 1935 to join the King's African

Rifles, make up some money. Knew nothing about the Empire, really. When I was posted to Nyasaland I hadn't got a bloody clue where it was!

Danny Misra joined the Rajputana Rifles at the beginning of 1937; not through a clear-eyed judgement about their military expertise or reputation, but because he was seduced by the sight of their 'spiked helmets and chin-straps of black metal, cross-belts with crests of battle honours, swords, khaki half-breeches, green puttees, black boots with silver chains, khaki jackets and red and green turbans. I didn't know anything about their war record, which was brilliant; I just fell in love with them.'

Before that, on graduating from the Indian Military Academy at Dehra Dun, he had spent a year with the North Staffordshire Regiment: an experience that gave him a taste of the wit and wisdom of the British Colour Sergeant.

I couldn't have joined a better regiment. I learned there the British sense of humour – that art of understatement. So different from officers of other countries, who were all the time trying to impress on you how big and great and rich they were.

Sergeant Lee was an ex-miner – a brilliant chap! He taught me to type, one-finger, 'The Quick Brown Fox Jumps Over The Lazy Dog'. I was getting on very slowly. After a while I noticed that Sergeant Lee had placed a fire-bucket full of sand on each side of me, without making any comment. I said, 'Why these buckets of sand?'

He said, straight-faced, 'Sir, I had the feeling that while you were typing, the paper might catch fire.'

I replied: 'Yes, thank you.'

It was not only regular servicemen who were getting military training in the 1930s. Territorial companies and militias had always attracted a certain type of young person; and in Australia particularly, the Anzac tradition had sparked an interest among teenagers in military training that somehow survived an almost complete lack of modern equipment.

'My father died of war wounds he'd got at Gallipoli and in France,' says Bob Taunt of Melbourne, 'and that probably influenced me to join the militia in about 1936–7. You went once a fortnight to drill – it was horse artillery then, we had horses – and you might have a camp once a year. We didn't really get vehicles until the war started, and then it was only one utility and a couple of staff vans. We used to do gun drill on a big tree laid down and we'd pretend it was a gun. It wasn't a bad training. When we joined up I knew what it was all about, having been in the militia; but half the fellows just came straight in off the Showgrounds, without a clue.'

Carlton Best, of Port of Spain in Trinidad, was an intensely patriotic young man. 'The British for me was everything. The King and Queen were the head of our family. Empire Day – I loved that! 24 May! "Land of Hope and Glory, Mother of the Free" – those were the songs we grew up with. Lovely days!' But what drew him to the Territorials – as Danny Misra in India had been drawn to the Rajputana Rifles – was simply their style:

> In 1936 one of the top-class police officers died and they had a military funeral for him. It was in my district. I saw some Territorials dressed in khaki, with helmets, boots and puttees. Oh, they were pretty, as far as I could see! And they marched so well! I said, 'Ah – I'm going to join *that*.' So the next drill night they had, I was down there offering myself. I had a problem: I learned that they were only taking men from twenty-four years old.
>
> I still put myself up. The English sergeant-major saw me. 'How old are you?' – 'Twenty-two, Sir!' He said, 'Uh-uh, you're not. But you have a good body and all that. We'll put you down as twenty-four.' So he enrolled me in the Trinidad Light Infantry Volunteers ... I was sixteen!

The great Depression of the 1930s hit the Empire–Commonwealth hard. It came as a particular shock to the self-reliant 'colonials', with their philosophy of hard work bringing hard-earned reward, to find themselves out of a job with next to no prospect of another. This period made a deep impression on the youngsters – some looking on from relatively privileged positions, others struggling with difficulties themselves.

Paul Radomski, New Zealand:

> A lot of people got laid off in Wellington during the Depression, and my dad was one of them. There was no redundancy payment then. He just didn't have any money – they might have had a few bob saved and they were living on that. I used to go out trapping rabbits on the hills, snaring them so we'd have something to eat. Men used to line up outside the wharf gates, mainly with horses and drays in those days, waiting for a couple of hours' work.

Thomas Hunter, Canada:

> Well, there was no work and my people were on welfare. My father died when I was thirteen and I went out to work from there, into a chrome-plating plant. I had a mother and two sisters; my father's death made me the man of the

family and I hadn't a choice. Jobs were tough to get, but I managed to squeeze in a couple of places. I wasn't really strong enough to do the work, but they tolerated me. $8 a week; 20 cents an hour. That was the average wage at that time: practically nothing. Kept us in rent, living here and there. We were very, very short of money. It was tough – that was Depression days. Nobody had jobs, everything was catch-as-catch-can.

Bob Gaunt remembers the poor whites queuing up at soup kitchens and some of his own friends walking around in tattered clothes, barefoot – astonishing sights, in prosperous white man's South Africa. Up to one-fifth of the whites were living on the poverty line, many of them upcountry Afrikaner farmers who had had to sell their hard-worked farms and leave the land – 'bitter Boers', who began to listen ever more attentively to what nationalist extremists with Fascist sympathies were saying about international affairs.

In Melbourne, Pierre Austin recalls the horse-drawn floats on which jobless ex-servicemen would play brass-band music, hoping for a few pennies; and a Captain Jacka who was reduced to selling door-to-door, in spite of the Victoria Cross he had won at Gallipoli with the 14th Battalion.

Meanwhile, beyond the oceans and round the curve of the globe, Chancellor Hitler had settled into his post and had begun to make a few changes.

There was no great mobilisation of purpose across the Commonwealth as the threat of war began to take shape. No common stance was taken up against the rise of Nazism, of Fascism, of racism, of intolerance and expansionism at the heart of Europe; nor against Japan's incursions into China, which had begun with the occupation of the Chinese province of Manchuria in September 1931, sixteen months before Hitler came to power. There was no Winston Churchill, as yet, to stand forward as a dogged symbol of right against might and articulate what so many felt, but couldn't frame, about decent people's determination and defiance. Those were the sentiments that the long-drawn-out succession of crises began to precipitate, as if by chemical reaction; but between most of the Commonwealth and what was happening lay a gauze of distance and a swirling cloud of misplaced hope that things wouldn't really turn out to be as bad as they were threatening to become.

By the 1930s one benefit of belonging to the British Empire and Commonwealth was being linked to a well-oiled and very far-reaching communications network involving radio, newsreels, newspapers, telegrams, ships, flying boats, aeroplanes and a highly efficient international postal service. Nor was expert comment lacking. There was a general awareness that the terms of the Versailles Treaty, supposed to emasculate Germany as a fighting power and bind her to reparation for damage inflicted during the Great War, had not really worked. The disastrous effects of inflation on Depression-hit Germany were well known. Hitler's aggression towards the Jews was deplored, his withdrawal of Germany from the League of Nations in October 1933 noted with dismay, the swift upturn in the German economy and in German confidence taken on board. Meanwhile, Japanese moves deeper into China against Chiang Kai-shek's nationalist government could clearly be seen, and their potential threat assessed, from Australia, New Zealand, Malaya, Hong Kong and the other Commonwealth territories of the Far East, as well as from Britain's own backyard.

Alec Dennis, Great Britain: 'The week I joined Dartmouth in September 1931 was the week the Japanese walked into Manchuria and nobody did anything about it. We were aware of that – I remember thinking, "Why doesn't somebody stop them?"'

Tom Somerville, New Zealand: 'Round about 1933, in the farming district where I was, we used to notice these migrants settling in the place; and they were Jewish people, out of Nazi Germany. Hitler was coming into power then, a lot of them saw the writing on the wall and they got out. But they wouldn't talk. They were used to secrecy and not expressing what they thought.'

In April 1935 Hitler introduced conscription and started to rearm Germany in earnest. On 3 October the Italian Fascist leader, Benito Mussolini, launched his invasion of Ethiopia ('Abyssinia' to many), the only sizeable state in Africa that had not yet been colonised. In March 1936 Germany sent forces to reoccupy the Rhineland territory on her western border, which had been turned by the Allies into a demilitarised zone after the Great War. No objection was raised by Britain or her allies. In July the Spanish Civil War broke out, with the Fascists rising against a left-wing Republican government. Germany and Italy would support the Fascists until their eventual victory in 1939, using Spain as a testbed for air and ground battle tactics. By the end of 1936 Germany, Italy and Japan had signed mutual-assistance pacts, forming themselves into an 'Axis' on which – they hoped – the future of the world would turn.

Lloyd Johnson, Jamaica:

We didn't know much about the persecution of the Jews; we didn't really hear about that in Jamaica, the world at that time was so far apart. But we got a lot of news, a lot of newspapers and so on. One of the things that also came to light was this Nazi feeling about this master race that Hitler had in his mind. I remember very well the papers writing about the 1936 Olympics, when the great runner, Jesse Owens, was snubbed by Hitler. We had that strong feeling that this man would be very anti-Negro, or anti-black. We realised that this man was also a racist. We felt that if he could be treating the Jews like this, and other people who were basically white in complexion – what would he have done to the blacks?

Bob Gaunt, South Africa:

I think the rise of Nazism and Fascism was first brought home to us at school when Hitler occupied the Rhineland in 1936, and by the Italian war against Ethiopia. That was when I first heard of the Ossewa Brandwag; this was an Afrikaner neo-Nazi organisation which wore brown uniforms and the swastika. They organised rallies to support the Nazis and made every effort to create ill feeling towards the United Kingdom and its aims. The movement was very strong in the Orange Free State and came out in support of Hitler's reoccupation of the Rhineland.

My housemaster in Bloemfontein was a member of the Ossewa Brandwag. It later came out that he was also a member of the Broederbond, a secret anti-British society. He was interned during the war.

In July 1937 the Japanese entered Peking. By November they were in Shanghai. In December Italy withdrew from the League of Nations, as the Japanese were about to capture Nanking and embark on the slaughter of tens of thousands of residents.

Alec Dennis, Great Britain: 'In 1937 I went out to China as a midshipman. The Japanese were extremely unpleasant. I watched the Japanese army march into Tsingtao and it looked a bit like Genghis Khan. On every street corner in the following few days there was a dead man laid out. You got a look at a world that wasn't cosy English village countryside life at all. It was perfectly obvious what was going to happen.'

In 1938, there was a sharp deterioration in the world situation. It was calculated that if war broke out in Europe, Germany would be able to field seventy-nine divisions; France, thirty-three; Belgium, fifteen; Britain, two. In March Hitler invaded Austria, in what was termed the *Anschluss*. He declared the country to be part of the Third Reich and placed Nazis in all the key administrative posts. There was no response from Britain. Next on

Hitler's agenda was the Sudetenland, another border area given up after the Great War, contiguous with Czechoslovakia and harbouring a big German population. Neville Chamberlain, the British Prime Minister, made three flying visits to Germany to meet Hitler and discuss his ambitions; they were limited to the reoccupation of the Sudetenland, Chamberlain reported when he came back with the 'peace in our time' paper in his fingers. In went the German troops in October; six months later they were in Czechoslovakia proper, cutting up the country. There were rumblings from Britain this time; but, in the absence of an effective pact with the communist bogeyman of Russia, the only power with the clout to give Hitler pause for thought, these seemed just a baring of gums by an all but toothless old lion.

Meanwhile, in the Far East, Japan was forging south and west into the central Yangtze region of China.

Danny Misra, India:

I had gone out to Hong Kong with the Rajputana Rifles in 1937, and in 1938 I got leave and went to Japan for four months, hopping along the islands – Kobe, Nagasaki, Tokyo. I also went to Hokkaido, where the primitive tribesmen lived – they grew very long beards.

I moved among the Japanese not as a spy, but as a visitor. I stayed in a Japanese home for some time – the father had been at Oxford, the son at Eton. I could not only sense that war was imminent, but also their ambitions. Hirohito was only a figurehead; the military ran the country. They had conquered most of China. It had all gone to their heads – an arrogant people.

To me, for political reasons, they were very nice, very charming. Their slogans were 'Co-Prosperity' and 'Asia for the Asiatics'. People seemed very nice, very able, very hard-working. They welcomed Indians. Their policy was to try and drive a wedge between the Indians and the British; trying to brainwash us.

I enjoyed it! I knew there was no such thing as a free lunch.

Across the map of Europe the final moves were being made. In August 1939 the Russians, seeing that they would not get permission to cross Poland to attack Germany in the event of war, came to an accommodation with Hitler and signed a non-aggression pact. That removed the last obstacle to a German reconquest of territory ceded to Poland, again after the end of the First World War. But Poland, finally, was where Britain and her allies had decided the line would have to be drawn.

Derek Watson, Great Britain: 'We didn't ever talk about Hitler in the regiment in the 1930s. Very few wireless sets out in Nyasaland; papers came out by boat or seaplane. I had the *Telegraph* – always out of date. Hardly even thought about a war till 1939.'

Rod Wells, Australia:

We'd sent away our troops to Gallipoli with only a week or so's training and we weren't going to make that mistake again. The decision had been taken not to send troops abroad again to fight. If they want troops, they're going to have to be volunteers.

There were two attitudes in Australia. One was that volunteering attitude and the other was: 'If a war does break out – well, we did enough last time. Let them fight their own bloody wars.' At that stage, many thought, 'The Japanese are just a lot of little yellow bastards. They'd never dare attack us.' A serious Japanese threat was never discussed. As for Abyssinia, when the Italians invaded it – well, that was just a place called Africa. There was a derogatory attitude to the Italians, too: 'a whole load of banjo-players. Useless at fighting.'

So when the war did break out there was no thought of the Japanese or the Italians as serious opponents. It was: 'What the hell are we doing? There's a *war* going on! The Old Country needs help ... Let's go and show them what we can do, eh?

Vernon Alexander, Tobago: 'I simply heard that Edward VIII, the one that abdicated the throne, he went to Germany when he was Prince of Wales, and he came back and told his father, King George V, "Look, you know Germany's preparing for war. You'd better prepare for war, too." And King George said: "Oh, bugger them, man. We'll take care of them." '

PART TWO
ACTION

TWO

Setting Out: 1939–40

Fancy interrupting a young man's cruise to Bali for a bloom-
ing war! Pierre Austin, Royal Australian Navy

'I remember so well,' says Sheila Kershaw, 'sitting in the sun at Olwen's father's house in St Fagan's, near Cardiff. It was this lovely sunny afternoon and it seemed totally impossible that it had actually happened. Chamberlain spoke in this deadpan voice without any emotion at all; it was just merely a statement of fact.'

On 3 September 1939, two days after Hitler's troops invaded Poland, Britain declared war on Germany. This time there was no question of the Old Country unilaterally declaring war on behalf of the entire Empire and Commonwealth. The colonies, it was true, were still going to have to do as Britain did – as was India, where the decision to declare war without consulting Indian opinion caused particular resentment. But the Dominions, at all events, were free to make up their own minds. Predictably, Australia and New Zealand were quick off the mark, declaring war on Germany immediately Britain had announced her declaration. In South Africa General Hertzog's government twitched about, looking for

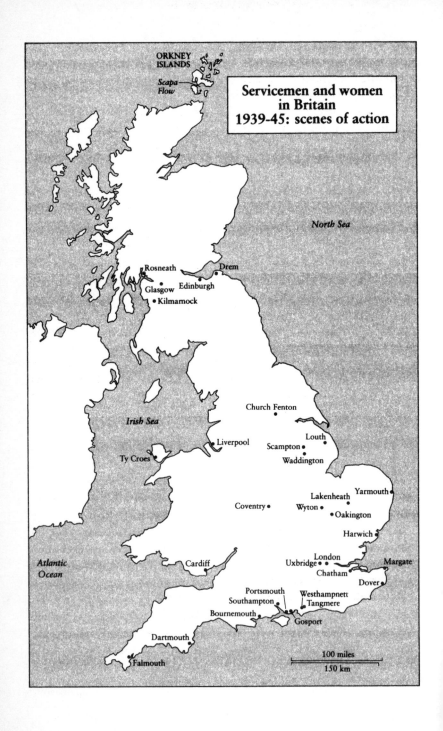

ORKNEY
ISLANDS

*Scapa
Flow*

**Servicemen and women
in Britain
1939-45: scenes of action**

North Sea

Rosneath •   • Drem
Glasgow • Edinburgh
      • Kilmarnock

Irish Sea

• Church Fenton

Liverpool •   • Louth
Scampton •
Ty Croes •   • Waddington

                     • Yarmouth
        Lakenheath •
Coventry •   Wyton • • Oakington

                  • Harwich

                London   • Margate
Cardiff   Uxbridge • •
               • Chatham
                     • Dover
*Atlantic
Ocean*

          Portsmouth •   Westhampnett •
      Southampton •   • Tangmere
Bournemouth •
              • Gosport

   Dartmouth •

Falmouth •

100 miles
150 km

ways to remain neutral. But Jan Smuts challenged the government in Parliament, defeated it, became Prime Minister himself and had the Union at war with Germany only three days after Britain, to the very vocal disapproval of Ossewa Brandwag and of many non-extremist but staunch Afrikaners. Canada, strangely as it seemed, hung back longest, preferring to have the decision formally taken by the Canadian Parliament in session – a delay of a week being the result. The Irish Free State, which was pressing for status as a republic and had already drifted clear of emotional attachment to British causes, opted for neutrality, to no one's surprise.

'The Dominions,' Lord Balfour had declared at the 1926 Imperial Conference, 'are autonomous communities within the British Empire, equal in status, in no way subordinate one to another in any aspect of their domestic or external affairs, though united by a common allegiance to the Crown and freely associated as members of the British Commonwealth of Nations.' By the Statute of Westminster, enacted five years later, the British Parliament abrogated its right to legislate on behalf of the Dominions, or to veto any laws passed by a Dominion's parliament. Many felt the Empire was crumbling and would never be able to act in a concerted way again. British politicians had a fair idea which way the Dominions would jump when it came to war with Germany. But the war would only be won if millions of individuals volunteered to augment the very small standing armies, navies and air forces of the Dominions and colonies.

Les Rowe, Australia:

The news broke in Melbourne on a Sunday; we were down on the beach. There was a ship out in the bay, a merchantman, and it fired a couple of shots – you could see it had a gun on the stern. A mate of mine who was in the Naval Reserve said to me, 'I suppose some poor silly bugger'll be going on that soon.' The words were scarcely out of his mouth when his father came down with a naval policeman to fetch him. He sailed on that ship straight away and was away for two and a half years.

We walked home, and I can remember quite clearly listening to Robert Menzies, the Prime Minister, saying, 'Mr Chamberlain has said there is no answer to the ultimatum and so it is my melancholy duty to inform you that Australia is now at war with Germany.' We hung around the streets, waiting for an Extraordinary Edition of the newspapers to be produced so we could read about it. And there it was.

I rushed around and tried to join the Navy, but they didn't want to know.

They took my details, but I was in the Middle East with the 2/48th Battalion by the time they got in touch with me.

Carlton Best, Trinidad:

On 3 September I was on this big savannah in the middle of Port of Spain, playing football. As I looked up, I saw my smaller brother and a policeman come across the savannah, beckoning. I said, 'Me?' He said, 'Yes, you.' I thought to myself, 'Well, I haven't done anything for the police to arrest me.' So I went. He was going round in his jeep, picking up all the Defence Force people: 'You are a volunteer? You have to go into barracks.' So I changed my football clothes and reported there. By evening we were in uniform, in trucks, heading for Point Fortin in the south of the island to guard the oilfields.

Pierre Austin had joined the Royal Australian Navy in 1938, and was now serving in the destroyer *Voyager*. 'When the news broke we were actually in Bali. Fancy interrupting a young man's cruise to Bali for a blooming war! A signal came through, and the Old Man said, "Good God!" He handed us this signal. It said: "Germany – Total – Germany".'

Bob Gaunt in South Africa recalls his father staying up most of the night after the invasion of Poland, listening to the BBC, and calling his son in from the garden on the Sunday morning to hear Neville Chamberlain make his declaration of war.

In Canada the Cayley family sat round the battery radio in their Toronto living-room while fifteen-year-old Peter – soon to join the Royal Canadian Navy – listened in disappointment to the British Prime Minister delivering 'a not very stirring address; it didn't exactly call one to action'.

Britain was shortly to get a leader uniquely gifted at calling people to action. In 1943, speaking after a Mansion House dinner in London, Winston Churchill would praise to the skies the commitment of the Commonwealth countries as he recalled the moment when 'this loosely and variously knit world-spread association, where so much was left unwritten and undefined, was confronted with the most searching test of all … In that dark, terrific and also glorious hour, we received from all parts of His Majesty's Dominions, from the greatest to the smallest, from the strongest and from the weakest, from the most modern and the most simple, the assurance that we would all go down or come through together.' Splendid phrases that roll as sonorously today as they did then. In September 1939, however, the Commonwealth had to make do with Mr Chamberlain's dry matter-of-factness as a call to arms.

As for the youngsters who would take the plunge and join the forces during this first year of the war, to face up to barrack-room life, service food and discipline, service pay, separation from friends and family, and the real risk of disablement or death in some foreign country far from home – like all the other millions who were to follow them during the next six years, their motives were as heterogeneous as their characters and backgrounds, skin colours and religious leanings, educational levels and cultural contexts. All they had in common was membership of the British Commonwealth, and a young person's desire to stretch the wings and be elsewhere . . .

Phil Rhoden, Australia: 'Some say that people enlisted for the following reasons – one, because they didn't have a job; two, because they had matrimonial troubles; three, they wanted to see the world; four, out of patriotic duty. I wasn't eligible to have a job, because I'd just got through my law course; I wasn't married; I didn't care if I saw the world or not. So – I joined because I thought it my duty to do so.'

Charles Bell, New Zealand:

> It was pretty well put by our Prime Minister of the time – 'Where Britain goes, we go!' – and that was the thinking of most of the country at the time. After all, we Maoris had done all this before. We'd sent a Maori unit to Gallipoli and France in the First World War. And it's not so long ago that we were engaged in warfare against Europeans in this country. A chief of my tribe even built a road up to Gate Pa to make it easier for the British to get their guns up there, so they could fight him better! Fighting was a kind of way of life for us. So it was to be expected that if there was a war over there, New Zealanders would be involved.

Aziz Brimah, Gold Coast: 'We knew that if we didn't volunteer the enemy would come. Our motives: one, the British helped us to quench our tribal wars. Two, if they have trouble elsewhere, it's proper for us to help them. Three, it's also in our own interest – these people have an expanding attitude to cover the whole world. If we did not go out to face them, they would come here.'

Sheila Kershaw, Great Britain: 'I'd joined the FANYs out in Kenya; I was more than capable of taking an engine out, taking it to bits and putting it together again. I was a decent shot, I'd learned first aid and I'd worked hard. I'd learned this series of skills which were of practical use, and I wasn't going to sit on the touch-lines! No – I was going to fight for my country; I was going to contribute.'

Paul Radomski, New Zealand: 'My father and mother were of Polish descent. The Germans had invaded Poland and I had a natural feeling for Poland. I was anti-German, yes – but *for* Poland more than that. And for the UK, too, for trade and financial reasons, because I could see that without them taking our sheep, beef and wool, we couldn't live.'

Ernest Khomari, Basutoland:

Our principal teacher in college was an Englishman from London. He was interested in showing us pictures of how the Germans were advancing and taking over country after country. I remember the picture which virtually drew me to join the Army. It was of a pilot getting married in London. During the ceremony sirens went off, confusion started in the church, people ran out to the trenches to take cover. From the town also, mothers carrying children came running to the trenches. Men going to their guns to shoot off the German planes and so on.

In this picture, the wedding couple also tried to escape. They got into one little red car and they were driving away, when a big building was blown by the Germans and fell right on their car, and they were killed. Also I saw a mother in the trench, breasting her child, and a bomb falling right on top, and bits and pieces falling on the mother. So I got very worried and shocked, and said, 'This man is going to do this the whole world over. So I'm going to volunteer to join, to stop him.'

Raymond Walker, Canada:

I went to Halifax and joined the Navy – the RCNVR – at sixteen. Lied about my age, like everybody else, I guess. And I had a birth certificate that was ... altered. Made 1923 into 1921!

At that time there wasn't too much work. It was a matter of getting into it, I guess. Everybody else was joining up. My friends that were a little older than I was – they all left Sydney Mines and joined up. And I liked the water, so ...

In the opening weeks of the war the first participants to see action were those who had a head start by having already joined the services. Pierre Austin in the Royal Australian Navy destroyer *Voyager* was ordered from his tropical paradise of Bali to the Mediterranean. 'We were part of what was called the Scrap Iron Flotilla, four World War One destroyers – *Vendetta*, *Voyager*, *Vampire*, *Waterhen* – and one a little less ancient, the *Stuart*. Only *Vendetta* survived the war. We all arrived in the Med in late 1939, wondering at that stage, in our innocence, why we didn't just go into Germany and finish them off.'

Desmond Sheen, a Sydney-born boy who was to win a Distinguished Flying Cross and bar, was one of many fighter pilots who had a boyhood love affair with flying. He had joined the Royal Australian Air Force in 1936 as a cadet. At that time the Royal Air Force in Britain was undergoing an expansion in response to the growing threat of war, and short-service commissions with free training were on offer to members of the RAAF. Des Sheen grabbed at the opportunity and came across to England early in 1937. He was soon in the air, in Hawker Fury and Gloster Gladiator biplanes. In 1938 he joined 72 Squadron and got his hands on a Spitfire, 'a beautiful aeroplane, very light, very manoeuvrable, lots of power – absolutely a delight to fly, it just felt right.' By the end of 1939 Sheen – based at Church Fenton in South Yorkshire – had already won his first DFC (presented to him in May 1940). On 21 October he and a colleague attacked fourteen He 115 seaplanes over the North Sea and shot down two. Then, in December, operating from Drem airfield near Edinburgh, he experienced the first of several very close calls. Attacking one Heinkel 111 bomber at low level, he was shot through the buttocks and the ear by the tail gunner of another. He managed to get his damaged aeroplane down into Leuchars, where the ground crew discovered that the Australian had had an extremely narrow shave. They found a German incendiary bullet, miraculously unignited, actually lying in the Spitfire's petrol tank. Sheen spent that Christmas, painfully, in Edinburgh Castle Hospital.

Worldwide, during these first few months of the war, there was aggressive activity at sea. German U-boat submarines operating out of German ports sank over 420,000 tons of Allied shipping before the end of 1939. The German pocket battleship *Graf Spee* alone sank 50,000 tons in three months, before being damaged and then scuttled off South America in December. Millions of German mines were laid around British coastal waters, virtually choking off free access to home harbours. Alec Dennis, by now a sub-lieutenant in the Royal Navy destroyer HMS *Griffin*, was on patrol one cold October night off Harwich when he saw the next ship in line blow up on a mine and sink with heavy loss of life. Many of the crew members' wives, staying in a hotel ashore, watched the explosion without knowing the identity of the victim ship.

Alec Dennis was soon to become involved in an abortive attempt to shore up Norwegian resistance to the German invasion which took place on 9 April 1940. Denmark, invaded simultaneously, capitulated within a

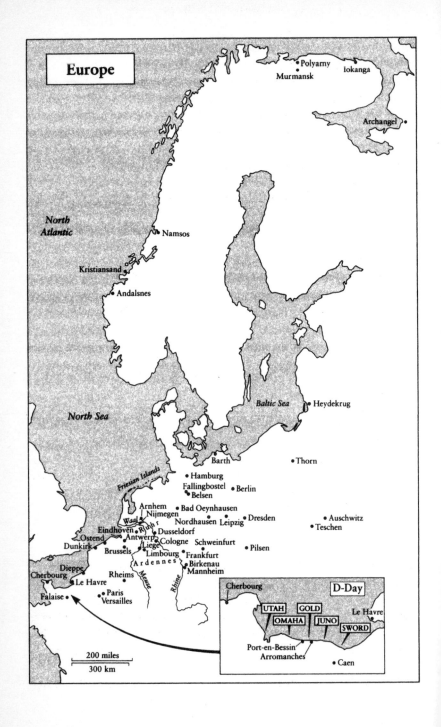

day. Finland had had to yield in March to an overwhelming Russian invasion, which Finnish forces had bravely and skilfully held up for over three months. Sweden had declared neutrality. A Norway landing was the Allies' only hope of retaining even a toe-hold in Scandinavia, and of denying the Germans a string of ports sheltered by deep fjords and with access to the open Atlantic. In the event the British, French and Polish forces landed in Norway between 14 and 18 April had all to be taken out again, under air attack and at great risk to the ships involved, within two months, after fierce but fruitless fighting. Alec Dennis covered both ends of the operation, starting on 18 April when *Griffin* took a batch of soldiers into Andalsnes.

> That was a pretty little fishing town. Next day the Germans demolished it – bombed it and burned it. Came out of there, and about seven o'clock in the morning I was woken up and told there was a trawler we didn't like the look of. A group of us went over in a whaler – the sea was pretty rough. As we got closer we could see she was phoney; a boat on the after deck was just a canvas dummy. She was disguised as a Dutchman.
>
> So Hero Dennis leaps on board with a gun, Hollywood kind of style, and a German comes forward and says, 'Cherman schip!' They had a fishing crew, a German naval crew and a bunch of rather tough Wehrmacht soldiers on board, and a whole lot of ammunition and mines and torpedoes and God knows what. Apparently these three groups had been at loggerheads and hadn't expected us to stop them. They surrendered right away, which was just as well. We got them all up on deck and shipped them back to the *Griffin*. Then she got called away and I was left with about seven of our chaps and about twenty or thirty Germans. They stoked the boilers and brought us food, and we set course for home. Unfortunately they'd thrown all the charts overboard, so we hadn't much to go on. Anyway I found my way back to Scapa Flow; it was really rather fun...

Something else the Germans had thrown overboard was the Enigma cypher machine, used to encode radio messages, whose secret lay still undiscovered by Allied Intelligence. However, they had omitted to dump some of the wheels which were used to change the machine's settings on a daily basis. Those left on board the trawler were quickly despatched to the Government Code and Cypher School at Bletchley Park, where they were analysed and used to decipher a portion of that month's German signal traffic.

Alec Dennis had hardly tied up in Scapa Flow before he and *Griffin* were back in Norway, evacuating the embattled remnants of the army from Namsos.

> Quite exciting. We went in through thick fog and didn't know our masts were sticking up out of it; but the Ju 87s did. Anyway, we got out of there – place was ablaze – and proceeded out to sea. A bit of a convoy – Mountbatten and the *Kelly* were there, that sort of thing. The Germans went for the destroyers and hit a French one, the *Bison*. She blew up, so the *Afridi* went alongside to pick up the *Bison*s and in doing so was left behind. Next wave of planes came along and blew up the *Afridi* – she had the celebrated Captain Vian on board.
>
> Anyway, we were detailed to go alongside *Afridi*. We picked up the *Afridi*s and the *Bison*s, and a whole lot of French *chasseurs alpins*, and a lot of our soldiers, and some Norwegians; we had an absolute shipful. Then – the most unpleasant experience I had, one I've never forgotten – as the *Afridi* was sinking by the bows there were a whole lot of sailors with their heads out of the scuttles. They couldn't get out. There was ammunition blowing up all over the place and they were burning down there in the fo'c'sle. It was ghastly: shattering, actually.

On land, from Poland to Norway, the Germans had had things all their own way so far. Now, in mid-1940, they were poised to strike westward, into and through Holland and Belgium, and on south into France. They would leapfrog over the northern end of the Maginot Line, the fortified border between Germany and France, and then encircle the French and British armies that were all that seemed to stand between them and the complete conquest of Europe. By comparison with the German army, though they outnumbered it in tank strength, the Allied forces were poorly off in terms of decisiveness of leadership, efficiency of organisation and quality of equipment. They were thinking and reacting defensively; while their opponents, with a series of victories under their belts, were thinking and acting offensively. It was as if the psychological effect of once more operating among the familiar names of First World War battlefields re-awoke that era's stasis and fatalism in the Allied armies, while it was galvanising their opponents into swift, daring movement.

The British Army, under the title of the British Expeditionary Force, had been rushed across to France a week after the outbreak of war – five divisions, almost the entire strength of the regular Army – and deployed near the Belgian border to face any threat from the German Army. Riding a Bren-gun carrier with the Royal Army Service Corps was Private Sam Meltzer, a half-Jewish Londoner from Islington who had been selling windows until he had enlisted in the Royal Army Reserve in July 1939. By the end of September Meltzer found himself stationed near Arras in north-eastern France. He was less than enchanted with the equipment the troops were using.

> We were still wearing First World War uniforms with puttees and carrying the old-fashioned Lee-Enfield .303 rifles. The officers and NCOs were from the Indian Frontier: they were pukka sahibs, come from India to train the troops.
>
> In France, training relaxed, if I have to tell the truth. I'd only been under training for three months and the square-bashing stopped; it became like a continental honeymoon, you know. You were in a little village; once or twice a week they would take you into the city, to Douai. It was a very relaxed atmosphere at that time. In fact, it was no more like war than what we'd experienced in camp at Blandford. It was phoney war. And we definitely thought we were invincible, because of the Maginot Line. But when they came, they didn't come through the Maginot Line – they came where we were.

The big German blitzkrieg across the Low Countries began on 10 May 1940 with paratroop landings in Holland and Belgium. That was the day when, across the Channel in London, Winston Churchill took over from Neville Chamberlain as British Prime Minister. On 14 May Rotterdam was bombed. Warnings had been given that it would happen if the Dutch did not surrender; but the Dutch played for time, there was a muddle over a possible halting of the attack and the ultimatum's deadline seemed to the Allied side to have been pre-empted by the Germans. Whatever the truth, the residential areas of the inner city were set alight by incendiaries; almost a thousand Dutch civilians were killed, and 29,000 wounded. The Dutch government surrendered the following day, at the same time as German Panzer divisions were driving into France across the River Meuse. The BEF, which had ventured east into Belgium as far as Brussels, drew back into France again. The Panzers were attacked on 21 May by the British and French near Arras, and slowed up in their advance; but they could not be prevented from reaching the sea. A month and a day later, with Paris in German hands, the French would sign an armistice at Compiègne which ended their official resistance to the invaders. The setting of the ceremony, insisted upon by the victors, was the railway carriage in which German signatures had signalled the end of the Great War and their own country's bitter defeat.

At the end of May, as the advancing Germans tried to encircle the remnants of the BEF and some of its French colleagues, Sam Meltzer was caught up in the retreat.

> The route we took back to the beach was the same route that they used in World War One. It was the same towns – Ypres, Cambrai, Douai. My father had been there, on the Somme with the Middlesex Regiment. My own first sight of the Germans was outside Brussels – the largest tanks I'd ever seen. Huge tanks, very well trained soldiers: the blitzkrieg stuff, you see. And quite truthfully – our line broke.
>
> You'll recall the story of the refugees on the roads. Those buggers were dive-bombing them. I was on my Bren-gun carrier; you could actually see the whites of their eyes in the planes, they came so low.

The beach that Sam Meltzer arrived at, eventually, was on the outskirts of Dunkirk – from where, between 27 May and 4 June, the ramshackle miracle of Operation Dynamo was to see 338,226 men evacuated to Britain aboard every kind of floatable craft, from fishing smacks to Royal Navy warships, under dive-bomb attack from the Luftwaffe and shelling from the ever-advancing German guns. 'Approaching the beach,' Meltzer recalls, 'they were shelling us from La Panne on the east and they were shelling us from Dunkirk on the west. On the beach itself there were masses of people lined up. The smell I remember – it was mostly of bodies which had been lying there unburied. It was a smell of death and of burning. There was bombing and strafing going on, of course, so after a few days a lot of people sort of trickled away from the beaches. They used to scatter and take refuge in the dunes at a place called Bray-Dunes. But the place to be, if you wanted to get home, was on the beach.'

The cheery, unselfish stoicism of the men under attack has become the very symbol of the 'Dunkirk spirit'. However, there were instances of less than admirable behaviour on the beaches, as reported by one interviewee who did not want to be identified for fear of offending his fellow Dunkirk veterans. This man wanted his side of the story to be told, partly to point up, by contrast, the steadiness of most of the soldiers, partly as a reminder that the varnish of civilisation had a tendency to crack off in the heat of war.

> Contrary to what is generally believed about Dunkirk, there was in fact a certain amount of panic. It became, in certain parts, every man for himself and suddenly the animal would come out in fellers. There was no line-jumping that I saw; but there were officers who ... pushed their privileges, let's say. So

much so, that when we got back to England we were severely reprimanded for not saluting our officers. That's the way we felt.

Yes . . . there was a certain amount of panic, and not only among the soldiers. When a boat full of men had been taken out to a ship, it had to be taken back again empty to the beach for the next load. But some of the sailors felt that they didn't want to, in case soldiers in the water would grab on to the boat and tip the ruddy thing up. The sailor might finish up in the sea himself and have to line up on the beach with everybody else. So some of the sailors shirked their duties and told the last soldier on board that he had to row the empty boat back for the next lot of men. This wasn't the 'spirit of the beaches', as it's often been referred to.

Watching soldiers running to hide in the sand dunes, Sam Meltzer realised:

I should be walking out to sea, instead of scattering. Which I did, and was picked up and taken to a little ship called the *Brighton Belle*, which I used to ride on when I was a kid.

The buggers sunk it, within sight of Margate. They dropped a bomb down the funnel. Orders were not to swim ashore, because of the Goodwin quicksands. The Navy picked us up; and that was when I did get a bit scared. I had on a French jacket, to keep warm. They picked me out of the sea and a British sailor said, 'He's a bleedin' Frenchman! Throw the bastard back in!'

Now all eyes, all over the world, were focusing on Britain. There seemed to be nothing to prevent the so far unstoppable German Army from hopping across the English Channel, under the protection of the so far all-conquering Luftwaffe, and sweeping through the United Kingdom as they had done through the Low Countries. On 16 July Hitler ordered the implementation of Operation Sealion, the crushing of the Royal Air Force by the Luftwaffe, to be followed by an invasion through barge-borne landing of troops. It looked like another foregone conclusion, although the Luftwaffe expected the coming battle to be tougher than those it had already won. But there were significant differences. Britain's air defences were efficiently marshalled into Fighter Groups; each of these gave instructions to several Sectors under its command, and each Sector then deployed the squadrons it controlled. Radar, which none of the German services was using at this stage of the war, gave invaluable advance warning of an impending attack. Production of fighter aircraft was rising in Britain, as it fell in Germany during the course of the air battles. And there were problems for the German Messerschmitt 109s, the single-engined fighters that rapidly took on the chief rôle on the German side. Their limited range meant that from their airfields near the north-eastern French coast they could only operate over the south-eastern corner of Britain. And they soon found themselves with a dual mission: to destroy the British fighters in aerial combat or in ground strafing, and also to shadow and protect the bombers which were trying to destroy the RAF airfields and radar installations. The RAF pilots, by contrast, had only one objective – to shoot down any German plane they encountered.

It would be the fighter aircraft that would decide the issue; and in July 1940 the two sides' strengths were not far apart. Britain had over 600 Spitfires and Hurricanes; German strength was a little over 700. The disparity could be said to have been made up by the superior determination of British men fighting to defend their own home country; yet determination, yoked to astonishing coolness and bravery, was also the hallmark of the Commonwealth pilots from Australia, New Zealand, Canada, Ireland and South Africa, who, along with Frenchmen, Poles and Americans, fought in the Battle of Britain on the Allied side.

Some had come, paying their own expenses, as freelance adventurers, generally with a flying background. Some, like Desmond Sheen from Australia, were on short-service commission with the RAF. Others came to the operational fighter squadrons via the Auxiliary Air Force, in which as peacetime civilians they had learned to fly at weekends. Glen Niven from Vancouver Island, the son of a Great War hero, was one of these – the family had come from Canada to settle in his mother's native Scotland early in 1937. Niven had been bitten by the flying bug, and in spite of short-sightedness had bluffed his way through the medical and into the air in a succession of more or less outmoded machines – Avro biplanes, Tiger Moths, Miles Masters, North American Harvards. Finally he graduated to Hurricanes. 'Flying a Hurricane was like driving a van. The Hurricane was a good solid hunk of stuff. You could drop it on the ground and it didn't worry. Quite slow, but manoeuvrable – you could do rolls by the ton.'

When the Battle of Britain started, Glen Niven was flying Hurricanes, but by 1 September 1940 he had been posted to 602 'City of Glasgow' Squadron at Westhampnett, next door to the Sector airfield of Tangmere. This was a Spitfire squadron, and Niven at last found himself at the controls of the fighter that everyone wanted to fly, the most glamorous aeroplane on earth.

Flying the Spitfire was like driving a sports car. It was faster than the old Hurricane, much more delicate. You couldn't roll it very fast, but you could make it go up and down so much easier. A perfect lady. It wouldn't do anything wrong. The Hurricane would drop a wing if you stalled it coming in, but a Spitfire would come wafting down. You couldn't snap it into a spin. Beautiful to fly, although very stiff on the ailerons – you had to jam your elbow against the side to get the leverage to move them. And so fast! If you shut the throttle in a Hurricane you'd come to a grinding halt; in a Spitfire you'd just go whistling on.

On 1 September 1940, as the untried Glen Niven was unpacking at Westhampnett, Desmond Sheen – already a veteran with several 'kills' and a DFC to his credit – was floating earthwards over the Weald of Kent about fifty miles away.

I didn't have much luck, because we were attacking a formation of Heinkels and I got shot down. I was looking down at the bombers and he came from above. I bailed out and came down in Kent, near Maidstone somewhere. Then about five days later we were climbing up over the coast near Dover when we got warning, a bit late – and again I got shot down. I was wounded, too, and had to spend another spell in hospital.

When it's you that gets caught, it's not very funny. The plane's gone – it shakes – half the wing has gone, the oxygen bottle blew up. It was just a mess. And I was wounded – a machine-gun bullet in more or less the same place as before. I couldn't control the plane. You've got to get out, it's instinctive. You've got to get clear of it, otherwise...

Things happen so quickly – very, very quickly. I passed out for a bit. When I did come to, the aircraft was going vertically. That's when I tried to get out. I got sucked out – and my feet got caught in the windscreen. I struggled, managed to get myself free, pulled the ripcord. The chute had only just opened when I went straight through a tree. That slowed me down, so I landed light as a feather.

A policeman came along on a bike. He handed me a flask and he said, 'You left it a bit late.'

I agreed with him.

Glen Niven:

We were living in a farmhouse in this field. We found a squash club with a bar and more or less took that over. A few chaps met a few girls, because there were WAAFs about the place. But you were really more interested in the flying, in what was going on the next day. We never thought, 'Oh, the filthy, dirty, swinish Germans!' We had no particular moral angle. You wanted to fly, fly, fly! You weren't very introspective or metaphysical about things. You wanted to get into the action because you were twenty, because you flew and because there was a war going on.

We were rather a race apart. In those days if you wandered into a country pub, you couldn't buy a drink. All the regulars would say, 'Ah, here they are!' and line up about six pints. Well, at that age, two pints and I was absolutely screechers. We thought we were the glamour boys, the top: rather above other people. And I notice even nowadays, if we're with other service people and somebody says 'He was a Battle of Britain pilot', they'll all go, 'Ooh, was he? Oh gosh!' There's still this sort of aura.

Joe Blencowe, an Oxfordshire lad working as an armourer at Tangmere, had a different perspective on the dashing young men:

The fighter pilots were only schoolboys. That's what most of them would have been called. They had the key few, the lads who'd had some very extensive training. They were your flight leaders, your squadron leaders. A wonderful experience, they seemed to show – a knowledge of how to lead people. The tight formations they flew! The younger fellows used to grumble, sometimes, because it was highly dangerous. They made me feel that I wanted to be part of their outfit, that what I was doing was too humdrum.

On the bomber squadrons you'd have had a lot more rapport between ground crews and pilots. The bomber pilot took far more interest in his aircraft than the young fighter pilot did. But we got little opportunity or time to make friends at all.

Des Sheen: 'You were up at dawn, and if you were lucky you were still there when it got dark. You just broke off for meals. Sometimes you had lunch on the broad outfield; or you went back to the mess, where you were probably called out again. I think the most call-outs I had was three in one day, but some people had five or six. Could be half an hour or an hour in the air at a time. It was a long day.'

Glen Niven:

My first engagement, I was chasing a chap across the Channel – he was jinking like mad. I said, 'You're quite safe – with my eyesight, I couldn't hit the broad side of a barn door.' Then, when I got back, Sergeant Andy Macdowell said to me, 'You great screaming twit! Didn't you see the one on your tail, shooting at you?' I said, 'Ooh, no – I didn't look!'

The only time I was scared was when I looked down and saw tracer bullets going by. I thought, 'Ooh, dear, there's something hostile behind.' He was a bloody good shot, this 109, so I did the only thing I could do – top right, bottom left. You put the stick *there*, and your foot *there*, and I don't know what happens to the aircraft, but it sort of does *that*! Then his cannon shell blew my wingtip off – it was like a giant hitting you with a bloody sledgehammer. That blew me upside down as well. I was a bit scared...

I don't think I ever hit anything, because of my eyesight. The first aircraft I ever fired at, he was coming towards me. So I said, 'Right, you bastard!' and gave him a squirt. He went whistling by – and it was a Spitfire.

Des Sheen:

Normally you'd attack in a 'vic' of three. The odd thing is that all the tactics we were taught before the war were useless. They were all based on the fact that we would be attacking bombers, but nobody realised that the Germans would have fighters on the French coast who would escort the bombers. It meant all our tactics went out the window. It was a question of more or less becoming individuals, getting in close, trying to shoot 'em down and avoid the fighters up top. Dog-fight tactics – we learned on the job.

Glen Niven:

The great thing was that during the Battle of Britain you were over Britain, so if something hit your engine, or it stopped, you would land in friendly territory. We had one chap shot down twice in two days. He just wrapped up his parachute and went to the nearest station; the same one both times, according to him. 'Cor blimey, back again, Sir?' He got in to London and just calmly caught the bloody tube out to Hornchurch, with his parachute, both times.

Joe Blencowe:

We were arming Spits and Hurricanes at Tangmere. Oh God, we saw enough action there. It seemed to me you got no sleep to speak of at all. We lost an awful lot of aircraft on the tarmac due to Jerry's activities. He was sneaking in at all times. Mostly in the very early morning they'd have a go for us, while we were still in the barracks asleep. You'd hear the bombs first – and then the warning sirens. We had a goodly number of nice young WAAFs – they worked hard, those girls – and quite a few of them got killed. When a raid came you were supposed to make straight for the shelters. Not everybody felt happy about those, but you were probably better in them than being foolhardy and staying out. I don't know – you look back and you think to yourself: it was good to be a Britisher. That sense of: 'Keep going!'

Des Sheen: 'Shoot the bastards down! That's how you felt. I think Douglas Bader put it the right way; he said, "What are they doing over *our* country?" Shoot 'em down ... if they don't shoot you down first.'

Glen Niven: 'We used to wander up and down the lawn in front of the farmhouse, chatting and joking about what we'd do when the war was over – "Pilot in the last war, Sir!" – holding out our hands like beggars on the street. But we knew we were going to win, even then. Because Britain Didn't Lose.'

Towards the end of September 1940, as German losses of fighters, bombers and aircrew mounted and the RAF seemed able to go on filling its empty seats and replacing its shot-down aircraft, Hitler decided to postpone the invasion and to switch from attacking the British planes and airfields to mounting a bombing campaign against British cities, particularly London. Nothing like the Blitz had ever been tried before. The Germans did not actually have the resources or equipment to carry their idea through to complete success – though no one on either side could be sure of that at the time. From 7 September London was bombed almost every night; from November onwards the attack was widened to include other major British cities. The campaign was to continue until May 1941, when the Luftwaffe had to concentrate its attentions eastward for the impending German invasion of Russia. During those eight months about 50,000 British civilians were killed and an estimated 3,000,000 homes destroyed – an appalling sum, a terrible indictment of modern warfare, but still only a small proportion of the toll in the Ruhr during RAF Bomber Command's nightly pounding of Germany with heavy bombers from 1942 onwards. In 1940 the Heinkel He 111, Germany's main bomber, could carry only a fraction of the load soon to be lifted by Allied bombers such as the Lancaster and the Flying Fortress. But the He 111 could still drop bombs of over a ton weight. The heaviest dropped during the Blitz was two and a half tons. Though these big bombs did serious damage where they fell, most of the ruin in London and elsewhere was caused by incendiaries filled with oil, benzine or phosphorus. But in spite of the burned buildings and shattered streets, and the burned and shattered corpses of civilian men, women and children, Joe Blencowe's sense of 'keep going' was very much the norm in Britain.

Mahinder Singh Pujji, a Sikh flyer who had just celebrated his twenty-second birthday, arrived in London from India in September, at the height of the Battle of Britain, and witnessed the whole of the Blitz from his London billet. Pujji, a real young fire-eater entirely in love with the romance of flying, had to curb his impatience for another six months before he could get into the air in a Hurricane.

> London was being bombed day and night, as you know, and we were billeted in this temporary hut at Uxbridge. Throughout the night the hut would shake and there would be bombs all over. I wasn't worried. I would just go out and see what was happening. We could see the searchlights looking for the German aircraft, and then the flashes of their bombing and the anti-aircraft guns. That was every night. I was more than longing to get into the action; I wanted to be *there*. Not just to fight anyone – but to *fly*...
>
> I personally appreciated the spirit of the Londoners. When we would meet them they were very friendly; and they were very courageous. If you would go to cinema and there was an air raid, then on the screen will come a notice saying: 'There is an air raid. Anyone who wishes to leave, there is a shelter. Please leave quietly.' I found no one would leave. It really fascinated me, because I thought, 'These people are really brave.'

It may not have seemed like it at the time, but Britain was not the only battlefield in the summer of 1940. On 10 June Italy had declared war on Britain and France. Mussolini could see his opportunity for further expansion in north-east Africa, with Britain fully occupied and likely to be defeated, and the Mediterranean ports of a beaten France available to the Italian Navy. In July, while Germany and Britain were beginning their three-month struggle for mastery of the sky over Kent, Surrey and Sussex, two Blackshirt brigades along with other local troops were massing in Ethiopia, near the border with British Somaliland at the top of the Horn of Africa. Derek Watson, by now a thirty-year-old captain in charge of a company of Nyasaland soldiers in the 2nd Battalion of the King's African Rifles, was sent up to the area to defend the camel tracks that led across the Assa Hills to the Somali port of Berbera. Altogether there were about three battalions on the Allied side. Outnumbered by ten to one, they were operating in broken, hilly country, trying to defend widely scattered positions with no proper signals communications or reliable supply system. It wasn't a recipe for success when Watson's C Company went into action on 12 August.

The Italians' Caproni bombers had been coming over and bombing us. We'd made round defensive positions, absolutely ideal for the people to come over and bomb. Anyway, the CO told me to take two companies and put them in a defensive position up on this hill. He said, 'It's perfectly all right, the Indians are there.' I said, 'Sir, have you looked?' – I could see them all streaming back, even as he was speaking!

Anyway, I took the companies up – hadn't got any trenching tools at all, only had what we'd taken to put the bloody wire in with. So we then had to build defensive walls out of stones. Had nothing to eat but bully beef; our rations were being brought up on camels, but the Italians started shelling us and the camels turned round and went. Never saw them again; never saw our rations again; never saw the CO again. We stayed there for three days. The Italians were all round us. When we ran out of water and food we up sticks and went, and it took us three days to get back.

It was completely chaotic. I actually sent a man with a message in a cleft stick, saying, 'What do you want us to do?' Never saw him again. There weren't even any telephone lines out, and no wireless – I hadn't got a clue where the CO had gone. No way of checking if the situation was changing – no way at all. Whole thing was a bloody shambles.

By 19 August the Italians had completed their occupation of British Somaliland (they would be ejected again in March of the following year) and Derek Watson's 2 KAR were evacuated from Berbera. As an exercise in warfare it had been a failure; but at least the Nyasa soldiers had come under fire, something Watson had wanted them to experience: 'Our training, to be frank, was bloody useless. We always seemed to have four maps and to be where the bloody things joined. Now my idea of training was to take the battalion on route marches twice a week – forty miles – and have someone shooting at them, and blowing up the side of the road and that sort of thing; give them some idea of what it would be like under fire. But that never happened during training.'

Getting a decent military training in a short space of time was proving to be a problem all over the world. The countries of the Commonwealth were trying to gear up for sending their men and women overseas with at least some of the right equipment and a smattering of knowledge as to how to use it. The challenge was to adapt the regular Army's 'Brasso-and-bullshit' approach to the needs of ordinary unmilitary young people coming in off the street from offices, farms, fishing boats, schoolrooms, the dole queue, who simply wanted to get on with things as quickly as possible.

In New Zealand Tom Somerville from the Upper Hutt valley made up his mind to enlist.

> Thought about it a lot, spoke to a few of the older men about it. They said, 'Well, it's a decision you've got to make for yourself.' Of course, there was the allure of going overseas, going away. I'd never been out of New Zealand before, I'd led a fairly sheltered life down on the farm. And there was always the thought of protecting your own country, England, the Empire. I turned it over in my mind. Will I? Won't I? Why should I?
>
> I went into training camp in Papakura. A hard life, parade ground stuff, long hours. We all got our share of spud-peeling. That's where I first learned never to volunteer for anything. One morning on parade the sergeant-major said, 'Anyone here can play the piano?' Four or five hands went up. They finished down at the Papakura yards, shovelling coal.

Jack Brown was another New Zealander who, at twenty-one years old, was thinking about enlisting. Brown joined with a chum, after they'd had a couple of beers at the Taihape agricultural show. His life had been a tough one up till then, a lonely working life as a cattle hand and shepherd on the big upcountry ranching stations of the North Island. But the Army didn't particularly prize self-sufficiency, as Brown found out in camp:

> Going from a lone job like shepherding, where you spend most of the day on your own, to an army camp with about fifty in a room – it took me quite a long time to adjust to being with a crowd of people all the time. I'd virtually lived a working life on my own, you might say. Sleeping with people grunting and groaning all round you: I found it very hard to adjust to. And the regimentation – I wasn't used to that. You think for yourself when you're out on the sort of job I was on. In the Forces, you don't think; they tell you you're not paid to think. I never, ever got used to obeying orders. Probably that's why I went through the Army as a private.

In Cape Breton Island, off the northern tip of Canada's Nova Scotia peninsula, Joe Oldford had been training with the militia since 1933, when he joined as a sixteen-year-old schoolboy. Now he enlisted in the Cape Breton Highlanders and found himself training 'with rifles that were from the First World War and Lewis machine-guns from the First World War too. We didn't really get uniforms for the first year or so. Some of us were doing beach patrol in pants that fitted so badly we had to cut the material and put a wedge in. In fact we had so little that this one fellow, the only piece of equipment he had was a water bottle. He'd come on parade every day with the water bottle strapped on. That's how he got his nickname – Water Bottle.'

Other Canadians were sailing for England, the vanguard of what was to become a large army-in-waiting pent up in that little island. Reg Burt, who had emigrated as a seven-year-old boy from Tottenham in London to Toronto, now joined an anti-aircraft unit.

On embarkation leave I went to say goodbye to my grandad, who was an old ex-Navy man. When he saw my Army uniform, he slammed the door in my face.

We went across on the P&O liner *Stratheden*, which had a crew of Lascars. They used to eat their meal from a communal dish, and they squatted down and ate with their right hand all the time. Of course, we found out that if your shadow went over the meal, then they'd throw it overboard – which became a fun game to us. We kept on walking by; they kept on throwing the meal overboard.

We were sleeping in the bottom of the hold, about sixty people with only one ladder up to the outside. Wasn't too safe down there. And it was hot during the trip; so we used to bunk outside on the deck when we could. What the Lascars used to do was hose down the decks, and if they saw us lying there they'd go right over us with their cold hoses. Wasn't too much love lost between us!

Horizons were being abruptly broadened, or prejudices confirmed, as the Commonwealth's young men and women went bumping up against a variety of alien cultures and peoples in a way that previous generations had never had the opportunity to do. Bombay was a place many of them remembered for its stinks, its squalor, and the visible poverty of the wharfside workers and idlers. In South Africa, and particularly Capetown, others got a rude shock – Mahinder Singh Pujji was one of them:

On our way to London we called in at Capetown. While I was having my dinner along with my friends – there were about six–seven of us, all in our RAF uniforms – the waiter came along and says, 'Look – are you from Egypt?' We said, 'No, we are from India.' He looked shocked and went away. Then the manager came. He says, 'I'm sorry, gentlemen; I'm not allowed to serve people from your country.'

Among us were two or three veteran pilots who had been flying from Delhi to London – very famous pilots of international repute. They were *furious*. They said, 'What do you mean? We have come to fight for the British and that's what you are telling us?' One got very angry; he hit the table, a glass table, with his shoes and it broke to pieces. He says, 'I want to know who doesn't want us here!' So a scene was created and very soon there were police, then there were officers; the High Commissioner and all those people came out. They all apologised to us; but we were led back to our hotel. Then we were explained: 'It's the local thing, it's not the British.' But – it was British rule at the time in South Africa!

Anyway, we at once realised that there was a discrimination in South Africa. In England, however, we didn't see it at all. It was a very pleasant surprise.

Pierre Austin from Melbourne had been drafted from his Scrap Iron Flotilla destroyer *Voyager* into the RAN heavy cruiser *Australia* during the early summer. As the Battle of Britain hotted up during July, *Australia* steamed north for Scapa Flow, the vast wind-whipped natural anchorage among the Orkney Islands where the British Home Fleet was based. Sailing from Scapa Flow out into the North Atlantic to fetch in convoys on the last stretch of their dangerous journey from America across U-boat-haunted waters, or steaming further north around Bear Island in search of the heavy cruiser, *Admiral Hipper*, and other German surface raiders, *Australia* was working closely with ships of the Royal Navy. Pierre Austin had plenty of opportunity to form opinions about his British counterparts.

We did feel that the Australians generally, over the whole spectrum, had more initiative – sometimes rather roundly expressed. There were, I know, a good many differences in the Army between the Australians and the British: for example, when you got a rather callow English officer with one pip on his shoulder insisting that a tough Australian sergeant should salute him in the street.

In the Navy we didn't have that, because the Navy had a very professional core. One thing we did find: we couldn't replace crew members with Australians, necessarily, being so far from home, so we took aboard some Royal Navy hostilities-only ratings. There, I know, there was occasional difficulty – lower-deck friction. They were less clean, less willing ... some of them.

Austin was soon to find himself under fire for the first time. *Australia* was one of the ships detailed to take part in 'Operation Menace', an attempt to put an occupation force into the port of Dakar in French West Africa. With the collaborationist Vichy government now installed in the unoccupied southern part of France, and controlling things in the French colonies abroad, it was felt that a swift strike against Vichy-held Dakar would deliver the valuable Atlantic-facing port into Allied hands. It was hoped that, by putting the Free French leader, General Charles de Gaulle, ashore to win over the defenders, the strike might even be a bloodless one. Unfortunately no one had assessed properly the mood of the hosts, who gave a very hostile response to the Allies' knock on the door at dawn on 23 September. Far from inviting them in, the defenders of Dakar delivered enough knocks of their own, via heavy shore batteries and the fifteen-inch guns of the French battleship *Richelieu*, which was in harbour, to hit the battleship *Barham*, the cruiser *Cumberland* and two destroyers, as well as shooting down nineteen aircraft from the carrier *Ark Royal*. A landing attempt by the Free French failed, a French submarine torpedoed and crippled the Allies' other battleship, *Resolution*, and on 25 September the would-be invaders retired, comprehensively outplayed – a small but complete disaster for Allied prestige and co-operation. De Gaulle had not even set foot on shore, let alone won any hearts or minds.

In the middle of all this was *Australia*, with Pierre Austin watching as the Allied force began to bombard Dakar and receive salvoes in return.

This was the first time I'd been under fire. You were too busy doing your job to react, although naturally you were apprehensive; you'd be silly not to be.

I was immensely impressed by one thing. When we were firing in concentration we had little bleepers that told us when our fall of shot would arrive. The only trouble was that everybody else's was arriving at the same time – you had no idea whose shot it was. But the French were very cunning; they screwed dye-bags into the base of their shells. You had green falls of shot, red falls of shot, purple, blue – they could tell whose was whose. It was so simple. At the first fall the crew were lying flat on deck while things were popping round us – great fountains of coloured water. One chap put his head up and in a loud voice said, 'Cor! Ain't it pretty!' It was a great tension-breaker.

The French fire was extraordinarily accurate at long range: we were hit with two six-inch shells, although they did no particular damage except wrecking the Captain's galley and our evaporators. We were firing salvoes. When a number of eight-inch guns go off, the whole ship jolts, everything shakes, bits fall off if they're not secured. It's damn noisy.

On the second day of the engagement, *Australia* was ordered to deal with a French destroyer. Pierre Austin watched, with mixed emotions, as the destroyer was fired on and driven ashore as a burning wreck: 'You feel tremendous pity, almost an empathy for those fellows, who were doing their job. I know she took very heavy casualties. And in this particular case, because it was a French ship and I had a French mother ... It was rather a peculiar position to be in. But it had to be done. That's all. And you go away from it and you think: Well, thank God it wasn't me.'

In Britain some young men were also experiencing action for the first time, with mixed results.

At the height of the Blitz [says Reg Burt] we were training at Colchester with tree trunks instead of guns. Eventually we got issued with a Bofors and were sent for anti-aircraft duty to the east coast, somewhere near Clacton in Essex. Our first experience of action, eh? Now, before you go out, you do an inspection and maintenance on the gun. You take out the breech block, grease it up, all this kind of thing. So we do our inspection and off we go to Clacton. We set up the gun and about two o'clock in the morning we had to stand to; the Germans were coming over. Everybody went to his position. We got the order to fire and the No. 4 stamped on the pedal. Nothing happened. So we went through the drill ... We had forgotten the breech block. It was back in Colchester.

Many young men must have been as inexperienced as Nila Kantan, but few can have had such a bewildering entry on to the war stage.

At nineteen years old I came to Bangalore. I was always dreaming of joining in the war. There was no conscription, there was no recruitment. So many people said, 'Let us volunteer!' I happened to meet one British officer and he said, 'Hello, lad, do you like to go abroad?' After two days he brought me a certificate, which said, 'I am prepared to go to any part of the world.' He took me to the collecting camp at Pune. They gave me a uniform and the rank of Indian Warrant Officer. Then, my God! I got in this troopship, without any training whatsoever – it was very peculiar.

Our convoy was known as Force Trout, escorted by three cruisers and six destroyers. There was a naval action – the Italians started attacking in the middle of the night. I tried to go to my action station, but the naval people were so quick that they completely blocked all the watertight compartments. I got stuck in one. When the ships started firing I began weeping like children – because I had never seen all these things. Then a naval officer came and said, 'Don't cry, lad.'

I first set my foot in Port Sudan in October 1940, after about twenty days. I went to get some Egyptian currency. Suddenly there was some sort of a sound and all the fellows vanished. It was an air-raid siren. I did not know what was happening. Then one sergeant-major came and said, 'Come on, lad, get to the shelter!' I did not know where the shelter was. I just lay flat. Then what happened – one bomb fell somewhere, one shrapnel hit my leg.

After everything was clear we went to Khartoum. The leg started paining. I went to the medical inspection room – and they hospitalised me for a month!

This was my first introduction to war.

As 1940 drew to a close, Johannesburg witnessed anti-war demonstrations. In Trinidad, by contrast, there were demonstrations by those not permitted to take part in active service because of the colour of their skins. Liverpool and London were burning with incendiary and high-explosive bombs. Rumblings of discontent could be heard in Delhi, Bombay and Calcutta over Indian involvement in the war she had not declared herself. In the Atlantic the U-boats were finishing off a highly successful year's preying on the still poorly defended merchant traffic – Allied losses would total 1059 ships, of 4,055,706 tons. In October the Italians invaded Greece – the New Zealanders Jack Brown and Tom Somerville and the Australian Bob Taunt would find mixed fortunes there next year.

In Africa the Italians were rampant, having expanded from Ethiopia and Libya. They had occupied British Somaliland; they had also entered Kenya and the Sudan to some depth. Pushing east from Libya into Egypt, they advanced until they were only 250 miles from the great Mediterranean Fleet base and military centre of Alexandria. There, in mid-September, they stopped at Sidi Barrani and consolidated their promising position in heavily fortified bases, with concrete bunkers and dug-outs and observation posts. They outnumbered and outgunned the Allied force facing them, which had been strung out in scattered positions across the desert to give a misleading impression of its numbers and capacity.

General Archibald Wavell was Commander-in-Chief Middle East – a post that made him supreme commander from Egypt to Cyprus, from East Africa to the Lebanon. A quiet, impressive man, thick-set and slow-spoken, a highly intelligent military leader, he had, in July 1940, suggested forming a 6th Australasian Division by amalgamating the 16th Australian Brigade and the 4th New Zealand Brigade, the only two then ready for action. Not altogether surprisingly, both General Freyberg of New Zealand and General Blamey of Australia had turned him down. 'I do not wish to disclose to the New Zealand Government', Freyberg noted to Wavell, 'the proposals as outlined by you to break up the New Zealand Forces, as they would make a most unfavourable impression in New Zealand official circles ... The answer to any such proposal would, I am sure, be an uncompromising refusal.' In other words: 'Back off!'

The temptation for British commanders to think of Commonwealth troops as British, and to wish to deploy them over the heads of their own commanders, was always a strong one. The British self-image of pluckily standing alone, of being the last back against the wall, could lead, all too quickly, to feelings of superiority over the 'colonials', as the official Australian history makes clear: 'When Dominion soldiers arrive overseas their cousins of the British command are inclined to regard them with the eye of a governess when some hitherto unknown children are suddenly mixed with her brood. When something unexpected and undesired occurs, it is safe to guess that the newcomers will be blamed for it.'[1]

Dignity was for generals to stand on. Private Bob Taunt of the Australian 2/2 Battalion, who arrived with the Western Desert Force in the ruins of Sidi Barrani around Christmas time, had no worries except how to keep warm at night and how to get under enough cover during the day. Shortly after New Year Taunt would be firing his field gun on the port of Bardia across the border in Libya, then chasing the Italians westwards – the first surge in an ebb and flow of friend and foe, east and west along the 600-mile strip of desert between Alexandria and El Agheila, which would not resolve itself until the great Allied tide of 1943 swept the Italians and Germans out of North Africa for good.

The year ended looking seawards. The struggle between the Allied merchant convoys and the German U-boats, aeroplanes and surface raiders that became known as the Battle of the Atlantic was in a desperate phase for the Allies, and would get worse into 1941 before a proper escorting system for convoys was worked out. The Canadian Navy was starved of fighting ships too, as Raymond Walker from Sydney Mines in Cape Breton Island confirms:

Canada only had a small Navy, only a couple of destroyers, at the beginning of the war. For a dollar apiece they bought some of those old four-stacker American destroyers. There was a bunch of them. And they also got some yachts from the States; they got those for a dollar apiece too. Vanderbilt, who had lots of money – they had his yacht. They named them after animals. There was the *Beaver* and the *Reindeer*, the *Lynx*, the *Otter*, the *Caribou*. In 1940 they put me on *Reindeer* as a stoker. We used to operate out of Sydney in Cape Breton, taking convoys. We'd escort them as far as Newfoundland; they'd meet up off Newfoundland to go off to England, and we'd leave them there and just patrol down the coast between Cape Breton and the Gaspé, and between Quebec and the St Lawrence. Because at that time Jerry subs were coming right in, right up the St Lawrence.

Once out in the Atlantic and beyond the limited range of air cover that could be provided from British airfields in Newfoundland, the convoys had to take their chance over some hundreds of miles of hostile sea before they could come under the protection of welcoming escorts and air cover from the UK. Pierre Austin in *Australia* sailed to meet many a convoy and remembers these excursions chiefly as being

cold: wet: monotonous. Sometimes we'd go half-way across the Atlantic to meet incoming convoys. We wouldn't always see them; our duty was, if *Hipper* or other raiders were out, to stand if possible between them and the convoy.

When you do see a big convoy, it's a curious sense of: 'We have an enormous responsibility here. That lot *has* to get through.' But that's the initial reaction: after that, it becomes just another bloody convoy!

Austin reserves a good deal of contempt for those among the dock workers in Liverpool whose thieving – at a time when the ships and stores they were robbing were part of an international do-or-die operation – incensed every sailor who became aware of it: 'These Liverpool dockyard maties were 100 per cent for themselves. Their attitude was: if they could scrounge, they scrounged. They even took supplies out of the life rafts ... Obviously there were some who worked jolly well. But there were just too many instances of those who loafed, scrounged and stole. In the ships, we all felt the same about them. But the people of Liverpool, generally speaking, were superb.'

On 19 December 1940 Tom Somerville left New Zealand with the 4th Reinforcements, heading away from home into the unknown for the first time in his life:

I got on the troop train at the little country station; friends waved me goodbye. There were crowds of people on the quayside at Wellington, standing there holding ribbons between the ship and the shore which would break as we sailed away. The ship was called the *Empress of Russia*. Fellows were up in the rigging, anywhere they could get a view. I remember one playing a bugle; it was quite touching, actually.

I had mixed feelings about leaving a dependent mother behind, who still had three children at school. But there was a lot of excitement about it. We were away! Lots of little boats were running around, and I wrote a note and dropped it overboard: just saying goodbye. It found its way home, eventually.

THREE

Low Point: 1941

The day I shot down my first aeroplane, I went into my room and I lay down. I didn't want to talk to anyone. What I had gone through – that could have been my death, you see.   Mahinder Singh Pujji, India

They were saying to us, 'Better get out of this, there's trouble coming. Rommel's coming!' We said, 'We don't get out of here. We're here!'   Vernon Northwood, Australia

'These men from the dockside of Sydney and the sheep-stations of the Riverina presented such a picture of downright toughness with their gaunt, dirty faces, huge boots, revolvers stuffed in their pockets, gripping their rifles with huge shapeless hands, shouting and grinning – always grinning – that the mere sight of them must have disheartened the enemy troops ... The "Australian barbarians" had been turned loose by the British in the desert.'[2] Such was the image the Australian soldiers loved to project, and it served them well in the North African desert campaigns. They had an early baptism in 1941 – the year was only three days old when they moved in to capture the Libyan port of Bardia. British Intelligence had reported the presence inside the fortified perimeter of 20,000 demoralised Italians; in fact there were 45,000, with 410 field guns, well protected inside concrete fortifications on top of deep wadis or desert gullies. They were, it is true, demoralised by the time the Australians came to attack on 3 January, by reason of having been pounded

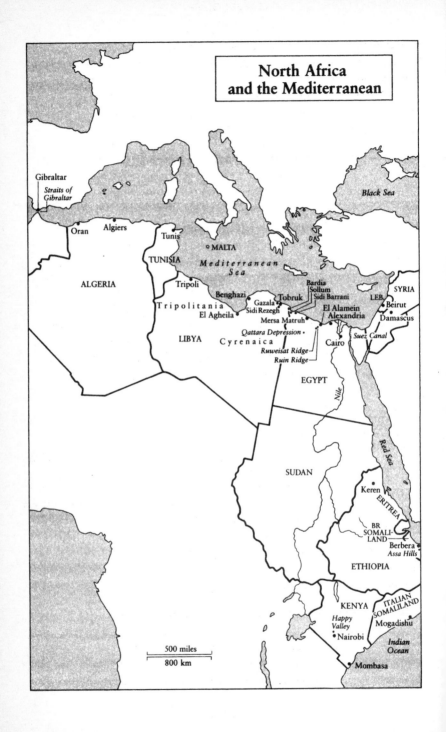

North Africa
and the Mediterranean

Gibraltar
*Straits of
Gibraltar*

Oran   Algiers

Tunis

TUNISIA

○ MALTA

Black Sea

*Mediterranean
Sea*

ALGERIA

Tripoli

Benghazi

Bardia
Sollum
Sidi Barrani

Tobruk

SYRIA

Gazala
Sidi Rezegh

LEB.

Beirut

T r i p o l i t a n i a

El Agheila

El Alamein
Alexandria

Damascus

Mersa Matruh

LIBYA

Qattara Depression ·

C y r e n a i c a

Ruweisat Ridge
Ruin Ridge

Cairo

Suez Canal

EGYPT

Nile

SUDAN

Red Sea

Keren ·

ERITREA

BR
SOMALI-
LAND

Berbera
Assa Hills

ETHIOPIA

KENYA

ITALIAN
SOMALILAND

*Happy
Valley*

· Mogadishu

· Nairobi

*Indian
Ocean*

500 miles

800 km

Mombasa

for two days and nights by naval, aerial and military bombardment. By 4 January it was all over and the Allies were free to push on along the dusty desert road to the west.

Bob Taunt of 2/2 Battalion was on signal duty just before the attack, acting as a conduit for orders, queries and reports passing between divisional, brigade and regimental headquarters.

We'd come up very quietly around midnight a couple of days before the attack and got our guns into position around Bardia. The town was cut off; no one could come out or come in. During the day I was in the telephone exchange in a deep dug-out we'd captured; at night we were in slit trenches a foot deep. We scrounged some galvanised iron, some sandbags for a bit of cover over the top. At that time, for us, it was a bit like the First World War – trenches and dug-outs.

They were firing at us; there were shells bursting all round, the Italians trying to reach a British formation behind us. You hear them coming over – *ssshhh! ssshhh! ssshhh!* – but the one that's really close you don't hear. Bang! It's there, without warning. It didn't feel too good, this first time for me under fire – but luckily their shells went in deep and threw up more dirt than metal.

We were limited in ammunition. We could only use about twenty rounds a day per battery. When we did the attack we put out a barrage, like the old First World War days, just ahead of the infantry, at dawn – and the infantry just walked and walked behind this barrage.

One of the big problems of desert warfare, in which several hundred miles often separated the battle front from anywhere with any facilities, was what to do with prisoners-of-war. And as the Italians began surrendering in their tens of thousands on the Western Desert Force's westward push, the problem became acute. The logistics of sparing fighting men to guard huge numbers of prisoners in crude wire enclosures, and providing the captives with food, water and sanitation while waiting for transport to be spared from more urgent duties, often meant suffering for captive soldiers. At this early stage of the war the sight of vast numbers of prisoners had not yet become commonplace.

The Italians surrendered after a while and we had thousands of prisoners. They were just coming at us in thousands, surrendering. Some didn't have white flags and we had to shoot 'em, open up on 'em with the guns. Then they put their hands up. You couldn't believe how many there were. You'd see 20,000 prisoners, marching along a thousand at a time, with one bloke guarding them at the front and one bloke behind. We put them in barbed-wire enclosures, and the British Army went backwards and forwards taking them off to Egypt, getting rid of them.

In the early part of 1941, Allied offensive operations were taking place in many parts of northern Africa, driving the Italians back from the positions they had taken up in 1940. Nila Kantan, recovered from his air-raid wound, went into Eritrea in January with a supply unit attached to the 5th Indian Division and advanced through hilly country towards Keren in the north of the country where the Italians resisted fiercely for two months.

Our duty was to ferry all the supplies and ammunition, including water. In other countries you will have water everywhere, but this is very peculiar in the desert campaign, we have to transport even water. I had to load, unload, take all the supplies, dumping them, even bury them. If somebody finds some buried drums in Eritrea even now, I wouldn't be surprised if we were the people who put the cache there.

I did not see much of the fighting at Keren, because I was back on the supply line. Sometimes our lorries were hit and they were burning. At first I used to be scared, but later it became a routine. The shells would be falling here, falling there, we never bothered. I have also some funny superstition. I thought, 'If I die in a battlefield, I'll go straight up to Heaven.' But no bomb, or bullet or shell came anywhere near me. So maybe I was not destined for Heaven.

Another area from which the Italians were being ejected early in 1941 was British Somaliland, the scene of the 'bloody shambles' experienced the previous August by Derek Watson and 2 KAR. The Allies had also entered Italian Somaliland, bordering the Indian Ocean along the east side of the Horn of Africa, and had won through to the capital, Mogadishu, by the end of February. Charles Adams from Capetown, South Africa, was there with the Cape Corps Regiment:

We had been sent to Nairobi and then up to the border with Italian Somaliland – the Italians had been trying to invade Kenya, and now it was our turn. We were part of the 1st South African Division and were attached to the 24th Gold Coast Brigade, supplying them with water. Poor quality water ... if you washed your face in it your hands would stick to your skin. It came in forty-five gallon drums, nine drums to a truck, and it was rationed – each man got about half a bottle a day. So there were plenty of thirsty people around.

Mogadishu I thought was a beautiful city – all that Italian artwork and architecture. But the Italians themselves – well, the Italian was never much of a fighter! We used to say that our 1st South African Division could defeat the whole Italian Army, because they were half-hearted fighters. Some were for Mussolini, some were for King Emmanuel. So they were divided among themselves.

South African whites feared, with some justification, what might happen after the war on the return of a large, disciplined body of non-whites trained in the use of firearms. Cape Coloureds, therefore, were not permitted to carry arms in the South African Army. Black recruits to the NMC were to be trained with assegais and knobkerries, the traditional weapons of the Zulu. Charles Adams felt belittled by the non-combatant role forced on him. So did Frank Sexwale, the black South African teacher. But the Indian, Nila Kantan, found dignity in the workaday labour of his supply unit:

I was very lean, thin, puny. I was not fit, so they rejected me for the infantry. I did not mind. Every job in the Army is useful, you see. The infantry is Queen of the Battle, they take all the credit; but I doubt very much if the infantry can do anything without the support of the services. Everyone is important, you see. Unless there is a pukka co-ordination, I don't think the infantry can do much. That is how we felt. The transport companies played a very crucial role. Without our effort, all the supply units, all the British and Indian RAC drivers, the ordnance and so forth – they could not have sustained the 8th Army. So I didn't mind. I was not a fighting man, in a sense – but we were very, very crucial to the action.

As the areas of conflict spread, and the reality of war came to menace more and more Commonwealth countries, so the number of Commonwealth participants grew. Some had been longing to join in since the moment of declaration of war and had only been waiting to complete their studies, or simply to become old enough to take part. For others, particular moments of revelation provided the spur. Dudley Thompson, Jamaica:

I was in a dentist's waiting-room in Kingston and just picked up one of the magazines left there. It happened to contain an article about *Mein Kampf*. Turning the leaves, I found out where in *Mein Kampf* Hitler denounced, with the most vicious vituperation, Jews and Negroes. I think we were described as 'semi-anthropoid, undeveloped human beings' – that sort of classification. And it stung me – I really felt stung by that. I said, 'I'm going to do my part to prove that he's wrong. I'm going to fly' – because I wanted to fly, the romantic attraction of the Air Force, you know – 'I want to fly and I'm going to be up there, in a Spitfire or something, and I'm going to meet some German – and I'm going to *show* him that I'm not an anthropoid. I'm going to beat him, up there.'

Etienne Marot, Mauritius: 'At nineteen ... it was adventure, more than anything else. My brother was in the Royal Air Force – a volunteer, he paid his own passage. I had a brother in the Army. I had to join. I had to be part of this. I think if I use the word "patriotism" it would be too big, too great. I was full of enthusiasm to be part of this mêlée, part of this problem of defeating an enemy.'

Frank Sexwale, South Africa: 'I thought, "Here's my chance to get some adventure." And with the hope, probably, of getting a little more money – I had to support my parents, and my sisters and brother, on my teacher's pay. I volunteered to join, but unfortunately I couldn't face my parents. I left without telling them, because they would not have let me go.'

Paul Gobine, Seychelles:

There were three reasons, to be truthful. In the first place: in the Seychelles at the time, life was hard. We knew by joining the Army we'd go to hardship; but you'll have a stomach full, you'll get some food to eat.

And the second thing: our loyalty. In school we always learned, 'Pussy cat, where you been? To London, to see the King.' The King of England was ... I don't know, we took him as one of the greatest people in the world. To serve the country and to serve the King; and at the same time, to leave the poverty behind.

And the third reason: to be a brave man.

Recruiting methods varied from country to country. In the case of Kenya, it was often the direct appeal of the recruiting officer, appearing in the flesh in classroom or market-place, that produced results. In other places the vivid imagery and punchy catch-phrase of an advertisement worked well. Keith Levy still remembers an RAF poster in Kingston, Jamaica, with its enticing slogan along the lines of 'Join the Royal Air Force – See the World – Learn to do a Good Job'.

A propaganda leaflet widely distributed in West Africa, and typical of the contemporary style, was divided into two halves. One, headed 'Britain's Way', depicted a black judge, teacher, nurse and policeman, and reminded readers that 'under British rule ... if a man does wrong he is judged according to the Law and Customs of his own people ... British Justice is the finest system in the world, and the fairest ... By means of education [Britain] wants Africans to learn, step by step, how to look after their own country and how to make good laws for themselves ... The

British Government wants to train more and more of your own people to look after you when you are ill...'

This was contrasted with 'Germany's Way', which showed brute-faced, swastika-festooned, whip-toting Nazi stormtroopers shooting and beating their African victims. 'The Nazi Minister for Labour has said: "A German is higher above an African than an African is above an ape." The Germans would take away your land, they would steal your crops and produce and they would force you to do what they wished, by torturing you and killing you if you refused to obey them.'

If some African tongues were in cheeks as their owners absorbed this, who can blame them?

In South Africa, too, a 'Note on Native Recruiting Propaganda' advised: '... while a blaze of colour might offend the susceptibilities of Europeans ... almost any colourful reproduction will appeal to natives. Films, depicting the native being transformed from an insignificant atom of a native territory to a swashbuckling brave of the NMC, have an enormous value.' The training films showed NMC recruits in full modern battledress, but brandishing assegais.

The NMC, or Native Military Corps, was part of the NEAS (Non-European Army Service) formed in June 1940 – the Cape Coloured Corps, of which Charles Adams of the Cape Corps Regiment was a member, and the Indian and Malay Corps were the other components. South African Government policy was clear on one thing: NEAS service personnel would be restricted to non-combatant roles.

Recruiting parties with loudspeakers toured the black towns and tried to get local chiefs to put the message across to their people. But appeals to blacks to join up to fight for liberty and freedom for all South Africans were not greeted with whole-hearted enthusiasm. The African National Congress – the radical political forum of the black community – had initially advised blacks not to serve unless the government would agree to arm them, though it had since softened that line. Those black South Africans who did join up soon found, as Frank Sexwale did, that their dreams of battlefield glory and of standing shoulder to shoulder with their brother soldiers were not to be realised:

After enlisting I did some sort of training – if you can call it training. We did squad drill every morning; later on we went to another camp to be trained as drivers. We used to do the drilling with assegais and knobkerries. I felt disgraced, because I was determined to go to war as a fighter. When we were not given

67

arms, then the whole thing fell through and I lost interest. I found that I had signed a contract that said 'for the duration of the war'; otherwise I would have walked out. From that point I was just hanging on in the Army. I think that's why I didn't try for promotion – because I lost interest.

It was just discrimination – it was a policy of the government. Who knows what the purpose behind it was? It's only now we realise that to them it was a white man's war. They fear that if we got an expertise with regard to fighting, we might come back and make a demonstration against their policies.

What a waste! They destroyed my spirit, I must say – they really destroyed me.

Black and coloured participation in South African wartime armies was nothing new. Eighty-three thousand Africans and two thousand Cape Coloureds had served in the First World War. The sinking of the troopship *Mendi* off the Isle of Wight on 21 February 1917, during which more than 600 black soldiers lost their lives, was still a sore issue with the African community, since no memorial had been raised nor any official acknowledgement made of these particular war dead.

Charles Adams was passionately proud of the Cape Corps Regiment's long history as an infantry regiment, and he also felt keenly the loss of status as a non-combatant:

I was a young man: I'd have rather liked to have been in the infantry. I would have been more happy there than in the supply corps. I wasn't a combatant because, when South Africa declared war, again this Ossewa Brandwag business comes in. They made the Coloured regiment non-combatant. They said in the paper that Jan Smuts is training the Coloured people to kill white people; so, to keep the peace in South Africa, to keep white people in South Africa happy, they would not allow us to fight. But of course that didn't make us very happy.

Over 40,000 Coloured men volunteered for service in the Second World War – that's an extra two divisions they could have had. And it's not to say those would have been divisions to take a chance on, because Coloured soldiers have proved themselves, 1st and 2nd Battalion, in the First World War, fighting against the Turks in Palestine and against the Germans in East Africa. We were an infantry regiment since 1793.

In the end 77,239 people served in the Native Military Corps during the Second World War as enlisted volunteers; 45,015 in the Cape Coloured Corps.

By the end of 1942 the policy of keeping non-whites unarmed had led to a widespread lack of interest among blacks and Coloureds in the prosecution of the war. South African members of parliament were beginning to put two and two together: at a conference on 18 November 1942 they raised the question: 'How was it possible to work up the spirit of the offensive among natives if the only training given them was that of watchdogs, patrolling a fence with assegais and at the sign of danger being ordered to withdraw? If the natives were given arms and trained as soldiers,' the politicians ventured, 'a different story would be told.'

By 1944 the Union Defence Force did have black and Coloured soldiers carrying arms; but that was too late for Frank Sexwale, Charles Adams and a hundred thousand fellow soldiers who had been unable to fight in the African campaigns.

At the end of February 1941, while Charles Adams was admiring Italian art and architecture in Mogadishu, Jim Tait – a dental student from Dunedin University, New Zealand – had landed in England as Ordinary Seaman Tait, RNZNVR and was doing basic training down at HMS *Ganges*, a shore establishment on the Suffolk coast which boasted an enormous rigged mast. 'I'm not a great one for heights,' Tait says modestly. 'I got as far as the crosstrees, that was compulsory. But I used to see these fellows from Newfoundland get up that mast to the top and sit on the little button up there. Gave me the horrors just to look at it.'

After *Ganges* the trainees went to Chatham, 'a real eye-opener. About a thousand sailors down those tunnels, hammocks everywhere – she was rugged! We were lined up and detailed off, six at a time, for various ships. Six of us went to the cruiser *Arethusa*; the next six went to a destroyer which sailed from the Thames and hit a mine the same night – all killed. Their first night at sea. I just needed to have been one place further along.'

Pierre Austin of the RAN was in line for promotion and opted to specialise in gunnery. That led to a course at the notoriously tough gunnery school on Whale Island near Portsmouth: 'I put one foot in, starting running and never stopped. Yes, it was tough; the accent was on discipline, discipline, discipline ... and discipline.' Discipline and mathematics: Whale Island's two gods. They were to smile on the gunnery officers of the Royal Navy the following month, when the Mediterranean Fleet caught up at last with the Italian Navy off Cape Matapan on the night of 28–9 March. Admiral Sir Andrew Cunningham, C-in-C Mediterranean Fleet, directed the chase from his flagship *Warspite*, and now had the satisfaction, after a year of hide-and-seek, of bringing his opponents to action. Alec Dennis was there too, as gunnery control officer in the destroyer *Griffin*. Dennis, closed up at action stations in the Director tower, had a good view of what was going on:

We were steaming into a pitch-black night at 20 knots, peering into the darkness through our binoculars. Suddenly we received an emergency signal to clear the screen and take station on the starboard side. Increasing to full speed, we started off, to receive in short order another signal from *Warspite*: GET OUT OF MY WAY, DAMN YOU. At this moment I spotted a dark shape ahead and got all the guns on to it. As we got nearer, it was obviously a large ship and one felt a little naked up there in front. Moments later, *Greyhound*, ahead of us, switched on her searchlight and in its silvery blue beam was revealed a 10,000-ton cruiser heading towards us, quite close, and looking magnificent in her light grey which stood out starkly in the beam. I gave an estimated range and opened fire. 'Ting-ting' went the firing bell. Then hell broke loose. The enemy ship virtually disintegrated in an appalling series of explosions, flinging one of her turrets high in the air. 'My God, did I do that?' was my first reaction, forgetting that there were twenty-four fifteen-inch guns in the three battleships behind us.

The enemy ship was the heavy cruiser *Fiume*; she was sunk, along with her sister cruisers *Zara* and *Pola*, and two destroyers. The main Italian fleet, whose C-in-C, Admiral Angelo Iachino, had given the orders that sent this force of cruisers and destroyers to its destruction, was elsewhere; but an earlier torpedo strike on the admiral's flagship, *Vittorio Veneto*, had crippled her too. It was the last time the Italian fleet would come out in search of prey.

The 600-mile-long battleground of the Western Desert, between Alexandria in Egypt and El Agheila in Libya, was only about fifty miles deep from the Mediterranean Sea on its northern edge to the Great Sand Sea on the south. These were two very definite touchlines – the water on one side, and the all but impenetrable sands on the other. Inside this fifty-mile-deep strip the Allied and Axis armies manoeuvred to outflank each other for the best part of three years. It was a fluid, shifting battleground, with the Suez Canal at the eastern end the ultimate prize for the Axis. The Allies held on to the canal, and to the great port of Alexandria at the mouth of the Nile nearby, for the entire desert war. At times the Axis armies, pushing eastwards, were only a few miles away. Had they captured Alexandria and the canal, Axis shipping would have had a direct route to and from the Indian Ocean, and the Mediterranean Fleet would have been deprived of its base. Beyond the canal and Saudi Arabia lay the oil-rich Persian Gulf. With its handily placed abundance of fuel at their command, the Germans and Italians could have driven on to invade India from the west. There, if things had gone well, these two prongs of the Axis might have linked up with the third, the westward-racing Japanese. Then only the Americas would have been outside a world-girdling Axis belt.

For their part the Allies were always looking west, beyond El Agheila and on past the port of Tripoli, which supplied the Axis forces as Alexandria did the Allied troops. Allied intentions were simply to push their enemy back west until he had nowhere to run, hide or stand; to chase him right out of Africa.

The man who so nearly brought off the grand coup for the Axis started his tenure in the desert as he meant to go on. General Erwin Rommel had arrived in Tripoli on 12 February 1941, newly appointed to command the German desert army, the Deutsches Afrika Korps. Within two months he had gingered up everyone, from high-ranking officers to ordinary soldiers; he had started an offensive, capturing El Agheila from the Allies; he had driven his enemy hundreds of miles back towards Egypt, in spite of temporary checks along the way. On 10 April, however – like a dog momentarily releasing its hold on an opponent in order to snap up an annoying flea – the pursuing Germans halted and turned aside to deal with Tobruk.

Tobruk, the main port in Cyrenaica (eastern Libya), was a vital card for both sides. Both Allied and Axis forces suffered throughout their North African campaigns from the critical problem of supply in a barren land. These mobile armies needed transport, repair equipment, ammunition, clothing; they also needed boots, food, medicines, tents, as well as spades, barbed wire, cigarettes, razor-blades. Their wounded had to be evacuated and more men were required to replace them. They needed petrol to animate their advances or retreats and water to keep themselves alive. But the nearer to its ultimate objective each side got – the Axis to Alexandria and the Suez Canal in the east, the Allies to Tripolitania (western Libya) and on west to Tunis – the further away it was from its chief supply port. Each side was like a man with his braces hooked round a post, trying to push another man through a door. The elastic becomes thinner and the resistance greater the nearer he strains to his goal until, weakening, he can no longer resist the counter-thrust of his opponent and is forced back on his heels again.

Tobruk lay roughly half-way between Alexandria and El Agheila. Both armies needed it, to supply themselves. Neither army, after bypassing it, could allow it to remain in the other side's hands. A besieged garrison in Tobruk, succoured by supplies being brought in by sea, might launch a sortie and cut the supply line of its enemy where it ran along the desert road past the garrison's 'front door'; a stab in the back which would drain away the opponent's lifeblood of supplies.

The Allies had captured Tobruk from the Italians on 22 January, during the big push west from Sidi Barrani and Bardia. Now the Afrika Korps fully expected to get it back without checking the momentum of their drive eastwards towards Alexandria. There was a garrison of 31,000 Allied soldiers in Tobruk, mostly men of the 9th Australian Division, along with the 1st Battalion of the Northumberland Fusiliers and a detachment of the Royal Horse Artillery. The Tobruk garrison was to hold out for 240 days, in spite of full-scale assaults, constant bombing and conditions that deteriorated from the austere to the appalling, until an Allied advance relieved the port on 8 December. A contemptuous remark by Lord Haw-Haw, the Irish-born propagandist on the German radio, would give them their immortal nickname – the Desert Rats.

Vernon Northwood, from Narrogin in the farming country of Western Australia, was thirty-one years old when he arrived in Tobruk with 2/28 Battalion at the end of March. Already promoted captain, one of the 'old men' of the battalion, he was on easy terms with the men of his A Company in a way that British Army regular officers could seldom enjoy.

The blokes came from the south-west of Western Australia, a farming community, and they were the salt of the earth. I knew a lot of them from back home. You could go to a feller and call him Tom and sometimes, if he thought he should, he'd call you Sir, and sometimes he didn't.

Some of the British officers I met later in Tobruk said, 'How is it that you can go down among these fellows and call them by their Christian names? And they either don't call you anything, or if we're there they might call you Sir. How can you do this and still have control?' And I said, 'Oh, I don't know, there's just this sort of feeling between us.' When they got over the straps you had to be severe with them and they'd have you in the poo for a while; but it soon passed over. If anything went wrong they'd be the first people to help you. You never had to throw your rank around in the Australian army. In fact, anyone who did – they were perfectly disliked.

Most of the Australians in Tobruk were raw troops. Some of the gunners had only fired their first practice shots the week before they arrived in the town, and some of the infantry had to be shown how to throw a grenade and what its lethal radius was, after they got there. The 2/28th were no exception; they had only been in the Middle East for a month. 'As far as we were concerned', remarks their historian, Philip Masel, 'there wasn't a German in the whole of Africa, and the Italians who weren't in the bag were still running and should now be somewhere near Tripoli.'[3] They were so poorly equipped that their first action on reaching Tobruk was to collect up all the equipment the Italians had left behind – guns, ammunition, mortars, petrol, food. There was so much Italian food available that the 2/28th's staple diet during the siege became a stew of British bully beef and Italian macaroni.

A Company was positioned on the Dirna road. Vernon Northwood recalls seeing the demoralised British troops, in full retreat from Benghazi, pouring back through Tobruk on their way east:

> That was what we called the Benghazi Handicap. There didn't seem to be any organisation. They were saying to us, 'Better get out of Tobruk, there's trouble coming. Rommel's coming!' We said, 'We don't get out of here. We're here!' Then all of a sudden the perimeter closed.
>
> On the first day, 10 April, ten o'clock in the morning, we saw the German tanks coming over the rise. The Royal Horse Artillery were firing over open sights, but they copped an awful bashing from the tanks. We could hear men screaming. They carried them to a bit of a ditch. I was up in a water tower, with a wonderful view, so I was able to report back what I was seeing. I was cold with fury when I saw the Germans machine-gunning an ambulance as it came up to get these fellers. Our men just took it in their stride though. Many of them had worked in the goldfields; they were men who knew what rough living was all about.

At this time the previous year Sam Meltzer of the RASC had been in France, part of the chaotic retreat to Dunkirk. Now, on attachment to the King's African Rifles, he was engaged in clandestine work in conjunction with that swashbuckling band of brave infiltrators, the Long Range Desert Group.

> I'd dress in Arab uniform. I always had an affinity for language and used it working behind the lines – and in front of the lines, sometimes. What we were doing was putting up detour signs for the Italians to follow into traps. They'd either fall for it, or run like hell – really, it was a pleasure to be there and take part.

The Long Range Desert Group – I think the reason a lot of people joined it was that it was a relaxed group. Naturally you grew beards. There was a lot of camaraderie in the desert, more so than anywhere. A lot of pride in the group – they were very close and the officers were more relaxed. They tended to be chaps whose Army careers weren't going too well: wild sort of chaps.

The group I was with was involved with setting booby traps, leaving thermos flasks or pens that exploded. I myself was not actually in the *crème de la crème*, but I would go behind the lines and come back with information. Many times we'd raid for supplies. Petrol was a prime target; I became quite good at that. I'd have been shot if I'd been caught wearing my Arab dress or my Italian jacket. And not just in those circumstances. If you're captured by Nazis and you have a name like Samuel Meltzer, and you're circumcised...

I volunteered for something even more hair-raising. The Germans had experimented with gliders when they'd invaded Holland and they hadn't worked. They were planning to invade England with these bloody gliders and they abandoned it. But somebody in Cairo got the idea that we could invade Greece with gliders!

They were made up like banana crates. Half of them would have fallen into the sea, the other half would have been shot out of the sky. However, thank God I got malaria and didn't go on the trip.

The Italians had been in Greece for six months when General Wavell sent an expeditionary force of 60,000 troops from Egypt to help the Greeks repel an imminent German invasion. The Greeks had been doing perfectly well against the Italians, penning them up along the mountainous Albanian border. But the Greeks knew they would be no match for the German Army coming south in all its power from an already conquered Yugoslavia; more especially, no match for the Junkers 87 'Stuka' dive-bombers and the strafing Me 109 fighters of the Luftwaffe. In the event the Australians and New Zealanders who made up the bulk of the expeditionary force, with their desert-battered equipment and their almost total lack of air cover, were no match for them either. Within a week of landing in Greece they were up near the Macedonian border; after another week they were already on the withdrawal trail south through the vineyards and olive groves, over the mountains and down to the blitzed ports of the Peloponnese.

The New Zealanders Tom Somerville and Jack Brown were among the soldiers who were sent to Greece. Their memories of the time they were there form a kaleidoscopic impression of heat, dust, haste and danger; a depressing, hangdog, terrifying and exhausting time, etched deeply into

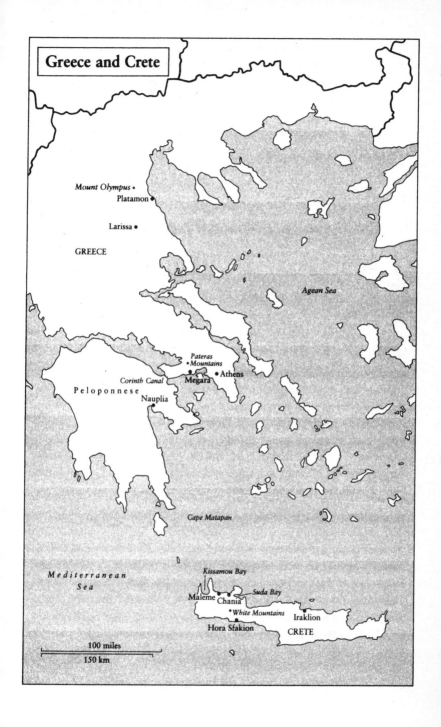

Greece and Crete

Mount Olympus •

Platamon •

Larissa •

GREECE

Agean Sea

Pateras
•Mountains
Corinth Canal •
Megara •Athens

P e l o p o n n e s e

Nauplia •

Cape Matapan

M e d i t e r r a n e a n
S e a

Kissamou Bay

Suda Bay
Maleme • Chania •

•*White Mountains* Iraklion •
Hora Sfakion • **CRETE**

100 miles

150 km

their memories. For Tom Somerville, with the 5th Field Unit of artillery, it was to last only a few weeks. Jack Brown of the 19th Battalion was to find his stay prolonged, against his will.

Tom Somerville:

We were evacuated from northern Greece back into the Mount Olympus range. And when we started the retreat – that's when we learned all about Stuka dive-bombers. This was on narrow roads, where the transport was all concentrated. There was always an alert – 'Here they are!' We'd be in any cover we could get. We'd never run; they said that the pilots got great sport out of a running target. You'd get under anywhere you could. I've been under a petrol truck. I've been under a load of ammunition.

You'd see a speck in the distance. Then they'd come in on you. It's all so instantaneous – and just as quickly it's all finished. They'd come rushing in, their sirens screaming; there'd be bombs going off all round and machine-guns rattling – they'd give us the whole lot. You're sure it's coming for yourself. That machine-gun sound seemed to hover in the air over you – a strange sensation. They'd come back along with the machine-guns going. Then they'd be gone. It's concentrated: but it happens over and over again. There were waves of them, you know – maybe five or six runs in a day, or more.

Morale was good, it was surprising. But everybody would be very shaken after one of these raids. Some would be swearing, and some would be cursing and shaking their fists at the planes; others would be taking it calmly. We had a little chap, he was quite a comic – Slick, we called him. There was a Bren gun mounted on the troop leader's truck and his job was to man this Bren gun. The Stukas came over and our officer was saying, 'Come on, Slick, give it to him!' He said, 'You come up here and give it to him yourself!'

Jack Brown:

We were in western Greece; it was very, very hilly – valleys and then more hills. We had no air cover whatsoever and the Jerries loved it, didn't they? They'd just sit right on top of us – and those Stukas, they give us hell. It was frightening – and when I say frightening, you really were paralysed. There could be forty or fifty of them sitting up there, and they'd open up that siren they had on them. You never knew where they'd be coming from – all you heard was *wooooo!* – that siren coming down to you. They'd come into a dive, but you didn't see the release of the bomb.

We had nothing to stop them. I still had my old Lee-Enfield .303 from the

First World War. You'd fire at them, in frustration, but you knew damn well it wasn't going to do anything to them.

Tom Somerville:

The tiredness was worse than the fear. We'd travel all day, with these Stuka attacks; then we'd be bombed by night, by the big Dorniers. We were sent down the east coast to Platamon; that's where the ranges sloped down to the sea. There was a castle on a promontory and the railway went under it in tunnels. We set up our gun there in a rocky river bed, supporting the 21st Division – it was a Good Friday. We fired thousands of rounds at armoured cars, tanks, motor cycles. But finally it got too much. We pulled our gun out in a hurry and the engineers blew the Platamon tunnels. We heard that, all right!

We went south through Larissa and set up among olive groves in swamp land. We could see the Germans coming down at night, a string of lights. They attacked us there; four of us dived into one slit trench, on top of each other. When we put our heads out we saw a big line of holes like sewing up the trunk of this olive tree, about a foot above our heads.

Jack Brown:

On Anzac Day, 25 April, we were right back defending the Corinth Canal, positioned in some pine trees. At daylight these big black birds came over – paratroopers. Still had me old rifle! So we took pot shots at them as they came swinging down. Not an easy target. Next minute there's a hell of a bang. Our guys had blown up the bridge over the canal and we were on the wrong side.

As soon as the paratroopers were down on the ground we knew we were done for. That's when I was wounded. A tommy-gun bullet went through my shoulder, so I was put out of action. It was just a bump on my shoulder and the whole arm went limp. The next minute I hear, 'Let's get the hell out of here – we can't stand up to this lot.' Away we went, up on to the hill. 'What are we going to do now? Better get round the back and see if we can pick up some transport.'

We did a day's hoop over the hills. There was a chap who was badly hit and I wasn't much better. He'd had it – his wound was starting to turn smelly. So to give the others a chance to get away I said, 'We'll turn it in.'

Tom Somerville:

Finally we reached ... I was never quite sure where it was. Somewhere south of the Corinth Canal; never heard the name of the place. We tidied up as best we could, destroyed all our guns, blew them up and got rid of the firing mechanisms. Poured sand in the oil filter in the truck engines and ran 'em until they screamed. It seemed a bit callous, but we had to deprive the enemy of them – we knew he was right on our tails.

We just left enough vehicles to get down to the beach. I drove a three-tonner. On the beach we dropped all the guys. Wrecked the trucks as much as we could and got down to another beach in one truck. That's how it was that we got separated from the crowd that went to Crete. There was a few of us walked out through shallow water to this lighter, and then we found ourselves climbing up a rope ladder on to a ship. They had a cup of cocoa waiting for us. Then everybody just flopped down – we'd had it.

Evacuating the expeditionary force from Greece was a fantastically risky job for the destroyers of the Mediterranean Fleet. With no air cover they could only travel safely at night, and they could only just complete the round journey from Alexandria to Greece and back during the hours of darkness – provided there were no hitches. That was an unrealistic proviso in the Mediterranean in 1941. If they were caught out on the open sea during daylight, the German dive-bombers and Italian torpedo-planes would be on to them in swarms.

On 25 April, the day that Jack Brown was shot through the shoulder on the Corinth Canal, *Griffin* came up in the late afternoon towards Nauplia at the top end of the Peloponnese with a convoy of four evacuation ships. It was 'a bit of a hairy time', according to Alec Dennis. Waves of Stuka attacks succeeded finally in holing *Glenearn*, a big landing ship. She filled with water and became virtually unmanageable. But such a valuable ship could not be left to sink; so *Griffin* was ordered to tow her back to Crete. It was, to put it mildly, a hell of a journey. 'The sun kept on going down ever so slowly,' Dennis says, 'and I kept on looking at it and thinking: For Christ's sake, get on!' They did finally get *Glenearn* into Kissamou Bay in western Crete, a feat of seamanship in the face of danger and anxiety for which – and for other services – Alec Dennis was awarded the Distinguished Service Cross. The aftermath of the disaster in which they would have become embroiled, had they continued into Nauplia with the convoy, is described poignantly by Dennis; it can stand for hundreds of equally bleak and saddening incidents experienced by sailors in every corner of the Mediterranean in 1941.

As it turned out, we were remarkably lucky. *Diamond* and *Wryneck*, the two other destroyers that went on, got sunk. The troopships had got delayed up at Nauplia and they didn't get away in time. The troopships got sunk – and the two destroyers had to pick up all these fellows in the water – and then *they* were bombed and sunk. The whole lot...

When we got back to Crete we were sent up to find out what had happened – there was no signal from anybody. We knew roughly where they must have been. They were obviously sunk. One of my Dartmouth term-mates and great friend, John Marshall, was on board the *Diamond*. Our instructions were not to wait beyond dawn, which would have been more or less suicide.

And so we get up there, but don't see anything. And then towards the very end of the night, of course, we *do* see a group in the water, then another one. And then: 'How long are we going to hang around before we all go?' So my Captain, Johnny Lee-Barber, had to make a very awkward decision. We hung around a bit longer and got about thirty chaps, out of 2000-odd. Apparently one little group got to one of the Greek islands in a whaler. But old John wasn't among them.

And we did the best we could...

I had to bury some of them at sea that evening. Having done a little service with a prayer or two and bunged them in the sea, the chief bo'sun's mate came along to me with a very sad face and said, 'Sir, there's another one.' We'd had a whole lot of oil-covered clothes and rags on deck, and among them was the corpse of a chap. It was dark by then, and I hadn't got the heart to pull the ship's company out – so we just popped him over the side. Said a prayer. Don't even know who he was. Probably had a mother, somewhere.

There would be no more fighting or soldiering for Jack Brown, left behind to nurse his badly wounded mate along in the hills of the Peloponnese:

There was a bit of a village below – Megara was its name. He and I just staggered off down there, thinking: well, we'll get picked up by the Jerries here. A Greek feller in his forties – one leg, crutches – hops out. 'Hey! Come in here!' Sat us in one of their air-raid shelters, brought us some food. At night-time they took us into one of their houses, got a doctor to come and have a look at us. My wound cleaned up pretty quickly, but the other feller's bullet had gone in his shoulder and come out his back, and left a pretty gapey hole.

They kept us there for a few days, with Jerry trucks and motor cycles whizzing past just outside the gate. And as soon as my wound healed up I headed out to the hills.

Tom Somerville made it safely back to Egypt. So did Alec Dennis and

Griffin: yet another return to Alexandria, the ancient sea port at the mouth of the Nile that the sailors, soldiers and airmen looked upon as a home from home. Coming in from dangerous and stressful duty, having shouldered responsibility far beyond their years, the young men and women could relax and let their hair down for a few hours in the arms of Alexandria, as Dennis quickly learned to do:

> You went ashore and there was everything – the restaurants, the bars where you had caviare with your drinks for free, the Sporting Club with horse racing, swimming, squash, tennis and golf. There was the Union Club where they had wonderful food – in fact, there was a Dutchman who was reputed to have gone there for the *sole chasseur* and never left. This was for the officers; the sailors all had lots of places to drink beer and enjoy themselves.
>
> We'd lay on bus trips for the sailors. One trip run by the ship's chaplain was to see the Sea of Nazareth. The sailors drank a great deal of beer in the bars there. On the way back in the bus they were all yelling, 'Stop, Sir, stop! Please stop!' The chaplain said, 'Why? There's nothing of religious or archaeological significance here.' We stopped the bus: he soon saw what the problem was...
>
> In Alexandria there was also, lower down the scale, Mary's House. It provided, on the ground floor, a bar which would lend money. Mary used to go round Alexandria in a Mercedes Benz and a mink stole, well known to one and all. Upstairs there were further pursuits – whatever – of a fairly high class, that kind of thing. Johnny knew some socialite woman and we got quite involved with her girls' concert party, which was a lot of fun.
>
> It was quite extraordinary; one moment you were out there in the Med, under attack, and the next you were in Alexandria having fun – I mean, a *lot* of fun ... we were terribly irresponsible.

Responsibility at sea, however, was a different matter – particularly in destroyers. In the Mediterranean the 'greyhounds of the ocean' were performing rather more in the role of sheepdogs, chivvying and fussing round their convoys, snapping at the heels of stragglers, being sent off at a moment's notice to pick up this group or land that party. Destroyers, however, trailed inextinguishable glamour and *esprit de corps* in their thirty-knot wakes. A destroyer's close-cramped community of about 150 men was constantly exposed to danger – the German surface ships were shut out of the Mediterranean beyond the well-guarded Straits of Gibraltar, but there was always the potential threat of the Italian Navy, and the very immediate and actual one of the Axis dive-bombers, torpedo-planes, high-level bombers and submarines. Destroyers attracted – in fact, demanded –

exceptional men as their captains; men whose wielding of absolute power and authority over a small group of other men, an essentially lonely job, often gave their behaviour a tinge of eccentricity along with a touch of genius. When they were good, as Alec Dennis explains, they were very, very good...

There was a generation of men between the wars who spent their lives in destroyers. They were exactly the right age when the war started; they had the experience and so on, and they knew what they were doing. They became, many of them, rather ... *unusual* characters. They became rather dictatorial – or very nice, you never knew which it was going to be – because they were in the habit of being God. What they did on board, so long as they stuck to the rules, went.

My Captain in *Griffin* was a man called Johnny Lee-Barber, a wonderful man and a superb destroyer captain. He was great fun; and he was very good with his wardroom. Strict as hell on the job, but when he was off duty he'd come down there and we'd laugh and we'd sing; and when you met on the bridge you were on the job again. A wonderful ship-handler, who saved the ship on many occasions. In fact, by May 1941 *Griffin* was one of only two 'G' class destroyers still afloat, out of the original nine.

However, the isolation and the strain could get to destroyer captains. I remember in Alexandria when Roland Swinley, Captain of the *Douglas*, came on board to have drinks. After we'd been talking for a while, he says, 'I can see you don't like me.' We said, 'No, Sir, we love you, really, you're great.' It was quite late, about ten o'clock at night; he said, 'Well, you'll all come on board *Douglas* and have dinner with me.' We said, 'But Sir, it's long past dinner time.' He said, 'When I say it's dinner time, it's dinner time.'

So three of us went on board the *Douglas* to have dinner with Roland Swinley. We sat at table and ate through the full dinner that had been waiting for the Captain for hours. The savoury appeared. He took one look at it and pressed the quartermaster's bell. Quartermaster came clattering down the stairs. 'Quartermaster, who is the Officer of the Day?' – 'Lieutenant Brasher, Sir.' – 'Tell him I want to speak to him.' Brasher had a decision to make: should he dress up in uniform, or come in his dressing-gown? He got it right this time; came in his dressing-gown. Roland looked at him and said, 'Brasher, are you Officer of the Day?'

'Yes, Sir.'

'Eat my savoury.'

And Brasher, who knew the form, made a most beautiful speech of acceptance, it really was nicely done – and the whole moment passed off in gales of laughter.

Weird, you know? Comes of being Boss for too long.

Crete became the byword for evacuation in the face of danger, and nineteen-year-old Private Bob Taunt from Melbourne was there. With the Australian 2/2 Battalion he had taken part in the 'Benghazi Handicap' and the tumultuous withdrawal through Tobruk; he had been sent to Greece, and had taken part in the withdrawal and evacuation from the Peloponnese. Now, in the last few days of April 1941, he was landed in Suda Bay on the north-west coast of Crete, one unit in the 32,000-strong garrison that was waiting to repel the expected assault by German forces.

> We were back in the foothills behind Suda, right out in the open – we had no tents. The people were very friendly to us, gave us a drink of milk from a goatskin as we came along, waved to us, that type of thing. There was a Greek living nearby who disappeared when the invasion came and left his house along with a lot of *krasi*, local wine in a big barrel. Our blokes got stuck into that wine. There was only two sober – myself and a bloke named Nick Mackintosh – and we had to dress them, put their rifles in their hands and everything. Lucky we didn't meet the enemy at that point!
>
> We were given American Remington rifles from the 1914–18 war; they arrived still in the grease they'd been packed away in back in 1918. We couldn't afford to practise firing them, because we only had fifty rounds apiece.

Crete, the ruggedly mountainous 150-mile-long island lying between North Africa and the southern tip of mainland Greece, was a valuable prize for the Axis. It would, theoretically, extend their air range into Egypt and Libya, and it would give them a central base to harry Allied naval operations in the Eastern Mediterranean. Its capture would also signal the final ejection of Allied troops from mainland Europe. And Crete, in the end, did not prove a particularly difficult plum for the Germans to pick, although a costly one in terms of casualties. Fourteen thousand Allied troops – Britons, New Zealanders and Greeks – had been in the island for six months under the very capable command of General Sir Bernard Freyberg, a New Zealander who had won the VC in the First World War. The garrison was more than doubled by troops arriving after the evacuation of Greece. But Freyberg and the other planners of the defence of Crete were expecting an assault from the sea. When it came, on 20 May, it came from the air, in the form of paratroops. That week, 5,678 of them were to die – many still in their teens. Some were shot in mid-air as they came drifting down from the planes; others were killed around their crash-landed gliders, or dispatched among the olive groves by Allied troops or by the Cretan resistance fighters. These last proved to be ferocious and highly competent guerrillas who would keep the occupying forces more than busy during the ensuing four years. After its occupation by Germany, Crete soon became the setting for a terrible war of attrition, of killing and counter-killing, mass murder and wholesale burning of villages, ambushes and reprisals. But on 20 May 1941 the Germans were confident of victory. Initially they took heavy casualties; but once they had secured Maleme airfield, to the west of Bob Taunt's position at Suda Bay, the result was not seriously in doubt.

> The morning of the invasion, all you could hear was this *rrrr-rrrr-rrrr*. Then you saw them. There were hundreds came past us, over us – Junkers. Then the parachuters, dropping out and going down.
>
> We moved up. We had a Cretan battalion next to us. They went forward, but came back pretty quickly – they didn't last too long. Then *we* were the front line. I was on a machine-gun. It was night-time by now and the Germans were due to attack the next morning. About twelve o'clock we were told, 'You're moving back. Bring all your rations. Don't leave anything for the enemy.' Next morning we were told we were evacuating.

It took the invading Germans eleven days to complete a crushing victory and seal their occupation of the island. But the German victory in Crete was not quite as crushing as it might have been, thanks to the work of the Mediterranean Fleet. Several thousand German reinforcement troops were intercepted, on convoy to the island, by Allied ships. Among these was the cruiser HMAS *Perth*, to which Pierre Austin had just been transferred from *Australia*:

> I was in the transmitting station in the bowels of the ship, so all I knew of the evacuation of Crete was loud bangings and rumblings. Just to the north and west of Crete we sank a number of German caïques full of troops. I didn't see that and I don't think I would have wanted to see it. Several of my friends were upset; they told me, "Those poor buggers were just left to drown, several thousand of them." '

And, of course, it was the Mediterranean Fleet that was responsible for trying to evacuate as many Allied soldiers as possible from the island, after having sustained many sinkings and deaths and much damage in landing them there. Some of the retreating soldiers got away from Iraklion, the capital town and chief port of Crete; but most had to make a foot-slogging journey across the White Mountains and down to the little harbour of Sfakia (otherwise known as Hora Sfakion) in the south-western corner of the island. Here, for four consecutive nights from 28 to 31 May, Admiral Cunningham sent in his battered ships and dog-tired sailors to pick up the exhausted evacuees, always at deadly risk as soon as daylight came, with little or no air cover. They managed to rescue about 17,000 soldiers. Bob Taunt was one of those who joined the raggle-taggle withdrawal to Sfakia:

> We route-marched all day and all night across the mountains, and those mountains are very, very high. We were bombed and machine-gunned by Messerschmitts. You'd hear them coming and just get off the road under the olive trees, anywhere you could hide. There was very little panic, really. Running doesn't do you any good, so you learn to stay pretty calm. I was in very good company, blokes that just about never showed any fear whatsoever; older blokes, you know, about thirty, thirty-five – really solid citizens. So if you're in good company, you tend to be a bit that way yourself, even if you're only nineteen.
>
> About nine o'clock at night on 29 May we moved down into Sfakia. You had to follow the leader down a goat track; you had to run down and keep the fellers in front of you in view, for fear of losing them. It was all rocks – I don't know how we didn't break an ankle. A whole regiment, six or seven hundred blokes, all running down that goat track in the moonlight.
>
> We got down to the beach about one o'clock in the morning and there were all these barges there. We went on the *Glengyle*, an invasion ship. We must have been some of the last to get on – they had to clear the island by dawn, to avoid the bombers. Not all got on. A mate of mine missed out and he was taken prisoner the next morning.
>
> All that day at sea we were getting bombed and machine-gunned. I remember HMAS *Perth* was in our convoy; she got hit and they lost about fourteen blokes. The Stukas were coming right down, but when the *Perth* started firing they pulled out bloody early! All the troops on board that had any guns were using them – I was firing my World War One Remington. And then next morning we arrived in Alex about dawn.

As HMAS *Perth* came alongside in Alexandria and unloaded her human cargo, Pierre Austin remembers, 'they said thank you very nicely and went ashore. Some looked very down, but with the majority it was a case of: "Here we go again!"

'We were all *very* tired.'

In mid-1941 it seemed to be all catastrophe, retreat and evacuation. Rommel and the Afrika Korps were besieging Tobruk, and pressing on towards Egypt and their great prize. Yugoslavia, Greece and now Crete had fallen. Malta, Britain's lone island fortress and base in mid-Mediterranean, was under constant attack from the air and looking increasingly likely to be invaded. The Mediterranean Fleet was losing warships faster than it could replace or repair them; merchantmen, too. True, in the Atlantic the German battleship *Bismarck* had been sunk by the concerted efforts of the Home Fleet and of Force H operating from Gibraltar. After an epic chase, *Bismarck* was destroyed on 28 May, the same day that General Freyberg was ordering the evacuation of Crete. But three days earlier *Bismarck* and her companion ship, the heavy cruiser *Prinz Eugen*, had between them sunk the pride of the Royal Navy, the battleship of which Dudley Thompson had been so proud as a boy in Jamaica – HMS *Hood*. An enormous explosion had literally ripped *Hood* in two. Out of the crew of 1410, three men survived.

In Occupied Europe, too, no belligerent action was possible by ground forces. But in the skies over northern France the RAF could at least put up a show of the offensive spirit so often invoked and praised by Winston Churchill. Thus the daylight sweeps came into being; operations in which British fighters flew at first on their own ('rhubarbs') and later with a few bombers as bait ('circuses') to tempt the German fighters up where they could attack them. The Spitfire and Hurricane pilots' orders were to shoot down Germans: failing that, to strafe anything that moved on the ground.

For Mahinder Singh Pujji, the young Punjabi pilot now serving with 43 Squadron, the launching of the sweeps was the answer to a prayer. At last he would be able to fly on operations and expunge the frustration of having had to watch the Battle of Britain take place without him the previous summer. There had been only one major problem during training – a matter of religion.

I probably am the only Sikh pilot who insisted on not taking off my turban, even while flying. It was an uphill task. I made a special request to the RAF that I don't want to take off my turban. They were curious, because there were other Sikh pilots who would readily take it off and put on their helmets. I told them that I feel it's my religion that I mustn't take off my turban. So they allowed me to have a special set which would come over the turban and over my ears, with a strap, to let me have oxygen mask and microphone. The British were very accommodating and showed a lot of flexibility. But I was the only one pilot who was allowed. Probably I was the only Sikh who asked.

On the sweeps we used to go out in three or four squadrons together – nearly a hundred planes. Each squadron would spread out, with instructions if you find any movement, anything, just strafe it, shoot it up. Troops, or ships, or boats on the rivers – destroy them. The Germans were sending up Me 109Es against us. We got into fights with them. They were very good; I came back with many holes in my Hurricane at times.

Hurricane – I *love* Hurricane! I think that was a wonderful aeroplane; I would prefer it to Spitfire. The only snag with the Hurricane was the speed. That was our handicap whenever we were up against German fighters – they were faster than us. Speed in the climb was the important thing. When you're going up in a Hurricane you're doing only about 180 mph; in Spitfire, 240. There's the difference. But Hurricane was very much more manoeuvrable. You could take it round in circles. I saved my life just by making a tight turn. I saw three Germans coming right on me; I saw them in the mirror. I immediately dipped and took such a steep turn, as I finished it I could see them miles away.

Two of the Spitfire pilots taking part in the sweeps were the short-sighted Glen Niven from Canada, and the modest and laconic Australian Des Sheen, by now a squadron leader. Towards the end of the year Sheen would be awarded a bar to his DFC, for completing fifty sweeps. Typically, even today he is extremely reluctant to talk about it. Stereotypical 'fighter types' who talk big about their exploits with bandits at Angels Five are in fact few and far between. Most do not want to be seen to be committing that ultimate sin: shooting a line. 'When you got back,' says Glen Niven, 'there used to be a lot of swearing. "Christ, did you see that bugger trying to shoot me down? Bloody hell!" – and then it would be "Right, now, what's for lunch?" You didn't talk about it too much. There wasn't an awful lot of this "Ooh, dear, I got awfully upset", or any bragging. If you did, everybody would shut you up: "Oh, stop line-shooting, for Christ's sake – have a drink." You didn't talk about it in that kind of way. Nobody was really all that interested.'

This modesty had several elements – reluctance to be accused of bragging, conforming to the group definition of good manners, a stiff-upper-lip culture of understatement. And behind that, as Mahinder Singh Pujji explains, the experience that could never be transmitted to an outsider and which needed no describing to those who had shared it: the nearness of one's own death and the other man's, the daily brush with one's own mortality at an age when young men are supposed to believe that they are immortal.

Fighter pilots are modest because they risk their life, not once or twice but three times a day. I was flying three times a day; sometimes in the early morning, at midday and in the evening they will call me. Each time, we are confronted with the enemy. So it's a question of either he goes or we go down.

I had another Indian bloke on my squadron, and the first few times when we came back home I tried to tell him what had happened to me. But he said he had an even worse experience. So very soon we realised that everyone has got those experiences; everyone has gone through hell. So there is nothing to tell anyone.

After a week I learned that I would rather keep my mouth shut. Everyone is a hero here. For every RAF pilot I have got great respect, because there are some who came down after shooting three–four aeroplanes and still they wouldn't tell you how they've done it, what happened. They wouldn't brag. We just kept quiet, we sat down. In fact, the day I shot down my first aeroplane I went into my room and I lay down. I didn't want to talk to anyone. What I had gone through – that could have been *my* death, you see.

That is the reason why the fighter pilot will normally never even tell you why he has been awarded a medal. I have been awarded a DFC and I hope you don't ask me why either. I know what hell I've gone through, but I could never make you realise it.

Many times I think of how I am alive: it's just Providence. It's not because of my skill or anything like that. There is no reason for me to be alive today. It's Providence, that's all.

The daylight sweeps probably cost more than they gained. The bombers, usually slow and low Stirlings, were vulnerable to flak and to the speedy Messerschmitts; while the precious, hard-won skills of too many seasoned Battle of Britain veteran fighter pilots – not to mention their lives – were lost while making what was essentially a gesture, however aggressive and morale-boosting.

By July 1941, however, the sweeps had another purpose. It was hoped, vainly as things turned out, that they would entice back to western Europe some of the German fighter squadrons that had suddenly been moved to the east to support a new German offensive there. On 22 June Hitler had committed the blunder that ultimately cost him the war, by launching Operation Barbarossa – a full-scale invasion of Russia. This was a grand over-reaching; a fatal miscalculation. The savage Russian winter, the enormous frozen mileages, the huge, brutal battles, the supply lines stretched beyond anything Rommel feared in his worst nightmares, the resisting spirit of the Russians, the skill of their armed forces – the sheer breadth and scale of an adventure that only a man with developing paranoid megalomania would have embarked on – drained the Third Reich dry. The Russians proved to be defenders far more resolute than Hitler had bargained for; and when the boot was on the other foot in 1945, they were to exact terrible payment from Germany during their advance to Berlin.

From 22 June 1941 the writing was on the wall; but few at the sharp end of the war could read it then.

June in the Middle East brought an Allied invasion of Syria by British and Free French forces. Syria, part of the French Empire, was controlled by a Vichy French administration; and there were strong Allied fears that Vichy and German forces based there might launch an attack on the Suez Canal from the east and go on to take Egypt 'by the back door'. The British Government also felt that with German troops massing on the Russian border they would shortly have a new ally whose supply routes, particularly for Persian Gulf oil, ought to be safeguarded against strikes from Syria. A six-week campaign saw the Allies installed in Beirut and Damascus, and an armistice signed – on 14 July, Bastille Day – with the defeated Vichy French. Nila Kantan went all through this campaign, fighting fires with the Fire Brigade attached to the 5th Indian Division. 'Very, very hard,' he recalls, 'and very, very bitter fighting.' Phil Rhoden, the Melbourne solicitor, took part as well, as a captain in charge of 2/14 Battalion's A Company, fighting French regular soldiers in mountainous country.

Everyone who served in the Western Desert was struck by its strange, impressive, unearthly landscape, and by the tremendous variation of temperature between day and night. No matter where in the world they had come from, nobody had experienced anything like the desert and nobody who fought or travelled or slept there ever forgot it. Gordon Fry from Capetown, just twenty when he first arrived in Egypt with the Capetown Highlanders, recalls dusty days and frozen nights:

The thing you can't really describe to anybody is the terrible dust storms you get in the desert. Shocking – you literally can't see a thing. No battle could take place in one of those. And another thing people don't realise was the cold. It was colder at night-time in the bloody desert than in Switzerland. It's that biting, dry cold that gets right into your bones. They couldn't get the trucks' engines to start in the mornings – they used to have to put boiling water in the radiators, because they were all iced up.

Jack Brown: 'Once you get used to the desert it's all right. But it was pretty hard to get used to it. It was very hot in the daytime, very cold at night. People don't realise that you can get frosts in the desert. And a frost in the desert is *really* cold. Getting up at two o'clock in the morning to go on ack-ack duty – damn cold!'

Nila Kantan:

The desert was a miserable thing. I wonder, 'Why the hell are we fighting here?' Godforsaken place: no water, nothing, no place to hide. Of course, Egyptian deserts were not completely flat. There are many folds. Two convoys can pass each other without being noticed at distance of a hundred yards. But the movement cannot be concealed because of the dust clouds there.

There's no such thing as Hindus or Christians in the desert. When we join the army we completely forgot our religion. Automatic – the situation makes us forget. No possibility of purification; nothing of the sort. We used to get a gallon of water a day only. Out of that gallon, 70 per cent went to the cookhouse. The rest of it was only for drinking, or our washing. Even the Sikhs, they suffered the most, with no washing, and all the dust and perspiration caked in their beards. I've seen British soldiers shaving with the tea...

Tom Somerville:

We just sat there and existed. The heat, the sand – the flies! The flies were terrible. They were there in their hordes, because there were so many badly buried corpses around. Then they'd come on to us. But we made our own fly traps. We'd get a four-gallon tin and we'd cut a flap about an inch square, three sides, near the bottom, and press the top part of the flap inwards. Then we'd hoard up our washing water and that would go into this tin, and we'd put a bit of white cloth over the top, and put a bit of jam on this flap. Of course the flies would wander in there – we caught a lot that way.

Then there was the Desert Rose. Ever grown a Desert Rose? Try growing one. You dig a hole, put a heap of stones over it, and put a four-gallon tin at an angle and anchor it down with the stones. That's a Desert Rose – and men gather there...

On 14 April, three days after the Axis attack on Tobruk began, the Australian General Morshead had been appointed Commander of the fortress.

Morshead was 'every inch a general ... the precise, incisive speech and flint-like, piercing scrutiny acutely conveyed impressions of authority, resoluteness and ruthlessness.'[4] His men knew him as Ming the Merciless. The Tobruk garrison needed such a man to look to, as the Axis siege tightened and conditions inside the perimeter worsened.

The Western Australians of 2/28 Battalion were holed up inside Tobruk with the Australian 9th Division for over five months and got to know the place rather well. The details of everyday life and daily warfare as a Desert Rat are scored into the memory of A Company's commanding officer Vernon Northwood:

First thing in the morning everyone stood to and expected – anything. Perhaps nothing happened – perhaps some shelling, some mortar. So you had to be watchful of that. Then about midday a heat haze would settle over Tobruk. Everything became distorted – a camel became a twenty-storey building. That was when you could move around safely, wander over to the platoons and have a talk to them. We encouraged the men to take their boots off and walk about barefooted in the sand – that's the only way we kept our feet clean. We took our shirts off and the sun baked the perspiration into salt, and we rubbed it off. You were always rubbing salt and dust off your body.

The water situation was pretty grim. You got a water bottle full of water per day for your own personal use. Tea was made when the food came up at night, so your breakfast and your lunch came out of your water bottle.

I had a little tobacco tin – I used to smoke a pipe then – and I shaved in it. Every man shaved every day in Tobruk. People don't believe that – but if they didn't, they soon got a skin rash. I wet my brush and I shaved in that tin. I cleaned my teeth and I spat the water back into the tin – didn't waste any of it. I used the balance of the water for the sponge to wash my privates. A little piece of sponge that could absorb water – you hung on to that. That was very valuable to you.

One of the problems was desert sores; if you got a cut on your hand or leg it started to fester. They were very hard to control. And the *khamsins* [desert storms], when they came, were terrible – they just covered everything with dust. But the worst feature was the flies – they were dreadful. The dug-out positions left by the Italians were very dirty; a lot of rubbish was left there, which the flies loved. And the fleas – the fellers said they've got heads as big as horses. I've never seen such big fleas. And they bit!

Enclosing the thoroughly bombed and wreck-choked harbour and few broken houses of Tobruk were two perimeters: an inner perimeter (the

Blue Line) approximately fifteen miles long, heavily mined and wired; and an outer perimeter (the Red Line) double the length of the Blue, fortified with concrete bunkers. Between Blue and Red Lines lay an arc of ground about two-thirds of a mile wide. Attacks by Axis tanks occasionally penetrated the defences, particularly the attacks on 14 April and 1 May. Both were repulsed and during the latter attack the Germans lost half their tanks. After this, Rommel was forbidden any more assaults by order of General Friedrich Paulus, who had been sent from Germany to oversee the progress of the Afrika Korps. So Rommel turned to the Luftwaffe to try to bomb the garrison into surrender. Without any fighter cover as protection the defenders endured 437 raids between April and July. Maurice Fischer, a tough Anglo-Indian scrapper from the Kolar goldfields near Bangalore who was serving with the Royal Army Ordnance Corps, found himself repairing guns and tanks in the workshops from 7 a.m. till 11 p.m., day after day, under intense bombing.

> I being in charge, when there was an air raid I had to switch off the generator. After that I tried to get into some tank; but the English fellows who were already in there, they'd closed the top. I thought, 'There's nothing better than getting under a tank' – so I got under a Valentine tank. A 500-lb bomb burst outside the damn wall, about thirty yards away. This lifted the tank up – up, and down. So they came looking for me to switch the generator on, shouting, shouting, shouting. I had lost sense of speech, sense of hearing, everything.
>
> Eventually they found me, they took me to the hospital. There were people outside, all wounded, shot up, crying. I said, 'See, Sir, there are other people worse off than me. I can wait.'
>
> The answer was: 'No, no – you're a technical man. You must be seen to straight away.'

But the attackers did not hold all the offensive cards: far from it, in fact. The defenders considered the area between the outer perimeter and the Axis front line to be their property. Their regular night-time patrols in this no man's land, and maintenance of permanently manned listening posts there, helped to boost their own morale and to dent that of the besiegers, both German and Italian, who tacitly acknowledged the defenders' sovereignty of the ground between the lines. It became psychological as much as physical warfare, in which, as Vernon Northwood of 2/28 Battalion illustrates, the vital thing was to maintain a sense of having the upper hand over the enemy:

> The CO sent me one day down to the forward positions – he wanted me to

have a look at the terrain from there. So a sergeant-major and I got out and ran like rabbits down to the forward positions, dodging all the way. The men down there were absolutely furious – 'You're giving away our positions!' I said, 'Look – we're using the maps we captured from the Italians. They've got the same maps, you know. Don't you think they know exactly where you are?' They hadn't thought of that.

The average Digger was told how important Tobruk was to hold, and he could see its importance to Rommel's supply line for himself. After all, he was patrolling at night 1000 yards out from the perimeter; he could hear the planes going overhead, he could hear the trucks going down the supply line.

Morale was further strengthened by the cordial relations between the 1st Northumberland Fusiliers – the British contingent in Tobruk – and the Australians. The tough conditions brought the two groups of men closer to each other than might have been expected, the Australians perhaps feeling that by their daring appropriation of no man's land they were proving something about themselves to the Poms. 'A bond grew between our fellers and the Northumberland Fusiliers,' recalls Northwood. 'We got on marvellously. We thought, "Well, they must think we're all right as soldiers." We felt like colonials; we were *Australians*, but British too. And we had tremendous trust in the Northumberlands – a real bond. That's something that young people thinking these days about the war don't understand – the closeness.'

And the grimness and tension of Tobruk were relieved, from time to time, by an unexpected laugh...

I went out on one reconnoitre patrol – officers weren't supposed to go, but I wanted to see what was going on. So we went out. I was moving up with the sergeant who was in charge and I suddenly thought: 'I can smell Italians.' I knew the smell of Italian cigars; they were all over Tobruk and I used to smoke them myself. I could smell a good strong one now. So I beckoned the men down – 'Down! Down! There's Italians around somewhere – I can smell them!' One of the men walked back to me, and said: 'Excuse me, Sir ... I farted.'

Finally, on 23 September, after more than five months under siege, 2/28 Battalion were relieved by the 2nd Battalion, the King's Own Regiment. On the quayside they watched the ship coming in to take them off to Alexandria. 'Out of the gloom,' Vernon Northwood wrote later, 'her destroyer lines unmistakable, she bore down on us: HMS *Kimberley*. "You pretty little bastard," breathed the man alongside me. His words expressed the feelings of us all.'

It was not HMS *Griffin* that carried Vernon Northwood and 2/28 Battalion out of Tobruk; but *Griffin* did go into the shattered harbour to take off other retiring members of the garrison's Australian contingent. Alec Dennis was struck by their lack of parade-ground polish:

They came along the harbour all anyhow, tin mugs rattling on their knapsacks, as cool as you like, all swearing. We got them on board and were about to cast off when we saw this chap shambling along on his own. We were all shouting: 'Come on, get a move on, we're just off!' Even then he didn't run, but just broke into this kind of casual trot.

We put them all over the ship, got their officers down in the wardroom for a drink. On the mess deck the men carried on as if they were still in Tobruk, opening their tins of bully beef and fruit, chucking the empty tins on the floor. A frightful mess.

As we were coming into Alex this fusillade of shots broke out from the upper deck. We thought it must be an air attack and they were shooting at the planes. But not a bit of it – a seagull was perched on a buoy, and the Aussie soldiers were taking pot-shots at it.

Vernon Northwood, although he was proud of the job his men had done, was sensitive to the impression they were creating with their informal dress and manner – especially among the British:

I did feel, sometimes, we were being judged. There were a lot of British officers who got back to Cairo after the 'Benghazi Handicap' and I think they were pretty surprised that Tobruk had held out. And they were wondering, 'What sort of fellers were able to do this?' So it didn't really help when they'd see someone half dressed in Australian battledress, but wearing an Afrika Korps cap. But you'll always get some clown, won't you?

When we arrived at Alexandria, General Blamey, the Australian Commander, was on the wharf and he sent one of his staff officers forward to find out, 'Why are the men so quiet?' I think he thought they were going to be waving, cheering, you know: 'We're out of Tobruk and good riddance!'

I said, 'They're just so tired.'

They were very thin, they were burned almost as dark as the local natives: but their eyes were so alert. It was most noticeable. They were on edge, they noticed everything. They were sharp, sharp as a razor – but so, so tired.

After 'Operation Battleaxe' – an abortive June counter-attack by the Allies – General Wavell lost the confidence of Winston Churchill and was replaced on 5 July as Commander-in-Chief Middle East by General Sir Claude Auchinleck. The Germans had consolidated their front line around Sollum, just across the border into Egypt; and Auchinleck now planned 'Operation Crusader', another offensive to relieve Tobruk and recapture the ground that the Western Desert Force (shortly to be rebaptised as the 8th Army) had lost in Cyrenaica. 'Crusader' started well, on 18 November; on 8 December Tobruk was relieved and Rommel started a long withdrawal back beyond Benghazi, all the way to El Agheila – the place he had started from nine months before. It was now his turn to feel his braces slacken against the post, to rest and regroup and resupply through his now shortened and unmenaced supply line from Tripoli; and the Allies' turn to be stretched and weakened, their supply line over-extended. The year 1941 would end with both combatants re-equipping as best they could, hostilities temporarily in abeyance, like two boxers on their stools between rounds.

Those three weeks at the start of 'Crusader' had seen some of the fiercest and bloodiest tank and infantry battles of the desert war. Especially demoralising for the South Africans was the disaster they encountered on 23 November at the Sidi Rezegh airfield about ten miles south of Tobruk. The Germans attacked the 5th South African Infantry Brigade from the south, unexpectedly, and rolled them over in short order, killing 224, wounding 379 and capturing nearly 3000. The dead, in the aftermath of the battle, were buried together in a common grave – white infantrymen and black Native Military Corps stretcher bearers side by side. Not for long, however. An order from South African Army headquarters soon had the corpses properly sorted: one grave for the whites, and another for the blacks.

Far away from the hot, bloody, fly-ridden world of the Western Desert and the bomber- and submarine-haunted Mediterranean, across the sea in another, colder corner of the world, two Canadian volunteers who had not yet been exposed to the realities of war were coming up against the not-quite-realities of training. Charlie Hobbs from North Bay in Ontario had volunteered in late 1940 for the Royal Canadian Air Force. 'I didn't know one end of a plane from another, but it seemed the right thing to do. It was a little more glamorous than footslogging. But it went a little deeper than that. There was a certain amount of pride in being a British citizen, a British Empire member. You could almost split it up three ways – one was the dollar bill, in other words employment; the other would be wanting to help Britain; and the third was the search for excitement. See, I was only nineteen.'

By June 1941 Hobbs had been through his square-bashing at boot camp and his elementary flying training in Quebec. Now he had arrived in Brantford, and was trying to polish up his flying skills on Ansons before qualifying – he hoped – as a pilot.

I was far from being a natural pilot. I would call myself a rather awkward pilot. However, I could fly and I got right up to the last day of my pilot training. My instructor said, when we got on the tarmac, 'Right, I'll take over now – I've got a date tonight.' So I didn't argue, I just sat there, and I should have been watching over my left shoulder, because there was another Anson on the ground and it was coming right at us. I didn't spot it in time, or tell him in time – and of course he didn't take any blame for that at all. We chewed the wing off it. They didn't like it. So they told me and asked me in the same breath whether I'd like to be a gunner, seeing I could do so much damage to a plane. So ... I became a gunner.

Peter Cayley, descendant of the Pilgrim Fathers' *Mayflower* carpenter, was seventeen when he joined the Royal Canadian Navy in the summer of 1941. His training had got as far as 'how to put on a gas mask and how to say Sir' when he was embarked on an armed merchant cruiser in Halifax, Nova Scotia, and sent off to England and the Royal Naval College at Dartmouth.

Dartmouth was very interesting and rather odd at times. We were a mixed bunch of English public-school types, a big contingent of Norwegians, the Canadians I'd come with, a group of Free French. Some of the Norwegians were twenty-five, twenty-six – full-grown men.

The officers weren't much good – they were dug-outs, apart from the chief petty officers and warrant officers. The Cadet Gunner, a man named Reggie Woodford, was *absolutely* superb. He ran the whole thing. His voice was ... penetrating enough.

Nowadays about twenty cadets live in the area where 200 of us were crammed in. We slept in hammocks, very close together. The food was terrible. Occasionally we were let out into the town. We were very much the age where we were interested in girls and beer. The Floating Bridge was a favourite pub. But I never met a local the whole time I was there. It wasn't on – there just wasn't time, we were being hurried through as quickly as possible.

Some volunteers had arrived from overseas fully trained; among them

95

was Sheila Kershaw, whose extensive training in pre-war FANY camps in Kenya – not to mention the contacts her former employer had with the organisation in this country – had secured her a job as a FANY driver with Western Command. Then she was posted to Ty Croes in Anglesey, a bleak corner of north-west Wales.

I was one of just two women there; and our CO was against women. I was driving the ambulance, a rickety old converted furniture van. We lived in an empty house with no furnishings; we had a black-out curtain for a tablecloth.

We had to be chaperoned; we had to have this little sergeant to chaperone us. He said that under no circumstances were we to disgrace the regiment by appearing with any stain or mark upon our camel-hair overcoats. Now, you *could not* keep a camel-hair overcoat clean. So before we were allowed to set off from Ty Croes to go to Bangor he went round both of us, wiping us down with petrol from the petrol tank!

Part of our duty was to stand by the Bofors anti-aircraft guns. I had a Welsh miner who used to help me lift the stretchers into the ambulance. That was one of the nicest things, I shall always remember – he was so well read, that man, and he had such enormously interesting, demanding ideas. We talked and we talked. He kept saying, 'Now, come on, Sheila, you take this book away and you read it.' The amount I learned!

Up there, of course, anything the workmen did, they sang at. So they sang in harmony, and the wind blew ... Beautiful! Beautiful!

Bob Gaunt had arrived in Glasgow on board the liner *Winchester Castle* in May. Travelling through London on his way to the interview board in Portsmouth that would recommend him for a commission, the eighteen-year-old South African was very impressed by the spirit of a taxi-driver who stopped to help him in the black-out:

He told me to hop in his taxi and he would take me to Waterloo. It was then light, and he took me on a drive past Buckingham Palace, Westminster Abbey and then to Trafalgar Square to show me South Africa House. To say I was worried about paying his fare is an understatement.

When we finally arrived at Waterloo he told me to wait in his cab and he would find out when my train would depart. He came back and told me I'd have to wait for about an hour, so he'd take me to have some breakfast. We went to a stall on the station and had a steaming hot mug of tea and sausage rolls. When it was time for me to catch my train I asked this kind person how much I owed and he replied, 'Nothing.' He told me he had a son who was a young lad of my age who'd been serving with the Royal Navy and he had been reported lost at sea the previous day. When he shook my hand I could see tears in his eyes.

That taught me, more than anything else, what guts the British people had. He'd just lost a son, but he was carrying on with his work. He wasn't sitting at home moping – the war was on, and he had to get on with his job.

Bob Gaunt's enchantment with the wartime spirit of Britain did not extend to all the naval officers he soon encountered. This was the other side of the social coin noticed by so many 'colonials' as they arrived in the mother country to be placed in the armed forces' training establishments. These Commonwealth youngsters often had a hazily romantic image of the British, engendered by their fathers' and uncles' stories of the gallantry, endurance and ironical humour shown by Tommy Atkins and Jack Tar during the First World War. It could come as quite a shock to bump up against the less endearing features of British service life – snobbery, parade ground bullshit and perceived assumptions of superiority. At Christmas 1941 Bob Gaunt found himself, along with some New Zealanders and Australians, at HMS *St Christopher*, a Coastal Forces base at Fort William in western Scotland. His response to belittling comments by the British officers was to climb Ben Nevis in the snow with a New Zealand chum and challenge the Britishers to do the same. Soon Gaunt had been appointed to serve as first lieutenant of a motor torpedo boat operating from Portsmouth. At HMS *Hornet*, the MTB base there, he ran into more negative attitudes:

The British Coastal Forces were mainly manned by young RNVR officers who'd been keen yachtsmen in peacetime. They'd mostly joined the Navy as ratings and been commissioned. The average age of officers serving in MTBs was about twenty-three; some were very much younger, with sub-lieutenants and, in a few cases, midshipmen serving as first lieutenants, navigators and spare officers. Some were even in command at the age of twenty. The large majority of these very brave young men didn't survive the war.

Some British officers were reluctant to accept Commonwealth officers, there's no doubt about it – because only the British were any good, and only those who'd been to public school. It led to friction. People separated themselves in the mess. Most of the Commonwealth officers would keep together, go ashore together; and all the Brits would keep together. That wasn't the case, I'm glad to say, once the boats had been in action. After that, everyone was judged on their personal qualities and some lifelong friendships were formed.

I don't think this separation happened in the rest of the Navy, but it was certainly true in the Coastal Forces. They found it hard to understand our attitude – I think we were possibly a bit too laid-back for them.

Thomas Hunter, the Scots-Canadian boy who'd left school at thirteen to be the breadwinner for his Depression-hit, fatherless family, had been in England with the Royal Regiment of Canada since early 1940. He'd found some British civilians pleasant enough, prepared to ask him and his friends home for a meal from time to time. But fundamentally, he felt, they didn't really want to know.

We were foreigners and that was it. The British didn't care for Canadians as a rule, until the fighting got started and we got entangled in the war, showed our prowess, proved that we could do anything and fight anyone. We felt we had to prove ourselves, and that's what the British didn't care for.

While the British Army was down in Africa, the only thing left to defend the country was Canadians, on the south coast and up around the shipping channel in Scotland. But the British wanted their own army there. There was a lot of friction. The English people were very austere; after all, those were tough times in Britain. We spoke a different tongue, a different language and did things altogether differently. So they treated us as foreigners. British NCOs were taken from British regiments and put in charge of us, and we didn't get along with them. The British have a different way of marching, a different way of doing everything. We just didn't go along with it.

A Canadian more recently landed in England was Charlie Hobbs, who had put the disappointment of his Anson wreck behind him and set himself to become an air-gunner. On a trip to London in October 1941 he'd found the citizens 'pretty starched, still pretty sure of themselves'. Like Thomas Hunter's army contingent, Hobbs and his Air Force colleagues were not unfriendly with the Britishers they met informally; but they, too, had problems with the inflexibility of barracks life and particularly with being drilled by British Army regulars who seemed to be making a point of ignoring the newcomers' status:

Here's where the trouble started: we went over as volunteers, but we were given rank. And our rank wasn't recognised by the Army, who were training us – no recognition whatsoever. A corporal in the British Army could put me, a sergeant, on a charge for not saying hello to him or something stupid like that. All sorts of us were getting into that kind of jam all the time.

Before we met these people we'd always done our own drilling. Why they couldn't have given us our own NCOs to drill us ... no one knows the answer to that. They had one tough old sergeant-major down at Bournemouth who gave us a real hard-boiled time, I'll tell you! I think there was a resentment there, a resentment of our free manner. We weren't rude to them, but we weren't subservient.

When I was sent to a gunners' school at Louth in Lincolnshire we just about went on a mutiny there. There were two bones of contention. One was the food. This was shocking: rotten fish, and it – was – *rotten*! These damn kippers! Some of it just wasn't right to eat. For all we had problems back home, we never had to eat bad food, you know? And the other bone of contention was the exercise in the winter. The CO was a colonel in the Guards, and he wanted us to get out and drill in our shorts when there's snow on the ground! Go on a run in the snow! These were Air Force boys, they weren't Army boys. What did they have to go out and run for?

Across the other side of the world, Rod Wells of 1 Corps Signals set sail from Australia, bound – as he thought – for Egypt: 'A day out of Fremantle, we got a signal. We weren't going to the Middle East after all: we were going to Malaya to help defend the naval base at Singapore. "Singapore?" I said. "Where the hell is that?" That was all I knew about Singapore.'

On 8 December 1941 everyone's knowledge of the Far East sharpened dramatically. All eyes, all over the world, suddenly switched to the map of the Pacific Ocean to find a tiny blob of an island named Oahu in the Hawaiian Island archipelago, an island provided with a deep-water inlet, charmingly named – Pearl Harbor. Then the eyes scurried on, across Midway Island and Wake Island, hurdling Guam in the Mariana Islands, before reaching the mainland of the Far East and searching out Hong Kong and finally the Malayan peninsula. There, at the southernmost extremity, lay the island fortress of Singapore, as symbolic of British imperial influence on land as HMS *Hood* had been at sea. The Americans in Hawaii, Midway and Wake had seemed as secure as the British in Hong Kong and Malaya. Now, all of a sudden, the old-established order had been sent reeling by a hammer-blow from Japan, a launching of swift, successful strikes across 6000 miles of land and sea. The attacks on the American Pacific Fleet at Pearl Harbor and at Midway (7 December) and the strikes against the other targets (8 December) were co-ordinated across the International Date Line to take place without warning, and more or less at the same time – a stunning piece of planning. Malaya, Singapore,

Hong Kong and the island targets would shortly be Japan's, along with most of the Far East. As for the US Pacific Fleet at anchor in Pearl Harbor, luckily for America, her four aircraft carriers were elsewhere. But the attack sank or badly damaged eighteen of the ninety-four ships and destroyed or damaged three-quarters of the aeroplanes there. A state of war existed forthwith between the two countries. Not that a Japanese attack had been unexpected; neither the Allies nor the Americans knew where the blows would fall, but they had been waiting for something like this to happen.

The problem for Japan, boiled down to simplicities, had been that she wanted an empire, but lacked the means to sustain one. The small string of islands that made up the country was short of both manpower and raw materials. Since 1931 Japan had been engaged in a long-drawn-out, brutally conducted conquest of China, taking advantage of in-fighting there between provincial warlords and a division in the country's leadership between Mao Tse-tung of the communists and Chiang Kai-shek of the nationalists. Alec Dennis, as a young Royal Navy officer, and Danny Misra, on overseas duty from India with the Rajputana Rifles, had both noted the dire effects of Japanese expansion in China in 1937–8 and had seen the war cloud swelling. Looking south across the Pacific, the militaristic regime in Japan could see what their embryonic empire needed – oil, rubber, rice, minerals, precious metals, medical extracts, unlimited cheap (or enslaved) labour – there almost for the taking in the far-flung Far Eastern colonies of Britain, Holland and France: Malaya, Borneo, Burma, the Dutch East Indies, French Indo-China.

In 1941 Holland and France were in the grasp of Japan's ally Germany; Britain's attention was fully occupied nearer home in the Atlantic and the Middle East. America was supporting Chiang Kai-shek in his opposition to the Chinese communists and also to Japanese expansion. The US had a military presence in the Philippine Islands, which had until recently been one of her colonial outposts in the Pacific. She had also slapped a raw-materials embargo on Japan. There was every temptation for Japan to go all out for an annihilation of the US Pacific Fleet and at the same time to smash America's air potential in the region by destroying her bombers based at two airfields on Luzon Island in the Philippines. That would open the door to a free hunt through the south-east Pacific, ripping open the soft colonial underbellies and fattening on their contents. And by occupying all the island archipelagos in a great triangle of the Pacific – its apex in Japan itself, its base extending from the Dutch East Indies way out west beyond New Guinea and the Gilbert Islands – Japan hoped to lock in place a defensive gate through which neither America nor any other opponent could break, if Japan should ever find herself forced on to the back foot.

The US General Douglas MacArthur believed his position in the Philippines was impregnable. The Dutch and French did not seriously expect to be able to defend their Far Eastern colonies in any case. As for the British, they suspected their position could be vulnerable in Hong Kong, Borneo, Malaya and Burma. But Malaya, at any rate, ought to be all right. Official opinion was that any attack would be bound to come from the south, from the sea. The island fortress of Singapore possessed its great naval base, its huge fifteen-inch guns covering all the sea approaches, its permanent garrison of 20,000 men. By 1941, with Britain's naval resources spread so thinly and under so much deadly pressure elsewhere, there were few illusions about the Royal Navy's ability to send significant, well-balanced forces to Singapore. But Winston Churchill's word on the situation, surely, was good enough. In 1940, as First Lord of the Admiralty, he had declared: 'Singapore ... could only be taken after a siege by an army of at least 50,000 men. It is not considered possible that the Japanese ... would embark on such a mad enterprise.'

As wartime Prime Minister, Winston Churchill was extremely unwilling to allow Australian troops to leave the Middle East and return home to Australia, which they very naturally wanted to do as the Japanese threat in the Far East became more and more clear. Australians had proved themselves tough, capable fighters in the desert, in spite of the mutual suspicion and quickness to take offence that characterised relationships at Senior Command level. But the average Aussie soldier, too, was feeling a little aggrieved. He had been proud to endure Tobruk, but the earlier disastrous campaigns in Greece and Crete had made him feel like colonial cannon-fodder. Now the Japanese were arriving on Australia's doorstep and he wanted to be back there to defend his own country. Australia had a new Prime Minister, John Curtin, whose Labour Party had just replaced the United Australia Party administration of Robert Menzies. General Blamey and John Curtin were both insistent that the Australian troops must be shipped back east, and Curtin crossed swords vigorously with Churchill on the issue as 1941 slipped into 1942. Many Australians, says Pierre Austin of the Royal Australian Navy, felt let down by Britain.

Churchill tried very, very hard to divert the Australian 6th and 7th Divisions, who were coming back from Egypt, when we desperately needed them. The only troops in New Guinea were our own militia and they were being pressed hard. The only other people coming across were Americans, you know – very raw and not a lot of use at that point.

The 6th and 7th had already sailed from Egypt and were half-way home when Churchill tried to direct them to bolster Burma. There was a very acrimonious exchange of telegrams between himself and our Prime Minister, Curtin, who wouldn't be bullied. The upshot was that Curtin said, 'They're my troops: get stuffed', which Churchill wasn't used to.

In the selection and deployment of Commonwealth troops in particular war theatres at the decision of the British war leaders, there were reasonable grounds for those troops to feel that they were pawns in a world-wide game being orchestrated – not without regard to its own imperial benefit – by Britain. Plenty felt like that among the men who were sent ashore, to all intents and purposes straight from the troopship into captivity, in the doomed colonial outposts of Singapore and Hong Kong.

On 17 November, three weeks before the Japanese launched their multi-pronged attacks, Private George Barron arrived in Hong Kong with the Royal Rifles of Canada on board the troopship *Awatea*. Barron was one of the older and steadier men, just a few days short of his thirty-third birthday. The Royal Rifles of Canada had been sent to Hong Kong, along with the Winnipeg Grenadiers, to boost the morale of the garrison there and as a deterrent to Japanese aggression – a notion suggested by the Canadian commander of the garrison, Major-General A. E. Grassett, when he had been relieved three months earlier. 'As soon as we landed,' George Barron says, 'we were shown the war positions. We knew then there'd be no escape. There was no way it could be defended. I said, "I hope everybody's got a good bathing suit, because it's going to be a long swim home."'

The little island's position at the nethermost tip of China meant that it was indefensible against any force invading from the mainland with sufficient determination and carelessness over loss of life. The Japanese had both these qualities in abundance. The garrison was short of modern equipment, of air cover, of sea defences. The Royal Rifles of Canada and the Winnipeg Grenadiers each had a substantial filling of raw recruits and were even shorter of equipment than the garrison they had come to 'boost'. The ship carrying their transport and heavy equipment had been diverted. Within three weeks they would be in action, green as grass, against tough, disciplined soldiers who knew what they had to do.

In the meantime the Canadians bashed the square, cleaned their bolt-action .303s and made acquaintance – almost all of them for the first time in their lives – with somewhere that wasn't Canada. George Barron was not the only one to be shaken by this first contact with an alien culture:

> Hong Kong was strange to us Canadian boys. We'd see people pulling cement mixers along by hand; you don't see that in Toronto! And a lot of people carrying stuff on bamboo poles on their shoulders. You'd see the women cutting grass and tie it in knots; that's what they use to cook their food with.
>
> Downtown, the streets was either very narrow or very wide. They were pissing and shitting on the streets, you know – they'd just drop their slacks and do it right on the kerb, the men and the women too. We were in a hotel one night and I went into the male washroom, and a woman came in and squatted down right beside me. I thought I'd made a mistake, so I went back and had another look at the sign on the door – I didn't want to get in no trouble! But no – I was in the right place and she wasn't. These things were kind of strange to us, because we'd never seen things like that before.

Towards the end of the year Rod Wells landed in Singapore. After a week in the island he was posted – attached to 2/15 Battalion, Royal Australian Artillery – north up the Malayan peninsula to Tampin, near Kuala Lumpur. The atmosphere was strange in those weeks: a kind of phoney peace. Like George Barron in Hong Kong, Wells was waiting for something to happen.

> We were on alert. There were two code words we had to look out for. 'Seaview' meant a situation of great gravity: prepare to demolish the signal base. The other signal was 'Raffles', and that meant that the invasion had started.
>
> We had a week of 'Seaview' alert. Then on this particular Saturday afternoon we'd come back from a route march and I thought I'd have a little sleep. I had a dream that I was back on the old farm at Dhuringile and the war was over. In the dream I threw a bucket of water over my sister as she was running round the old farmhouse. Then my father tapped me on the shoulder. I woke up and found that a signalman was tapping my shoulder with a signal in his hand. It said: 'Raffles.'

It was 8 December and the Japanese had landed at Kota Baharu, up in the north-eastern corner of the peninsula. Rod Wells and his party soon evacuated the police station they were working in and burned it down. Then Wells was recalled back to Advanced HQ and commenced an anxious withdrawal southwards down the peninsula towards Singapore Island. On the second day after the invasion, 10 December, the Japanese struck another tremendous blow against British imperial strength and pride when their aircraft caught two of the Royal Navy's finest warships, the battlecruiser *Repulse* and the 35,000-ton battleship and flagship of the Eastern Fleet, *Prince of Wales*, without air cover in the Gulf of Siam just east of Malaya, and sank them both. The loss of two such ships – like *Hood* and like Singapore, potent symbols of the British Empire – caused shock all round the world. The jolt was especially keenly felt by Commonwealth sailors.

'The only time I can remember being really depressed about the outcome of the war,' says Peter Cayley of the Royal Canadian Navy, 'was during my time at Dartmouth in December 1941, when the Sergeant of Marines came into the mess and said that *Prince of Wales* and *Repulse* had been sunk. He just sat down – he was utterly flabbergasted. That shook our confidence as much as anything.'

Alec Dennis of the Royal Navy, agrees, though he remembers more a sense of sadness than of shock:

> It didn't surprise us at all that these two ships, which had no air cover at all, would get sunk. They were the might of the British Navy, two very impressive-looking ships. They went to Singapore, which was not in good shape, and lifted everybody's spirits: 'Now we've got these two great ships, everything will be all right.' And of course everything wasn't all right; they were sunk and that was the end of Malaya, because there was nothing to stop the Japanese at all. The Japanese by then had the reputation of being unstoppable. 'They never miss' was the cry. Yes – when *Prince of Wales* and *Repulse* were sunk the blow to morale was enormous.

Rod Wells: 'On Christmas Day my CO told me, "You ought to know this, even though you shouldn't – a defence exercise was carried out around Singapore in 1937, and the conclusion was that there was bound to be a land battle and that they'd need at least another one to two infantry divisions and 478 aircraft to defend Malaya. And they also concluded that these reinforcements wouldn't be made available." '

It was beginning to look to the Australian soldiers in Singapore as if they had been sent into a powder-puff fortress; one that could never have been properly strengthened against attack by sea, land and air even if the political will and adequate resources had been there, and which had been written off through Pommie parsimony or Pommie colonial arrogance. As a strong line of defence against a Japanese thrust towards Australia,

Singapore was patently going to fail. It looked to many Australian eyes, then and there, as if Australia itself had been written off.

'It was down to Churchill and Roosevelt,' Rod Wells says. 'I can see their point. The main thing at that time was to build up the base of operations in Europe. If Australia had to fall, it had to fall. But it wouldn't have lasted, anyway. No matter how long it took, we would have cut off the Japanese supplies. They wouldn't have been able to maintain any control over Australia.'

On arrival in Hong Kong in November the Royal Rifles of Canada had been billeted in Shampshui Po camp on the Chinese mainland, looking across to Hong Kong Island. After the Japanese invasion the Canadians would come to know Shampshui Po extremely well.

On 8 December 1941 George Barron was waiting to go into the dining-room for breakfast when he heard a flight of planes pass overhead, followed by the booming of anti-aircraft fire. It was the start of ten days of firing at the Japanese planes, guarding the gate to the ammunition dump and watching the smoke thicken from burning factories while waiting for the expected infantry assault on the island. It came on 18 December, at which time George Barron was in Pillbox 38A. From the hour he first saw the Japanese until the surrender of the garrison on Christmas Day a week later, Barron was in the grip of events outside his control, rushed from one place to another in a whirlwind of incidents that scooped him up and swept him breathlessly along.

I was on guard duty outside the pillbox just at daylight and I could see movement on the road. I thought it was a Hindu battalion at first, wearing turbans. Then our HQ ordered us to get out and began trench-mortaring the Japs. So now we're stuck between our own fire and the Japs' fire. We got the locks out of the Vickers guns, climbed over the barbed wire and got down the hill, running as fast as we could go. Then we went across Sai Wan Bay, with the planes diving straight down on us. It was quite a time. Quite a time. It's more scary, being attacked from the air – you've got the bombs *and* the bullets.

I got into the bushes. Tried to run, fell down, got up, fell down. I'd been wounded in the leg, although I hadn't known it at the time, running from the pillbox. It was shrapnel – I always said from our guns. Shrapnel was coming down just like rain; it was a wonder any of us got out alive. I'd ripped my hand and arm, too, getting over the barbed wire.

Anyhow, I got the others to go on and I stayed in the bushes. The Japs were down at the water's edge, firing across the bay at the bushes. I lay there with my head in my arms and could hear *bzzz-bzzz-bzzz* going by my ear. But none of them hit me. I lay there till late in the day; then I rolled over into this big nullah that they'd dug to catch the storm water during the rainy season. Cigarettes, matches, money, clothes – everything was soaking wet. I sneaked along the nullah right below the Japanese and got to a village. The Chinese had stripped that place as soon as the English had moved out. Doors, windows, window frames, electric fittings – you wouldn't believe it unless you'd seen it.

Finally I got up to Fort Collison on the east side of the island. They had two British soldiers there, with bayonet and sabre wounds in their backs. They dressed up my leg, and we went up over Mount Collison and down over Shek O Beach. Found a Chinaman with a boat; started to cross over to Stanley village, with the Japs and the British both shooting at us. Two-inch guns – *boomf!* In the water, all around us. And it was raining like hell. Finally the shooting stopped. Oh, God! . . .

I was so thirsty. I'd filled my water bottle with gin at Collison, because that's all there was – the Japanese had bombed the water supply. But I couldn't drink that gin. I found a stream that was moving over a whole lot of rocks and stuff, dumped out the gin, filled my cans with water. Then in Stanley village they took us into the police station and they give us tea – hot tea. And, oh God – it tasted good.

They put me in the hospital, bandaged my arm and leg. I didn't want to stay, but they said, 'That's your bed – get in!' Next morning the doctor said, 'Can anyone walk?' I said, 'I can.' He put me in a truck and they took me to an emergency hospital in Port Stanley. On 24 December I left there and went off with my unit; and on the twenty-fifth – Christmas Day – the war ended for me about four o'clock in the afternoon, when we all surrendered.

When the Japanese broke into the hospital in Stanley village, after I'd been moved, they walked in and they bayoneted the wounded men in that hospital where I'd been. And they raped the Red Cross nurses that were with the patients, and they dragged them all outside, threw gasoline on them and burned them. That's true. That's gospel true.

FOUR

Turning Round: 1942

*I went into my cabin and had a bloody good cry. I was only
twenty.*   Bob Gaunt, South Africa

It was a happy New Year for Japan. She began 1942 sitting on top of
the Far Eastern world. Hong Kong was hers; Guam and Wake Islands
too. Her aircraft had destroyed the effectiveness of both the US Navy
and the Royal Navy in eastern waters, giving her troops enough breathing
space to sweep on to more quick and dramatic victories all over the South
Pacific.

She had also, ultimately, sealed her own defeat as comprehensively as
Germany had done with 'Operation Barbarossa' and for the same reason:
a half-sleeping, uneasily bystanding giant had been turned into a shocked
and furious opponent. And the American giant had a pile of money behind
him and a heap of resources into which he had already been dipping
generously to help his midget buddies across the pond. In March 1941
President Roosevelt's Lend-Lease Bill had become law, allowing Britain
and any other Allied country to tap American money and war materials
on a 'borrow-now-repay-later' basis. In July American marines had taken

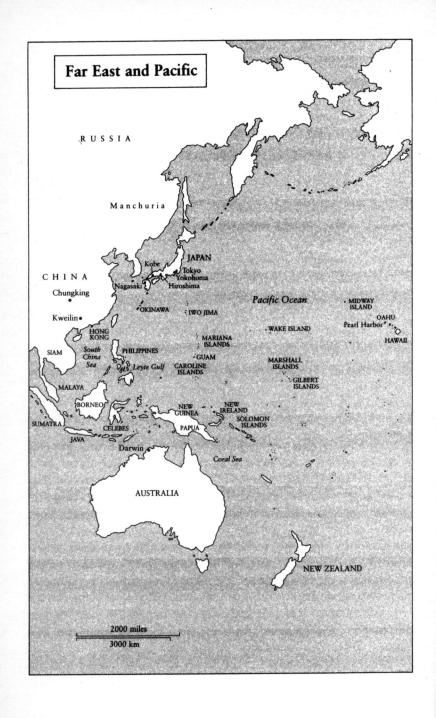

Far East and Pacific

RUSSIA

Manchuria

CHINA

Chungking

Kweilin

SIAM

MALAYA

SUMATRA

JAVA

BORNEO

CELEBES

Darwin

AUSTRALIA

NEW ZEALAND

JAPAN

Kobe

Tokyo

Yokohama

Nagasaki

Hiroshima

OKINAWA

IWO JIMA

HONG
KONG

South
China
Sea

PHILIPPINES

Leyte Gulf

Pacific Ocean

MIDWAY
ISLAND

OAHU

Pearl Harbor

HAWAII

WAKE ISLAND

MARIANA
ISLANDS

GUAM

CAROLINE
ISLANDS

MARSHALL
ISLANDS

GILBERT
ISLANDS

NEW
GUINEA

NEW
IRELAND

PAPUA

SOLOMON
ISLANDS

Coral Sea

2000 miles

3000 km

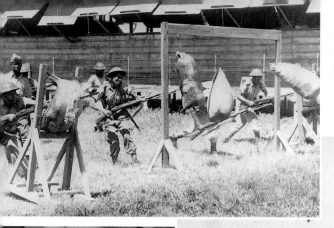

Trinidadian men of the South Caribbean Force go in enthusiastically with the bayonet during training.

Above A Gold Coast villager, watched by a British recruiting officer, applies tongue to bayonet while he is sworn in as a private in the Gold Coast Regiment.

Left A Trinidad soldier says goodbye to his wife before embarking for Italy in October 1944.

Moment of departure on active service overseas for men of the King's African Rifles.

Top Des Sheen (Australia), laconic Battle of Britain fighter pilot, with his Spitfire.

Right Mahinder Singh Pujji (India) in the turban he insisted upon wearing while flying his Hurricane fighter.

Above Mahinder Singh Pujji today.

Top Flight Sergeant James Hyde (Trinidad) allows squadron mascot Dingo to sit on the wing of his Spitfire.

Left Paul Radomski of New Zealand (left), as a young RAF bomber pilot relaxing with a colleague.

Above Paul Radomski today.

Above On board a Royal Navy warship going to the defence of Greece in early 1941, an Australian soldier and a British sailor try to out-shake each other for the benefit of the official photographer.

Right Officers of HMS *Griffin* at the time of her 1941 operations in the Mediterranean. Alec Dennis (second right) stands next to his much-admired Captain, Johnny Lee-Barber (end of line).

Below A wounded Maori soldier, evacuated from Crete dressed only in his underwear, is helped to disembark at Alexandria on 31 May 1941.

above Aftermath of the Dieppe Raid, 19 August 1942.

inset Thomas Hunter (Canada), just before the raid.

below 'Dieppe Victors Come Back Singing' (Daily Mail). In stark contrast to the newspaper headlines, the traumatic shock of witnessing the slaughter on the beaches shows all too clearly on the faces of these Canadian survivors, photographed on board the ship that brought them back to England.

Left Bob Gaunt of South Africa (right) poses with youthful but dashing colleague on board their motor torpedo boat.

Below Sister MTB 238 at speed.

Below Sub-Lt Jim Tait, RNZNVR, (right) with his brother Sub-Lt (later Admiral) A G Tait, RN.

Right Jim Tait today.

Below Italian submarine *Cobalto*, carrying a boarding party that includes Jim Tait, just after being fatally rammed by Tait's ship HMS *Ithuriel* during Operation Pedestal in August 1942.

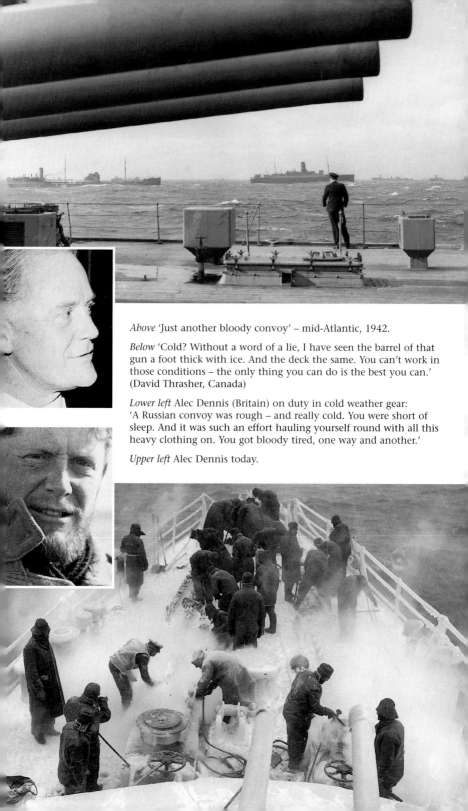

Above 'Just another bloody convoy' – mid-Atlantic, 1942.

Below 'Cold? Without a word of a lie, I have seen the barrel of that gun a foot thick with ice. And the deck the same. You can't work in those conditions – the only thing you can do is the best you can.' (David Thrasher, Canada)

Lower left Alec Dennis (Britain) on duty in cold weather gear: 'A Russian convoy was rough – and really cold. You were short of sleep. And it was such an effort hauling yourself round with all this heavy clothing on. You got bloody tired, one way and another.'

Upper left Alec Dennis today.

Two under-age volunteers.

Left Juanita Carberry (Kenya) as a 17-year-old FANY in Nairobi, and in her Chelsea flat in London today.

Right Frank O'Donnell (Canada) aged 16, in New York in 1941, and as a barrister in Toronto today.

Below A Kenyan FANY dispatch rider takes a message – a not entirely unstaged photograph!

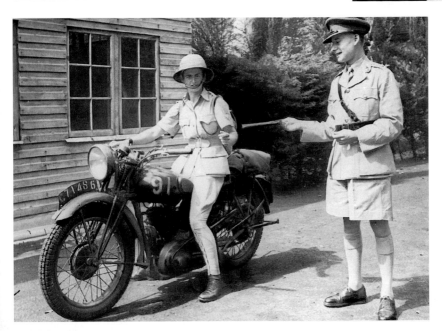

over garrison duties in Iceland from the British, and US Navy ships had begun to accompany North Atlantic convoys. Now, after Pearl Harbor, United States forces would be right there in the ring, with the majority of Congress and people behind them. Their participation would ensure an Allied victory, as Winston Churchill foresaw:

> Now at this very moment, I knew the United States was in the war, up to the neck, and in to the death. So we had won after all! ... We had won the war. England would live; Britain would live; the Commonwealth of Nations and the Empire would live ... The British Empire, the Soviet Union and now the United States, bound together with every scrap of their life and strength, were, according to my lights, twice or even thrice the force of their antagonists ... Many disasters, immeasurable cost and tribulation lay ahead, but there was no more doubt about the end.[5]

For Rod Wells, the Australian farmer's son, there was every possible doubt about the end. 1942 began disastrously and went on that way. He was withdrawn from Johore Baharu on the Malayan mainland, where he had been maintaining signals communications for the withdrawing Allied forces, and pulled back on to Singapore Island. There were some days as a member of the 'Snake Gully Rifles', while big guns fired into the defenders' positions – a splinter from one shell sliced Wells's sleeping bag in two just after he had vacated it. On 7 February came the Japanese assault across the Johore Strait. There was brave resistance from the defenders; but the naval base still frowned seawards with most of its big guns, and the north-facing nape of the island's neck was to prove as vulnerable as Hong Kong's. Within a week the Johore Baharu causeway was destroyed, the island's reservoirs were all in Japanese hands, the water taps were turned off and General Yamashita offered a choice – surrender, or have the city of one million inhabitants bombed flat. Surrender by the British Commander, Lt-General Arthur Percival, followed on 15 February. George Barron of the Royal Rifles of Canada, a prisoner of the Japanese in Hong Kong, heard about the disaster almost as it happened:

> We had a radio in a bully-beef box. Every night we'd listen to the BBC. The night before, we put it on and the BBC said, 'No word from Singapore today.'
> In the morning I had to go over to the guardroom. They were all laughing in there, but when I went in you could have heard a pin drop on the floor. Their sergeant threw me a piece of paper. It said, in red ink – I can still see it now – 'February 15 – Singapore fell today.'

The unthinkable had come to pass. Churchill's 'mad enterprise' had been undertaken and concluded in just over two months by 35,000 soldiers under disciplined command, moving on foot and by bicycle through bush and off-road terrain, thinking ahead and adapting as they went, living hard and always following one blow with another. The Japanese had bamboozled, harried, penned up and finally captured more than 130,000 Allied troops, at the expense of 3507 dead and 6150 wounded.

One soldier whom they didn't catch, however, was Major-General H. Gordon Bennett, the Australian 8th Division's commanding officer. General Bennett was a red-haired and hot-natured man, whose reputation as an anti-authoritarian fire-eater went down well with the Australian soldiers. On 14 February, the day before the surrender, Bennett ordered his shell-starved gunners to fire only in direct defence of the Australian perimeter. He cabled the Australian Prime Minister, John Curtin, and told him that he would surrender to avoid further bloodshed, 'in the event of other formations falling back and allowing the enemy to enter the city behind us'. But he did not keep the British General Percival informed of these moves – nor of his preparations for escape, which he accomplished after the surrender on 16 February, getting away in the early hours with twenty others in a small boat and managing to reach Java and, eventually, Australia.

Feelings were mixed about his action. Back home General Bennett was congratulated by politicians but cold-shouldered by many of his military colleagues. They felt he should have set an example by sticking more closely to the spirit of General Percival's orders: 'Officers will remain with their troops and protect them until they are taken into legal custody ... There must be no talk of mass escape.' A case was also made for prag-matism: a free general was of more use than an imprisoned one. 'General Bennett had been making his arrangements,' comments Rod Wells, 'and he took off. And the typical rank and file said, "Good on yer, mate. You did the right thing." Well, actually, he didn't; he did the wrong thing. He was still legally in command of his troops. That bothered me. Here we were, building up morale as best we could, doing what we could – and someone goes and shatters it by walking out. I felt that very deeply, and I think a lot of other people did too.'

Later, in the Japanese prisoner-of-war camps, the Australians found a new name for their running shoes. They christened them 'Gordon Bennetts'.

*

One thing that everyone in Singapore knew about the Japanese soldiers was their capacity for brutality towards captured enemies and civilians. There had been evidence enough of that in China. Now that the Japanese had Singapore, they killed probably as many civilians as they had captured soldiers. Most of these were expatriate Chinese. But this mass murder, because it was not publicised, did not hit home around the world as did the bayonetings and shootings at the Alexandra Hospital in Singapore just before the surrender. In the afternoon of 14 February, as a reprisal for what the Japanese soldiers said was use of the building as a firing point, they entered the hospital. While some sadistic soldiers played 'games' with the pulleys and weights attached to the limbs of patients suffering from severe fractures, others were bayoneting to death everyone they could find – doctors and nurses on duty, patients in their beds and even on the operating table. Over two days, at first wholesale and then in batches taken at intervals from a locked room, the Japanese murdered about 250 unarmed prisoners. Among them was Captain Lance Parkinson, an officer working with the Royal Army Medical Corps. He was bayoneted while a captive, walking along a corridor with his hands up in surrender.

Back in England Captain Parkinson had been Medical Officer in the camp at Ty Croes, Anglesey, where Sheila Kershaw was working as a FANY ambulance driver. They were married six months before Lance Parkinson was posted to Burma. He had fallen back on Singapore, together with the rest of the Allied garrison in Burma, after the Japanese invaded on 8 December. His wife would receive confirmation of his death in a bizarre fashion by the return, through mysterious channels and many unidentified hands, of his gold cigarette case, which the young couple had jokingly called their insurance against disaster.

After the surrender, Rod Wells was among the tens of thousands of Allied servicemen sent to Changi, a well-appointed British Army married quarters before the war. Now it had been bombed, shelled and looted.

> There was no power, no sewerage. We had to get those going, and we had to take wire and build a wall round ourselves. Well, they had the guns – and if you wanted to feed ... In fact, those first weeks in Changi weren't too bad. The Japs virtually kept out of it. Changi as a whole, in fact, wasn't really all that bad. A lot of Changi-ites'll tell you different; but to chaps on the Burma Railway, and in other camps, Changi was considered almost as a home away from home. After one of those places you'd do anything to get to Changi.

Rod Wells was soon to experience one of those places. Of the two commodities the Japanese were critically short of – raw materials and manpower – the second could be supplied from among their prisoners and the civilians they had conquered. Their most notorious project, the jungle railway from Siam to Burma, was beginning construction, and slave labourers were needed. Perhaps 300,000 civilian prisoners were to die constructing this line, in conditions more appalling than anyone who had not suffered them could guess. About 12,000 Allied prisoners died on the works too. Some of these were in 'A Force', 3000 of the fittest prisoners who were picked from those in Changi and sent off to Burma. Rod Wells missed selection then, but he was in the next batch, 'B Force', which was numbered off and sent away a few weeks later, in the opposite direction. 'They said', Wells recalls, 'that we'd be going where there would be little work; we were told we were going to a land of milk and honey.'

The capture of Singapore put the Japanese in control of the Strait of Malacca, the narrow channel between the Malayan peninsula and the island of Sumatra which formed the main sea thoroughfare between the Pacific and Indian Oceans. The capture of Malaya gave them a land connection through to Siam and on west into Burma. India was the prize that lay beyond Burma: India, where Japan might hope to have joined hands with the other two Axis powers by the end of the year, to complete the ring of steel. More immediately, the fall of the island fortress caused enormous shock waves, profound despair and disillusion with Britain as an effective defender of her vast Commonwealth of Nations. Every kind of failure and weakness, from complacency to deviousness, could be and was imputed to Britain. The image of the mother hen protecting her chicks beneath sheltering wings, or of the imperial lioness guarding her cubs with the sharpest claws and teeth in the business, simply wouldn't wash after a débâcle like Singapore.

It was, for many Commonwealth volunteers, a definitive episode; a moment when they were forced to contemplate a future outside the imperial family, a future in which they would have to find for themselves a national identity and security that Britain could no longer guarantee.

All over the world, however, the Commonwealth family members were still coming forward to offer their services...

In New Zealand, the romantic half-Maori boy, Charles Bell, was still under-age. But that wasn't going to deter him from trying to wangle his way into service overseas with his beloved Maori Battalion:

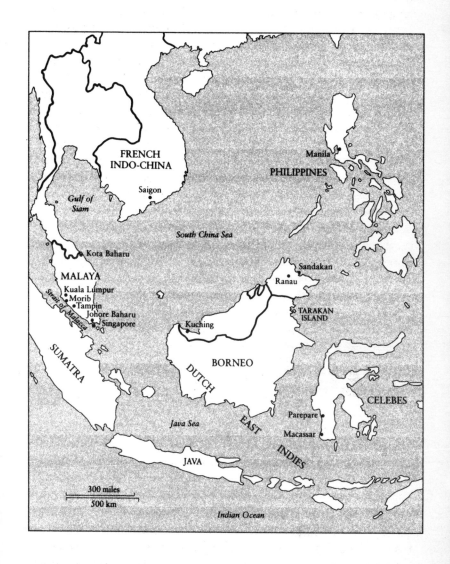

FRENCH
INDO-CHINA

Saigon

Gulf of
Siam

South China Sea

Manila

PHILIPPINES

Kota Baharu

MALAYA

Kuala Lumpur
Morib
Tampin
Johore Baharu
Singapore

Strait of Malacca

Kuching

Sandakan

Ranau

TARAKAN
ISLAND

BORNEO

SUMATRA

DUTCH

CELEBES

Parepare

Macassar

Java Sea

EAST

JAVA

INDIES

300 miles

500 km

Indian Ocean

I tricked the guards at the railway station in Wellington and I waited down at the railway yards. As the train slowed down I jumped on it with my gear – kitbag, the whole lot. When I got into the wharf area there was no way I could get up the gangway onto the *Aquitania* with the rest of the Battalion reinforcements, because they were being checked off on a list. There was this huge square hole in the side of the ship where all the ropes went in; so when the train pulled out I took a flying jump off the wharf and landed in this hole. I banged on the doors in there and a crew member opened them up. I told them what I was doing and they took care of me for three days, until the ship was due to leave.

On sailing day the wharf gates were opened up to let relatives in to say goodbye. I made the mistake of going up to look over the rail, and saw some girls I knew from the Maori Club of Wellington. So I scribbled a note to my Auntie Rita and dropped it to them in my cigarette case: 'Goodbye, I'm leaving New Zealand.' They dashed off to Auntie Rita; and the first thing she did was to get in touch with the MPs to get me off the boat. Well, I got a message to go below and there they were, waiting for me. The master of the ship said to me, 'If you'd waited a couple more hours till we'd got out past the Heads, I wouldn't have turned this ship around just to put you off.'

They took me off the ship and put me into an army jail thing over in Port Dawson – and as the ship went out the sergeant in charge of the jail took me down to the water's edge to wave her goodbye.

Other under-age volunteers were more successful, or just luckier. In Kenya, Juanita Carberry – in flight from her unhappy childhood on a coffee farm in Happy Valley – was in search of somewhere she could feel at home:

I joined up at seventeen – went to the FANY headquarters in Nairobi and lied about my age. They taught me to be a despatch rider, on Ariels and BSAs and Triumphs. And I learned radio and telephone exchange – all in and around Nairobi. I loved it. It was fun. I didn't know much about the war overseas, although I had a couple of boyfriends in the South African Air Force who were shot down and killed in action. There were a lot of chaps around Nairobi – South African troops, a lot of Yanks – we were in demand, always asked out to this and that, dances and so on.

I was a girl, so I got on fine with the Yanks. When we were in uniform we had to wear these stockings, ghastly horse-shit-coloured stockings. But the Yanks made things out of old parachutes. Silk – that was the big thing. There were American Air Force chaps who were ferrying aircraft across from West

Africa – one of them wanted to marry me, but I wasn't interested in that sort of thing at all. I remember the day he left; he must have gone into a flower shop and ordered the entire contents, because two vans arrived at FANY Headquarters and every single fire bucket was stuffed with flowers.

I was very happy in the Army way of life. Other people wanted to wear civvies – I couldn't care less what I wore. I was only too pleased not to have to think what to wear. Army uniform . . . that's fine by me. I just loved the Army. I liked being in Communications and felt very loyal to the Signals. I felt I *belonged* to something.

Another Kenyan seventeen-year-old who joined up at about this time was Mutili Musoma, who came from the village of Machakos south-east of Nairobi. Unlike his cowherding parents, Musoma had had the opportunity to go to school:

My parents didn't known the gain of education; they wanted me to look after cattles. One day recruiting soldiers came to the village. I thought to myself, 'I better skip, go and join the Army.' We had so many difficulties in the area. Many of my friends were going. Said I, 'I'm not going to remain by myself, I'm going to follow my friends.' I decided that only myself.

I skipped very early morning. I went without giving notice to school. I did not inform my father.

Frank O'Donnell, racing through High School in Canada, was even younger, a precocious sixteen-year-old too bright for the schoolroom but not yet old enough to be allowed to emulate his older brother and join up. There was only one thing for it:

I ran away from home. I hadn't attained my proper weight yet; I still had some growing to do, in many ways. But the recruiting sergeant didn't say, 'Get lost, kid.' He wanted to know how old I was. I gave him my birthday, as far as the month and day went; but I added a couple of years. It must have been pretty obvious, but I guess in January 1942 they needed bodies anyway.

I told them I'd get some proof of my birth date. So I wrote a letter, put it in an envelope and sent it back to Toronto. And after a few days it came back; it had been mailed by my pal there. It was a letter that I had composed, of course, certifying that I had been born on such-and-such a date. So I guess they put it on the file – and I suppose if I looked it up, it might still be around somewhere!

Wilmer Nadjiwon of the Ojibwe Indians, from the Cape Croker reservation on Owen Sound, saw his friends start to go off and join the

115

Canadian Army right from the beginning of the war. But there were various pressures on him not to join them.

> I was working in a brick factory when war broke out. It was a job, and they weren't too easy to come by. Many of the boys joined up straight away, right out of the reservation; the Army meant good pay, a dollar and a half a day. But I hung back for a while. Actually, my father didn't want me to join. He said he had no respect for military service, because he wasn't treated very good after *his* service in the First World War. He said, 'You won't get no thanks for it' – in other words, it was a white man's war.
>
> I agreed with him, up to a point. But fighting was part of our tradition. As your friends left, you became uneasy with yourself, saying, 'Haven't I got the guts to do it? What am I doing here, when they're all over there?' So in 1942 I stopped in at a recruiting office with a friend – I was just bumming around with him, I wasn't intending to join. He said, 'Just wait for me; I'm going to sign up.' Well, he was in getting a medical and the sergeant was talking to me – he knew my dad, he knew most of the boys from the reservation. And before my friend came out ... I'd signed up.
>
> Now, when you first go up there and get your first army gear, your shaving kit, your pack and that – they give you a blanket. And they say: 'Take care of that – because that's the one we'll bury you in.'

Red-headed Geraldine Turcotte now stepped out from behind the ready-to-wear counter in Timmons, the town she'd moved to from Sturgeon Falls, and volunteered, one of the 17,000 women who were to serve with the Royal Canadian Air Force (Women's Division).

> The minute that war was declared I'd wanted to join. Oh yes! But they weren't ready for women in 1939. But the men had been joining up; and, you see, now they realised that if the women were recruited, then they could send more men to the front. Everything had to be administered, eh – and they had the men in the offices, whereas they should have been with the Army, the Navy or the Air Force. And if *I'd* been allowed to fight with a gun I would have done. Well, boy – we were in London in the rocket attacks – you couldn't get any closer to the war than *that*!
>
> We were made to understand that we were recruited so that men could fly. That was always made very plain. Right from the offset we were aware that that was the reason we were involved.

Recruiting for the Indian Army in 1942 was not a straightforward matter.

For one thing, although the process of 'Indianisation' – phasing out the presence of British officers and NCOs – was going forward, it was progressing much too slowly. Graduates from the Indian Military Academy at Dehra Dun, where Danny Misra had been a cadet, were especially upset at the slow pace of reform. Although Dehra Dun had been styled the 'Indian Sandhurst', King's Commissioned Indian Officers were still not permitted to command British troops. British officers in the Indian Army in 1939, at which time they outnumbered their Indian counterparts by ten to one, drew two or three times as much salary when pay and allowances had been taken into account. By January 1941 the proportion of British to Indian officers in combat units of the Indian Army had actually increased to about twelve to one. By the end of the war it was to fall to not much above four to one, and pay and conditions would be on a par – but in 1942 the position looked, and was, unfair.

Then there was the growing strength of the Quit India movement. Back in August 1941, on board *Prince of Wales* in Placentia Bay, Newfoundland, President Roosevelt and Winston Churchill had signed the Atlantic Charter. The charter confirmed their commitment to the destruction of tyranny and the vanquishing of those seeking 'territorial aggrandizement'; and, more practically, the US committed itself to a loan of $1 billion to the Soviet Union, which had been invaded by Germany three weeks earlier. The charter went on to express the signatories' respect for 'the right of all peoples to choose the form of government under which they will live'. What was sauce for the Nazi goose, Indian nationalists were quick to point out, should also be sauce for the imperialist gander. They felt that Roosevelt, in expressing the general dislike of Americans for 'colonialism', had wrung a signed commitment to Indian independence out of Churchill. In mid-1942 Congress considered an offer made by Sir Stafford Cripps – sent to India on a ship-steadying mission by the War Cabinet in London – to deliver everything that the Indian nationalists seemed to want. Indian political leaders were to be included straight away in the national Indian government. After the war there was to be independence for India, in or out of the Commonwealth, with or without the provinces where Muslims were in the majority: the Muslims could decide whether to stay or go. Congress rejected the suggestion and instead, passed a Quit India resolution. Britain should leave – now. Britain could not agree to that. There were riots and suppressions, and a rise in nationalist resentment by one more notch.

As Krishen Tewari's doctor father in Jullundur was listening to the advice of his good friend Colonel Kilroy, nineteen-year-old Krishen himself felt pulled between two sets of loyalties:

> The reason why I joined the Army was because Colonel Kilroy insisted that the war had started and my father must send two of his five sons into the Army. There was in fact a little hesitation at one time – some members of our family said, 'Why should you join the British Army to fight on the British side? We want independence!' At the same time there was the Quit India movement of 1942 also, which we read about. There was a conflict, there's no doubt in my mind, at that time. We would have ... discussions. It was not so much anti-British as hesitation whether we should join the Army to be on the British side or not. But I think better sense prevailed.
>
> Colonel Kilroy insisted that we boys should be toughened. And so he arranged for us to train with a Dogra Battalion. They were tremendously tough, tremendously disciplined. We admired them very much – they *charmed* us into joining the Army.

Equipment for the new recruits of the Commonwealth had improved a little since the rudimentary early days of 1939–40, though the rifles were still First World War .303s and some of the artillery crews were still learning how to fire tree trunks rather than real guns. But one aspect of basic training none of them was to forget – the NCOs who bullied them through their paces.

Frank O'Donnell:

> At Berryhill in Quebec they marched us right, left and centre. We learned how to polish boots – oh boy, did we!
>
> We had a corporal down in Berryhill – we were a mixed group of French and English speakers – who'd line us up in the morning and he'd say: 'By ze right, number!' And we'd give him bilingual numbers: 'One – *deux* – *trois* – (pause) – four – *cinq*!' He gave some of his orders in a bilingual way too; for instance, he'd say: 'On ze carbeen ... will go ze knife ... put!' – which meant 'fix bayonets'.
>
> Then I went down to Kingston to learn signals. I learned the rudiments of morse code, which they spent hours and hours teaching us – days and days, weeks, months – never used in action, not once. They taught us semaphore, with flags – never used. I'm not sure that if we'd been there a couple of weeks longer they wouldn't have taught us Indian smoke signals.

Krishen Tewari:

At Officer Training Academy in Bangalore we had British commandant, British deputy commandant. My Company Commander was British – I can still remember his name, Long Lanky Longfield. We had mostly British instructors for physical training and drill. I still remember the sergeant-major in Bangalore. He was my height, five feet five-and-a-half, and he was rounded like a football and tough as anything. On the drill ground he'd say: 'You might have broken your mother's heart, but you're never going to break mine! Now come on – double up – SIR!'

Geraldine Turcotte:

I was sent to Ottawa for basic training. Do you know that it was so new that we didn't even have boardwalks? But we managed. We had a sergeant-major – he was a real rip-snorter! And it was good, because he didn't stand for any nonsense and he didn't have any favourites. The training didn't do you any harm, believe *me*.

I went to No. 16 Senior Flying Training School at Hagersville near Hamilton, on signals in the orderly room. We had a great social life with the men. Oh, yes – I made sure of that! We had a canteen – and oh, we had fun – oh, yeah! One thing you had to do when you were on an SFTS was flying – low flying. I went low flying with this one guy, and I'm telling you – we scared more cows than you'd ever shake a stick at. Right over the fences, you know. Oh, my God . . . Sick? You bet! But you couldn't shoot your biscuits, you know – not in front of the men. As soon as we landed, though, I was out of that plane and into the washroom like a shot! Oh, you bet!

What became known as the Battle of the Atlantic, the attempt by Germany to prevent Allied convoys crossing between America and Europe, had been increasingly dominated by U-boats and aircraft rather than by surface raider attacks. Germany's purpose was, quite simply, to starve Britain of food and war materials until she capitulated. The initiative swung between one side and the other, with the weight generally rather in favour of the U-boats for the first three years of the war, ever more heavily with the Allies thereafter. In the first few months of 1942, now that war had been joined with the United States, the German submarines enjoyed a run of success in the western Atlantic against American convoys that had not yet learned the hard lessons learned by the British and Canadian seafaring forces. Over 300 merchantmen were sunk by U-boats in the coastal waters off America between January and June 1942; total tonnage sunk in the Atlantic by U-boats in those months came to over 3,000,000.

The U-boats hunted in wolf packs, with one spotter summoning all the others; the escorts with the convoys hunted the U-boats, and by mid-1942 had driven them back into mid-Atlantic again. But the U-boats could not yet be mastered, as they were later when their positions at night or in foul weather could be determined by specialist short-wavelength radar fitted in aircraft. For most of 1942 it was still a question of convoy discipline and endless alertness in the escort ships, allied to astute use of Asdic sets to locate the U-boats by echo and depth-charges to finish them off. The submarines went on sinking merchantmen and escort ships; in 1942 Allied losses world-wide were 6,226,207 tons, representing 1159 ships. The vast majority of these sinkings were in the North Atlantic, something like 450,000 tons *per month* in 1942. In May 1942 it was 585,431 tons. Merchant ships were being sunk faster than they were being built. The marauders probably never numbered more than ten or a dozen at any one time in the North Atlantic. German successes in cracking British naval cyphers in 1941 and early 1942 meant that the U-boats generally had plenty of warning about Allied intentions and dispositions – and about Allied counter-measures. British imports fell dramatically. In the Battle of the Atlantic, 1942 was a desperate year, and the brunt of the battle, as always, fell on the ordinary seaman, who had to work on an ocean which could always produce prodigious winds and seas at the drop of a hat, and who had to keep going through exhaustion, fear and discomfort. Stoical courage was shown, in particular, by the merchant seaman, who had no way of fighting back against his enemy. His very likely death (between 20 and 30 per cent of the Merchant Navy's total manpower died during the war) would in all probability be a horrible one, some grisly combination of drowning, smothering in oil and burning alive.

David Thrasher, from the little Canadian village of Combermere in north-eastern Ontario, was in his late twenties when he joined the Royal Canadian Naval Volunteer Reserve in August 1941. Within a few months he was a gunlayer in the corvette *Louisburg*, and served throughout the war in her on escort duty with Atlantic convoys. Corvettes were tiny ships – the crew of *Louisburg*, numbering just fifty-eight, was about a third that of a destroyer – but highly effective at submarine hunting. If destroyers were the greyhounds of the ocean, these were the fox-terriers.

Now, on a convoy you're given a position and you're supposed to keep that position. The convoy might be several miles long – destroyers out front, frigates to the side. But winter in the Atlantic – you couldn't always keep your station.

The weather was *bad*. Oh, God – nobody knows how rough it was. You're on a skating rink. We had the ropes rigged round for safety. Corvettes roll something terrible in a sea. The way they're built, they bend in a sea and the water goes right over the stern. Jesus, there's nothing heavier than water when it hits you! And cold? Without a word of a lie, I have seen the barrel of that gun a foot thick with ice. And the deck the same. I've been in the St Lawrence when you didn't have to drop an anchor. The ice in that Gaspé was two feet thick! You only had to stop and you were frozen in. You can't work in those conditions – the only thing you can do is the best you can. You put on lots of clothes, a rubber suit, a big life-jacket – you can't *move* for clothes!

You're on alert all the time – you never know what in hell minute you're going to the bottom. One of those ace U-boat commanders, he'd surface right in the middle of the convoy – taking a hell of a risk, suicide really – and he's set the torpedo on a ship. Couldn't miss. You see a flash and an explosion. And that's it. Sometimes you see her go down, sometimes you don't. A torpedo can split a corvette in two; I saw it happen. There's so many escort ships – so many. And yet they still put them to the bottom. God only knows how much this man put to the bottom. But he went to the bottom himself eventually, with his crew.

Now when you get a contact, the first thing you get is what they call a 'ping' on the Asdic. You hoist a black flag to show you've got a contact. There's a paper graph attached to the Asdic; it'll put down the course, the depth and the size of that thing. Sometimes it's a sunken ship, sometimes it's something else. Sometimes it's a submarine. This one – he was sitting down there with his motors off, and the only thing we can do is run over him.

Our Captain – he had a big red beard – he made a signal to the Commodore in charge of the convoy, that he's attacking. We've already got the depth the U-boat's sitting at down there. We set the charges pretty much according to what we had on the graph. We used eight depth charges; that's about 300 lbs of TNT. We got going out of there, quick! You get going; then you turn around and watch for whatever's coming up. If there's nothing come up, it's up to the Commodore again. This feller knew what he was doing. He lets our Captain go in for another run. The first attack, those submarine men might survive – but the second attack's fatal. The submarine gets blown to the surface. Up she comes – I saw that – yes, indeed.

Seasickness in the rough seas of the North Atlantic was a widespread problem. It was also a nuisance and a potentially fatal distraction from duty. David Thrasher used an age-old remedy:

There's a thing called chronic seasickness. Some of these Newfoundlanders, they'd sailed practically all their lives. But the first big wave we'd hit – oh, God! Now as true as I sit here, I was never seasick once. I used to get one of those big mugs – and by Jesus, most of the time there was 'spirits up' I'd get that three-quarters full, if there was a good officer on. Some of them, they'd throw it out the porthole rather than give you an extra ration.

Pusser's rum! Oh, God – it'd make your hair stand up. Sometimes your tongue'd be thick, but you'd never throw up. I can honestly say that drinking pusser's rum is what kept me from being seasick.

Now, with the war nearly three years old and having spread to all corners of the world, many of the Commonwealth volunteers had already fallen into the hands of their enemies. They were the sons of farmers, doctors, railwaymen. Some had only just left school. Some had had to make a life for themselves against tough odds; others had hardly known a moment's discomfort. They were nobody special – just average young men, who had never thought they would pick up a gun, or drop a bomb on a city.

Their experiences in prisoner-of-war camps varied enormously, depending on who their 'hosts' were, where they were incarcerated, what stage the war had reached at any given time. Survival, physically, depended largely on husbanding your strength, avoiding disease, maintaining personal hygiene, evading punishment and supplementing the universally meagre camp rations any way you could – the Red Cross parcel was everyone's saviour. Whether you could manage any of these good-health practices depended entirely on the circumstances you found yourself in.

Mental survival was another matter. Boredom, sexual frustration, anger, claustrophobia, bitterness, meaningless obsessions: these chipped away at the veneer. Those who found something to keep them occupied; those who already had, or now discovered, codes to live by; those who found out how to trap the beast of mental anguish when it came out and push it back into its locked box before it could tear them apart – they were the survivors. None of them, whether they learned to cope or not, would come out of the prison camps unscathed, nor fail to hear echoes of their captivity for the rest of their lives.

The twelve months on the run that followed the Allies' 1941 downfall in Greece were the loneliest in Jack Brown's life, months of quiet desperation that he would never forget. The experience he had built up during his shepherding days in the high back country of New Zealand stood

Brown in good stead now, for he was to find himself more isolated and thrown back on his own resources than ever before.

The village of Megara, where the one-legged Greek and his friends had sheltered the wounded New Zealander, lay about twenty miles east of the Corinth Canal, with the Pateras Mountains rising behind. Hiding out in the hills were other fugitives who had been left behind during the April evacuation. Brown joined them in the mountain caves from where, at the end of May 1941, they watched the great armada of troop-carrying planes and gliders going over to the invasion of Crete. Then the local people decided to split up the hunted men. Jack Brown was allotted to an elderly Greek couple in Megara. He grew a drooping moustache, dyed it and his fair hair black with charcoal, learned a few Greek phrases and tried to pass himself off as a local. It was a miserable, skulking life; at first in the village itself, later in the garden hut of his kind but apprehensive hosts, or back in the caves of the Pateras Mountains. The penalty for harbouring a fugitive soldier could very well be death – not just for the harbourers themselves, but quite likely to be visited at random on the local community as a reprisal.

I spent twelve months on the run and that was one of the toughest things, nerve-wise – one of the toughest things I ever did. You didn't know which of the Greeks you could trust, so you didn't trust anybody, only the actual people who were looking after you. They were a very poor country and the Italians were paying quite a little bounty for us; the Germans had gone out of Greece by this time, and the Italians had taken over. With starving kids there, who could blame the locals for turning someone over?

So I was shopped, some time in April. I was in a cave up in the hills and the patrol had been told where I was. They came in, one each side of me with a pistol in their hands, so what was I to do? I couldn't brazen it out. They'd used Greeks for the job, so they knew I wasn't Greek. They took me down to the police station in Megara. I wasn't all that happy, because I was in civilian clothes – they took great pleasure in pointing that out to me. I didn't know whether I was going to get out of it alive. That wasn't such a good week.

In the event Jack Brown was not shot as a spy. His captors handed him over to the Italian Army, and he was soon put on a ship and taken across to Italy, to a holding camp at Bari, where they began by taking his trousers away so that he could not escape. The trousers were returned once he had been processed. Then followed a long journey north, to Gruppignano near

Udine in north-eastern Italy, within sight of the Dolomites. Here, in midsummer 1942, Brown entered Campo 57.

The camp was made up of two compounds of eighty-foot-long huts, with about fifty men to a hut, sleeping in two-tier wooden bunks. The huts were stuffy in summer, and cold in winter when there was fuel for no more than four hours' heating and the men shivered at night under their single blankets. The camp was run by a disciplinarian Italian, a colonel of *carabinieri*; but inefficiencies in the system he was supposed to administer – delays in censoring and distributing letters, pilfering of parcels – caused hardship and frustration among the prisoners. Campo 57, in fact, was neither better nor worse than most Italian prisoner-of-war camps. The prisoners suffered just the same; particularly men like Jack Brown who had been accustomed to independence, to making their own decisions and acting on them.

Camp life is very demoralising. You just sit. Nothing to do, not much food. The whole thing is surrounded by barbed wire, lights all around, machine-gun nests up in the guard towers. We were pretty well jammed in. Quite a few blokes couldn't handle it. They used to take to the wire – virtually commit suicide, you might say.

The basic rations was a little dixie of watery stew once a day and not much else. Well, you can see the size of me now and I was down to a seven-stoner at one time, so you can imagine – I was hungry! We were very, very dependent on Red Cross parcels. If it hadn't have been for those we wouldn't have come back. I think they were a ten-pound weight. Different countries had different styles of parcels: in a typical New Zealand parcel there could have been some tins of butter, tins of meat, chocolate, raisins, dates, prunes – that type of thing. In the Canadian parcel they used to have a big tin of KLIM milk powder: that was a very popular one.

I was missing presumed killed for a year, so the first notification my people got that I'd turned up alive was through the Red Cross. We were given a little card to write home: 'I am well' would have just about covered the card.

After about twelve months we were put into working parties of fifty each and sent out to work on the farms. It was maize, wheat and sugar-beet growing country. It was good, in that it gave us something to do. And out on those farms – well, I think we were the most expert thieves around. Sounds awful, I know.

Half-way across the world Rod Wells was working too, for his Japanese captors, in the 'land of milk and honey' which they had promised him. 'B Force', assembled in Changi camp at Singapore, had been shipped off to Borneo and landed at Sandakan on the north-east side of the island. Sandakan was to become – for Australians in particular – one of the most notorious names in Second World War history. For now, though, in spite of the hunger and creeping disease, it seemed to Rod Wells endurable:

> About five miles inland of Sandakan we built this aerodrome. We were living in huts that had been built by the British colonial authorities to house Japanese traders.
>
> We were visited by Hoshijima, the Camp Commandant. He told us, 'You'll be obedient, work hard, be loyal to the Emperor.' And of course our aim in life was to upset him – which we did. We formed an underground organisation. I found myself as the prisoner rep of the wood party, which supplied the fuel for the camp's electrical power station. There were Malays and Chinese working on the local rubber plantations. One day I got permission to go behind a tree for a pee. A Malay turned up. He went, 'Ssshh! I want to help you!' So we built up on this. Getting drugs for the camp hospital was the most important thing; but we were also starting to bring in the bits and pieces we needed to build a radio.

In Hong Kong the Japanese had made no provision for the ten thousand prisoners they found on their hands on Christmas Day 1941. George Barron of the Royal Rifles of Canada was among them. Barron, along with over 7000 others, was herded into Shampshui Po barracks, beside the naval dockyard on the mainland near Kowloon, to make the best they could of its now bomb-damaged, burned and looted buildings.

> Shampshui Po camp had been stripped completely bare by the Chinese – all the doors, window frames, furniture, electric fittings and so on. There was really nothing left at all. The food was pretty bad. They used to bring in rice, bags of rice, from the godowns. It was musty and dirty, and full of rat shit and mouse shit. They could wash out the must and the dirt; but the rat shit and the mouse shit – soon as it got wet, it stuck to the rice. Actually, I think that there was more nourishment in the goddamn rat and mouse shit than there was in the rice! And we ate a lot of Chinese vegetables – water lily roots and all that kind of stuff, in a stew; and sometimes we'd get a piece of water buffalo.
>
> We were working on the airport, just manual work, making the airport bigger. They'd divide us up by rank, give us picks and shovels and away we'd go. We'd be brought back to the camp late at night in a boat.

We had to keep our spirits up. There was a whole bunch of us from Toronto, and we used to sit around a table, shoot the guff and say: 'Six months and we'll be out of here. The Americans will be here and get us out. Give it six months.' We learned to take it six months at a time. Of course, when a Zero came over and tried to chase two American planes – oh, we were out, cheering like mad! And the Japs went *uh-uh-uh!* at us with the fixed bayonets.

If you kept your head down, avoided disease and secured enough food, you might with luck survive Shampshui Po. But you could never predict the temper of the guards, who had complete power over thousands of helpless men and could wield it as they chose: 'There was a guard there who was a real bad egg. He was from Vancouver. He said, "You bastards made it tough for us when we were going to school; now it's my turn." He used to act as an interpreter and come in with two six-foot guards with their bayonets fixed. If you said something to him and he didn't like it, he'd haul off and belt you. What can you do about it? You wanna get stuck by a bayonet? Oh, he was bad. The Vancouver Kid, we used to call him. They hung him, after the war.'

The Japanese were sending drafts of prisoners to work in Japan. They had the military files on their captives and quickly identified the linguists, doctors and other specialists they wanted. They also sent parties of the fittest men they could find in Shampshui Po to Japan for heavy labouring work. Few of these were to survive the war.

The guards soon marked George Barron down as unsuitable for shipment to Japan, and with good reason – he had already had four or five doses of malaria and had been suffering from both wet and dry beriberi, in addition to the universal Far Eastern POW's scourge of dysentery. Tropical diseases, of course, ran riot in the cramped, insanitary conditions of Shampshui Po, among run-down and depressed men who were overworked, seriously malnourished – average weight loss in the camp was fifty to sixty pounds – and without proper medicines. Pellagra was one extremely painful affliction, which dried and cracked the skin; another was dry beriberi or 'electric feet', which first numbed the toes and then stabbed them with constant shooting pains, preventing the sufferer from relaxing, walking or sleeping. For George Barron, one of the hardest aspects of captivity was that the Japanese seemed immune to human sympathy or understanding.

The worst thing about it was that they didn't treat you like human beings. This is what happens in the camps: they'd tell our CO, 'We want 800 men by tomorrow.' He'd say, 'Sorry, but we've only got 600. There are men in the hospital, men convalescing.' They'd say: 'We want 800 men.' So we'd have to select convalescent men. They didn't give a shit. They didn't care.

When it came to giving out hypodermic needles, they wouldn't give any to the Canadians. They said we'd been issued with some before we got here. We had an epidemic of diphtheria among the Canadians. Another disease – I don't know the name of it, but it killed a few of our guys. Their testicles all swelled up, and they'd sweat. Wet beriberi – some of them got all swollen up with wet beriberi – they can't drink water, they can't drink anything. Oh, it was terrible. I'd be up all night, just waking up guys with dysentery, to get them to the latrines.

And if the Allied prisoners-of-war were treated with such careless brutality, the wretched Chinese civilians of Hong Kong could look only for death if they crossed the path of the occupying powers.

One Chinese guy used to leave a note on the boat which took us to work, telling us the news. They threw him off the boat into the water – left him to drown. Another Chinaman – I don't know what he'd done, but they dragged him through the camp with his hands tied behind his back and a rope around his neck. One guy's pulling him with the rope and the other guy's walking behind him, sticking him a little bit with the bayonet, just to keep him going. They pulled him right over to the water, to the China Sea, and they stabbed him in the back, and then they shot him as he went in the water. It happened right in our camp. Maybe they caught him stealing something? I don't know.

Danny Misra of the Rajputana Rifles had left Hong Kong, the 'best station in the world', in 1940 when his regiment's tour of duty in the colony came to an end. He'd had a wonderful time there, learning to drink and dance, and to avoid too serious an entanglement with the charming young ladies of the Indian–Chinese community in Hong Kong: 'Beautiful girls, and I will say with all humility that they were quite keen to marry up with us and get back to India.' He had also learned the local dialect and a smattering of Japanese; he had been some distance inland into China; he had spent four months wandering through Japan, absorbing himself in the culture; and he had a thorough knowledge of Shampshui Po barracks, having been based there himself while helping to train the defenders and improve the defences. In short, Danny Misra was just the man that the newly formed British Army Aid Group was looking for in March 1942.

The BAAG had been created on the suggestion of Lieutenant-Colonel L. T. Ride of the Hong Kong Volunteer Defence Force, who had managed to escape from Shampshui Po and make his way to the important British and US intelligence-gathering outstation in the Chinese city of Chungking, the nationalist capital. It was decided to set up a unit within the Indian Army, operating under the Headquarters Intelligence Branch in Delhi, which would base itself in China to harass the Japanese and support their victims by all available means. The BAAG aimed to encourage not only the 20,000 Indian prisoners-of-war in camps around Hong Kong, but all POWs, Chinese and other persecuted people throughout the Far East, to escape to Free China. But the Indians were of particular concern, because of the formation, in the late summer of 1942, of the Indian National Army, the creation of the Indian radical nationalist Subhas Chandra Bose. The INA was raised from Indian POWs and from other Indians living in South-East Asia; they were encouraged to believe that by joining the Japanese in their struggle for 'Co-Prosperity' and 'Asia for the Asiatics', independence for India would quickly follow a Japanese defeat of the colonialist Allies. The temptation for Indian prisoners-of-war to exchange their shackles for a place in an INA unit was strong as Danny Misra explains: 'The Japanese said to our POWs, "If you want to live properly, join the INA." Our people said, "We have taken the oath." Indians of my generation, at that time, had a tremendous sense of honour. For those who joined the INA, the lap of luxury – that was the propaganda. And, of course, it meant that a POW could escape from malnutrition, from beatings, from dysentery, from beriberi.'

Up to 40,000 were to join before the end of the war – proving, as things turned out, remarkably ineffective in the field. On the INA's inception, however, the organisation was seen by Allied strategists as a threat within the POW camps that must be combated as a matter of real urgency. The prisoners must be offered inducements as strong as those held out by the Japanese, to keep them to their oaths of loyalty. Medicines, morale-boosting news, parts for radios must be smuggled into the camps, and an effective 'underground railway' established to smuggle the prisoners out. At the same time intelligence could be gathered about the defences of Hong Kong, about conditions in the camps, the morale of both prisoners and Japanese guards – and, in the wider world, the movement of shipping, troops and war goods in and out of Hong Kong and other Japanese-held ports.

It was a prize worth making an effort for; but the BAAG would have to find a co-ordinator for the Indian section with extensive local knowledge and Hong Kong contacts, a feeling for the Japanese and a cool head. An Australian escapee from Hong Kong, Colonel 'Doc' Wright, remembered the bright young soldier that he'd taught to play cricket, and recruited Danny Misra as having exactly the qualities required. Soon Misra was hopping over the Himalayas in a DC3, with a brief to establish an Indian section of the BAAG in the Free Chinese city of Kweilin, in Kwangsi Province, about 300 miles north-west of Hong Kong.

We were based in a palace in Kweilin, with a Red Cross flag flying, and the Chinese looked after us very well. The team was made up of beachcombers, adventurers; very much a happy team. We had a few little comforts, sometimes a party, occasionally a bottle of Scotch. It couldn't run on military lines – it was very informal. Our agents or couriers in Hong Kong were the Hong Kong Indian girls, nice girls from wealthy business families. They all had English names – Nancy, Mabel, Margaret. They would go into the prison camps as Red Cross representatives, taking in much-needed medicines and tonics.

The thing started beautifully. Having established the couriers, we had to establish somebody in the camp itself whom I could communicate with. We were very fortunate in having a Captain Ansari of the Rajputs – a Muslim from Hyderabad. He was the ideal man to join us. We used to write to each other in Urdu in invisible ink and the girls would take it in with their medicines.

Our prisoners inside the camps would be sent out on fatigue parties. Fortunately for us, the Japanese sent only one driver and one soldier with fifteen POWs. Our agent would meet them. He would speak to the driver and say, 'Either you come with us to India, or that's the end of your story.' Most of them came with us. Some – the fanatic ones – refused. They were bumped off by the prisoners on the fatigue party; they'd fix him with his own rifle.

In another camp we bribed the cook to put sleeping pills in the guard's food. The guard went to sleep. Our men came out, formed up – left! right! left! right! – marched out of the camp. The dhows were waiting for them. They came up along the Chinese coast and made their way to Kweilin, where they were put in an aircraft and taken back to India.

The Japanese put out a notice in Hong Kong: 'Major Misra – 5000 military yen, Dead or Alive.' So I wrote back to them, 'Don't be so bloody silly. I'm worth much more than 5000 military yen.' Shortly afterwards, I got a letter of apology from the police headquarters!

In these hole-in-corner ways, working with constant ingenuity, the BAAG managed to extract several hundred people from captivity, while easing the burden of many more with medicines and with the morale-boosting knowledge that they had not been forgotten and left to rot. The BAAG agents in Hong Kong, those 'nice girls' and their strong-arm colleagues, were people of very special calibre. They had to know Hong Kong like the backs of their hands in order to arrange secure rendezvous points and emergency escape routes. They needed their own secure bolt-holes too. They had to play a neutral hand between communists and nationalists in the colony, to avoid being betrayed, or done away with, by either rival. And, above all, they had to be ice-cool, very brave and beyond suspicion by the Japanese. If they were caught – as several were – torture and death were inevitable. Captain Ansari was one to tread this *via dolorosa*.

> Eventually the cat was out of the bag. The Japanese got to know that Colonel Wright was running the show and that I was in charge of the Indian section. So they set a trap. Two horrible people – INA Indians – came to Captain Ansari: 'Can you help us get Major Misra's assistance to escape?' I smelt a rat. I sent a message down to tell him not to get involved, but too late.
>
> The Japanese charged Captain Ansari with treason. They offered him his freedom if he would join the INA. He refused – 'I can't break my oath.' They tortured him and beheaded him. He got a posthumous George Cross.

On Christmas Day 1941, at almost exactly the moment that George Barron was entering Japanese captivity in Hong Kong and Rod Wells's commanding officer was confiding Singapore's indefensibility to his subordinate at Johore Baharu, Pierre Austin was stepping on board the RAN cruiser *Australia* at Sydney after an enjoyable few weeks' leave at home. Austin had left *Perth* after the evacuation of Crete and was now rejoining his old ship as a fledgling sub-lieutenant. 'We sailed from Sydney on Christmas Day,' says Austin, 'and we didn't come back in again for six months.'

At the end of April 1942 the cruiser was in the Coral Sea between Australia and New Guinea, part of a task force sent there to stop the Japanese swooping in round the Papuan peninsula from the west and capturing Port Moresby from the sea. The capital of the big, dinosaur-shaped island was the vital stepping stone that the Japanese had to have if they were to hop the short distance across to the northern coasts of Australia. Carrier-borne and island-based planes had already bombed Darwin, in the Northern Territory of the Dominion, on 19 February, the Japanese thereby demonstrating their muscle and concentrating everyone's mind on their closeness to mainland Australia. The Americans, too, had a strong task force in the area, which included the two carriers *Lexington* and *Yorktown*. The Japanese forces also contained two carriers,

Shoho and *Shokaku*, to support the Port Moresby landings; these had been detached from the main Japanese Navy, which was hoping to bring the US Navy to battle further north in the Pacific and destroy its carriers and therefore its threat to further Japanese operations.

The course of events in the Battle of the Coral Sea sprawled over the period between 28 April and 8 May. It was a remarkable battle in several ways. Carriers had never before directly engaged each other, as they did on 7 May via their aircraft; the two main forces of ships never even caught sight of each other; and the engagement, although it ended with even losses at a carrier apiece (*Lexington* and *Shoho*), proved to be one of the hinges on which the course of the war swung – for the Japanese turned away and abandoned their attempt on Port Moresby. They were never to repeat it by sea.

At action stations in *Australia*, Pierre Austin was keeping a sharp lookout when the battle opened:

They found us without any air cover – *Australia*, *Hobart*, *Chicago* and another ship. We were attacked simultaneously by torpedo-bombers and high-level bombers. We were very fortunate – we only had one casualty.

I was in a four-inch anti-aircraft director. I was too busy doing my job to see the planes launching their attacks, but all of a sudden I found myself covered in sooty water, and the ship shaking and shuddering. At one point I stood up in the director and saw a Japanese torpedo-bomber come flying down the side of the ship, having dropped his torpedo, and firing at us as he went by. I remember thinking: 'Cheeky bugger!' He was blown out of the sky for his pains.

What you see of the planes depends on how quickly you pick them up. We picked up the torpedo-bombers fairly quickly, though it would have been better if we could have got them earlier. We were just plain bloody lucky – a torpedo ran the whole length of our side without touching us. We thought it was going to blow *Chicago*'s stern off, but it missed that by a fraction as well. Unlucky pilot! As for the high-level bombers – the first we knew about those was when the shit descended.

It was roughly the same level of attack as sank the *Prince of Wales* and *Repulse*. At one point *Australia* received fifteen simultaneous near-misses. *Chicago* signalled, 'Do you require medical help?' The Old Man signalled back: 'No casualties – require clean underwear.'

I think at that time, with the Japanese on your doorstep – yes, you did feel the significance of what was happening. But I don't know that you have very elevated feelings as a young man in a battle. You feel those later, when you're sitting at home reading the newspaper. Then you think: 'Really? It was *that* important? Hmm. Well, well...'

Over in Scotland it was the boat builders on the River Clyde that caught Bob Gaunt's eye, when the teenage South African was finally selected to serve in motor torpedo boats:

My first boat was a Vosper, which I joined in Glasgow while she was still being built. The boat builders on the Clyde were women – real sweeties, of course. They were girls of eighteen or nineteen, real Scots lassies; all pretty tough, but really, really nice. They were building our boat, so it very much belonged to them. Carpenters, fitters: you name it, they were doing it. There were only nine sailors in our crew and they used to have – as they say – 'good runs ashore' with these women at night. They absolutely spoiled us completely; they used to take the sailors dancing and take them home to meet the family.

I was nineteen years old, and of course they used to tease me like mad, try and make me blush. I only wish I'd been in a position to do what I thought they wanted!

Another young man charmed by the girls of the Old Country was Charlie Hobbs of the Royal Canadian Air Force, about to finish his training as an air-gunner and wondering how to get hold of the wherewithal to go dancing. Once again, Hobbs was unimpressed by the attitude of the British officer in charge of the young Commonwealth airmen:

The day before our gunnery course ended, we were told we'd be going on thirty-three days' leave. The CO had made no plans for us. What would we do for thirty-three days? Our money wouldn't hold out, he must have known that. He just shut us off the station, that's what it boiled down to, and left us to our own resources in a foreign country with, at the most, £10. The fellers – about sixty-four of them – decided to hold a giant crap game and the winners would take it all. Well, Jack Cameron and I won all the money! So we had a whole pile of pound notes – we were loaded with money; we ended up with maybe £500. That saw us very nicely through our leave.

Bournemouth, you know, was a wonderful place for a feller with a uniform on. Great big dance hall, and the local girls very pleased with us – very much so. We even went out of our *way* to please 'em. No shortage of opportunity!

The Canadians were keen not to be mistaken for American servicemen, who were over in Britain at the same time. 'Over-paid, over-sexed and over here', the Yanks were running into difficulties with the British public, as Charlie Hobbs noted: 'The Americans brought their problems on themselves. For instance, I watched a great big sergeant come into a little local pub that had been there for a thousand years; he walked to the bar and said to the landlord: "Hey, boy!" That didn't wear well. Then he pulled out a roll about the size of a horse – "Here, you keep this!" The guy felt insulted. It wasn't the best way of getting on.'

In mid-May 1942 Charlie Hobbs had yet to go on an operational flight, but there were other Commonwealth airmen who already knew exactly what it meant to be on active service with RAF Bomber Command. British bombers had been in action since the early days of the war, at first in daylight, then, from late 1940, at night-time, dropping leaflets, mines and bombs over the North Sea, over Occupied Europe and over Germany. The navigational difficulties inherent in night flying, and a lack of sophisticated bombing techniques and equipment, meant that the greater proportion of these attacks were ineffective. By the beginning of 1942 Bomber Command had dropped about 50,000 tons of bombs on European targets, with much less effect than they or the British public would like to have believed. British civilians, fresh from their experience of the Luftwaffe's 1940–1 blitz of their cities, desperately wanted someone to hit back on their behalf at Germany, to strike at the aggressor country itself; and Bomber Command looked like the only candidate capable of carrying out the job.

'Strategic' bombing of industrial installations was the objective; 'area' bombing – exactly what its name implied – was the practice. Development of radio and radar navigational aids, heavy bombers and bombs, and better training and equipping of bomb aimers, would begin to make bombing more effective in 1943; but in 1942 Bomber Command was still learning. The process involved, inevitably, mounting losses to anti-aircraft fire and to the German night fighters who were also beginning to hone their skills. Losses among Bomber Command crews at the beginning of 1942 were just under 7500 – about a tenth of the overall losses among RAF bomber crews by the end of the war. These men had been flying in already outdated two-engined bombers such as the Whitley and the Hampden or the slow, low-flying, fabric-bodied Wellington, or in the heavier four-engined Stirling with its bombing ceiling of only 10,000 feet and its doggedly slow speed. The vulnerability of these planes over Germany, and on the long runs in and out across occupied countries, made a Bomber Command crew member unlikely to survive more than a dozen operations. By 1942 the RAF's pride and joy, the four-engined Avro Lancaster, was becoming available in limited numbers, and with this strong, speedy high-flyer (it had twice the ceiling of a Stirling) the crews felt they had a better chance of travelling and bombing in safety – especially when operating over the Ruhr, Germany's heavily defended main industrial area.

Paul Radomski, the Polish-descended New Zealander from Wellington, arrived in England late in 1941 after training on Tiger Moths and Oxfords, and was posted early in the new year to 149 Squadron at Lakenheath in Suffolk as a twenty-year-old pilot flying Stirlings.

The crew was all Pommie. They accepted me quite well. You get to grow together – you get a sort of feel of family, that you've got to protect each other. If you had to fly with someone else it wouldn't be the same. I mean, you've known these people for over two years; you've flown with them, you've shared a pot of beer with them, you've shared a bit of danger. You do get that feel of family.

The first thing we were on was daylights, dropping pamphlets over Paris. I don't know what they said: we were not allowed to read them. It was a court-martial offence to be caught with one of those. I expect they were calling on the French to resist. Then we went 'gardening' – mine-laying in the Friesian Islands, mining that passageway between the Dutch and German mainland and the islands. It'd be a dirty, dark night, and you'd have to drop your mines from under fifty feet or they'd explode. Do you know how we did that? We'd have a trailing aerial, like for your wireless; we'd let that out so much and the wireless operator would keep his fingers on it, and when the bead on the end of it hit the water you knew you were fifty feet and you let your mines go. Highly technical!

In February 1942 Bomber Command was given a new chief, Air Marshal Arthur Harris, and under his direction began to step up the intensity of its area bombing – even though Harris himself had been a strong advocate of strategic bombing. Paul Radomski remains convinced that the crews of 1942–3 were bombing accurately and that 'Bomber' Harris unjustly carried the can for the mass slaughter of German civilians.

I believe that man had no choice. He was ordered to do what he did, he did it and he's been maligned after. He was a hard man, but he had his orders. He was given the Ruhr to clean up; he was not allowed to bomb civilians, not like that mass bombing they had afterwards. Over the target you had to fly so accurately it didn't matter what was coming up around you. When you dropped your bombs a photoflash used to go and a camera would turn over. And if your target wasn't in that print you couldn't count that as an operation. *And* you were sent back over the same course the next night.

I'm not saying that pinpoint was possible, but at least we got close to it. The Fiat works in Turin – we did that from 100 feet, with hand-held bombsights. It was a hell of a long way to go; and you either finished it then, or you·had to go back again the next night. So your only thought was keeping steady, concentrating on getting that ruddy photo. The target *had* to be in that photograph. If a few went astray – well, we can't help that.

I saw civilian deaths in London; I saw quite a few civilian deaths from raids. I've helped out. If you were on leave and there was a raid you were called in to it. I've pulled many dead bodies out. So I don't agree with it, on either side. But it was happening.

Bomber crews entrusted their lives to each other on every operation, but the man with the ultimate responsibility was the captain of the aircraft. As a pilot you needed luck to preserve your own life and the lives of your crew – but you could help luck along if you were blessed with the natural, instinctive skill of doing the right thing at the right time.

They had these master searchlights – they were blue. They'd just suddenly flick over there, and the other searchlights would all come and cone that plane and about eighty guns fire at it. It was a very lucky person who got away from one of those. I was coned one night off the French coast, and I never want to do it again. We were flying at about twelve and a half and I just pulled everything back – dropped my flaps and pulled my nose up. And I side-slipped. I didn't know whether she would *do* a side-slip, but I found out. In less time than it takes to tell I dropped 10,000 feet. The crew – they were praying, I should think. They couldn't do much. I just slammed everything on, pulled my flaps in, put her into a bit of a dive to get my speed up, and I sneaked out under the searchlights – out above the waves. Pulled her up again and flew home.

Sometimes, not even the pilot could do much . . .

On one occasion I was told, 'We've got three minutes' petrol left, Sir,' so I knew we couldn't get home. We'd been badly shot up, lost gas. I'd been trying to raise Detling, a Tiger Moth 'drome in Kent – I was going to put her in wheels-up there. But they didn't hear me – though they heard me in Scotland, apparently.

So I ordered a bale-out over Kent. I headed her out to sea, but she didn't make it. Buggered up a farmer's fence-line, that's all. They'd all jumped out by then, and I'd gone too. Landed in the middle of this plum orchard. It was early in the morning and I knocked at the farmer's door. A light came on upstairs. I told him who I was. He says, 'Stand back from that door!' and presents a shotgun at me! Anyway, his wife says, 'Come in.' And when I took my jacket off and he saw the New Zealand flashes up, I was all right.

The nature of the job, the intense strain, made the bomber crews grow up quickly. Most felt, and after a dozen or so operations began to look, older than their age. But a bunch of very young servicemen could always let off steam in time-honoured fashion – by the plentiful use of bad language, combined if possible with cocking a snook at authority:

Each wireless op had a sector to monitor. Now, we had carbon mikes built into the motors; and if he heard German voices, like a ground station, he'd just stab this key down, blow them off the air. Oh, it would blow the BBC off the air – we did, no trouble at all. That gave us the idea: if we can back-tune to that, we can back-tune to Radio Berlin. So we back-tuned to Radio Berlin and sang filthy songs for them.

One night we were coming home, two o'clock in the morning, and heard the BBC news – 'Our bombers attacked last night. Four of them are missing.' And out of the air comes this voice: 'That's a pack of bullshit!' They tried to find out who that was ... We'd sing over the BBC and that sort of thing, fairly cheeky – because we were young and stupid, I suppose.

The air could be pretty blue at times. The Air Force had a patter: 'Tallyho, Tallyho, Jerry at So-and-so', you know. Well, one night we're going along quietly, when up comes Jimmy, he's the rear-gunner: 'Christ, there's a fucking Jerry on our tail!' He shouldn't have said it that way, but he did – nobody took any notice of it, of course. Then he dropped into the correct patter, gave the range and so forth. Then, as they were closing in: 'Prepare to turn port – prepare to turn port – prepare to turn port ... turn left, you bastard!'

They made a recording one night – they wanted to play it over the BBC. They put equipment on several of the aircraft, to record the talking of a crew at night. But they didn't play it. No, they didn't play it. I don't know why ...

The picture in North Africa, in June 1942, had changed dramatically since the start of the year, when the 8th Army had pushed General Rommel and the Deutsches Afrika Korps back west as far as El Agheila in Tripolitania. Rommel was now, in effect, the man easing his back against his post; the Allies were straining forward, the braces of their supply lines stretched to their thinnest and tautest. They were overreaching themselves, at the very limit of their forward momentum. On 21 January 1942 Rommel, sustained by supplies freshly landed in Tripoli, felt strong enough to commence his second – and, as it turned out, final – great surge eastwards along the 600-mile corridor of desert that was already littered with so many burned-out tanks, wrecked lorries and crashed aeroplanes, and with the badly buried bodies of soldiers and airmen of a dozen nations. The Afrika Korps drove the 8th Army back again along the desert road. Within two weeks they were back at Gazala, only thirty miles west of Tobruk. Here both sides gathered themselves for the best part of three months; then, at the end of May, Rommel surged onwards again. Having penetrated inside the Allied lines, the Axis forces gathered strength for a renewed push forward; then burst out eastwards again towards Tobruk, with the glittering mirage of Egypt and the Suez Canal once more floating ahead of them, looking real enough to grasp before the year's end.

The surging, tidal nature of the back-and-forth desert war lent itself to periods of calm between the advances, retreats, skirmishes and battles. Not every memory of this time is of bloodshed and the drama of action. The Punjabi pilot Mahinder Singh Pujji had been posted to the Middle East to fly American Kittyhawk fighters after completing 1941's offensive sweeps over France in his beloved Hurricane. He remembers the difficulty he experienced, as an orthodox Sikh, in getting anything like a decent diet:

In the Western desert I was just starving! The only thing which was available there was beef – dog biscuits and bully beef. Beef I don't eat – my religion. Dog biscuits I could only eat if I dipped them in tea long enough for them to get soft. So my diet was dog biscuits and tea; that is all it was. I'm surprised myself that I stayed fit. For two years I didn't eat any English food. I *hated* English food – your cold meat, et cetera. I took breakfast in the morning, and in the afternoon those chocolates, Cadbury chocolates, you know. They were specially given to me, a double portion. Chocolates, dog biscuits and tea: for two years I lived on that.

As for drinking, I am a good actor. I would shout to the barman, 'Give me a gin and lime, please!' Everyone was too drunk to know exactly what I was drinking. It was water – I had previously arranged it with the barman. I could do so because I was the Flight Commander; I was the boss. He'd say, 'Yes, Sir.' Then that water will come to me, and the Air Marshal or whoever it was would say, 'Ah well, cheers, Pujji! Cheers! Good show!'

I didn't meet another pilot who didn't drink. It's no pleasure to me to drink. Once the Air Marshal says to me, 'Pujji, you're scared of it!' I said, 'Sir, don't say that. I am not scared of anything in the world.' He said, 'Ah – you're scared of whisky.' I said, 'I'm not; but if it doesn't do any good to me, why should I waste all that money?' He said, 'I'll buy it for you.' I said, 'All right, Sir, just to convince you, I'll drink with you.'

He sat down there with another two–three officers. He offered me one whisky; he offered the second and the third whisky. My head started getting very warm. But I didn't show it; I'm a good actor that way. Then, luckily for me, the Air Marshal turned to his friends and told them, 'Ah, we're wasting our good whisky on Pujji!'

Paul Gobine, the Seychelles Islander, was in North Africa too by now, serving with the Seychelles Pioneer Corps. He has none too fond memories of conditions: 'In the desert we are rationed with one bottle of water a day and three biscuits, harder than devil's shit, piece of cheese, a bit of jam. Your clothes was infected with lice. We wash our clothes in petrol, we cannot wash it in water. And to take off your pair of socks there – you have to get miles away and then burn it! You could smell it ... it was really, really horrible, you know? But, thanks God, we survived it.'

In June 1942 the Allied Army was pouring back towards Egypt from Gazala in what the soldiers were soon calling the 'Gazala Gallop' – a repeat of the 'Benghazi Handicap' of April the previous year. The 8th Army, in retreat, was not a reassuring sight. Les Rowe, moving west against the tide with the Australian 2/48 Battalion, remembers how 'we started off up the desert road, a little narrow road in those days, and here's this broken army streaming back past us, and all the Tommies were yelling, "You're going the wrong way!" You were seeing the wreck of an army.' And Charles Adams, the Cape Coloured driver with the South African Army, recalls 'a chaos – a traffic jam. I remember one morning a German Junkers 88 came over, and the convoy was just nose to tail. If that gunner had opened up I don't think I would be here now. He came so low and he even laughed – you could actually see him laughing! But he didn't fire. The infantry – they're quite happy, can't be bothered. They just want to get back there to the Canal.'

The Allied commanders seemed in two minds about whether Tobruk was worth hanging on to. The port's defences had not been maintained properly since General Auchinleck issued an instruction in February that 'it is not my intention to hold [Tobruk] once the enemy is in a position to invest it effectively. Should this appear inevitable,' the instruction went on, 'the place will be evacuated and the maximum amount of destruction carried out in it.' Yet on 14 June he told his commander in the field, General Ritchie, 'Tobruk must be held, and the enemy not allowed to invest it.'

By 19 June the Afrika Korps had Tobruk surrounded and cut off. The South African garrison commander, Major-General H. B. Klopper, had been promoted to that rank only a month before and had no battle experience. The defences and organisation he had inherited were a shambles, and he had no hope of holding on to Tobruk once Rommel had arrived to direct in person the final tank assault on 20 June. The only decision to make was whether to allow the defenders to get out, if they could, before their otherwise inevitable capture by the Germans. The officers advising General Klopper were divided on the issue, and no definitive order to evacuate – or for individuals to use their initiative – was given. The garrison surrendered at 7.45 a.m. the following day. Mountains of stores and ammunition passed into Axis possession and 33,000 South Africans, Indians, Gurkhas and Britons went into captivity.

Among them was Gordon Fry of the Capetown Highlanders, who had arrived in Tobruk just before the 'Gazala Gallop' and had been defending the fortress on a twenty-five-pounder gun. The chance of escape that had slipped through his fingers would haunt and tantalise Fry throughout his subsequent captivity.

The thing where we were a bit upset was: Tobruk fell on a Sunday. On the Friday night we heard they'd broken through, from the chaps on the 'Gazala Gallop' who came through Tobruk but didn't stay. We had our little truck all packed up – the officer, myself and the other two – and we said, 'Let's go!' Then the order came through: 'If anyone leaves Tobruk now, they'll be classified as a deserter.' So we stayed; but we should have gone. That's what irked me during my time as a POW. 'Well, why didn't we go?' We felt they should have said, 'Every man for himself. Those who can get out, get out.' We could have got out before the Germans came round and surrounded us. By that time the ack-ack battalion behind us were firing with Bofors guns against tanks. Then the order came through to spike the guns, and that was it; we were all taken. It was a fiasco. This was how the ordinary rank and file felt about it; that they didn't give us a fair chance to get away.

Being captured is a great bewilderment. You don't realise what's happening; you're in a daze. You spike your guns – you put a round in the top and a round in the breech and you fire the thing with a long lanyard. The barrel peels back like a banana. Then you've got to smash up the sight; then your rifles. You try breaking a Lee-Enfield. It's quite a job.

Where our blokes were a bit stupid – they went and destroyed all our rations, and they went and buggered up the water supply. So of course the Jerries said, 'We can't give you any water or food. You've buggered it up, so it's your look-out.' When they were taking us from Tobruk to Benghazi, about ten of us on the back of this little truck, they had radiator water in the back. It was rusty, but we drank it. We weren't worried about Gyppo guts or anything – we just drank it.

While all this destruction, defeat and retreat were going on out in the desert, the mills of military justice still had to be kept grinding back at base. Ernest Khomari from Basutoland, who had been inspired to join the African Auxiliary Pioneer Corps when shown graphic pictures of a bombing raid on London, was serving in Egypt on attachment to the 28th Field Punishment Centre in Alexandria.

Commonwealth soldiers of every colour who were serving minor punishments were sent there for seven days. They were roughly treated and they never came back again. Lunch squashing in the cell, with water on the floor; work in the quarry, preparing roads. All you do is stone-breaking. And then you marched them quickly. When they are far away you call them: 'About turn!' and they come back, after they have dumped the stone at the double in the quarry. And so on, the whole day. We make them to feel that seven days to them is seven years.

About this time, Mahinder Singh Pujji was shot down:

I was in a Kittyhawk and I found my instrument panel suddenly shattered. I heard no sound, because the aeroplane was making a lot of noise. Later I found that a bullet had gone through my overalls – the same one that had shattered the panel. I preserved that as a souvenir for many years.

Then I didn't know what to do. Suddenly the aeroplane started dis-integrating. I immediately throttled back and I landed with a damaged aero-plane in the middle of the desert, right in the sand. Every aeroplane had water and these sort of things; so I sat on the top of the aircraft, waiting. I knew to the north was the Mediterranean Sea – I couldn't walk that far. South there was nothing. East and west also. There was no choice for me to walk on any side.

I was there for about nine–ten hours, when I saw a dust column. As it happened, it was our soldiers running home, retreating. I was picked up. And they said: 'Nothing doing! No more flying for you.'

By 7 July the 8th Army had withdrawn deep into Egypt, all the way back beyond Mersa Matruh to the last dip of the coastline before Alexandria. Rommel, following them all the way, was as near as he would ever get to the final breakthrough. Now a series of battles developed around the ridges that stood up from the desert between the coast and the impassable low sands of the Qattara Depression a few miles inland – ridges from which whoever was strong enough to hold them would command all the surrounding country. One of these, just inland of the coastal railway line, was named Ruin Ridge after the shells of a couple of buildings that stood there. The Australian forces were to suffer a huge blow, to manpower and morale, trying to capture it.

The 9th Australian Division was still sweating it out in the desert six months after the 6th and 7th Divisions had gone back to Australia to begin training to fight the Japanese – and plenty of soldiers of the 9th Division were sucking their teeth about that, as Les Rowe of 2/48 Battalion confirms: 'I know of cases where blokes were getting "Dear John" letters and there was that feeling of resentment. Churchill came out to the desert at that stage, and he came up past us and they all shouted out, "When are we going home? When are we going home?" And he said, "Only one more fight and you can go home." One of the Australians bid him for a cigar; he gave him one, and said: "Nobody else!"'

It was Vernon Northwood and the south-western Australian farm workers and small-town dwellers of 2/28 Battalion who were asked to capture and hold Ruin Ridge. The battalion made two abortive attempts on 18 and 22 July, during the second of which they fell back in error when they could have gone on to take the ridge. The Australians felt that the British tanks supporting this attack had got too far ahead of the infantry. There had been a squabble, before the attack, between General Auchinleck and the Australian commander, General Morshead; the Australian felt that his men had done enough attacking, and he lacked confidence in British armour – justifiably, on the whole, in spite of the bravery of the tank crews. All Allied tanks in North Africa were British Army, and none was the equal of the German Panzer, nor able to withstand the heavy shell of the German eighty-eight-millimetre gun. Their tactics, too, had tended to show up in a poor light compared with those of the Afrika Korps. It was perhaps inevitable that, in the absence of any armour of their own, and considering the natural rivalry that mingled with the kinship they felt for the Old Country, the Australians and New Zealanders should blame the bloody patronising Poms when things were going badly – as they undoubtably were during the first seven or eight months of 1942. Equally inevitable, too, that British sensibilities should be ruffled by the coarse colonials. '[The British] have an inbred "tribal" spirit,' comments Sir William Jackson, 'which makes them take an inordinate pride in the capabilities of their own regiment or arm of the service. This has great advantages which should never be underestimated; nevertheless, it does make co-operation between "tribes" more difficult. Each "tribe" or arm tends to believe it can do the job best and would prefer to do so on its own.'[6]

Or maybe it was the *khamsin*, the fierce desert wind, that stiffened so many necks in the desert.

The third attack on Ruin Ridge, carried out on the night of 26–27 July, was fuelled by a certain amount of 'we'll show 'em' sentiment. What happened, in all its stark drama, is related by Vernon Northwood, who received a Mentioned in Despatches for his cool bravery.

The attack started just after midnight, a bright moonlit night, with visibility about 800 yards. As we were going forward I saw a gun coming up on the ridge on my left, about thirty or forty yards away. I thought, 'That can't be one of ours.' We waited and watched, and then two truckloads of men came up and they turned this gun round – and it was an eighty-eight-millimetre, an anti-tank gun. They were vicious, worse than we encountered anywhere.

We could see men coming forward, obviously going to take up firing positions to protect the gun. So by word of mouth I turned my company to face that flank. I realised whatever had to be done had to be done quickly, so I said, 'We're going in with the bayonet.' I got two platoons roughly in line; couldn't wait for the third platoon to come up. I told the men to roll away, because they'd have our position marked. And then I said, 'Right, into them.'

It's really hard to lead a bayonet charge from fellers lying on the ground. For the moment I'm the only man up, and I really thought, you know: 'Oh God – I'm a one-man bayonet charge!' You get a horrible feeling – where *are* they, where are my blokes? I was shouting, all sorts of things, obscenities – 'Get the bastards!' Because you've got to get yourself into a state of frenzy, or you can't attack a group of men with a bayonet.

You know that if they're in a position to run, they will. They won't face you. A moonlight night, moon glinting on bayonets, and they know you're charging with those bayonets. A person in a dug-in gun position will stay there and fire till the end, but a rifleman will get up and run. They don't want to be facing you, they don't want to see you in such an excited state. If they've got their back to you there's a chance you won't bayonet them. This is all completely automatic – it just happens.

So I started, shouting my head off – and all of a sudden I heard this noise behind me and I got the fright of my life! All my fellers screaming! My hair started to stand up on the back of my neck. It was an awful noise.

Anyway, I'd only gone fifteen or twenty paces, I suppose, and then . . . First of all I got a bullet through my steel helmet, which cut my scalp. That threw my head back. Then I got one through my neck – I've still got a bit of metal in there. Then I felt a cut through the top of my arm and then – wham! – a bullet through my left wrist. A compound fracture; that arm's three inches shorter than the other one now. It felt just like a kick from a horse. The bullet through my wrist hit the bone, and it threw me round and round, out of control like a crazy thing. My rifle and bayonet flew out of my hands, and I just pitched to the ground. Someone shouted out, 'The Skipper's been hit!' and I called back, 'I'm all right,' and they went on. I looked up at the ridge: the gun had gone, but I saw this group of men standing there and realised they were our prisoners.

Northwood picked himself up, handed over command of the company and went groggily forward up on to the ridge. There he found no sign of the ambulances and supply vehicles that should have been arriving to support the assault. So he started back, accompanied by a medical orderly, to find out why, backtracking along the line of advance towards a German minefield. Here the two men ran into a German army doctor and a couple of German soldiers who had been taken prisoner. Northwood – still losing blood and feeling faint – took them under his command and brought them along with him to show him the way through the minefield.

Then I found one of our men in charge of about ten more prisoners. He said, 'I don't know what to do with them. Shall I shoot them?' I said, 'No, you clown' – or words to that effect – and took them along with me as well. Now there was one wounded man and a stretcher bearer, and we had thirteen prisoners – and you're not quite sure who's the prisoner in those circumstances. I'd learned some German at university before the war, but of course I couldn't think of one word now.

Anyway, the doctor set off and we kept behind him. By then there were eight vehicles ablaze on the minefield and even as we got down to the edge of it another one went up. As soon as a vehicle blew up, of course, the Germans turned their fire on it. The prisoners were worried about crossing this minefield, so was the doctor – and so was I. I could see there was no sense in trying to get across, so we went back and eventually met up with some of our people, and they put us on a vehicle and took us back to the Regimental Aid Post. So I only got away because I came back to see what was going on with our supply vehicles – otherwise I would have gone into the bag next morning with the rest of the battalion.

Vernon Northwood was lucky. Colonel McCarter, 2/28 Battalion's commanding officer, had signalled 'We're here – Mac' at 0230 hours, as they took possession of Ruin Ridge. But their convoy of stores and ammunition was ablaze on the minefield and under the fire of an anti-tank gun, and their communications had been cut. They could not be informed of the failure of another force to break through to them and by morning they were surrounded and under intense shell and tank fire. The fruitless messages sent by Colonel McCarter tell the story:

0905 – 'We are in trouble.'
0942 – 'We need reinforcements.'
0943 – 'There are tanks all round us.'
0944 – 'You had better hurry. Rock the artillery in.'
1003 – 'We have got to give in.'

When the dust had settled, 730 men of 2/28 Battalion had been captured or were casualties. Only ninety-two front-line troops were left to form a nucleus round which a new battalion would be built, in time to take part in the biggest desert battle of all.

This was the low point. Once Rommel was resupplied with fuel and ammunition there seemed little to stop him making one more giant effort and breaking through to Alexandria, Cairo and the Suez Canal. Many of the Allied soldiers thought he would, as did some of the generals. There was defensiveness and a whiff of defeatism in the air. But then, in mid-August, Churchill and the War Cabinet in London produced just the shake-up required, with a double replacement among the desert commanders. On 15 August General Sir Harold Alexander replaced General Auchinleck. More significantly as far as the immediate situation in the desert was concerned, General Ritchie had been replaced two days beforehand as Commander of the 8th Army by General Bernard Montgomery. Fate played a hand here: the appointment was to have gone to General 'Strafer' Gott, an experienced desert campaigner, but he had recently been killed when his plane was shot down.

Montgomery had plenty of enemies, people who did not care for his self-righteousness and his taste for self-glorification. But he was most definitely that rare bird: the man for the hour. The effect he had on the troops, on the company commanders, the brigadiers and the generals was galvanic. Tom Somerville, the quietly observant New Zealander gunner, had been up and down the desert with the 5th Field Unit since his evacuation from Greece sixteen months earlier and had seen the deterioration in the 8th Army's morale at first hand. His assessment of General Montgomery's impact sums up what most of the desert soldiers felt:

We'd sort of stagnated in the desert, that's all we'd done. Auchinleck only had one thought: retreat, retreat, retreat, all the way down the desert. They'd got defences around Cairo and all down the Nile – not too good for morale. We'd got into fairly bad shape. There's an Egyptian word, *maleesh*, and it means, 'Ah, she's right, boy, she's OK.' It was just like that.

But then Churchill came out to the desert in early August and he saw what was going on. General Gott was killed; so, against Churchill's wishes, Monty came. He'd been chosen to be in charge of the North African landings, but he came and took over two days before Auchinleck was relieved. Auchinleck was very angry about that. Anyway, Monty arrived and took over – and what that man did was just amazing, really. Something about him – he could sum up the whole situation.

He shifted his Headquarters to the coast, so he'd have a clear place to work. At the same time he drew in the Air Force to the same mess that the Army Headquarters were in; previously they'd been fighting two battles, with neither one knowing what the other was doing. He sacked a lot, too, most of the old timers, and he had a lot of young fellers round him. A lot of them didn't known anything about the desert; but he told them, *his* way.

We got a letter to say that there would be no surrender and no retreat, and we're going to hit Rommel for six, clean out of North Africa. We used to laugh at that! Before Monty came we'd been slouching up to our meals, no shirts, unshaven: he said that everybody'd got to have a shave first thing in the morning, and you'd got to dress for meals in the heat. But you noticed the difference in yourself – it picked the whole place up. And he kept in touch, in good contact with us all the way through with those letters of his, encouraging us.

And he was so strict! He had his own caravan and he'd go to bed at a certain time, and he wouldn't be woken in the morning before time. He plotted the whole Alamein breakthrough on 23 October and went to bed and slept on it – slept right through the big barrage! How would a man do that? Self-discipline – a military man, right to the very core.

Montgomery was the man for the hour. Most generals review the battle *after* the event – Monty said what he was *going* to do and he did it, even though it sometimes cost a lot of lives.

He had purpose.

The situation out in the Mediterranean Sea had been fluctuating this way and that since the evacuations from Greece and Crete a year earlier. The Allies had two forces of ships in play throughout 1941. Force H, based on Gibraltar and under the command of Vice-Admiral Sir James Somerville, fulfilled the role of 'doorkeeper' of the Straits of Gibraltar at the western end of the Mediterranean and was also available for operations into the Atlantic against German surface raiders (it was Swordfish torpedo-planes from Force H's carrier *Ark Royal* that had damaged *Bismarck* sufficiently for the Home Fleet to catch up and destroy her). The Mediterranean Fleet under Admiral Sir Andrew Cunningham was based on Alexandria and had responsibility for the whole of the Eastern Mediterranean.

Of vital strategic importance to the Allies was the small, rocky island of Malta, lying half-way along the east-west convoy routes through the Mediterranean. In May 1940, with France crumbling and things looking desperate for Britain, the Foreign Secretary Lord Halifax had actually proposed offering Malta, and other British possessions or protectorates, to Italy's leader, Benito Mussolini, in return for Italy's neutrality and Mussolini's intercession with Hitler for peace terms favourable to Britain. The proposal was outvoted by the British War Cabinet, luckily for the outcome of the war in the Mediterranean and in the Middle East. Malta was superbly equipped with naval dockyards and vast dry docks capable of repairing a ship of any size. It was also a well-placed base, lying between Tripoli and Sicily, for aircraft that could provide cover for east-west convoys between Britain and Alexandria; and for aircraft and submarine operations against Axis forces in all corners of the Mediterranean, with reconnaissance being as important as bombing.

After Italy entered the war on 10 June 1940, Malta had also raised a twinkle in Allied strategists' eyes as a possible jumping-off point for some landing operation, in the unforeseeable future, in Sicily or Italy. But Italy's position as an enemy immediately posed a serious threat to Allied operations in and around the Mediterranean. For periods it became impossible to pass Allied convoys through the narrows between Sardinia, Sicily and the Tunisian coast; men and supplies for the North African campaign had to go the long way round by the Cape of Good Hope, up the eastern coast of Africa and through the Suez Canal. Malta was within easy striking range of bombers from both Sicily and Italy, and air raids quickly became frequent and very heavy. Allied tenure of the island became a matter of hanging on by the fingertips. But the benefits of possession of Malta could not be allowed to pass into Axis hands; nor could they be allowed the propaganda coup of capturing the island, or of halting the convoys that supplied it with aircraft fuel and spares, ammunition of all kinds, armaments and civilian supplies for a population that was otherwise in real danger of being starved out.

The 'Malta Run' from Gibraltar or Alexandria was one of the most dangerous naval operations a wartime sailor could be engaged on. A convoy was almost certain to be attacked by bombers and torpedo-planes. Enemy submarines were a constant threat, minefields were frequently sown afresh and there was always the possibility of a major intervention by the Italian Navy. Destroyers, the factotums of the escort groups, generally bore the brunt of these attacks as far as the Navy was concerned, although of course the tankers and freighters, and the incredibly brave seamen who sailed them, were the prime targets of the hunters. In all the mayhem of 1941, fifteen Allied destroyers were sunk in the Mediterranean along with 158 merchant ships; in 1942 losses amounted to twenty-five destroyers and seventy-three merchantmen.

At the end of 1941 Admiral Somerville was appointed C-in-C Eastern Fleet to replace Admiral Sir Tom Phillips, lost when *Prince of Wales* and *Repulse* were sunk off Malaya. Admiral Cunningham left the Mediterranean some months later, appointed to head the British naval staff mission in Washington. His replacement as C-in-C Mediterranean Fleet, Admiral Sir Henry Harwood, had been in the saddle for less than a month when two simultaneous convoys were run to the beleaguered island of Malta from either ends of the Mediterranean. 'Harpoon', sailing from Britain via the Straits of Gibraltar, entered the Mediterranean on 12 June with six merchant ships protected by one battleship, two carriers, three cruisers and eight destroyers; these were to peel off half-way, and the merchant ships would complete their trip after being met by another escort force of one cruiser, nine destroyers and four minesweepers. Twenty-eight escorting ships to protect six merchantmen; and in the event only two of the merchantmen reached Malta. The four others had been sunk, along with two destroyers; five other escorts had been severely damaged. Fifteen thousand tons of supplies were landed; 28,000 tons had been sent to the bottom. The convoy had been attacked by about 200 aircraft (twenty-nine had been shot down) and the escort had also encountered and driven off Italian naval forces of superior strength. Jim Tait, the softly-spoken New Zealander, was a sub-lieutenant in the destroyer *Ithuriel*, part of the force sent to meet 'Harpoon'. He recalls, in laconic style, firing on the Italian ships at 15,000 yards range: 'I was the gunnery officer in charge of A and B guns. We did hit one of the cruisers – killed six. There was excitement, guns firing. You really could see a shell, I discovered. The Italians were firing at us, and you could actually see the shells at the top of the trajectory.'

At the same time, 'Vigorous' had sailed from Alexandria – eleven merchantmen, protected by seven cruisers, one anti-aircraft ship and twenty-six destroyers. Ship shortage was so acute that a dummy battleship was provided instead of a real one and there was no aircraft carrier for the escort.

During three days at sea the escorts used up a deal of time and fuel manoeuvring to avoid a reported squadron of Italian heavy ships, and fired away so much of their ammunition at attacking aircraft that they had insufficient stocks to protect themselves and the convoy all the way to Malta and back. So 'Vigorous' had to turn round and go back to Alexandria with its precious cargoes undelivered. Six of the eleven merchant ships got back; of their escort, three destroyers and a cruiser had been sunk and many others damaged. 'Not exactly inspiring' was the verdict of Alec Dennis, who was there in *Griffin*:

> The planes were attacking the big ships: we were on the screen and saw an awful lot of mayhem going on. One of the ships was the old battleship *Centurion*, which had been a target ship and was now being used as a dummy *King George V.* She had phoney turrets and was full of concrete. She was one of the prime targets and sent up clouds of concrete dust each time she was hit. It must have been absolute hell for her crew. One merchant ship I remember being hit – there was a huge ball of flame as she went up.
>
> A little bit later on, the Italian torpedo-bombers came in. They were brave; really brave men. We shot one down. Very unpleasant; it exploded in a ball of fire and ended up in the water in a pool of black oil and stuff.

In August Jim Tait and *Ithuriel* escorted 'Pedestal', one of the war's most famous convoys. On the run from Gibraltar to Malta the escort lost the aircraft carrier *Eagle*, two cruisers and a destroyer, and suffered the customary varied damage among other ships. Of fourteen merchant ships that set off from the Clyde, only five arrived in Malta; among them was the fuel tanker *Ohio*, a war hero if ever there was one, having survived hits from a torpedo, bombs and a crashing aircraft, as well as a shaking from near misses that stopped her engines. She was towed into Malta half full of water; her master was later awarded the George Cross for his skill and bravery. During the voyage, Jim Tait became involved in a dramatic episode:

An Italian submarine broke surface not far away from us, and our Captain – a man called Maitland-Makgill-Crichton, a hard name to forge – decided to ram the thing. I was on A deck, just in the bow. The Italian submarine – the *Cobalto*, she was called – came sliding down the side of us. The Captain was shouting, 'Board it! Board it!' So I and one or two others threw a boarding ladder over and we jumped aboard the submarine.

It was badly damaged, and drifted away and eventually sank. I've got pictures of me standing on the bow of the submarine as it slipped down. We swam around – it was warm in the Mediterranean – and were picked up with the Italian survivors.

Peter Cayley from Canada was on the escort screen in the destroyer *Westcott* when a U-boat torpedoed and sank the *Eagle*. He remembers the impersonality of the scene. 'The order came: "Lower all scrambling nets"; then we had to pull them up again, with men still in the water, because we were ordered away to hunt the submarine. As with so much of war at sea, unless you're hit yourself – when it gets very terrible – it's all very impersonal.'

Alec Dennis concurs: 'You were sinking a U-boat, let's say, and they weren't people down there. It was just your professional job. These blasted aeroplanes coming down were a bit more personal, but you didn't really think of the pilot there, with a wife and children – you just thought of a machine coming down.'

The Mediterranean was not the only theatre of operations at sea where young men were in the thick of action in mid-1942. Back in home waters the motor torpedo boats of Coastal Forces kept up a constant harrying of German and Vichy French shipping in the North Sea and the English Channel. The young South African, Bob Gaunt, describes an encounter on 7 August off the Cherbourg peninsula of northern France, which catches all the hectic immediacy and the camaraderie of service in MTBs:[7]

We'd just picked up a brand-new boat, MTB 237. We had a wonderful crew. Our coxswain was Leading Seaman Stiff, about twenty-two years old. The machine-gunner was McPherson, a real dour Scot, a real rough chap from the Gorbals, but a heart of gold. One of the torpedo men was called Morran, a Cockney, and his best friend on the other tube was Ordinary Seaman Pound, a relation of the First Sea Lord, Admiral Sir Dudley Pound. Our spare officer was Fish Salmon. The telegraphist was a youngster called Russell, about nineteen years old. In the engine room were Petty Officer Batchelor and two stokers – one was called Blackie, he was always covered in oil. A splendid crowd. The Captain was *Sir* Guy Fison, an Old Etonian. And this night, 7 August, we had on board Peter Dickens, who was to become one of our most famous MTB commanders.

There were three boats – MTBs 232, 241 and ourselves. The idea was to go across to the Cherbourg peninsula to intercept a special ocean-going tug, the *Oceanie*, and her convoy.

We lay down-moon, stopped. First thing we knew, there was the enemy right ahead of us – this big ship and these escorts. So we started up engines and went in to attack. We were pretty quickly illuminated by star shell; but that always happened. What *was* unusual was the heavy calibre of their guns and their repetitive fire. I was in the wheelhouse, navigating; and the next thing I knew, this bloody great big shell exploded beside me. Fish Salmon and I were both blown completely out of the wheelhouse and landed on the fo'c'sle. Never felt a thing, not a thing! In fact my skull and spine had been cracked, but I didn't find that out till after the war.

Russell was still in his wireless office; on the right of him the wardroom and the galley were on fire, and on the left of him was our small-arms ammunition magazine which was also on fire. Rockets and so on, shooting all round him. So I went down to give him a hand to get out. As I was doing that, Fison shouted, 'We've got no steering. Go and rig the hand steering.' The enemy ships were within 300 yards of us and they were just pouring everything they could into us. Three hundred yards! The for'ard fuel compartment was on fire by then too. This splendid chap, Stiff, came with me and we rigged the hand steering; then I went forward with our mechanic Batchelor and we put the fire out with extinguishers. Then he got the engines going, steering by hand. We were in the absolute centre of the convoy by then – you could have thrown something and hit the main target, we were so close. We'd fired our torpedoes and missed; I think they'd gone underneath the target because the range was so close.

We steered away and the increased draught of getting under way set the main fuel tanks on fire. Then the boat really started to burn. The after tanks had exploded, throwing people to the deck and Fish Salmon to the top of the mast. The main tanks forward were blazing and the magazine was on fire. So I managed to get into the wheelhouse to try to put it out. Morran and Pound stood above, handing down every extinguisher they could find. The heat and the smoke were most intense. It was stupid – there we were, trying to fight 2400 gallons of 100-octane with hand extinguishers! We did this till there was nothing left. Then I had this terrible, frightening experience of the bulkhead to the fuel compartment opening up in slow motion and all this fuel just pouring out, on fire. Coming straight through, coming towards me, with ammunition going off all round. And then dear old Morran and Pound grabbed me by the hands and pulled me up, out of all the petrol. Now, to me that was bloody gallantry. I'll never forget these two chaps pulling me out and saying, 'Come on, Sir, it's going to be all right.' And I mean – they were both covered in fuel ... Then I was on deck and I passed out, because I was so full of cordite and fuel fumes.

The crew of MTB 237 had to abandon ship. They jumped on to MTB 241, which had been bravely steered alongside the burning wreck by its young New Zealand commander, Sub-Lieutenant McDonald. Then, having signalled their base at Portsmouth that they had casualties, they were taken back there. But not to a hero's welcome: 'Both the sentry and the Officer of the Day were asleep. Dickens went to bang on the Captain's door, and said something like, "Sir, this is a bloody disgrace. We've just fought a battle against the enemy; one boat has been lost; another is badly damaged, with enough serious casualties for us to have made a signal. And not a soul in this benighted dump gives a damn!"' A bureaucratic nonsense ensued. None of the five medical officers on the base turned out to attend to them. The crew were refused breakfast because they 'should have ordered it the day before'; they could not exchange their burned and filthy clothes for clean ones because of 'stock-taking'. And even after they got their new clothes, says Bob Gaunt, 'they couldn't go on survivors' leave, because they couldn't get their rail tickets or ration cards – because the office was closed for the afternoon. Anyway, eventually I got them what they needed and saw them off; then I went into my cabin and had a bloody good cry. I was only twenty.'

Many of the young Commonwealth servicemen, away from home for the first time, found it hard to cope with feelings of loneliness and homesickness. Bob Gaunt says:

It may be difficult to appreciate how strange it was at eighteen years old to find oneself, within three weeks of leaving one's little town in South Africa, serving in a ship with people from a country one had never visited, who had grown up with such different social and environmental backgrounds.

When that MTB action took place I'd had my twentieth birthday only a week or so before. I'd been away from home, in the Navy with no other South Africans, for nearly two years, and felt bloody lonely. I think this feeling of isolation that some of us had was just never appreciated by the Brits. I'm sure that many very young chaps from the Commonwealth shared this experience. It left an everlasting impression on me.

A Commonwealth serviceman in wartime Britain could find himself in awkward situations. Sometimes a young man, far from home and feeling at a disadvantage, would react by standing crossly on his dignity, as with Dudley Thompson from Jamaica when he went to sign up after arrival in England:

I saw that one of the questions on the form was: 'Are you of pure European descent?' I wrote 'Yes', because some of my friends had been turned down because they were not. And they were told so. There was a difficulty, particularly in the early stages of the war, getting in if you were coloured. I thought this was bad, really bad; this was stupid; this was prejudice, really wrong. So I said 'Yes', because I wanted to fight – I wanted to fight against *that*.

There was an old sergeant in charge, a Poona type, walrus moustache and all. When he came to check the form, he said to me, 'Question so-and-so, about pure European descent – you've answered "Yes". Do you understand the question?' I was face to face with him – I drew myself up to my full five foot seven and said: 'What gives you the impression that I do not understand the English language?'

It was the Canadians, however, in those days before the build-up to D Day and the attendant mass influx of US servicemen, who were finding it hardest to get along with the British. Canadian flyers were already in action: among them was Charlie Hobbs, now trained as an air gunner. His first operational sortie was on the first 'Thousand Bomber Raid' on 31 May, when 14,500 tons of bombs were dropped on Cologne. 'They told us not to hit the cathedral,' he recalls. 'Well, we couldn't have hit it if we'd wanted to; in fact, the best way to make it safe would have been to aim at it!'

Hobbs and his friends were baffled and irritated by one quirk, in particular, of the British way of life:

The class system – it showed up, and the Canadians resented it; any show of class. For instance, when we were stationed at Upper Heyford, we were close to Oxford. And here's this gorgeous old university, with the fellers going to lectures with the fancy scarf around their neck; and here *we* are from 5000 miles away, fighting their battles for them! Now that didn't make sense to us. They could have accomplished the same thing by taking off the stupid scarf and getting into it themselves, couldn't they? I'd say that there was a resentment on our part, and they brought it on themselves. It was almost a defensive thing with them. At the time it wasn't our cup of tea, let's put it like that.

At least Charlie Hobbs was able to purge some of his contempt in action. The Canadian soldiers in Britain – some of whom had been there since early 1940 – had as yet been offered no action, no possibility of getting to grips with the enemy. Instead, they had been drilled until they were sick to death of drilling, under British officers and NCOs they had learned to dislike. The disenchantment was not all one way. Sam Meltzer of the Royal Army Service Corps sums up the British resentment of the Canadians:

They came to Britain poorly trained, or untrained – no arms, no boots. We trained them; but the British High Command didn't really trust them. There was a feeling in 1942 that the Canadian Army hadn't really done a lot. They were there in England, wining and dining the ladies, making more money than our boys. Whenever British soldiers returned to anywhere in England the Canadians would immediately be moved away for fear of trouble. There was a *lot* of resentment: 'They're over here screwing the ladies, while our boys are out there doing the fighting in the desert.'

The feelings of the Canadians at the time are expressed by Reg Burt, who in mid-1942 was still performing anti-aircraft duties around the English coast – more action than most of his fellow soldiers were seeing:

In one incident our Prime Minister, Mackenzie King, came over to speak to the troops in Aldershot, and they booed him right off the stage. See, in the Canadian Army you had to volunteer to go overseas. And of course Mackenzie King was quite against conscripts going overseas. He wanted the French vote, the Quebec vote; and the French were opposed to conscription. In Canada people could be conscripted into the army all right, but not for overseas. So if you wanted to, you could stay back in Canada the whole six years of the war. Those who did, we called 'zombies'. The Canadians booed Mackenzie King off the stage because they wanted more men. We were quite angry about this failure to send the zombies overseas.

Everybody was kinda restless. They wanted a second front, all the guys; everybody was talking about 'going over'. That's why Dieppe came into it, because a lot of the Canadians were getting quite upset.

Was the Dieppe Raid put in train to test the ability of Allied forces to take and hold a Channel port, or to give the disaffected soldiers of the 2nd Canadian Division in Britain something to get their teeth into, or to show the disillusioned British public that the Canadians were not just freeloading? Or was it undertaken – as seems likely – to prove to the hard-pressed Russians that the Allies were serious about opening a Second Front in Europe? Winston Churchill, writing with hindsight after the war, remarks: 'Strategically the raid served to make the Germans more conscious of danger along the whole coast of Occupied France. This helped to hold troops and resources in the West, which did something to take the weight off Russia. Honour to the brave who fell. Their sacrifice was not in vain.'[8] Dieppe may have taken a very small weight off Russia. It certainly put paid to any Allied notions of a full-scale invasion of north-west Europe in the near future. As a military operation the raid, carried out on 19 August 1942, was an unmitigated disaster. As a confidence booster among the Allies it was a complete failure.

The Dieppe Raid was planned by the Directorate of Combined Operations under its Chief, Vice-Admiral Lord Louis Mountbatten, with the advice of General Montgomery and other experienced service leaders, and with Churchill's enthusiastic backing. He definitely viewed the operation as a guinea pig for a future all-out invasion: 'I thought it most important that a large-scale operation should take place this summer, and military opinion seemed unanimous that until an operation on that scale was undertaken no responsible general would take the responsibility of planning for the main invasion.'[9] As envisaged, the plan was for a landing force of about 6600 Canadian, American and Free French soldiers and British commandos to make a frontal attack on the strongly defended channel port of Dieppe and the coastal defences each side. A sustained naval bombardment and aerial strafing was to precede the landings. Some units were to hold their objectives for specified lengths of time; others were to destroy installations, to note the state of the defences and to bring back information when the marauders re-embarked and sailed back to England.

In the event, the raid had to be postponed for six weeks from its original June date. Intelligence gatherers miscalculated the quality of the defending troops and the siting of their positions. The naval bombardment proved ineffective. Delays on the crossing meant that many troops had to land in broad daylight under the fire of thoroughly alerted defenders. Almost all the defences were found intact. Those on the western flank of Dieppe were successfully attacked and destroyed; those on the east were silenced. But as the main assault body came stumbling ashore from the landing craft under the cliffs of the town itself, a terrible massacre took place on the beaches.

Ray Walker of the Royal Canadian Navy, the Cape Breton Islander from Sydney Mines, had been training at Rossneath in Scotland when he was 'volunteered' for duty with diesel engines. He thought he was going into submarines. Then, in a guarded building in Plymouth, he and some fellow sailors were told: 'You're going to go on a little visit to the coast of France – a place called Dieppe.'

The Scots-born Toronto boy, Thomas Hunter, had been in Britain with the Royal Regiment of Canada since early 1940. The first he knew of the impending raid was when 'we were told we would be making an invasion and there'd be lots of casualties. That's all they told us.'

Documents captured later in the war show that, in spite of the postponed date, the Germans had no specific prior knowledge of the raid. But both Walker and Hunter are convinced otherwise. 'We were sacrificial lambs,' Hunter says. 'The Germans had binoculars all along the French coast and they could see us training on the beaches from Hastings right along to Bournemouth. They were there waiting for us – they knew it was just a matter of time. In fact, one German at Dieppe actually asked us: "What took you so long?" I know of a couple of guys that deserted; they got wind of all that was coming and they went AWOL. I saw them after the war, told them they were lucky they weren't in it. They knew what they were doing.'

Ray Walker arrived off the coast on a Free French gunboat, at daybreak on the nineteenth. 'the bombarding was going on, the shore battery was picking us off in the water, and Jerry was there. I don't think we had enough air cover, for one thing. They should have done away with that shore battery. They were just picking them off left and right in the barges, as soon as they hit the beach. They were lucky any of them got ashore at all. Some of the barges were coming back out, and instead of pumping water out of the bilges they were pumping blood. It was terrible. I saw it – something you don't forget.'

Thomas Hunter had slept through the briefing given to his company. The Royal Regiment of Canada had to wait for an hour for some commandos to disentangle themselves, and were forced to make their landing on Blue Beach, below Puits just east of the main town, in daylight. Blue Beach was short (250 yards wide) and narrow (fifty yards deep), pebbly in part, with a twelve-foot, wire-topped sea wall to be surmounted before reaching the sixty-foot cliffs at the back of the beach. A pillbox at each end commanded the whole beach. Puits had only sixty men to defend it with mortars and machine-guns, but they were securely positioned inside concrete pillboxes and gun emplacements. The idea was for the attackers to gain the clifftop and surge to the right, to take from the rear the strongpoints that overlooked Dieppe. In the event, says Thomas Hunter, hardly anyone got further than Blue Beach. The place was, quite simply, a death trap.

All in all, it was a very, very poorly planned operation. We were slaughtered – the machine-guns in the pillboxes just raking away, killing everybody as they came off the ships. When we got off we were up to our chests in water, and had to pull a three-inch mortar on its buggy through the water and up on to the beach. The guy that was pulling the mortar on the other side, he got shot. I couldn't pull it myself; it was over 300 lb, too heavy to pull through soft sand. So I dropped it in the middle of the beach, and headed for the cliff and got out of sight.

We got into a little alcove, Jimmy Elliot and I, and we were firing at the pillboxes – he was firing at one and I was firing at the other, aiming at that eight-inch slit. We had rounds and rounds of ammunition, and just kept loading. I really don't know how we weren't killed: I never fathomed that out. The Germans were throwing potato-masher grenades from up over our heads. They'd come down beside us and I'd just throw them out towards the water; they'd go off and not harm us at all.

Out on the beach there was heaps of dead guys, and medical orderlies out in the middle bandaging wounded men, doing what they could for them. The Germans weren't killing too many ordinary soldiers; they were getting the NCOs and the officers. They could see their stripes and their pips. Get them out of the way and the rest of the troops'll follow. That was their idea. Officers, that's what they concentrated on – you could see it quite clearly.

A few hundred yards off the beach, Ray Walker was waiting to land with a bunch of Royal Marine commandos. He and his group had been told to get ashore and steal an E-boat; but at present he did not look like getting as far as the beach. 'The noise was just continuous, all the time – Bang! Bang! Aircraft, dogfights, planes hitting the water, bombs hitting right alongside of you, shells ... I was on deck all through that. Then the Free French gunboat I was on got hit by the shore battery. The commandos were taken ashore with the small landing barges, but we never got ashore. We just lay outside, laying smoke screens – I coughed for about two weeks after.'

In his alcove in against the cliffs, Thomas Hunter was expecting to be killed at any moment.

We were quite cool and calm, Jimmy Elliot and I. There's nothing you can do about it. Where would you go, up against a sixty-foot cliff? There was pillboxes each end of the beach and the water was thirty, forty feet away. We couldn't possibly swim back to England, it was too damn far; and all the ships were out of reach, so ... we were stuck. We had to stay. It was a feeling of hopelessness: 'How did I get into this mess?' There was no way out. I told Elliot, 'We can't do much about it now. Let's just survive as long as we can.'

Eventually someone up ahead of us put up a white flag. That meant surrender, put your gun down. The Germans came down from the cliffs, came and stood beside us, took our rifles. A lot of them spoke good English. They were quite easygoing. Everyone felt relief, I think. It was just slaughter – no one wanted it.

It was all over by 8.30 in the morning. Hunter was among the 2195 prisoners marched off to a long journey east, by railway truck into Germany and prisoner-of-war camp. Behind him on the beach lay 906 dead Canadians. The Royal Regiment of Canada had lost 209 killed and 262 prisoners-of-war. Only sixty-five of the regiment made it back to England. These were the worst Canadian losses since the Somme in 1916. The raid, with a grand total of 3367 troops killed, captured or wounded – well over half the number that took part – had been a catastrophe for the attackers. For the defenders, of whom about 600 had been killed or wounded, it had been a comparatively easy containing operation.

Next day's *Daily Mail* headline blurted: 'Dieppe Victors Come Back Singing.' Over in Canada the *Winnipeg Free Press* wrote of the 'sheer joy of getting to grips with Jerry'. These were First World War sentiments, for a botched assault that had cost a First World War butcher's bill. The Canadians, after their first big offensive operation of the war, found themselves playing second fiddle to the British commandos in the public prints. General Roberts, the CO of the 2nd Canadian Division, was awarded a DSO, but Dieppe damaged and cut short his career. Mountbatten had blotted his copybook. In Canada, once the casualty figures were known and the proportion of dead, wounded and captured Canadians appreciated, pride was mixed with further disillusion.

For Thomas Hunter three years of captivity lay ahead. 'I still can't understand why it was Canadians who were sacrificed at Dieppe,' he says. 'I think Churchill had a dead set against Canadians, a personal grudge. I think he's still turning over in his grave. He had a hatred for Canadians, maybe because we were gallivanting, or taking his women around Britain – I don't know. Yes, I think Churchill had a great deal to do with it. However – it was war, and you can expect anything from war.'

For Ray Walker, return to England meant a continuing active involvement with war service in the RCN. But he would find that Dieppe had been scarred into his psyche: 'I think about it now. I'll tell you what gets me – when I hear a service band playing the "Last Post". Then I feel like I want to break down and cry.'

Over on the other side of the world, meanwhile, attention was focusing on a string of Pacific Ocean islands north and east of Australia. From April onwards the Japanese had been trying to get a toe-hold in the Solomon Islands, which run 600 miles in two parallel lines north-west towards New Guinea. If they could establish themselves securely in these islands, and also capture the New Guinean capital of Port Moresby, they would have cemented the southern wall of their Pacific empire and would also be in a much better position if they chose to assault Australia.

Their first attempt to take Port Moresby, by sea landing, had been thwarted at the beginning of May at the Battle of the Coral Sea, where Pierre Austin in *Australia* had watched the 'cheeky buggers' being shot out of the sky. But by the beginning of July Japanese forces had landed on Guadalcanal, a large island in the lower, more southerly line of the Solomons, and were building an airfield there. At Tulagi on Florida Island, just north of Guadalcanal, they had already got an airstrip operating. Unless they could be dislodged the Japanese would soon dominate the skies over the Solomons, enabling their ships to run with impunity along

The Slot (the channel between the two lines of islands), snapping up and fortifying the islands one by one. So the Americans decided on a landing on Guadalcanal and Florida, to wrest the islands back from the Japanese. It was to be a long and extremely bloody campaign. The Americans quickly secured the Guadalcanal airfield, but then had to winkle out very well dug-in opponents in thick jungle terrain and mountains, as well as beating off attack after attack during the following six months as Japanese troop carriers came down The Slot at night and landed fresh assault parties.

At the outset of this campaign on 7 August – the same night as Bob Gaunt was fighting the flames in his MTB in the English Channel – the RAN cruiser *Australia* arrived in the channel off Guadalcanal. She was part of a screening force commanded by Rear-Admiral V. A. C. Crutchley VC, attached to the American 'Amphibious Force' under Rear-Admiral R. K. Turner. So Pierre Austin was present at what turned out to be, for the Allied naval forces, a crushing defeat. A Japanese cruiser force from Rabaul arrived in the early hours of 9 August, pounced on the unsuspecting Allied cruisers and tore them apart. Had the Japanese admiral pressed on to attack the transports landing American troops, the whole Allied recapture of the Solomons could well have been smashed. He did not: but at the time, the Battle of Savo Island appeared to be an unqualified disaster.

We were thoroughly screwed: it was Matapan in reverse. They sank four heavy cruisers for no loss. *Australia* was Admiral Crutchley's flagship: he was very much a 'see-the-whites-of-their-eyes' man. The Americans landed on Guadalcanal on 7 August and took Henderson Field airstrip; I think they underrated what the Japanese riposte would be.

We went in and did a preliminary bombardment, got the troops ashore. Everything was well established by nightfall both on Florida Island and Guadalcanal. We'd had a torpedo-bomber attack and some dive-bombers – once again, spectacularly unsuccessful. Very little damage inflicted and they lost pretty well the ruddy lot. We knew the Japanese had a cruiser force on the way, but the estimate was it wouldn't reach us before a given time.

Admiral Crutchley split the escort. Three American heavy cruisers, *Quincy*, *Vincennes* and *Astoria*, were patrolling to one side, and *Australia*, *Chicago* and *Canberra* – three more heavy cruisers – on the other side of the passage between Guadalcanal and Florida Island, two large chunks of land. And in the entry to the bay between them was Savo Island. We'd been at action stations for a couple of days by that time, and it was pretty hot and humid, with tropical rainstorms.

Turner, the American admiral, had taken his carriers away from the area, which left us very vulnerable and in two minds whether we should continue unloading troops, get on with it and consolidate, or not. Admiral Crutchley had to confer with the Marine general; so we in *Australia* had moved out of line and away from the area of attack, when a Japanese flare appeared overhead – this was during the dark hours. Then all hell broke loose, on one side. We couldn't see who was firing at who. Then all hell broke loose on the other side; we still couldn't see who was firing. Came the dawn – *Canberra* was burning and in a sinking condition; *Quincy*, *Vincennes* and *Astoria* were sunk; *Chicago* had had her bow blown off. Four heavy cruisers lost.

We had to get out of it. For a short period, at least, we had no presence and this meant that the Japanese could institute a thing we called the Tokyo Express. Fast battleships and cruisers would come belting down The Slot from Bougainville, running in troops and supplies to help their defence of Guadalcanal.

The statistics from this action tell the whole sorry story. The full complement on the Allied side was 345 officers and 4417 men; on the Japanese side it was 353 officers and 4002 men. The Allies lost 1024 killed and 709 wounded; the Japanese lost nobody.

We didn't get back home for about a month. At the end of my leave I was saying goodbye to my cousin, and I said, 'Dorothy, I don't want to go back.' The first time ever. I'd had it.

On 9 August, as Pierre Austin was listening to the detonations and watching the gunfire flashes that told of the destruction of his unseen colleagues off Savo Island, another son of Melbourne – Phil Rhoden, the young lawyer who had been recalled with 2/14 Battalion from the Middle East – was shivering, along with his men, among frozen mutton carcases in the hold of the US Liberty ship *James Fenimore Cooper* about 800 miles away. The battalion were on their way north from Australia to New Guinea, to meet and halt the Japanese southward advance across the island towards Port Moresby that had followed their landing on the north coast on 21 July. The battleground where the two opposing forces would meet to decide the fate of New Guinea – and, by extension, of Australia – was the dense mountain rain forest of the razor-backed Owen Stanley Ranges, which run as a spine down into the tail of the island. Rain, mist, jungle sores, mud, leeches and malaria are endemic here. Maps of the mountains –

outdated, inaccurate, pre-war quarter-inch maps – showed a motor road, the Kokoda Track, crossing the ranges. This 'road', along which all the men and materials for the battle would have to pass and around which all the fighting took place, was in fact a zigzag path where two people could scarcely pass each other, that rose and fell laboriously, often by steps, from one valley to the next ridge and down again. Wheeled or hoof-borne transport was out of the question. All supplies would have to be taken in on men's backs.

A pre-war report on the state of the Kokoda Track had concluded: 'Impossible for white men carrying loads; natives may carry up to fifteen pounds.' When 2/14 Battalion set off on 16 August from Port Moresby, 546 strong, they were each carrying loads of forty-five pounds minimum. Even their towels and toothbrushes had been cut in half to reduce the weight and bulk of their burdens. Every man took his turn at carrying his section's Bren gun. Over the first three miles the track rose 1200 feet, then dropped 1600; then it rose again 2000 feet in the next four miles. It took the rear companies – always the slowest, as they had to wait for delays up front to be sorted out – twelve hours to accomplish nine miles, a remarkably good rate of progress. They marched for ten days like this, until they reached what Phil Rhoden calls 'a little village on the Moresby side of the Ranges, called Isurava. And there the 2/14 Battalion met the Japanese – and the Japanese met the 2/14 Battalion.'

What followed, over the course of four days' savage jungle fighting, is told in Rhoden's dry, economical style:

I was Second-in-Command of the unit. Taking the track as an axis, the entire battle area would be a couple of cricket pitches' length in off to the right, and to the left maybe half a mile of high ground. Everything was in such a small area that you could see, and hear, everything that was going on.

The Japanese had flat country to get to Isurava, so they'd had an easy go by the time they met us. They'd been continually landing troops and they'd built up a force of about 12,000 to call on; we had our 546 Australians. And the track was so narrow that we could only feed one company at a time into the battle.

The first day, 26 August, was given over to patrolling by both sides. On the twenty-seventh, more of the same – but much more firing at each other. All we had were rifles, Bren guns, tommy-guns and grenades. They had heavy machine-guns, mortars and mountain guns, and of course grenades and all the rest.

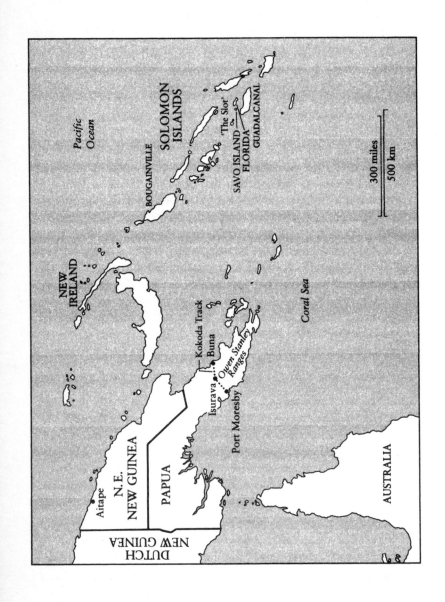

Anyway, comes the twenty-eighth and first thing in the morning all hell broke loose. They fired and fired with all their weapons. Platoon positions changed hands seven times during the day. But not one inch of ground was given. I suppose we lost about twenty of all ranks during the day. Then on the twenty-ninth, more of the same, only much more intense. The usual outbreak of firepower by the Japs in the morning, which continued intermittently all day. One platoon position changed hands eleven times on that one day. Here again, everyone stood firm. We suffered twenty-one dead that day and forty-eight wounded by 'stumps'. There were plenty unaccounted for as well.

Two remarkable things happened during the day. A fellow called Charlie McCallum – his platoon was hard pressed. They had been overrun four times, and four times got their position back. On the fifth engagement, when things were looking a bit grim, he grabbed a tommy-gun from a wounded comrade and went in with his Bren gun firing from his right hip and his tommy-gun firing from his other hip. When he ran out of ammunition and had to change the clip on the Bren, he kept firing the tommy-gun; and so it went on. Then the platoon had to withdraw and he covered their withdrawal. He was put up for the VC, but he got a DCM. A most remarkable thing.

Then at about 5.30 p.m. the unit position was getting a bit wobbly and the Battalion Headquarters was going to be overrun. Everything was committed at this stage – fighting on every front. We gathered together a few troops, a few volunteers, some of them wounded, and a fellow called Kingsbury led a patrol against the Japanese who were attacking Battalion HQ. He, too, went rushing forward firing his Bren gun from the hip under intense machine-gun fire and cleared away the Japanese so that we could retake the position. Kingsbury was killed by a sniper. He was posthumously awarded the Victoria Cross. It was the first VC won in the South Pacific and the first on Australian Territory; and he was the first Victorian to win a VC.

I believe myself that Isurava was the turning point in the war against the Japanese, and that action of Kingsbury's was the thing that triggered it off. That four-day battle is coming to be seen as a time when a delay was imposed upon the Japanese, a delay which they didn't want – and they started from that point onwards to run out of steam.

The following day, 30 August, disaster struck 2/14 Battalion when the Japanese mounted a big afternoon attack from two flanks simultaneously and overran Battalion Headquarters. The battalion's CO, Lieutenant-Colonel Key, was reported missing, as was the adjutant.

At first light [says Phil Rhoden] it was realised that the CO wasn't coming back again and the Brigadier sent a message that I was to take command. So I had something to think about then.

The next fortnight was a fighting withdrawal. Our job, together with 2/16 Battalion, was to withdraw, make a stand, withdraw again – always keeping ourselves between the enemy and Port Moresby. That required great discipline; no one was to move until the last moment. You wouldn't see them until they were on you, just a cricket pitch away. One of our strengths was that they hated the bayonet. So if they came up close we gave them the bayonet. And they didn't like it.

By now 2/14 were in touch with their fellow battalions in 21 Brigade, 2/16 and 2/27. The three battalions, fighting beside and for each other, fell back through the Owen Stanley mountains day by day. There were plenty of desperate moments, and the Japanese had pressed them almost to the outskirts of Port Moresby before 2/25 Battalion came up to relieve 2/14 at Ioribaiwa on 16 September. By then the fighting strength of Phil Rhoden's battalion – which had set off up the Kokoda Track 546 strong exactly a month before – had been reduced, by a battle casualty toll of 248 and a long sickness list, to just eighty-seven men.

The Japanese, unable to break through and with men now required for the intense fighting in the Solomon Islands, began to fall back themselves. The soldiers on the Kokoda Track whom Rhoden had fought, trapped without supplies between Australian troops advancing from the south and American soldiers who landed in November on the north of the island, had turned to cannibalism before the year was out. At the beginning of the new year their remnants would finally be driven into the sea at Buna, where they had landed six months before.

Phil Rhoden sums up the jungle battle of Isurava:

Looking back on it now, there's a great temptation to rewrite it all. But you mustn't do that, you can't do that. When I look back – well, I don't like to think of it; it's not something I often do. Because it was a dreadful time, because it was an anxious time. It was all so close. There was no question of getting your fieldglasses out and having to identify something a mile away, like we had been doing in the desert. You were all part of the action. The CO is just as vulnerable as Joe Blow behind a tree in the forward section. I was visiting forward troops, getting round wherever there was an opportunity to go. You're there encouraging, you're there planning, you're there assisting, you're there for people to talk to. And it's all happening, it's all so jumbled in point of time and space. In that situation there's one focal point that people look to – hopefully to get the right advice. You had to somehow do your best, because other people's lives were at stake.

Putting it on a higher plane – if there is a higher plane than a man's life – there was also at stake, in the short term, Moresby; which, if they'd got, would have made Australia terribly vulnerable. In the long term, to the Japs, the glittering prize of landing in Australia. There would have been very little to stop them once there, with the Australian Army and Navy fully committed and the Air Force lacking in planes. So that was why Isurava was so important.

This comes back to the business of being Australian. Because you were fighting, literally, for Australia, without the assistance of Americans or anyone else – you were doing it on your own, as Australians, and you were becoming Australians fast, whether you liked it or not. We *had* to do it; otherwise our loved ones at home would have been ... gone.

If Isurava marked a turning point in the Far East war against the Japanese, another turning point was rapidly approaching in the North African desert. With the 8th Army pushed back on to its own home ground in Egypt, its back against the very walls of Alexandria, it was odds-on that General Rommel and his Afrika Korps would gather themselves for one last great eastward push through to the Suez Canal and the oilfields of the Middle East. Had General Ritchie still been in charge of the 8th Army, it might well have happened. But now the Allied soldiers had General Bernard Montgomery, the man of purpose, to stiffen their upper lips and brace their backs. The desert pendulum was about to swing one more time, decisively and unstoppably; a swing to the west.

In late October the opposing lines filled the whole width of the desert between the Mediterranean and the low-lying, marshy, impassable Qattara Depression. By now Montgomery had more than twice as many men and tanks as Rommel. The German general, at the extremity of his over-stretched supply lines once again, knew that he could not outflank the 8th Army as hitherto; he could only try to break the southernmost part of the Allied line, then race north behind it to fall on Montgomery's main forces from the rear. He tried it at the end of August, fruitlessly, a last throw of his offensive dice.

Montgomery, on the other hand, could wait and fatten his army on men and supplies coming in through Alexandria. When he was ready, on 23 October, he launched diversionary attacks in the south of the line, then brought his forces north to add weight to the infantry thrust he was developing along the coast through the Axis minefields and anti-tank positions. The idea was to weaken the defenders, before punching through to the open desert with tanks. Once there, he would be able to roll up opposition and drive whatever opponents remained back along the well-trampled and much fought-over desert battleground – this time, he and all his troops believed, all the way back to Tunis.

The plan worked, gradually, over the course of two weeks of heavy fighting, manoeuvring and out-manoeuvring. There were tremendous tank battles and infantry confrontations, delays and diversions. At one point Hitler issued a 'fight on at all costs' order which overruled Rommel's on-the-spot decision to withdraw. But realities, and the 8th Army's supreme Montgomery-inspired self-confidence, had their way. By 8 November the Afrika Korps was in full retreat westwards for the second time; the Allies were pushing towards Tripoli and beyond, to Tunis, for the third time since the opening days of the desert campaign back in 1940.

For another reason, too, 8 November was a significant day. 'Operation Torch', the landing of Allied forces at Casablanca in Morocco, and at Oran and Algiers in Algeria, began on that date, with the object of taking French North Africa from the Vichy French. The stage was set for the final squeezing of the Axis forces out of the whole of North Africa.

Participants from many Commonwealth countries were present at El Alamein, either in a fighting or in a supporting role. Paul Gobine, the Seychelles Islander, helped with the deceptions and ruses; Les Rowe fought throughout the battle as an infantry private with the Australian 2/48 Battalion; Tom Somerville served his twenty-five-pounder gun with the 5th Field Unit of the New Zealand artillery. Charles Adams, the Cape Coloured driver, worked behind the Allied lines and chafed at not being where the action was; Frank Sexwale of the Native Military Corps, his black compatriot, felt likewise in his job as an office clerk within earshot of the battlefield. And Nila Kantan, the 'very lean, thin, puny' youth from Andra Pradesh, kept the 5th Brigade of the 4th Indian Division supplied through the thick of the fighting and, when the battle was over, helped to clear up the mess.

Les Rowe:

Alamein was the culmination of a whole lot of training. When you've been on the losing end of the stick for quite a while, it's a different thing entirely when you realise that it's all coming together. The front had been stabilised, Montgomery had taken over, and we rehearsed and rehearsed and rehearsed.

The Army can psyche you up, you know. They had us at a stage where we were wanting to get at 'em, you know what I mean. And the evidence is there that this is the big one, this is the one time when it's not going to fizzle out on you.

Paul Gobine:

Montgomery addressed us. He come and visited us at Alamein. He says: 'We have to keep the German on the run.' He say, 'No more evacuation – let's go!' Montgomery was a great fellow, but I know the Americans didn't like him. They try to interfere; he went to them and he said, 'You don't smoke in my quarters! I don't give a damn for you, I don't take my order from you!' – you know? He was a great, great, great man.

At Alamein the German were more superior in quality of weapons than what we had. So we do tactics. We start building wooden tanks, camouflaged well. When the German reconnaissance plane photograph all these false tanks, false lorries with their little lights – they start bombing them. So the Germans were taken by surprise when the 8th Army began to advance on them with all their real tanks.

Tom Somerville:

Twenty-three October was a great turning point. There was a whole lot of preparations for it, there were odd movements of troops to fool the Germans where we were. They kept it a dead secret – there was no leave at all, no troop movement, no vehicle movement. Anyone in an endangered place was kept in the dark, because they were likely to be captured. The infantry, for instance; the night before, they were taken forward – poor beggars – and they dug in, in slit trenches, and they had to lay there in full view of the enemy, all day until the following night. They couldn't move, to answer the call of nature or anything else. They weren't told what was happening: they were an endangered species.

Les Rowe: 'We were taken up by a guide. It's like being shown to a seat in the pictures: "OK, you go down this line." They had little torches that only shone one way; so when you looked, it was just like a cinema. Then it was just lay on the sand and wait, with a World War One rifle in my hand.'

Tom Somerville:

The night before, truck-loads of ammunition came in and we prepared it. Some we buried, some we put under camouflage nets. Cases and cases and cases of shells. We spent the whole of that day talking about it, wondering what was going to happen. We'd been given Zero Hour: 9.40 p.m. on 23 October. Everyone was a bit churned up about it. They brought us a meal, and that was just about the best meal we'd ever had. There was South African guavas there, nice fresh meat cooked up – we called it our sacrificial meal. We knew what the outcome could be if it went wrong.

Anyway, we sat around and sat around. Cups of tea ... Finally it worked round towards the hour. One shell fired – and then it all started, a line of flashes as far as you could see from north to south, until a cloud of dust gradually closed down.

Les Rowe: 'At 9.40 at night, when the barrage started – well, you've got to have experienced it to know how it was. What it must have been like on the other end of it ... There's a big difference between outgoing and incoming fire, you know! The sounds of it must have been absolutely unbelievable. It lifted up and we were off, walking steadily, the officers and everyone keeping us in line, and the first poor buggers we came to had blood running out of their ears. They were just about dazed.'

Charles Adams:

We were lying about three kilometres away when the guns all went off. It was just like thunder; the flashes were as bright as daylight. For forty-five miles it was just guns – oh, just amazing! Thousands of guns. I wonder how Jerry felt on the other side. During the day you could hear the Navy hammering the Jerry lines, giving them a whack. Then every night the artillery opens up – just to let them know we're still there, to keep them nervous, because they don't know when is the British going to attack.

Yes ... I would have liked to have gone up with the main push – I would have liked to have been in the fighting.

Frank Sexwale: 'Sometimes I did the driving and taking up supplies, but mostly I was in the office as a clerk during the battle. When it started – I remember it very, very well. One heard the barrage, then the noise of tanks and infantry, tanks rushing to the front, bombardment from the sea and air, supplies going in, ambulances coming back with the injured and the dead ... all that. I was a spectator – no chance of taking part as a combatant. It was a British war, a white man's war.'

Les Rowe: 'The sand's very hard there – you can't dig a hole in it without you've got a pneumatic drill. So you're walking forward on this firm sand, keeping in line: in effect, you're walking till they tell you to stop. The idea

was we were supposed to get through their line, and turn round and finish up attacking back the way we came. But it didn't work out like that.'
   Tom Somerville:

We raised the range every few minutes and the infantry were creeping in behind that line of barrage. A fantastic noise. But after a bit we couldn't hear it – I suppose our ear-drums weren't coping. We'd stop every now and then for the barrel to cool off a bit, and then on we'd go again. There's a rhythm you get: pass the shell – into the breach – fire – open the breach – out comes the empty – in goes another shell. Next morning we cleaned up such a stack of shell cases and empty shell boxes...
   Then they told us very briefly that it had been a success. But you wouldn't have known it as far as we were concerned, because the infantry attacks and the tank attacks and the German counter-attacks were going on just the same.

Les Rowe:

Well, of course, you can take ground off Jerry – but you've got to hang on to it. One of their masterstrokes was their ability to re-form quickly and counter-attack. You've got to get your anti-tank mines out, and your wire. You've got to get your ammunition up, all your supplies – and then you've got to be prepared to stand the onslaught when it comes back at you. Well, that's virtually what it was like. You attack one night, the next day you spend fending them off, then you attack again – very often the next night.
   Day Two was very bad for us. Trig 29 – very, very bad; terrible casualties. They're starting to tell on you, people being killed and so forth. It's having its effect.
   At Trig 29 we were attacking from below; only ten feet below, but it enabled the people holding that point to overlook us. You could see flashes, star shell, all sorts of stuff going up ahead of you. You'd have to chuck in a grenade, maybe man a Bren if the gunner had been wounded or killed.
   The battle itself was a game of chess – each side guessing where the armour was. But as infantry we didn't know much about the tank fighting, though I did see a tank battle from the plateau. We just went on night after night, losing men all the time, for the ten days. In action it's like a kaleidoscope – things going on all the time round you, things you have to do and see to. That stops you feeling scared when you're actually fighting. It was the times in between, when you were dug in, between being bombed or shelled, when you had the time to think: it could be me that gets wounded or killed.

Nila Kantan:

In 'Operation Supercharge' on 3 November we were asked to break through on Ruweisat Ridge, just inland of Alamein, and allow our armoured divisions to pass through and trap the Germans. As a supply unit I would say our role was something less than a participant and something more than a spectator. There was a gap we were guarding, a wadi, and we never allowed the Germans to come through that when they were attacking. When we had captured our objectives we had the order to make way for our armour to cross through.

Then came the thunder of these armoured divisions, passing through us. I have never seen so many tanks going in one go. Two divisions, I think, passed through. If you want to know the size of two armoured divisions – if the head of the column was in Bangalore, the tail would be in Madras! So many tanks, so many armoured vehicles, so many personnel carriers. Numberless tanks passing through, thundering. And their dust clouds – we breathed dust, we ate dust, we drank dust.

Tom Somerville:

All this went on until 5 November. We stayed around the gun, firing intermittently, day and night. We did get the odd newsflash every now and then, one of Monty's little letters. But the end of the battle – that was the strangest feeling. We never felt it really *had* ended, because we had a lot more fighting, chasing Rommel all the way back to Tunis. It was a peculiar feeling when the end finally came; it's hard to describe it. Suddenly a holiday comes to an end; everything's finished and you've got to go back to work. But this ... no more bombing, no more shelling, no more rushing round ...

Les Rowe:

At the end of the battle when the 2/48th were relieved, out of a whole battalion – eight or nine hundred men – only forty-odd blokes were left. And I was one of them.

This Tommy ASC company had been told they had to come up to pick up the battalion, and they weren't very happy with their trucks out in the open on the sand. They had about fifteen trucks lined up for us, and we said, 'We'll only want two of those.' They wanted to know where the battalion was. And we said: 'This is it.'

There was one unexpected, distant after-shock of the battle for Sheila Parkinson (née Kershaw) of FANY, back in England:

My brother had joined the Royal Horse Artillery and was sent out to North Africa. He went across to Alamein and was blown up in a tank there. On his twenty-first birthday my mother had given him a silver cigarette case, which she'd had engraved with his name and college – he was always losing everything. And once again, by some extraordinary means, it crossed the Mediterranean via either Italian or German hands, and came back to the college and so to us – exactly as my husband's gold cigarette case had made its way back to me from Hong Kong.

So that the two cigarette cases were the final identifying of both of them. Strange, wasn't it?

Towards the end of 1942 Alec Dennis of the Royal Navy found himself serving with the Eastern Fleet and more or less penned up in Mombasa, Kenya's chief port on the east coast of Africa. The Eastern Fleet, a collection of superannuated and war-battered ships put together to present at least some kind of opposition to the Japanese in the Indian Ocean, had had to play fox to the very much better equipped and more powerful hounds of the Japanese Navy. It was a 'keep out of trouble, strike where you can' policy which got on the nerves and threatened the morale of everyone involved – including Dennis, by now First Lieutenant of *Griffin*. However, a welcome diversion brought a happier end to 1942:

I had to go and capture a French island called Mayotte, in the Comoros, just off Madagascar. That was amusing. We went roaring in at dawn through the reef and up to the harbour, and I got landed in the whaler with my braves. All the Frenchmen were asleep. The Governor of the island was in bed with somebody else's wife up the other end. So we had no problem at all. All these signs of decadence: peeling posters, the whole place unbelievably ramshackle. We just took over the island, and all the sailors got drunk on the brandy. That was an interesting experience – the only island I've ever captured.

Back in the UK, at the end of the year, seventeen-year-old Frank O'Donnell from Pipestone, Manitoba – still too young to drink, or vote, or even (legally) fight for his country – was doing his best to have a Merry Christmas in Kilmarnock:

One day we got in a conversation with a man in a Kilmarnock pub. He was interested in ferrets. So my friend and I allowed as how we'd got a ferret over in the barracks and we'd sell it to him for ten bob. The arrangement was that he would leave the ten bob with the barmaid and we'd bring the ferret over after parade, you see. So he went along with that.

We went back to the barracks and we got a shoe box. We put a dirty pair of socks in it. We put a few holes in the top of the shoe box and tied it up, brought it back to the barmaid and said, 'The ferret's sleeping. You mustn't disturb it. Put it under the bar and give us the ten bob.'

So somewhere in Kilmarnock there's a man who's paid ten bob for a dirty pair of socks, and he's madder'n hell! No wonder the Canadians got a bad name ... We were just boys, you know.

FIVE

Gathering Ground: 1943

*When I tasted this ice-cream made without sugar, I says,
'My God – the war is really on!'*
                                              Dudley Thompson, Jamaica

E. K. Powell, Jamaica: 'I tried to get in at sixteen. I went to the recruiting officer and he said to me, "How old are you?" I said, "Sixteen, Sir!" And he said, "Boy, go back home, and come back next week when you're eighteen." So I got in, you know. If my mother had found out ... she didn't even know. The first she knew was when I wrote to her from England, from Cardington in Bedfordshire, in March 1943, to say I was in the Royal Air Force. She really was upset with me.'

Kofi Genfi II, Gold Coast: 'I had never been away from home. And it wasn't easy to leave home – no, no. It wasn't easy, leaving your wife and children. I had three children – I have thirty-six now; I don't pride myself with it, it shows how bad I am – but then I had three children and a wife. I had to leave her behind. She was sorry – but you couldn't do anything, because you have been enlisted and so you are forced to leave her.'

Connie Macdonald, Jamaica:

There was a mood of fear in Jamaica then – they put the fear of God in us. We

173

were definitely positively told that the Germans wanted us because we were a stepping stone to the coast of America. So we were on our tenterhooks all the time.

Like England, Jamaica is an island. We depended on boats bringing things in. So if you are short of oil because the boat coming in was torpedoed, then the whole bloody island has no oil. Many country parts of Jamaica in those days didn't have electricity. So you had a bottle, you filled it up with paraffin and you put the cork in. You turned the bottle over, the paraffin soaked the cork, you lit the cork and that was your light for eating, for doing homework or anything. I can tell you, a lot of people got their eyebrows singed! Oh, yes.

Down in Kingston town, at a place they call Parade, they had two lists put up – a list of men reported missing and a list of men reported dead. And that list would go on and on ... Sometimes you'd go and you'd see the name of your cousin; you'd go back a few days later and see your friend's brother reported dead.

So we damn well knew there was a war on. And that's why I joined up in the ATS and went as an admin secretary into the British Military Hospital at Kingston.

All over the Commonwealth, with the war now more than three years old, men and women were still joining up, still doing their basic and specialised trainings, still longing to get on that troopship and leave home. Charles Bell, the half-Maori who had been caught trying to stow away on a troopship, made it at last into his revered Maori Battalion – and then, to his disgust, found himself allotted to coastal defence duties in New Zealand. It was to be another year before Bell could watch the Heads of Wellington Harbour slip away behind him, as he headed out for Italy.

In Canada, the peppery Geraldine Turcotte had more or less settled down to Air Force discipline. But there were still one or two spats with authority at home before she was able to volunteer for overseas duty:

My senior officer was really insolent to me one day, and I said, 'Lookit, let's go into your office.' We went into her office. I said, 'You take off that jacket with the pips on it,' I said, 'and I'll take *my* jacket off, and we'll just be two women!' Oh, yes, I did! I had a pretty good temper on me in those days. I could control it, but don't let anybody do anything that was mean – no, I couldn't stand that ... or cross me in any way! Well, you know – you have to stand up for your rights. If you don't, you're not worth your salt.

Anyway, they wanted women to go overseas. So I said, 'This is my chance!' So I went down to Sergeant Brown – we'd been friendly for a long time – and

I said, 'Brownie, this is our chance. What d'you think?' – and she said, 'Ho! Let's go for it!' So we marched down to the WD officer and we said, 'Here! We want to go! We'll give up our stripes, we'll do anything. Just get us on that boat!'

I'd enjoyed the station, but now I wanted to see the real thing, the sharp end. It was just in your blood. You wanted to be *there*!

For Jamaicans in Britain in 1943 there were plenty of cultural shocks in store. Coming from an island where sugar cane could be got for the chopping to one where sugar had been rationed almost out of existence brought Dudley Thompson up against reality: 'I remember being on a train going into London and vendors outside the carriage windows selling ice-cream – Walls ice-cream, I think it was. I bought some ice-cream for the boys and passed it into the carriage. Then I tasted it. Of course, we were not used to the strictures of England, the shortage of sugar. When I tasted this ice-cream made without sugar I says, "My God – the war is really on!"'

There were problems with the sugar ration for E. K. Powell too. As a guest in an English friend's house he noticed the family staring while he gaily spooned sugar into his tea, and was desperately embarrassed when they pointed out that it was rationed. This was the first that he had heard of rationing, having been cushioned from its effects in the airmen's mess at Cardington. Things went better for Powell, however, with the local girls, for whom the fit young Jamaicans were a great attraction:

We were sort of ... favourites, you know? Most of the people in Bedfordshire never saw black people before. We would run up from Cardington towards Bedford along the River Ouse, then come back down – something like two and three-quarter miles. The girls used to line the fence, because somebody told them there were some black men there, running. I suppose they were just fascinated, really.

At that age, mark you, we didn't have girlfriends – but there was one who liked me. We went to the Bedford Corn Exchange for dancing. Now, you know the British had this attitude of tapping on the shoulder; an 'excuse-me' dance. I mean, there were so many fellers after this girl – she was tall and blonde. So I said to her, 'Why do you like dancing with me, with all these fellers after you?' And she said: 'Oh – when I'm dancing with you, I am seen.' That's what she said! – 'When I'm with you, I am seen.' That was her motivation.

The air war that the newly arrived young men and women were joining was centred, as before, on the bombing of Germany. But things had changed since mid-1942 when Charlie Hobbs flew on his first operation with the Thousand Bomber Raid on Cologne. Now a combined offensive with the US 8th Air Force was under way, the RAF Stirlings and Lancasters raiding by night, and the USAF Liberators and Flying Fortresses by day under some fighter protection. Enormous damage was inflicted on cities and industrial targets as the bombers extended their range further into Germany and down to northern Italy. Tens of thousands of civilians were killed. Night navigation had been revolutionised by radio and radar developments, and the accuracy of bomb aiming was improved by the use of Pathfinders, highly trained crews who could locate and mark the target for the following streams of bombers. By the end of 1943 the RAF and USAF between them would have dropped over 200,000 tons of bombs on Europe.

But the German defences had also been improving. Their night fighters, guided on to the big planes by radar, pounced on the bomber streams going and returning. Flak installations, radar early-warning stations and powerful searchlight batteries were strung along the coast of occupied Europe and ranked in defensive lines to the north-west of the Ruhr and Berlin. It became more difficult to reach, bomb and return safely from such heavily defended targets at night, while during the day the American planes were being shot down at ever-increasing rates: sixty-five out of 291 – over 20 per cent – on one particularly bad sortie to a ball-bearing factory at Schweinfurt, east of Frankfurt on the River Main. Being a member of a bomber crew was, along with serving as a merchant seaman, one of the most dangerous and nerve-racking of all war jobs.

In January 1943 Charlie Hobbs was a rear-gunner with 83 Squadron, a Pathfinder outfit based at Wyton in Huntingdonshire. On the ground the twenty-one-year-old Canadian was very partial to dancing, to beer and to young ladies; but once in the air behind his four Browning machine-guns the job was all:

Once you're in the air, and you're going on an operation, you're all eyes – that's all there is to it. You're just one big set of eyes. That's right; you never stop. You're not necessarily looking for fighters, though that's primarily what you're doing. You're looking for anything that should be reported; might be ships below, might be other bombers nearby. You're a watchdog – with teeth.

I never shot down any fighters – not that I know of. I fired at them; but at night, you don't know. Unless that plane explodes, you don't know whether you got him or not. Hell, sometimes an encounter wouldn't even last four or five seconds. I think it was on our second trip that a Jerry came right across our rear end. I gave him a full burst when he went by, and he just didn't turn in after us. Now I don't know whether I hit him or not; but he certainly lost his nerve or his dare, anyway.

Over the target, the most vulnerable member of the crew – at least in his own estimation – was the bomb-aimer, stretched out on his belly with only a thin skin of metal between the flak (whose sound Charlie Hobbs likens to eating apples in church) and his vital organs. Dudley Thompson, having survived the shock of wartime sugarless ice-cream, was quickly trained as a navigator-bomb-aimer and joined 49 Squadron, another Pathfinder outfit, at Waddington in Lincolnshire, as one of only two Jamaicans on the station. He gives a graphic description of the bomb-aimer's job at the critical moment of the operation.

You're lying in the nose of the plane, lying flat on your parachute. You have on all your flying clothing, sometimes an electrically heated suit. You have on your heavy uniform and heavy mittens, you have the oxygen mask on. Everybody's behind you – you're right out in front, in the nose of that aircraft, just the perspex between you and Heaven – or Hell. You're right there, looking at the enemy.

You get over the target and you line up your bomb-sight, which has a sort of reflective light on the glass. When you are within a certain area you take charge of the navigation; you are in charge of that aircraft. The pilot takes his instructions from you. So you're going: 'Left-left ... right ... left-left ... right' and getting back grunts – 'Uh ... uh ...' – that's all that comes through to you. 'Left-left ... right ... steady – steady – steady ... Bomb doors open!' You feel a change: instead of going with the wind the plane takes a different lift altogether. There's a loud cracking of the ice coming off; a very loud crack, like a shot. And then: 'Bombs fused! Left-left ... right ... running up ... running up...'

You have your target map in front of you. You're hearing all sorts of talk and jokes, all kinds of things going on: 'Watch out, something's on the left there! ... What's that coming in on the right?' The rear-gunner saying, 'I don't see anything.' And the pilot's usually dead steady quiet. He's got a very demanding job; every little comment means something in an aircraft like that, demands a response from him.

'Left-left ... right ... left-left ... right ... steady ... steady ...' That's all you're doing; you're looking at that line on your bomb-sight and you're lining up that bomb-sight, really lining it up. A quarter of an inch up here means hundreds of yards down there. So you're getting it dead steady, and of course the aircraft is wallowing around because of air turbulence and the bomb doors being open. 'Steady ... steady ... steady ...' – pilot's doing his best, the line's moving and you're trying to hold it – 'steady ... steady ... steady ...' – your nose is getting nearer – 'steady ... steady ... steady-y-y ... Bombs gone. Boy – you're gone, too!

Like Paul Radomski, the Polish New Zealander piloting Stirlings with 149 Squadron, Charlie Hobbs lays emphasis on the accuracy of the RAF's bombing and rejects the suggestion that it amounted to a policy of indiscriminate destruction.

We abhorred what had happened at Coventry in November 1940. That probably attracted many Canadians into the Air Force; it was one of the strongest builders of pride and purpose. We all felt the same way about it – this was not a prime target, and the Luftwaffe had just wiped it out and killed I don't know how many thousand civilians. Now we resent the suggestion that we didn't go after targets, that we went after people. That is not true. We went after targets. If people got killed, that wasn't what we were primarily out to do. I can't stress that point too strongly. The area that we unloaded on was a target area, not the city of X. That's what they're trying to imply, by saying that we just bombed wherever we wanted. Indiscriminate bombing – that was not the case. We hit *targets*.

After the war I didn't feel guilty about taking part in the bombing – not one bit. I was *sorry*, about the damage that was done to beautiful things. That's as far as it went. You see, Canada's not old enough to have the charms of antiquity that they have in Europe. We don't have any of these beautiful 1000-year-old cathedrals to protect. Thinking as a young Canadian, it was impossible for me at that time to picture exactly what we were destroying.

The young men going out on these bombing operations had been plucked from ordinary civilian lives, from every kind of background and cultural tradition. Now they had to cope with highly complex, technical jobs, in conditions they could only have imagined in nightmares. They were well aware of the odds they were facing. They did not need a statistician to tell them that they would be lucky to survive twenty trips; they could see the gaps at the mess table after each raid quite clearly for themselves. Most, because they were young and fit and confident of their abilities, were able to keep a grip on their fear. And fear, says Charlie Hobbs, was something they all felt.

I had fear, I was never on a raid that I wasn't afraid. Anyone that tells me they went on ops and weren't afraid – they're just not living in the same world with the rest of us. I didn't live with fear, though; I wasn't terrified all the time. When you know you can do your job you're not as afraid; you just automatically do it. Like a turret is a mechanical device and you learn to handle it without even thinking about it, like driving a car. More than once I've been afraid – very afraid. But never to the point where I was petrified, frozen, and couldn't do my job.

It could suddenly affect people, though. We had a Scottish feller by the name of Crowe, Jock Crowe. Jock was lying on the floor of the plane as the bomb-aimer, looking through his sight, and he had his map on the floor down in front of him. He sat up to tell the pilot something and a bullet came right through his map. He developed an instant stutter, and he's still got that stutter as far as I know.

The New Zealander Paul Radomski, by now a veteran of almost a year's operational experience as a bomber pilot, had a natural phlegmatism that helped him cope. But he, too, remembers the effects of tension and suppressed fear on others:

I have known some to be disturbed in their sleep. You'd hear them screaming. In fact, I'm still in touch with one chap who was flying Spits off Malta for eighteen months. Not long ago I said to his wife, 'Can I take Jimmy out?' She said, 'Take him out and get him drunk, he might get a good night's sleep for once.'

I'll say this to you: everybody has their breaking point. Luckily, I didn't reach mine. I have seen people break and I felt sorry for them. The Air Force were bloody cruel. They had what they called a 'lack of moral fibre'. If you would not fly, you were stripped and sent to the prison camp. Uxbridge. That was a real stigma.

I can see how people could break, yes; but I can't condone it. There's a difference. I mean – here you've got a young chap of nineteen, let's say he's a sergeant. He's got his girlfriend. How would he feel if he could get out of prison camp, going home and seeing her? I think there was a lot of that. Fear of what other people might think; that kept a lot of people going.

I'm not saying the Air Force were right or wrong, but they'd put a hell of a lot of money into training their people and they couldn't afford to have them going like that. If one person had got away with it – we'd have all said: 'Bugger you!'

Charlie Hobbs:

The British had a very, very uncaring method of handling 'lack of moral fibre'. You see, they would not recognise shell-shock, which is purely a physical thing. We had fellers that got shell-shock badly; often you'd see them on a squadron, because the CO wouldn't turn them over for Administration to deal with. Because they knew what they would do with them. They would send them to the glasshouse and they'd have given them a dishonourable discharge after two years of hard labour, taken all their medals away from them. Shocking? – shocking is right! Now that was one of the reasons why, at times, we hated the British. When I say 'the British', I mean their system. That is a typical example.

Death, of course, was the figure that stood at the end of the road. Not death as the soldier generally experienced it, in bloody technicolour close-up; nor death as it impinged on the sailor, partly impersonal in terms of sunk or shot-down machines, partly personal in terms of burned, drowned, oil-smothered corpses fished out of the sea or littering the deck after an attack. Death for the airman almost always happened just round the corner; intangible, unseen, unheard. Soldiers and sailors could imagine the details of their own deaths from what they had seen, heard and smelled; a bomber crew member, says Paul Radomski, hardly ever saw his friends or enemies die:

They just didn't come back, and that was it. I don't think I've ever seen anyone get killed – I've seen them not come back. It's not like in the Army, when somebody's killed alongside you. The crews in the next hut – they just haven't come back, and that's it. Someone would clean up the hut, pack their gear up, and a few days later you'd have a new crew in there. You sort of get used to it. If a chap had a family you'd send his money home. But if he was a single man – and the majority of them were – you'd put his money on the bar and booze it away: 'We'll have one on So-and-so.' There was an expression that was used throughout the Air Force: 'Gone for a Burton.' It was things like that … that got you away from the stark reality.

You know it's not going to be you that doesn't come back. It's going to be that chap, or that one, or that one. But you know it's not going to be you.

But on the night of 16 April 1943, it was Charlie Hobbs.

We took off from Scampton in our Lancaster. We were off to Pilsen, in Czecho-slovakia, to hit the Skoda works there. It was a ten-hour trip, there and back – a long, long trip. We'd contracted to do forty-five operations and I'd done over forty, so this was to be just about the last trip of my tour before a long rest. We were Pathfinders; it was our job to find our target, to drop our bomb markers, then turn around and get the heck out of there.

We got all the way to our target with no serious problem. Then, on the way back, we got coned by searchlights just outside of Mannheim. Glen McNichol, our pilot, dived down very close to rooftop. I tried to use my guns on the searchlights and put about 2000 rounds into – something!

We flew on about half an hour and we were getting our height back up to a few thousand feet. Then one of the engines conked out; it had obviously been hit by flak. That left us with three engines. We flew for say, another hour, and this time one of the other engines caught fire. We put that out chemically so we wouldn't have to dive it out; otherwise we wouldn't have had much height left. From now on, height was critical. A Lancaster flies well on two engines, but it takes you a long time to get your height back up.

So we got into France. Then a third engine conked out. The intercom was gone, so the pilot sent Harold Beaupre, the navigator, back to tell me that they were going to bail out. He told me to come forward, so I prepared myself and started to go forward. Then a fighter came in out of nowhere. I hadn't seen him. He just came in and blew us all to hell – just blew my turret right off, and set the plane on fire.

I got up front. In the meantime everybody had bailed out except the pilot, who was holding the plane steady, and the mid-upper gunner who'd been wounded. So I stood beside Nic, the pilot, and I said, 'I'll go back and see if that fire can be put out.' I was gone about five minutes, but I couldn't put it out with just the hand extinguisher. When I got back to Nic he says, 'Take off my harness. We're too low to bail out now.' He was as cool as a cucumber, this guy.

So I did, and I just stood beside him; I had my arm just leaning on the back of his seat. In came the fighter again. It killed Nic on the next shot. The plane went up a little bit, then straight down. We hit the ground from about 1000 feet – right into a stone house. Nic was killed outright, he was dead before we hit.

I must have been thrown clear. I was out cold. When I came to I was still in the wreck. I stood up. Couldn't find Nic at all, but I found the mid-upper gunner, Willis. He had something wrong with his leg. That's when I found I had no use in my arms; they just would not function. The jolt, I guess. So I wandered off and went down the road a little piece and a Dutch boy followed me – he was a slave labourer on one of those farms. He pulled off my parachute harness for me, and my overalls and my flying boots. I was able to walk. I wandered back to where Willis was; he'd just cleared himself of all this wreck he was under. I knew where the fellers had hidden, because I'd heard them – they'd gone to a farmhouse nearby, all but one of them. I'd no sooner got there and got a dish of water to wash the blood off me when the Germans pulled in and surrounded us. Said if we'd give our parole they'd take us off for first aid. Which they did.

By February 1943 the Allies' North African campaign was drawing to a close. The outcome was not a foregone conclusion; the Axis armies in Tunisia – German and Italian – still numbered about 300,000. But the successful landing to the east during 'Operation Torch' in November, and the rapid advance westwards of Montgomery's 8th Army, would eventually squeeze them up into the western 'horn' of Tunisia, around Tunis itself.

The 8th Army, after its three years of hard fighting in the desert, was wise in the ways of make-do-and-mend and other old soldiers' manoeuvres, as the New Zealander gunner, Tom Somerville, describes:

There was a canteen on the desert road, a big roadside place; everybody stopped there. Our gun sergeant said to me, 'How about if we have a breakdown, Slim?' – everybody called me Slim in those days. So we got outside this canteen, and our boys were all ready, and in. So Bert and I got the spanners out and were tapping away at the pipes underneath the bonnet, and the traffic had to stop behind us. The whole convoy had to stop; and as soon as they saw what was happening, they all came flooding into this canteen, very grateful for our 'breakdown'.

We made our own furnettes. We'd have a cylinder of tin, a five-gallon tin, and we'd have a cone – you'd slip the cylinder down over the cone and run some solder round, and there you'd have a furnette. Used to burn petrol in it – a Benghazi Burner.

Every fifteen minutes we'd stop and have a brew-up of tea on our Benghazi Burners. Then there'd be a row of jokers standing out there on the sand, earnestly looking at the ground. And there'd be another row, further out, squatting behind a tree – but there were no trees...

Nila Kantan, coming west on the long trek with his Indian supply corps, was overwhelmed by the contrast between Tunisia and the desert countries where he had been living for so long:

We were all accustomed to the drab, dull desert scenery. When we passed through the centre of Tunisia and saw fertile valleys, orchards, terraced fields – it was all enchanting. So much beauty: we thought we had been transported to Paradise. And then these French people and French children, racing across our vehicles and shouting something in French – they were very happy.

Then when we neared Tunis, we met the British 1st Army coming from the east. What a contrast between these two armies! They were fresh from England – absolutely the glowing, fresh complexion. Brand-new uniforms and vehicles, all camouflaged to merge with the green environment. And we, who had advanced nearly 2000 miles from Alamein – we were unkempt, unshaven with beards, shattered. Our vehicles had no windscreen, no mudguard, no headlamps, no superstructure, everything secured with wire. We were dark and very bad-looking; they thought we must be some aliens from some other world. 'What – is *that* the 8th Army? These bloody junglies – what can they do?'

Then we went straight and caught the throat of the Afrika Korps. Then they begin to respect us very much. We were crowned with glory. Completely!

Rommel, by now a sick man, had been invalided back to Germany on 6 March. It was the end for the Afrika Korps. On 13 May Nila Kantan happened to be walking by as Rommel's successor, General von Arnim ('absolutely spick and span, and immaculately dressed – Prussian military etiquette') took a salute and surrendered. 'The British soldiers came and hugged me. I said, "What the hell is happening? Why do you hug me?" They said, "Don't you know what happened there? He surrendered!" Then I became very happy, very elated.'

But the stamp of three years of desert warfare would not be quickly erased; three years of life-and-death intimacy with the harsh, unfathomable character of the desert. 'As I was coming back from Tunisia to Alexandria I stopped at all the places where there was the wreckage. Every hundred yards a knocked-out tank, or a plane shot down, or a steel helmet. All those broken signboards: Knightsbridge, El Adem, El Agheila, Tobruk. All those places I have fought; I would never again see those places. Everything was so quiet, so calm, so perfect. So many memories came crowding in my mind. I wept. I did not want to leave.'

Frank Sexwale's memories of his service in the desert are far less affectionate. 'A white man's war,' he says, 'a British war. South Africa belonged to Britain; everything that the Afrikaner did, he got the notion from the master, Britain.'

In the case of Sexwale, a black South African, much of his disillusionment was grounded on his strong dissatisfaction with his own country's domestic policies on racial discrimination and 'separate development'. But non-white Second World War servicemen and women of the Commonwealth had more generalised causes of complaint in two areas in particular: pay and promotion. When all was said and done, your pay and promotion prospects in most branches of the services were better if you had a white skin, worse if you did not; and this in spite of the British Government's declared policy that there should be no colour bar in either the services or in colonial administration. Herbert Morrison, Secretary of State for the Home Department in the War Cabinet, remarked that giving the African dependencies self-rule would be 'like giving a child of ten a latch-key, a bank account and a shotgun'. Whatever the merits of his political stance, it was a revealing simile. Some politicians and senior figures in the War Office did not believe in equality of opportunity; did believe, in fact, that they were dealing with people who could not measure up to their British counterparts.

In terms of promotion, the Jamaican, Dudley Thompson, says:

If an individual went for a board, recommended for a commission or promotion, all sorts of spurious arguments were put, like: 'Oh, we know that it's going to be difficult having men of colour as officers over other people.' There were feelings that men of colour had not properly proved themselves as full combatants.

Even in recruitment there were all sorts of obstacles placed against people of colour. I can remember seeing an advertisement in some Scottish Sunday newspaper for young women to join the WAAFs or the Land Army – 'No coloured people need apply.' In Trinidad, in the early stage of the war, there were almost riots because people wanted to join up and they were kept back. They were told, 'We don't need you.' The colonial government there was under pressure and was having to ask itself, 'How can we be exerting colour prejudice against these people, when these people are fighting against the same thing as we are? We are being embarrassed; what can we do?' There were running battles between the Colonial Office and the War Office, and it was the Colonial Office that was largely carrying the ball for us.

One London-based official in particular, Lieutenant-Colonel Cole of the Colonial Office, had doggedly set himself to champion the cause of equal prospects of promotion and pay for Commonwealth aspirants.[10] On 25 October 1941, for example, he received a letter from a War Office official about a West Indian signalman, O. St Elmo Smith, who was seeking a commission. The letter recommended that Smith should be considered only for command over 'an African Transport Unit or Labour corps'; it would be undesirable for him to 'hold any command over British soldiers'. Colonel Cole writes back, 'Reading through the correspondence ... one does get the impression that this man's colour had militated against his acceptance for a Commission in the Army.'

Another 1941 case in which Colonel Cole's advice was sought was that of Private H. K. George of the Highland Light Infantry, a soldier from the Gold Coast who had applied for consideration for a commission in the Royal West African Frontier Force. 'As I think you know,' Colonel J. H. Woods wrote to Cole from the War Office in Cheltenham, 'the Government has decided that all who hold British Nationality shall be eligible for consideration for commissions. On this ruling this man must be considered, but where he is used is another matter. At the same time if he is once commissioned, it will not be very easy to keep him out of Africa without making it pointed.' Africa, of course, would be a more likely place for a commissioned George to exercise command, since the idea of him commanding British (i.e. white) troops or of exercising command in Britain was unthinkable at the time.

Colonel Cole comments, reasonably:

In view of HMG's assurance in respect of equal treatment of coloured British subjects ... I do not think that it would be possible for [the Colonial Office] to object to the posting of an officer to the RWAFF on any colour ground ... There will be a certain amount of misgiving in some quarters on the appearance of an African on equal terms with British officers and, after the war, Africanisation of the officer corps might have some adverse effect on voluntary recruitment, for a time.

... Personally, I think that it will have a very good effect if a limited number of African officers are given the opportunity to command Africans. My view is that, in principle, we can not, and we should not, attempt any colour discrimination in the selection of Army officers for service with the African military forces.

Private George was subsequently found unfit, at his Commission Interview Board, for training at an OCTU. But in October 1941 the first African candidate did arrive in Britain to be trained as an officer. In 1942 Sergeant Seth Kobla Anthony (known with crunching Army humour as 'Blondie'), another Gold Coast man, was granted a second-lieutenant's commission in the Gold Coast Regiment, having been judged a 'great success' by his OCTU. Even then there were hiccups – Anthony's first pay cheque was held up for six weeks, so that he had to borrow money. 'A poor return for a man hundreds of miles away from home who is ready to fight for the Empire,' fumed his major in a strong letter to the Colonial Office. 'He cannot but take away with him a sense of injustice as well as a very poor opinion of Army organisation.'

It was just as well that the major did not see a telegram from the Governor of the Gold Coast, Sir Alan Burns, sent to the Colonial Office just after Sergeant Anthony had started his OCTU course, in which the Governor disclosed that the War Office was intending Anthony to receive Malta Artillery rates of pay (two-thirds of British rates). The WO also intended that he should not actually be commissioned until he had returned to the Gold Coast – on the grounds that he might die on the way back, and the War Office would then be liable to pay an officer's gratuity to his dependants! 'A further example of meanness and unimaginative discrimination,' was Burns's comment.

Obstacles to promotion to commissioned rank were a bone of contention for these non-white servicemen and women with potential as officers; but, after all, only a limited number of non-regular volunteers would want to attain commissioned rank in any case, regardless of their racial origin. What concerned everyone was pay; and here the national – or perhaps the colour – differentials were clearly marked out.

The problems arose partly from the muddles associated with Britain's possession of so many small, scattered territories, nominally under the aegis of Whitehall but in fact largely run by their British governors and officials and, to a greater or lesser extent, their local officials. For example, in 1942 a captain in a Caribbean island's local defence force could expect to be paid 23s.6d a day in St Vincent, 21s. in St Lucia, 16s.6d in British Guiana and 10s.6d in Dominica. Similar rates for a sergeant would be 4s., 6s., 6s.6d and 2s.6d; for a private 1s.9d, 2s., 2s.6d and 1s.6d. Local officers received the same pay rates as the British, but the British received an additional Colonial Allowance of 1s.8d a day – except in the Bahamas, where it was 5s.3d, and in Jamaica where it was nothing! This was plainly a nonsense, and in 1942 all pay was unified across the Caribbean; but Other Ranks received only two-thirds of the British allowances, because of the perceived difference in their cost of living.

The differential in family allowances between British and other servicemen was a real cause of resentment, particularly among newly appointed African officers such as Second-Lieutenant Anthony. In Anthony's Gold Coast Regiment, for example, African officers' family allowance had been recommended at two-thirds of their British counter-part. Africans sensed a grudging attitude, a reluctance to accept black soldiers on an equal footing with the whites. Their suspicions were not unjustified. 'We originally approved the grant of a lower rate of family allowance to African officers,' says a War Office minute of 26 November 1943, 'on the logical ground that a family is cheaper to maintain in Africa than in the UK. There may, however, be political reasons for disregarding this argument – (a) to avoid the usual cry of racial discrimination, and (b) to encourage by special treatment African candidates for commissions ... I am bound to say I see little or no reason for giving African officers the same rate of family allowances as British. I cannot believe that the cost of maintaining an African family is anything like the same as the cost of maintaining a European family in England.'

To this unimaginative statement the Resident Minister for West Africa shrewdly riposted that 'this suggests that an African of this [officer] class should *aim* at a standard of living below that of the European ... a suggestion which is contrary to present policy in West Africa'. And Colonel Cole adds his own contribution: 'The African officer must conform to the standard set for military officers and that standard is measured by the European element ... He has to maintain the status of an officer if he is to keep the respect due to his position in command of the African ranks ... He must not be treated as a child of charity in these matters, and liable to be regarded with a measure of contempt by the African soldiers as "dan godi" [the son of "thank you"] which would be fatal to any chance of success with African officers.'

The African officer, if paid the same allowance as an unmarried European subaltern, would receive 3s.2d a day. Add a wife and children and the rate would rise to 8s.6d a day; about £3 a week, which – considering that basic pay was about £8 a week – was certainly worth making a fuss about.

The basic pay of an African NCO was about two-thirds the rate of a British NCO. Allowances ran at the same differential: 1s. a day for warrant officers, 6d for sergeants. African privates, stuck right at the bottom of the Allied basic pay scale, were still being paid at the rate which white British Tommies had grumbled about before the First World War:

> *A shilling a day,*
> *Blooming good pay,*
> *Lucky to touch it,*
> *A shilling a day.*

As for an African private's allowances, Colonel Cole of the Colonial Office commented: 'It is the case that while such allowances as war pay, or family allowance, have been bestowed all over the Empire to locally enlisted personnel e.g. Malta, Cyprus, Palestine, West Indies, Gibraltar, Ceylon, Mauritius, etc., the African soldier has received neither war pay nor statutory allowances. He remains where he started in the matter of his daily pay. I would contend that he has merited, in this war alone, consideration at least equal to the others.'

Pay differences did not go unnoticed. John Mumo, a Kenyan serving in the East African Army Medical Corps, remarks: 'On the battlefield there was no distinction, but back in camp it was different. Even our pay was different from the white soldiers. The askaris, the ordinary Kenyan soldiers, didn't like that.' And Aziz Brimah from the Gold Coast, soon to be fighting in Burma, confirms that 'British privates were paid much more than Gold Coast NCOs. In Burma it didn't bother us. At that time you only thought of getting something to eat, more bullet, more water – and then fighting. That was all our interest at that time. But later, we thought about it. And all this made us to help Kwame Nkrumah to put up the revolution for our independence after the war.'

Rates of pay were governed by the low cost of local labour in Africa, as well as in other colonies. But the war situation, in which everyone was making the same effort and taking the same risks for the same common end, did bring about changes. In 1943, when African troops were beginning to be sent to Burma, an expatriate allowance of two shillings a month was proposed by the GOC West Africa ('far too little', someone at the Colonial Office tartly scribbled in the margin). This was soon doubled. Later that year the Colonial Office suggested raising the pay of troops from the Seychelles and Mauritius to full British rate, from its current two-thirds. A tremendous amount of paper and ink was expended trying to work out how to allow Seychellois and Mauritians to be seen to draw the same money at the pay table as their British colleagues, without swelling the men's family allotment – a proportion of their pay automatically put aside and sent home to their families. The Governor of the Seychelles, in particular, foresaw social unrest in the islands if the men's families had spent the extra money before those who had earned it could get home to claim it.

South Africa set its own agenda. The recommendations of the South African Parliament's 1943 Select Committee on Soldiers' Pay and Allowances exemplify the situation there. On basic pay: Coloureds should receive half the white rate, Africans two-thirds of the Coloured rate. On pensions: Coloureds two-thirds of whites, Africans two-fifths. For 100 per cent disablement: whites would get £200 a year, Coloureds £75, black Africans £50. Whites' child allowance would extend up to age eighteen for a boy, twenty-one for a girl; blacks' to age fourteen and eighteen respectively. Whites should get thirty days a year leave; Coloureds twenty-four days; blacks eighteen days. And so on...

All these examples serve to show the very wide differences across the British Commonwealth in prospects for promotion and in the application of pay and allowances. In the tone of Colonel Cole's notes from the Colonial Office, and in the suggestions of the Governors of various dependencies, one can already detect a realism about the aspirations to equality of Commonwealth people and a setting of British shoulders to the wheels of progress towards independence, rather than a futile standing in their path. Not that the realism was unequivocal. 'The true philosophy in these matters', suggests an unsigned minute in the Colonial Office files for 1942, 'must be that, where we have large military forces serving the Crown composed of people of many races and colours, we must seek to avoid fundamental differentiations in terms of service which are nakedly based on race or colour.' That *nakedly* seems to beg a question or two.

The feelings of black soldiers about their white officers varied widely too. The Kenyan medical orderly, John Mumo, says, 'All our commissioned officers were British. As far as officer-askari relations were concerned, it was just a matter of military discipline. When we were obeying orders we didn't have at the back of our minds that this was a white man giving us orders. We were all just soldiers.'

But Frank Sexwale's angle on the relationship was rather different:

Relationships between the South African officers and their men were master-servant. It broke our spirit. If you are not armed, then the white man is a superior and you are an inferior person. Army discipline stipulated that an African sergeant should take orders from a European private. It was a question of being a white man and a black man. Exactly what was happening in this country: they carried the policy from here into battle.

English, Australian, New Zealand officers – we were friendly with them. But when South African officers came around, conversation just stopped. With the other nationalities, on leave in Cairo, we could have social contact, a few drinks. But it was never like that with South African officers or white NCOs.

It became so painful that in later years I was reluctant to talk about it. It was nothing to be proud about, being a soldier under the South African government. We were never soldiers, in fact – we were just black civilians in uniform.

Whitehall was well aware of the likely problems if black officers were to serve in Africa. Along with the War Office and Colonial Office correspondence about Private George's potential commission is a minute dated March 1941: 'If there was a likelihood of a West African officer being sent to serve in East Africa where he might come into contact with South African officers, etc., the GOC in East Africa ought no doubt to be consulted.'

White Commonwealth soldiers, finding the South Africans' rigid colour segregation unacceptable, would sometimes challenge it. Nila Kantan's British colleagues unwittingly brought him shame and embarrassment when they were passing through Tobruk one night and decided to stop at the NAAFI canteen.

I told them, 'I am not coming.' He said, 'Why?' I said, 'This is a South African area. You see this? Black canteen – white canteen. Black urinal – white urinal. You see? Everything distinction. So they won't serve me. I am not a white man,' I said.

He said, 'What nonsense, what you are talking. We are here. Come along.' I went in. They ordered. He served only the Britishers and not me. They said, 'Why, what about him?' He said, 'No, he won't be served here. He'll have to go to the black canteen.'

I told the British soldiers, 'You have humiliated me.' Then they threw all the plates and everything. The Military Police had to interfere. I said, 'Come on, let us get out of this place.' They also came. We opened our own tinned rations; then we ate that.

I didn't like South Africans at all. I felt very much humiliated among them. They were all of the same mind. I have seen the black soldiers being abused venomously, in that unpronounceable language called Afrikaans. These soldiers were not armed, you know; they were all non-combatants. It was stupid. He is fighting for a cause, I am fighting for a cause. There should be that comradeship. But nothing of the sort. Very sad. That was one of my most gloomy experiences of the Second World War.

Ernest Khomari, the volunteer from Basutoland, had been occupied in Egypt on guard duties at the 28th Field Punishment Centre in Alexandria. Most of the Basuto soldiers of the African Auxiliary Pioneer Corps were engaged in heavy labouring duties in Syria – digging, road building, portering. Recently they had been learning anti-aircraft gunnery, so as to release British AA gunners for infantry duty. Now two companies of Basuto men embarked from Alexandria on the troopship *Erinpura*, bound for Malta where they were to help build and extend aerodromes and offload ships. But half-way there, on 1 May, they were spotted in a rough sea by a reconnaissance plane and attacked at dusk by thirty bombers, followed by a torpedo-plane which scored a direct hit on *Erinpura*. About 600 men died, most of them trapped below when the ship went down.

Ernest Khomari had a remarkable escape, and the tale he tells of his experience is fully worthy of a Sinbad:

The Germans put up a light, so that it became like day. They came to our boat, they identified that it was us and they torpedoed it – most dreadful – like a bomb, and the water flew away. The people down below were the first to get trouble. They came rushing up through the decks – you could see these people rushing, some of them walking on top of another. It was a panic, really.

I was down on the third deck, inside the ship. We felt a big bang and we made a decision to run to the top deck. I was a fit man at that time and I just walked over the weak on the stairs – just walked over them. The sirens were on. We ran to the top of the deck. We were given instructions by our officers that you don't move any way until you are instructed. The ship was slanting much. A bomb exploded above my head: all these people around me were killed instantly, but I didn't have a scar – nothing. Then a sailor-boy, an Englishman, came dressed in white. He had a lifebelt with a red lamp. I followed him up to the top deck, walking over the corpses. When I came to the top I looked into the sea, to find so many pieces of things in the sea. So many people, too – you could only see their heads, because of the lifebelts. One lifeboat only was on the water; the rest were still fastened around the ship.

The Englishman threw himself inside the sea; but I couldn't do that. I could not swim. I saw a big rope and tried to catch it. I don't know what made me fall, but I fell inside the sea from a great height. Then I paddled to the lifeboat. I remember everybody was trying to get on to the boat. I got on and I thought to myself, 'Well, now I am safe.' Then there was shouting: a thick rope, as thick as my arm, was still tying it to the ship. Then the ship fell over, right on to the lifeboat, and smashed it. And I went down, sinking, suffocated. I prayed for death on me: I thought it was prayer time.

Before you die, you do a lot of kicking. And when you kick, and you are inside the water, you fly up, like that! Then I was on top of the water. I took a breath. The lifeboat was beside me, upside down. The German boys saw that little boat; they came down again to it and bombed it. I was able to get two of the planks and I was floating. The sea was very rough at this time. The tides were big tides. I thought they were going to cover us. But that didn't happen. We were lifted up, up ... then dropped down – it felt like fifteen or twenty kilometres.

During the course of that I picked up a little suitcase, and I found it was the payroll! So I sat on the suitcase. It had a belt, with a bayonet and a revolver. I put the belt on. But then I missed the weight; the suitcase was on top and my head was inside the water. So I let the suitcase go.

The shark itself is a thing which has got a very little sight. It sees only whitish things. I had a white canvas shoe on my left foot. A shark saw it, it grabbed my foot and it dragged me down. He got me so well that he went many kilometres down with me. I stabbed it with my bayonet, and you know what it did? It tore my laces and got off my shoe. Then the lifebelt burst and blew me like a bullet to the top of the water.

I got on to one of the rafts, and picked up some wounded soldiers and put them on the raft. There was one officer who was a very good survivor, and he was boxing down my comrades and putting his own men on the raft. But I was very fit, a very good boxer – so I boxed *him* down and he went away.

We were floating like that in the sea. Some people were making prayers, some of my people were singing war songs. We saw a destroyer boat coming to rescue us and we paddled there; but the ropes were not where we could get hold of them. So off it went. Then we had to look for another one. We paddled there, too – like a bloody fish, we were so fast! Two more ships were full and they left us. The third one, when we came close to it, I took a jump from the raft, like a lion, and I was hanging on the side of the destroyer. It was smooth; you couldn't climb it or get a step hold. So I told the others who were hanging there to step on my body and get on the top. I had the hope that they would rescue me once they were on the deck. But they didn't. They forgot about me. Then my muscles gave out and I fell back on to the raft.

I was shouting, but no one was there to hear me. But then a sailor man came and said, 'Hey, George, let's go!' He took me right down into the engine room of the destroyer. We got to Benghazi; and there I could only see about sixteen men of my company. Most of them were drowned.

Pay attention and listen!
Listen to a pitiful thing!
This Eighth Army and Fifth Army,
They are still going forward in their work.
They attack mightily
To push back the Germans,
They capture countries,
They run with tanks.
The Spitfire dived!
Lightning shot up.
It left grief, it roared on!
The day was clear and beautiful.
With the Spitfire we Allies fight for victory.
We started in Africa, we reached Mellita.
We found battle, fierce battle
Fought by Maltese and the English;
And we Africans too fought in this battle,
For even this too we have learnt, we have learnt to fight.
Soldiers of different races were mixed;
And the Canadians too were there
When Sicily and Italy were taken.

Basuto soldiers' war song

The 'Operation Torch' landings in French North Africa in November 1942 had shown the Allies that landings *per se* need not invariably be associated with disaster. The shadow of Gallipoli had stretched forward over the years from 1915 to haunt not only the Australians, but also British planners of war operations; not excluding Winston Churchill, who had forcefully pushed through the catastrophic landings in the Dardenelles. Dieppe had seemed to confirm this, and had also lodged the image of the Canadians alongside landings and disaster. But in mid-1943 the time seemed right, to the Allied planners, for the opening of the long-awaited Second Front in Europe. In February the Russians had completed the encirclement and defeat of the German army besieging Stalingrad, and they had the invaders on the retreat in the south of the country. It would help the Russians enormously if the Germans were obliged to withdraw men and materials from the Soviet Union and commit them elsewhere. America wanted a Second Front opened as soon as possible. The British had the experienced 8th Army redundant in North Africa, flushed with the confidence of victory, and the 1st Canadian Division chewing its nails off with frustration in Britain.

The Americans had originally favoured a cross-Channel assault from England, but the lessons of Dieppe had been thoroughly borne in on their Commonwealth allies. Once committed to landings on the north coast of France, there would be no alternative to an all-out drive for Berlin and victory, a definitive insertion of all the Allied eggs in the one basket. The island of Sicily, lying where it did off the toe of Italy and within easy reach of reinforcements from Tunisia, seemed a safer bet. If an invasion became bogged down there, the setback could be contained within one small island. If things went well, the armies might carry on across the narrow Strait of Messina and begin an advance through mainland Italy.

The problems of a drawn-out, bitter, attritional slog up the heavily defended Italian peninsula, whose considerable German garrison would be reinforced once the invasion began, were plain to see. There were some internecine tensions too. General Dwight D. Eisenhower of the United States was to be Supreme Commander of the invasion force, comprising the US 7th Army under General George Patton and the British 8th Army under General Montgomery. Eisenhower had to be persuaded away from his preference for invading Corsica and Sardinia, which could have offered mainland invasion sites further up the Italian peninsula than Sicily. Then Montgomery's suggested alterations to the Sicilian invasion plan seemed, to some US officers, to give the British too many publicity plums in the form of towns to capture, while leaving the Americans to advance through inglorious (though picturesque) villages and countryside. There was also the ticklish question of how to use the Canadians so that they would be operating as a large, identifiably Canadian body as demanded by their C-in-C in Britain, General McNaughton, yet would not be exposed as cannon-fodder for another fruitless slaughter to mirror the disaster at Dieppe. General Montgomery had reservations about using such untried troops in such a hazardous operation. But the Canadian Prime Minister, Mackenzie King, whom some had thought to be deliberately holding back the Canadians in Britain because of French Canadian pressure at home, let it be known that his country would take a very dim view of any further inaction on the part of its troops – to say nothing of the troops themselves, some of whom had been stalled and unhappy in Britain since December 1939.

The date of the commencement of 'Operation Husky' was set for 10 July 1943. One of the most important tasks was for paratroops of the 1st

Italy and Sicily

Turin • Milan •

Gruppignano •
Udine •

Trieste •

Po
Po Valley

Massa •
Gothic Line
Rimini •

Florence •
Leghorn •
Monteccio •
Foglia

ITALY

Adriatic Sea

CORSICA

Rome •
Liri Valley
Arielli
Ortona •

Route 6
Gustav Line

Anzio •
Monte Cassino •

Minturno •

Naples •
• Vesuvius
• Salerno

Bari •

SARDINIA

Tyrrhenian Sea

Strait of
Messina

Palermo •

Messina •
• Reggio di Calabria

SICILY

Catania •
Primasole
Bridge

Pachino •
Cape Passero

100 miles

150 km

Airborne Division to capture the Primasole Bridge on the route to Catania, half-way up the eastern side of Sicily and well in advance of the general area of assault in the southern toe of the island. Ronald Henriques from Jamaica, who had volunteered for paratroops after arrival in England, was one of those detailed for this dangerous job: 'We dropped with the first landings; Americans drove our planes. That was the first time I'd dropped into fire. When you're dropping, you don't actually see those shots fired at you; you probably might hear it. You come down pretty fast, you know. You're terrified, at first, but after a while you get accustomed to it. The boys used to say, "Come on, Ron – let's get going!" You just got to have some luck, you know?'

The 1st Canadian Division, about 20,000 strong, came ashore from their landing craft around Pachino, near Cape Passero in the extreme south of the island. Among those landing was the 2nd Field Regiment of artillery, with the Kilmarnock ferret-fancier, Frank O'Donnell, in tow – still two months short of his eighteenth birthday, rather seasick and extremely glad to regain dry land:

We went on that ship in the Clyde and we were on the damn thing for twenty-eight days before we landed in Sicily – twenty-eight days stooging round the Atlantic. The day before the landing there was a hell of a storm – God, the waves were up to the deck and that wind was blowing *fierce*. We were supposed to go in on landing craft which were suspended from the side of the ship; they were to be let down by pulleys and so on. We weren't at all sure how that was going to work. Anyway, by the time the day came the storm had subsided, so we went in – this would have been early in the morning; the commandos had gone in a couple of hours earlier. We didn't know it, but the ship that carried the guns for our particular unit and battery had been sunk in the Mediterranean, so we had no guns.

Going in, we hit a sandbar. The water wasn't that deep, but it was deep enough for me, because I couldn't swim. It wasn't over my head, but for a moment I thought it was – we'd been told it would be knee-high and got a surprise when it was neck-high! Anyway, we got in all right – there wasn't much opposition that morning, though later on there were a few air raids aimed at the ships. The objective, we'd been told, was the airfield at Pachino. We saw a few Italian prisoners being marched back, a couple of our guys with wounds coming back.

We didn't have any guns, of course, so there was confusion about what we were supposed to be doing. Eventually they used us to haul ammunition back and forth. Before the Sicilian campaign was over we finally got some guns from the British 8th Army – these were old twenty-five pounders. They weren't shooting very straight. They were all worn out, the calibration was all wrong. They were rejects from the desert.

The 1st Canadian Division suffered very few casualties that first day, getting ashore and established at a cost of seven killed and twenty-three wounded, and taking 680 Italian prisoners-of-war. It was a great success and Mackenzie King looked forward to a publicity coup back at home – the Canadians' first uncostly and effective operation. However, in spite of his and Churchill's appeals to US President Roosevelt for the Canadians to be included in the communiqué breaking the news of the Sicilian landings, the broadcast from Algiers on 10 July omitted mention of the Canadians – for 'security reasons', according to General Eisenhower. Ten minutes later the Pentagon issued its own communiqué naming 'British, American and Canadian troops': too late to appease Mackenzie King, who went public with his own message asserting that the Canadians ought to merit an equal mention for an equal job done. This was not the last instance of insensitive handling, for four days after the landings General McNaughton was refused permission to visit his troops in Sicily; his presence might, it appeared, distract the men from their duty. McNaughton had to wait another five weeks, by which time the 8th Army had reached Messina at the north-eastern point of Sicily, the fighting was over, and 100,000 Italian and German troops had withdrawn across the straits into mainland Italy.

The culture shock of Sicily, after being cooped up in Britain, hit young Frank O'Donnell hard:

It was all hills – it was rugged terrain and dry. The roads were powder, so every movement sent up a huge cloud of dust. And it was *hot*.

We were kept out of the main cities; we weren't allowed into places like Palermo and so on. We didn't have much to do with the local Sicilians, because first of all we hadn't been there long enough to know any of the language – later we got used to it – and secondly, they were so poverty-stricken that they were hardly of any interest to us. We were pretty well living on our rations. They did get brave enough to come out and beg food from us, but it was kind of a hands-off approach on both sides. You might find a few chickens and things like that, but most of the farms were so poverty-stricken that really there wasn't anything worthwhile to interest a soldier who was looking for something to eat.

They were just so poor. We'd pass a shallow grave – casualties of ours – and the feet'd be sticking out without boots on. The peasants needed the boots. We didn't like that. I guess later on we got used to it, as we got more used to war. But at the time it didn't make us very happy.

Before the Sicilian campaign was over, 160,000 Italians had been killed or taken prisoner. Altogether nearly 400,000 Italians had been lost since the war began; more than twice that number were committed in fighting on various fronts. It was too much for an essentially non-industrial, non-militaristic country. On 25 July Benito Mussolini was dismissed and imprisoned by King Victor Emmanuel; a fortnight later Italy signed an act of surrender. Now the Germans in Italy, deprived of their ally in the field, dug in their heels for a long campaign; in essence, by holding the Allies up at one prepared defensive line after another, to make their progress north as slow, difficult and painful as possible – an object in which, given their already fundamentally hopeless position, they succeeded brilliantly.

Gordon Fry of the Capetown Highlanders, last glimpsed drinking rusty German radiator water after his capture at Tobruk in June 1942, had been penned up in a succession of Italian prisoner-of-war camps. He'd volunteered for farm work in Northern Italy, thinking that he would be better fed and have an enhanced opportunity to escape, and had 'never felt so ashamed in my life' when the British prisoners lined up to boo him and his compatriots as they left their camp near Rome. However, after Italy's surrender the Italian guards lost interest in their charges, and on 8 September – a week before his twenty-third birthday – Fry and two friends decamped. They passed from farm to farm for the best part of three months, killing time, waiting for the Allies to arrive from the south to liberate them. One farmer and his household proved particularly friendly: 'They didn't like the Germans. "*Tedeschi!*" – oh, they hated them. All they wanted from us was a note to say they'd helped us, because they'd heard about the Indians and the Australians and they were dead scared of them.'

At last, near Christmas, the farmer decided it was time for his guests to go.

One afternoon two real Al Capone types pitched up in this little car to take us to Milan. They gave us guns, and said, 'If anyone stops the car, just let them have it.' It was so cramped in the car and we all wanted to go to the toilet. So they stopped in this station. When we went into the toilet there were Germans there. It was one of those where you talk over the top: you could see their feet and their heads, kind of thing. Quite a moment.

They took us to this place where they had all the contraband in the world – the foodstuffs, the tea and the coffee, the silk stockings, the lot. They were obviously smugglers. Next morning they took us to the border. We get to this place, an inn. Of course the bloke's not there, the guide. Eventually he pitches up and says: 'No, too late – *domani*.' So we said, '*Niente* – we're going now.' He says, 'But it's light!' We say, 'We don't give a damn. We're going!'

So we go to where we can see the sentries, and looking down we see the border fence. Now he says, 'I'm going to go down there and cut the fence, and when I make a sign, you come.' Well, of course, as soon as he touched that fence all the alarm bells began to ring. So we didn't wait for him to call us – we were down, and through, and up the other side. Of course the sentries were firing shots all over the place. We get to where there's a tobacco patch and something that looks like mealies; so we got in there.

The guide had pushed off by this time. We didn't know if we were in Switzerland, or in some sort of no man's land. We made our way to this little cottage where there's this old Italian. We're talking to him when all of a sudden, round the corner, here comes this bloke. So we thought: 'Oh, God – right on the border and we have to get caught by a German!' But my mate says, 'It's OK – he's Swiss.'

They took us to this pub on the other side and everybody bought us drinks – and we got absolutely sloshed!

While Gordon Fry's ordeal was ending, Charlie Hobbs's was just beginning. After surviving the crash of his Lancaster bomber in France, the Canadian rear-gunner was hustled off to the Dulag Luft transit camp for captive airmen near Frankfurt. Here he was interrogated by the Gestapo.

They wanted information. They tried everything to get you to tell them things. They wanted to know what squadron you flew on, who your CO was and so on. You gave them name, rank and number; and you just sat there for a long, long time before they finally gave up. They used all sorts of threats. For instance, they fired off a shot in the hall and said, 'There's your buddy from the crew – he wouldn't talk.' They hadn't killed him, of course, but at the time you didn't know that.We hadn't a stitch of clothes on, so they really had us at a disadvantage. I was scared all right – I was just a kid. You don't feel you've got a friend in the world when you're in that kind of position.

Another Allied prisoner-of-war was in an even worse position in July 1943. Rod Wells, the Australian farmer's son who had been shipped by the Japanese to Sandakan in Borneo after the fall of Singapore, had been working with another Australian prisoner, Captain Lionel Matthews, to make useful contact with the local people. By now there were about

2000 Australian and 750 British prisoners-of-war in the Sandakan camp – designated the 'land of milk and honey' by the Japanese. It was scarcely that to the underfed, overworked and diseased prisoners. Captain Matthews had been trying to foment an uprising among the Filipino, Malay and Chinese workers; he had gone some way towards achieving it when someone – under torture – divulged his, Wells's and several other names. One of the pieces of information the Japanese extracted was that there was a radio in the camp, painstakingly constructed from items smuggled in from outside over the past year. On 22 July 1943 the captors made their move, as Rod Wells describes.

> They got a list of the parts from the Filipinos. I'd been keeping notes in code on everything that was happening to us, because those of us who were thinking long-term realised that we probably didn't have much future.
>
> Lionel Matthews was arrested that day and I had an unpleasant three days waiting for the axe to fall. Then they lined everybody up. Hoshijima called me out and said, 'You have radio set.' I said no, and he swung out and cracked me across the jaw, and dropped me and kicked me. They picked me up and put me on a vehicle, in front of the two thousand men on parade. Hoshijima said to them, 'You see this man? You will never see him again.'
>
> Then the Kempei Tai – the Japanese version of the Gestapo – took me over. I had raw rice pumped into me, down into my throat and lungs, stuffing me. Then they poured water in on top. Raw rice, of course, swells tremendously. About three hours later ... I cried for death. For three or four days after that I didn't have a motion. When I did, it bled and bled for months.
>
> They put a plank of wood across my chest, a bit of four-by-two. Two men jumped on this plank, one each side. They broke two ribs, cracked another. Then they threw me back in the cell. Pain for weeks – I couldn't touch my ribs. But it healed up by itself. I wasn't going anywhere, except to sit cross-legged all day.

After four months, when they realised they would get nothing more out of Rod Wells and Lionel Matthews, the Japanese transferred the two Australians out of the camp. But the misery continued for those still at Sandakan. Towards the end of the war the Japanese were in fear of what would happen to them if the Allies – by then threatening to invade Borneo – should discover how their prisoners-of-war had been treated. So the entire complement of sick and starving men at Sandakan was moved out in sections on the Sandakan Death March to Ranau, a journey of 165 miles on foot through thick jungle. On a rice ration of three ounces a day the prisoners staggered forward. Those who fell out were shot.

On 29 May 1945 the Sandakan camp was put to the torch. Three hundred men too ill to move were shot to death. The remainder of the prisoners, 536 men, were herded along the twenty-day journey to Ranau. Three hundred and fifty died or were murdered along the way. On 25 June 1945 – seven weeks after the end of the war in Europe – 183 prisoners arrived in Ranau. After another month only thirty-three were still alive. Six managed to escape: the rest were machine-gunned to death.

Burma, on the eastern borders of India, had been one of the British Empire's half-forgotten corners long before the British forces that fought there during the Second World War designated themselves the 'Forgotten Army'. The country, shaped like a quarter-size India, falls south from its Chinese northern border for 1000 miles through jungle-covered mountains, along the pair of river valleys called Irrawaddy and Sittang, to a ragged mass of rice paddies, swamps, islets and tidal creeks known as chaungs around the many mouths of the Irrawaddy. The capital, Rangoon, is situated on the eastern side of this stubby southern toe of Burma; a long, thin spur trails further south, down the western side of the Siam–Malay peninsula. Burma yields oil, rubber and chiefly rice, for which reasons alone it was a desirable asset for the Japanese when they opened their Far Eastern campaign on 8 December 1941. To them, Burma was also strategically threatening as a conduit for American supplies to the nationalist Chinese army they were fighting; these supplies were passing into China along the west-east Burma Road in the north of the country. Securing the country would enable the Japanese to choke off the supplies; it would also guard the northern and western flanks of their Malayan and Siamese and Indo-Chinese conquests. And, later on, Burma might provide a springboard into India.

In January 1942, while Japanese forces were advancing down the Malayan peninsula to capture Singapore, others were moving across the Siamese border into Burma. By 9 March Rangoon was in their hands; then, reinforced, they pushed quickly north up the Sittang and Irrawaddy valleys, meeting, beating and driving before them Indian, Chinese and British forces. By the end of April they had taken Mandalay and Lashio in the north, cut the Burma Road, and pushed the Chinese back into China and the British and Indians back into India. It would take the Allies another three years, almost to the day, to drive the Japanese out of Burma again.

The British and Indian 14th Army – the 'Forgotten Army' – was commanded by General Sir William Slim, at first under General Wavell (who had been appointed British C-in-C in India after his removal from command in the Middle East) and later under Admiral Lord Louis Mountbatten in his role as Supreme Commander, South-East Asia. As the 8th Army regarded the Suez Canal in Egypt, so the 14th Army saw the Indian border as the wall against which it would resolutely place its back. The Americans under General 'Vinegar Joe' Stilwell felt the same about the Chinese border with Burma. They were most interested in helping the Chinese nationalists beat the Japanese in northern Burma and in China; the British were focused on recapturing their colonial possession by penetration from its western border with India. Both allies, painfully and with many arguments and setbacks, would have to reconcile and unite these differing roads to the same destination – the ousting of Japan from the entire region. Both would have to learn to contend with deadly and bloody fighting, in and out of monsoons and dry seasons, over and through some of the most difficult and disease-ridden country in the world, against an enemy who would rather die than yield.

As men and materials were beginning to build up back in England for the coming invasion of Europe, so India was filling up with Commonwealth soldiers, sailors and airmen waiting to enter Burma to fight the Japanese. Those who arrived in 1943 found the war here at a low ebb. The 14th Army had recently tried and failed with its first offensive effort, a thrust into the Arakan peninsula to the west of the Irrawaddy. The Arakan area of north-west Burma would be the 14th Army's main battleground over three campaigns. On this first offensive, started during the dry season late in 1942, they had hoped to capture the port of Akyab on the southern Arakan coast – important both as a potential jumping-off point for the recapture of Rangoon and as a means of cutting off Japanese sea supply routes to their forces up in the Arakan. But without effective amphibious support it all came to nothing and by April 1943 they were back in India, demoralised.

At this low time in the Far East the Eastern Fleet had been reduced to cruisers and destroyers, and Royal Navy morale had for too long received no boost from grand successes at sea. The South African, Bob Gaunt, was sent out to India as part of two flotillas of motor torpedo boats that had been fully stretched in wild actions in the English Channel. These young men bitterly resented the inaction that was forced on them when they arrived:

It was a complete waste of time. We'd all had immense experience in the Channel; we knew what we were doing. The boats were very fine boats; we all felt that they – and we, with all our operational experience – should have been in the Med, or continuing our work in the Channel. Our crews were far from green; they'd all seen action. But we just sat in harbour. No one was the slightest bit interested in us. The whole thing was a political move, I think – if the Japanese attacked India, at least we'd be seen to be there to meet them and put up some sort of a show.

I was lucky; I returned to England pretty quickly. But the others – they were volunteering for anything. Submarine, special service, midget subs: anything to get away. And the final insult came when the two flotillas were recalled to Trincomalee and they were used there, at times, to deliver the *mail* and the *laundry*. Eventually the Indians took them over, couldn't maintain them – and they were paid off and scrapped. Absolute bloody waste. Absolute disgrace. Someone along the line should have been court-martialled and strung up from the yardarm . . .

Training to fight formidable enemies in formidable terrain had to be rigorous and as realistic as possible. Over in Kenya, Derek Watson had been appointed Commanding Officer of the 4th Battalion the King's African Rifles, which was composed of Ugandan soldiers. 'I was put in charge of them because we'd had a bit of trouble. One of them had hit an officer or something of the sort . . . they were a bit bobbery.' Any bobberiness was soon ironed out of the men once Watson had taken them over to India and got them under training near Chittagong:

Well, I made the battalion march for a long distance, forty miles. Then we dug ourselves in and they were thoroughly tired. I had them on a bank; and I got our guns to fire over their heads. Then I got my mortars to fire over their heads. I gave them two hours' sleep after that – then I got my jitter parties to open up on them. You've got to find our how tired people will react under surprise attack. The askaris stood to quietly. It paid us dividends later in Burma. We had firepower discipline if there was an attack; they'd learned to hold their fire.

Training was realistic, too, for Krishen Tewari of 25 Indian Division, at Coimbatore in the jungles of south-west India:

We learned to live comfortably in the jungle and this was of enormous help in Burma. We learned to respect the forest. It was good, hard training. I remember the battle inoculation we were given. We had to crawl with all our equipment and rifle and so on – full kit – under a barrage of machine-gun fire. There were little explosives set up on the ground where we were to crawl and they would go off with a big bang. They couldn't do any damage, but they were loud bangs!

One of our cadets, a gentleman who was a little bit on the fat side – a big bang went up close to him. There's a natural tendency to shrink, to protect yourself, and his bottom must have got stuck up. A bullet went straight through both his cheeks. Very uncomfortable for him for a few days; but fortunately no vital parts were touched.

Now the first time I came under fire it was shellfire, not bullet fire. My reaction was . . . indifference, actually. It might have been because of that battle inoculation we had had. We had learned not to react, to ignore it. We developed a fatalist attitude of 'Every bullet has got a name written on it. If it's your name, you will get it in any case, so – why worry?' You know what the Gita says: 'You do your duty; don't worry about the rest.' That has been a tremendous philosophy in my life. 'What is to be, will be.'

When the Accra chief's son, Aziz Brimah, arrived in Madras with the Gold Coast Regiment he found an unexpected invitation to attend a meeting in a cinema, where Mahatma Gandhi would be the speaker. The Indian leader was making the most of the opportunity to scatter the seeds of independence on so much fertile soil, blown by the war into his own backyard. 'Gandhi was wearing his usual loincloth and spectacles, and with a stick,' Brimah recalls. 'He said we have come here to fight a war. We'll see that some Indians are sitting on the fence, while other Indians are fighting for their independence. We mustn't be discouraged by it; but we must learn from it that when we get back we must spearhead our own drive for independence. We didn't think much about this at the time; but we stored it at the back of our minds.'

The enormous extent of the British Empire and Commonwealth meant that its component Dominions and dependencies rarely had much of an idea how any of the others lived – apart from sharing a common interest in Britain and the British. It was a shock to most Commonwealth soldiers, for example, to see and smell the poverty of wharfside Bombay and downtown Madras. And the shocks were not all on one side. 'When we were coming in on our ship,' says Aziz Brimah, 'rumours went round among the Indians: "The Africans are coming! They are cannibals; they chop [eat] people; they have tails!" So when we went to bathe in the streams, people asked us not to take our pants off – our blue PT pants – in

'Every job in the Army is useful, you see. The infantry is Queen of the Battle, they take all the credit; but I doubt very much if the infantry can do anything without the support of the services. Without our effort, they could not have sustained the 8th Army. We were very, very crucial to the action.' (Nila Kantan, India)

Right Vernon Northwood then and now.

Australian characters on the front line, (above) dug in at the siege of Tobruk, 1941, and (below) at ease after a patrol in the New Guinea jungle.

Below right Phil Rhoden then and now.

Australian troops cross an improvised bridge over a deep ravine in New Guinea.

Two sides of the colour bar. Seth Kobla Anthony of the Gold Coast Regiment (left) gained his lieutenant's pips in a pioneering breakthrough against institutionalised prejudice in the British Army, while Frank Sexwale of the South African Native Military Corps (below) became bitterly disillusioned with his own Government's racial policies, which denied South African blacks the opportunity to fight. Sexwale and his colleagues were issued with spears and clubs during their training.

Below Frank Sexwale today.

West African soldiers with head-loads follow their leader, a European officer, through the dense jungle of the Kaladan Valley in north-west Burma.

Cassino, Italy – a photograph take on 15 March 1944 after 2,500 tons of bombs had been unleashed on the town. 'Oh God, that was atrocities, really. Five hundred planes, bombing Cassino town. When they finish, then others come. They reduce that place to nothing ... no monastery, no town, no nothing at all. All gone.' (Paul Gobire, Seychelles) *Inset* Paul Gobine today.

Above Indian stretcher bearers carry a badly wounded man down a steep mountain track at Cassino. 'No vehicles could go where we were. On our shoulders we carried all the things up the hill. The gradient was 1 in 3; almost on all fours we had to go.' (Nila Kantan, India)

Below New Zealand gunners fire on Cassino. 'When we came to fire on the monastery - well, we were only too glad to see such a strongpoint pushed off that ridge. But we made a mess of it; only made it easier for the Germans to hide in the rubble.' (Tom Somerville, New Zealand)

Two branches of the women's services: Connie Macdonald, Jamaica, of ATS (above), and Sheila Parkinson, Britain, of FANY (below).

case they would be frightened by our tails! Then the British authorities themselves began to spread the story: "We are bringing in the Africans. When they catch you, they will chop you alive." This was the best way they had of putting fear into the Japanese.'

Japanese soldiers and Indian civilians were not the only ones to believe such tales. From September 1943 onwards the countryside of southern Italy was rich in rumours, too. All kinds, conditions and colours of men were to be seen on the move northwards; for after bustling through Sicily the Allied armies had now launched themselves on to the Italian peninsula. On 9 September, a week after the initial landings across the Strait of Messina, a mixed British–American force assaulted the beaches around Salerno, just south of Naples and half-way between the toe of Italy and Rome. Paul Gobine, the Seychelle Islander who had built dummy tanks to fool the Germans at El Alamein, went ashore with the Seychelles Pioneer Corps.

> We landed at Salerno, at Green Beach. Everywhere was covered with warships that start shelling on shore. We disembarked up to the chest in water, with our rifle, our haversack. Some pioneers from Basutoland and Zululand had disembarked before us and had been wiped out; I could see the bodies. The Germans were firing at us. We just say, 'Oh, God ...' and cross ourselves, to protect ourselves from everything. And luckily, God was on our side.
>
> We hit the beach and start digging trenches, take cover. Bullets went passing us, ack-ack overhead. But thanks God we had the Navy; it was bombing, was shelling the mountainside behind Green Beach.
>
> The next day we advance about one kilometre. We in the Seychelles are mostly Catholics, so we went to church. All the people, they ran away. They said we were cannibals. '*Nero mangare bambino*!' – black men eat babies! So we went to the priest: 'No, we are Christian. We are only in the British Army – we are not going to eat you!'

However, misunderstandings soon adjusted themselves. The Seychelles Islanders did not feel bound to behave towards the Italian civilians in the same way as their British colleagues:

> At the time there was no fraternisation. If an Italian woman is seen with a chocolate, for example, the British troops would slap her and take it. But we did not. We gave them things. We don't know what side they were on – some were Fascist and we don't know which one is on our side. I was very quick to

learn the language, the rudiments of Italian; I can talk and write it even now. As a young boy, you know, you go there, you meet a young girl, you fancy her at the time; you've been in the desert, here and there, for a long time. So we establish friendship ... Then the Italians became to love us ... but they didn't love the British troops at all.

Did I have a girlfriend there? Oh, of course! My first baby was born in Italy. Now she's a doctor there, a specialist. She's a grandmother herself!

The runaway, Frank O'Donnell, arrived in Italy from Sicily with the Canadian 1st Division, landing at Reggio di Calabria on the toe-tip of the peninsula a few days after his eighteenth birthday – at last permitted, legally, to take part in the war. In Italy O'Donnell learned what military bullshit really meant, on both sides of the Commonwealth divide.

One of our majors decided that the outfit was going to show a good face on some important parade or other. Olive oil was easily obtained in Italy. So the guys got rags and they put olive oil over every vehicle, over every gun – and man, did they ever shine in the sunlight. Then the wind blew up, and the sand ... By the time the parade came you'd think we'd fought the desert war ourselves!

Bullshit wasn't confined to the Canadian Army. I was in a hospital in Italy with a terrible go of jaundice; in a British hospital, which was a tent hospital. In that hospital the British were something else. All those soldiers – wounded, sick, whatever – were ordered, in the morning, to lie at attention. To *lie at attention*, in their beds! Then the inspection could take place. I was happy to get moved to a Canadian hospital; I wasn't quite used to that kind of thing!

The news of the death of her elder brother at El Alamein – coming only nine months after the murder of her newly wed husband by Japanese soldiers in Singapore – had devastated Sheila Parkinson. She had been promoted Junior Commander in the FANYs, and now desperately needed a new challenge to focus on. The opening of the Italian campaign seemed to offer the chance she was looking for. Young women in the ATS (Auxiliary Territorial Service) were needed in Italy as clerks, drivers, switchboard operators and for general administration duties. All Sheila Parkinson wanted to do was to get away and do something that was going to hold her attention:

I went down to Hobart House near Buckingham Palace, to be interviewed to go to Italy with this advance lot of ATS just after the landings. Well, it was perfectly normal: the young ones who were being interviewed were going to go out where men were men, and they were intending to find boyfriends among them. This was their life, and it was a lovely thought. They were all waiting there, longing to be chosen.

I was, in fact, chosen; but I said I'd have to go away and think about it. I knew it wasn't for me. All these young things, most of them ten years younger than me, looking for boyfriends; and I wanted something that was quite different – more serious, more demanding. So I turned it down.

By this stage of the war there were scores of thousands of Allied prisoners-of-war in the hands of the Germans and Japanese. The Japanese, as Rod Wells in Borneo and George Barron in Hong Kong had discovered, considered that servicemen who had allowed themselves to be captured, rather than fighting to the death or committing suicide, were deeply dishonoured and worthy only of contempt and harsh treatment. The effects of this maltreatment were compounded by the rampant and virulent nature of diseases in the tropics, and by the inability of the Japanese to organise adequate transport and distribution of such food and medicines as they were prepared to allot to their prisoners. They had acquired their empire, scattered over many thousands of miles of sea, in just three months; so it was scarcely likely that they would have the experience to deploy these resources, even if they had possessed them.

The Japanese had never ratified their signature on the 1929 Geneva Convention on the treatment of prisoners. The Germans, on the other hand, had. Treatment of their Russian prisoners-of-war by the Germans was scarcely better than that of the Jews in the concentration and death camps of the Holocaust. For other prisoners – Commonwealth servicemen included – conditions generally stretched to the limit the stipulations of the Convention, but did not ignore them as blatantly as did those in the Japanese camps. However, all prisoners everywhere had to face the same demons – boredom, frustration, self-castigation, enforced idleness, hunger, the creeping fear of mental instability and, worst of all, the gnawing uncertainty about when it would all end.

The Canadian infantry private, Thomas Hunter, captured under the Dieppe cliffs during the disastrous raid in August 1942, had ended up in Stalag VIIIB at Teschen in Silesia. Under the control of this camp were 11,500 Commonwealth prisoners, and almost all were parcelled out among fifty-three *arbeitskommandos* or working groups. Some were sent to labour in the coal mines; others were put to work on local farms. Hunter, who had left school at thirteen to earn his fatherless family's bread in Depression-hit Toronto, coped well with the hard manual farm work.

It eased your mind, anyway, that's what I found, just turning the soil and planting. As long as you're working and doing something your situation didn't penetrate the mind too much. You were in a place where you couldn't go anywhere or do anything, so you just ... tell yourself it'll pass. You tried to be busy all the time, either marching or walking up and down, just keeping your mind busy and your feet busy, trying to stay healthy. You knew you had to keep your mind clear. There was a library, and I did as much reading as I could. If everybody kept reading they would find themselves quite easy. But I know a couple of them were taken away because their mind went; they were raving and were taken off to the asylum. I saw one guy – what was it? Something about he could get four aces out. He was playing cards all the time. He was there all day, you could see him going off his mind. The Germans came and watched him; eventually they took him away.

The commandant was an ex-officer in the Navy and he was a pretty tough cookie. He wanted us all treated rough, as prisoners. They brought some women into the camp – escapees from Russia, I think – and they ran them through, naked, chasing them and whipping them at the same time. Oh, some terrible things went on there...

The British compound was next door, and some of our guys went and played soccer with them. It was very easygoing between the nationalities, except for the Indians. They didn't want anyone to walk through their hut while they were eating, because our shadows poisoned their food. They had their own toilet; nobody else could go there. They didn't enter our group, they weren't communicating with us; they were pretty well on their own. The Germans let them wear their turbans and pray religiously in their own faiths.

The Germans had guard dogs that were supposed to keep us in at night. They were supposed to attack us if we left our hut. But we just used to take a little piece of meat or something – the dog'd go away. So the head of the dog pound came along and said to the prisoners: 'Please don't feed our dogs; you're ruining their training.' We weren't very sympathetic to that request – no, not a bloody bit!

Jack Brown, the New Zealand shepherd who had been captured in April 1942 after a year on the run in Greece, spent about a year in Campo 57 at Gruppignano in north-eastern Italy. As news of the successful Allied landings and then the Italian capitulation reached his guards late in 1943, they disappeared and left the camp gates open. But before Brown could decide whether to risk escaping the Germans arrived. The prisoners were taken to Stalag VIIIB, Thomas Hunter's prison camp. But Jack Brown did not stay long at Teschen. Labourers were wanted in Leipzig, 300 miles to the north-west; so an *arbeitskommando* of seventy-five New Zealanders, Britons and South Africans was assembled and sent off there in October to labour at shovelling coal into railway trucks. Little did the crews of RAF Bomber Command suspect, as they unleashed their incendiaries and high explosives on Leipzig, that their own comrades-in-arms were among those suffering below.

The Englanders came over and bombed us. Oh my God, did they! The RAF bombed us out of our quarters twice. The alarm would go at night; no lights, cold as hell, snow on the ground, but you'd get out of bed sharpish! If you happened to be working on the railway when the alarm went, they took you into the nearest air-raid shelter which nine times out of ten was three parts full of Germans. And you virtually just about had to have your guard with you to protect you. I mean, we were the bad boys, so we got it both ways. You can imagine – these damn things up there overhead, and we were getting out of the road of them, and these German civilians weren't very happy about it either – 'You cursed swine' and so on. We were not very popular people.

The town was flattened – I mean, it was flattened for miles. People who hadn't seen it for themselves would never realise how a town could be flattened. They were brick buildings five or six storeys high and they just crumpled in the blast, flat. We were put on digging trenches to put the bomb victims into. They just brought them in by the truckload and in they'd go. That was our first real look into what was going on. They were brought in just as they were picked up: women, children, the old people. That didn't help us a whole lot either.

After they started these bombing raids we were on a lot of cleaning up. Clearing roadways, clearing away buildings and that type of work. These things don't ever leave you. The smell of the people buried in the ruins – they'd been buried there for weeks – the stench was something terrible. You got sort of hardened to it, in the respect: 'They're only bloody Germans, anyway.' You *had* to look at it like that.

Even nowadays you don't talk about it, because people really don't under-stand. It's a very hard thing to visualise. How *could* you visualise things like that, if you hadn't actually seen them?

'Freedom means everything to me,' says Charlie Hobbs. 'To be able to make a decision and do it, and not have someone tell you you can't do it – that's what freedom means to me. Provided I stay within the laws, I want to be able to do what I like. I could never exist under a communist system or even under some forms of socialism. Canadians in general are all that way – they're a free-spirited people.'

Charlie Hobbs had never been a yes-man; had never taken too well to other people's routines, to having to steer someone else's course. Now he would have to learn to do just that; to control the nagging irritation, to damp down his fires, to rein in his individuality and surrender himself to the sluggish, tightly channelled, colourless, endless stream of prison camp routine. From Dulag Luft near Frankfurt, through Stalag Luft I at Barth and Heydekrug Luft VI in extreme north-eastern Germany, to Thorn (in Poland, north-west of Warsaw) and back again into Germany, to Fallingbostel near Hanover – Hobbs was shifted and shunted around as the exigencies of the crumbling Third Reich dictated. At each new camp the same anxieties and rebellious tension would flare up; the painful knack of surrender to the deadening, sanity-saving routine would have to be learned all over again.

You learned to live with being a prisoner. You got into a routine, and you just followed the routine. You'd 'walk the circuit', as they called it. We had to do our own cooking. All that sort of stuff kept you busy. The days didn't go fast, but they went by.

Uncertainty – that is the problem. Really, that is the whole problem . . . yeah. You just didn't know when it was all going to end. The rumour-mill was always going: every Friday the Turks came into the war, you know! But it was routine – routine that got you through.

The Geneva Convention gave us some protection, for the simple reason that we were holding German prisoners too. But they didn't live up to the Convention, not worth a damn. They didn't clothe us, they didn't supply us with the amenities; no toilet paper, no toothbrushes, no razor blades, none of this stuff. They didn't even give us plates to put our food on, or pots and pans to cook it in. We had to make our own. And here's the ultimate: when a Red Cross parcel did come through, which wasn't regular, the officer in charge made us open every can. Well, the food would spoil if you opened all the cans, and you couldn't eat it all in one day, and we only had one dish to put it in – so you're dumping condensed milk in with meat, butter in with sugar; it was ridiculous.

When people got on your nerves you walked away from it. And that happened often – you were living at awfully close quarters. You'd have at least twenty-five men in a small room, and from eight o'clock in the evening through to eight o'clock in the morning you were in there – you were *locked* in there. I think people's characteristics grow in your mind; if there's something you didn't like about them before, there's plenty you didn't like about them now! You had to be very careful when you're playing bridge, or games like that, that you played with the right players. Otherwise you'd just go right out of your mind, there'd be so much irritation.

If someone did overstep the mark they'd be disciplined very cruelly. The favourite one was to use the outhouse, which was a low one; forty seats there and maybe waist deep. They'd just drop him down there; and if he fought it they'd step on his hands and make sure he was in there for quite a little bit of time too. That was enough to kill a man. And then, of course, when he comes out of there nobody'll talk to him, and that's the way it would stay for a long while. That was all the punishment any man needed – because the worst thing that can happen to you there is to be ignored completely.

The character of the POWs' own leaders was of vital importance in maintaining morale. Luckily for Charlie Hobbs and his fellow prisoners, their Senior British Officer was exactly the man for the job, a man who would stand no nonsense from anyone. Under his protection, the 'kriegies' did what they could to make life difficult for their guards.

We had a very strong leader, British leader, by the name of Dixie Deans – a Warrant Officer 1st Class in the RAF – who did wonders with the Germans. He knew their mind – he was famous in the prison camps. In Air Force camps it didn't matter what the man's rank was; if he was the leader, he was the leader, and he'd be chosen by the people. Now when we got sent to Thorn in Poland they already had a Senior British Officer there – an Army man, because it was an Army camp. He immediately tried to discipline the Air Force fellers, and we appealed to Dixie Deans. We said we didn't want any part of that military crap, you know. So Deans had it out with the man, and he went at him hot and heavy. This was a colonel that he was up against, too. They got it sorted out and no more problems. Left to ourselves, we would have disciplined ourselves; but the Army tried to throw its Army authority at us, and it didn't work.

Now our guards – if they were Home Guards, then they were no different from our own. But if they were Hitler Youth, they were a bunch of bastards; that's the only word for them. They were brought up, from the day they were born, practically, to be mean – and they *were* mean. They thought nothing of doing things that you and I wouldn't do in a lifetime: cruel things. The only thing they feared – and this was a tempering factor – was to be sent to the Russian front. They personally, every one of them, feared the Russians. And with good reason, after what they had done to the Russians.

Well, in the morning these guards would count us. We were in groups of fifty men, all around in a big semicircle. The guards would begin their count. But they couldn't count, in a pinch – they were not the brightest. Not too nimble-minded. They'd get to *eins – zwei – drei*, and sombody'd move and they'd have to start all over. We could run one of these counts for two hours, you know, just to count fifty men!

Anyway, one morning we showed up on parade. Nobody moved. They counted us in fives – *eins – zwei – drei – vier* . . .– they got to nine, and then they got to ten – and there was two pairs of empty shoes. So then they caught on and they did a sheep count. They lock you in a big sports field, and they run you through a funnel and they count you in twos. Well, the fellers had a good idea that they could mess up this count too. They messed it up left and right – must have gone through about three times – and finally they had the count up so high it was ridiculous. If the Germans figured there were 700 men we'd show them 800. You see, when you'd gone through the funnel you were free – so you just joined the circuit, walked round and joined the crowd going through again. They never caught on to that. Oh, dear, dear, dear . . . it took *hours*.

So finally Dixie says, 'That's enough.' He said to the German Commandant: 'In exchange for future favours, we will give you an accurate count in ten minutes.' And we did. That's how much control and respect Dixie Deans had.

As 1943 drew towards a close the Japanese moved the Australian signals man, Rod Wells, from the prisoner-of-war camp at Sandakan and brought him round by ship to Kuching, on the Sarawak coast of northern Borneo. Here he was thrown into jail, broken in body by months of torture and neglect in solitary confinement, and left to wait for whatever the next year would bring.

Half-way across the world, the Germans and Russians were still locked in their titanic struggle inside the borders of Russia. In many ways all other actions in other theatres of war were now side-shows to this; on its outcome, everyone knew, hung the outcome of the war. The Germans were so heavily committed that no other interpretation was possible. And by the end of 1943 they were being driven back, with terrible losses, suffering and misery on both sides, in the south through the Ukraine, along the central front after a comprehensive defeat at Kursk, and in the north by a series of Russian thrusts which would result in the lifting of the epic 890-day siege of Leningrad in January of the new year.

The Royal Navy had been running convoys to the Arctic ports of Murmansk and Archangel since the German invasion of Russia in 1941, giving the Russians some kind of supply line in war materials. Just as importantly, the Arctic convoys were a symbol of the will of the Allies to support each other against their common enemy, even before America brought her big battalions into the war and while Britain's own lifeline was being all but choked off by U-boat successes in the North Atlantic. These Arctic convoys were among the roughest and most dangerous naval operations of the war. Seas could be mountainous and were deadly cold; freezing fog was endemic; daylight lasted twenty-four hours in summer, as did darkness in winter. Ice was a danger the further north the convoys went; Archangel, on the south-eastern inward curve of the White Sea, was frozen up in winter. Ships were vulnerable to attack by German aircraft from airfields in northern Norway, by U-boats when surface conditions permitted and by surface raiders operating from Norwegian fjords – raiders such as the battleship *Tirpitz*, whose very existence proved far more destructive than her guns. The most disastrous Arctic convoy of all, PQ17, having sailed for Archangel on 27 June 1942, was ordered to scatter in face of a suggestion (unfounded) that *Tirpitz* might be out and about. At the same time the convoy's escort was withdrawn. Twenty-four out of the thirty-six ships were sunk in the ensuing hunt by German aircraft and submarines.

Not all Arctic convoys were attended by such mayhem, but they were all unpleasant in their various ways. Alec Dennis of the Royal Navy, by now First Lieutenant in the destroyer *Savage*, remembers escorting a convoy to Murmansk:

That was the roughest sea I'd ever seen in my life. The waves had rolled all the way across the Atlantic and up there, and you were swooping up and down these things. Very uncomfortable. It *was* rough – and really cold. My feet got terribly cold and I can't sleep with cold feet. So I'd have a pair of boots and leave them with an electric light bulb on in each; then as soon as I came off the bridge I'd go down and put my feet in them and then after a bit I could go to sleep.

We were watch and watch – you'd be up there from eight to midnight. By the time you've come down and taken enough clothes off and got your feet warm it's taken you an hour; then you had to dress up again, well before it was time to get up there once more. Then you'd be on watch from four in the morning till eight. So you were kind of short of sleep. And it was such an effort hauling yourself round with all this heavy clothing on. You got bloody tired, one way and another. I remember on one occasion lying on the deck in the throes of seasickness, saying, 'God, why am I alive?'

But ... you got used to it.

Something the Arctic convoy men never got used to was the inhospitality of the country they were supplying. Dennis remembers Murmansk as 'a dreadful place. Black rocks – white snow – black, black, black ... dark. Drunken pilot. Very forbidding, no welcome. And this was supposed to be your haven on arrival! It – was – grim!'

Peter Cayley of the Royal Canadian Navy was on Arctic convoy escort duty too, and did his best to fraternise with the locals: 'We went in to fuel in a little place called Iokanga, which was a very barren harbour. It was just rock; there was barely a dwelling house, hardly a tree in sight. We went alongside a tanker and refuelled. Then the local commissar came with his three chums. They didn't bring us their vodka – no, they wanted our gin. We gave them supper. They didn't talk much English, but I remember after dinner they sang to us, rather impressive Russian songs. Then they said: "Now you sing for us." We didn't have any songs as stirring as theirs, but we did our best – it was "Down at the Old Bull and Bush"!'

The Russians did not greatly impress Alec Dennis with their manners, even when he and the wardroom of *Savage* did at last receive an invitation:

The Russians never said thank you for any of the arms and transport we sent them – until they unbent to the extent of inviting us to the Red Navy Club in Polyarny, which was a naval base with a lot of sleek-looking submarines and rather useless destroyers which always came out when the shouting was over.

The Red Navy Club was interesting. Red banners everywhere – Lenin, Marx, Stalin – the Gruesome Twosome, the whole lot. They gave us a show, the choir and the singing and all that kind of stuff; and then there was a dance. All these rather square women sat round the walls. Up starts the music, and you would go and approach a woman. They were all terrified! She'd look at the KGB man – little nod, like that, and she'd dance with you. As soon as the music stops, zip! she'd scuttle back to her seat. The atmosphere of fear – you could almost touch it. And that was their thank you to us for sinking the *Scharnhorst*.

The sinking of the battleship *Scharnhorst*, one of the sea epics of the Second

World War, took place on Boxing Day 1943 and closed the year on a high note for the Royal Navy. *Scharnhorst* had left her anchorage in Altenfjord on Christmas Day with the intention of attacking the twenty-two ships of the Russian convoy JW55B. British intelligence had long ago broken the Germans' Enigma code, and Admiral Bruce Fraser, C-in-C Home Fleet, was fully aware of his enemy's movements throughout the interception and chase of *Scharnhorst*. Dennis tells the story:

We anchored in Hvalfjord in Iceland and were invited on board to dinner with the Admiral, Bruce Fraser. I drank some of his brandy, which I shouldn't have. Anyway, he was absolute charm itself – a lovely man, made you feel at home right away. After a while he told us they were expecting the *Scharnhorst* to come out and what we were going to do. It was just like Nelson, with the pepperpots and whatnot: he would be on a certain course, he would open fire at 12,000 yards, the destroyers were to be up here and so on – it was all planned out. I thought, 'This sounds right, for a change' – after all the *ad hoc*ery we'd had before.

Anyway, sure enough, *Scharnhorst* attacked the convoy and was coming back. Bloody rough, really a full gale, huge great waves, you could barely stand up. We went to an interception position between her and her base in Norway. Seemed too good to be true, really. We were doing twenty-five knots, the ship almost uncontrollable, weaving about all over the place. I was on X gundeck, aft. After a while somebody fired off star shell, and there was this most marvellous gunnery duel between the *Duke of York* and the *Scharnhorst*. They used tracer shell and you could see them going up, making a great arc, a magnificent arc. And the joy of it was – they weren't shooting at us!

Anyway, *Scharnhorst* turned off north and we pursued her, four destroyers, waiting to make our torpedo attack. It was still damn rough, we had to cling on. Then she started shooting at us, anti-aircraft stuff, to burst overhead. We had a few people wounded. One young man on my gun suddenly went 'Yipe!' and tore off his tin hat – a splinter had burned its way through his tin hat and his balaclava helmet, and he had a hot head.

We were thinking we'd never catch up. Then, suddenly, she turned around in an absolute cloud of smoke, came out of it and came down in an ideal position for us to make a torpedo attack. It was quite an exciting moment or two. We had an Old Etonian on the Torpedo Control – Warrender – charming fellow; I thought, a bit wet; on practice he'd always get it wrong. This time, being an Old Etonian, he got it right. We fired off all our torpedoes; there was no doubt we got one or two hits. You could see and hear a great '*boooomf*!' – she was only three or four thousand yards away, and that's close. This magnificent-looking ship, sort of silver-grey; she looked wonderful, coming down. She was a lovely ... just a lovely ship. Anyway, we got all our torpedoes off, shoved off, got the cocoa open and did no more, really.

After that it was just a shambles. Wretched *Scharnhorst* – she just got clobbered by everybody, because she'd stopped by then. It was really ghastly. Those poor fellows – out of 2000, they only picked up about thirty. Once you're sunk, you're a victim of the sea. If ever that fellow feeling between sailors lapses, it'll be a sad day for humanity.

SIX

Big Push: 1944

Down at the end of the street was ... an awful mess. Boy,
oh boy. So, you know – it was food for thought. It took me
a while to get over seeing that. But you didn't let on. It was
... within you. Geraldine Turcotte, Canada

W ith the war well into its fourth year and having spread to every corner of the globe, there were unmistakable signs of cracking and subsidence in the house of Hitler. During 1943 he had lost his one European ally, Italy. His forces were gone from North Africa. In the Balkans they were fighting a very cruel and unresolved war against local partisans. In Russia they were slowly retreating on all fronts. They were also in retreat in Italy, though their succession of defensive walls or lines across the peninsula would hold up the Allies in bitter fighting for another year. At sea the German Navy had just lost *Scharnhorst*, and their other chief surface raiders were either sunk or penned up in French, Baltic or Norwegian ports. In the Atlantic the balance had tipped against the U-boats with the deployment of more hunting and destruction technology in ships, and the introduction of long-range aircraft capable of finding and destroying submarines. In the air the RAF and USAF between them had dropped over 200,000 tons of bombs on Germany, whereas the

Luftwaffe had dropped fewer than 2300 tons on Britain. Slowly but surely the world of the Third Reich was contracting, shrinking inexorably inwards towards Berlin, the eventual vanishing point.

This would be the year when the eyes of the British Commonwealth were on three land areas in particular: on Italy, on Burma and, after 6 June, on northern Europe too. At the start of the year Britain was a giant holding camp, a stupendous arsenal continuing to swell with men and materials pouring in for the impending invasion of Europe. The rest of the continent still lay under German occupation, but the steady Allied advance north through Italy showed what could, and would, be done shortly in northern Europe. In Burma, however, the mood was far less confident. The Far East in general was still the area most in the balance, with the Japanese once more on the offensive and forging westwards to the very gates of India herself.

By February 1944 Juanita Carberry had been working in the Signals Office at FANY Headquarters in Kenya for the best part of a year, and was enjoying the Nairobi night-life with her American boyfriends. Now the war in the Far East was to come right home to the eighteen-year-old:

> Some of our girls were sent up to North Africa, while others ... you may have heard of a ship called the *Khedive Ismail*? I'd volunteered for service overseas and been turned down because they found out I was under-age. If they hadn't, I would have been on board that ship. She was carrying ammunition and was a troopship as well. She loaded a lot of Kenyans – Wrens and FANYs and ATS – for Ceylon. Going over to Colombo she got hit by a torpedo off the Maldives and there was a tremendous loss of life – 1300 people. I was working in the Signals Office; messages would come in and I had to decide whether they were a security risk, whether they had to go into the cipher office or could be transmitted in plain language. And I sort of froze over this message, because it had all the names of all my mates on it. All killed.

At the beginning of 1944, the situation in Burma was critical. The British 14th Army launched their second offensive eastwards into the jungles and mountains of the Arakan peninsula, with the intention, as before, of capturing the port of Akyab as a launching pad for a drive south towards Rangoon. Almost simultaneously the Japanese commenced their own dry-season offensive – a diversionary attack in Arakan, followed by a main thrust westwards into Assam around the settlements of Imphal and

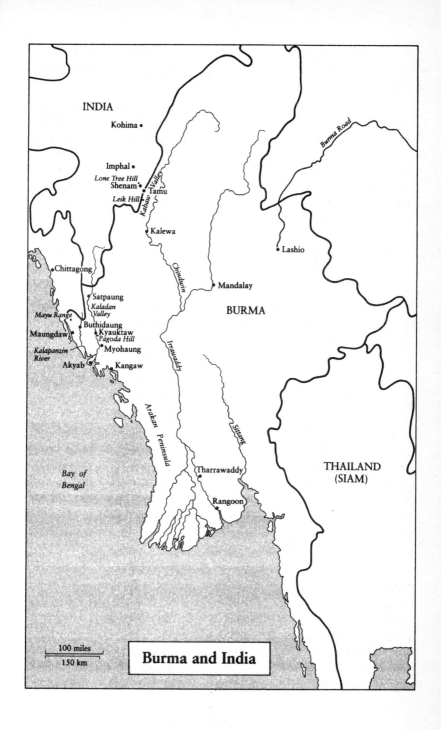

INDIA

Kohima

Imphal
Lone Tree Hill
Shenam
Leik Hill
Tamu
Kabaw Valley

Kalewa

Chindwin

Chittagong

Satpaung
Kaladan Valley
Mayu Range
Buthidaung
Kyauktaw
Pagoda Hill
Maungdaw
Myohaung
Kalapanzin River
Akyab
Kangaw

Arakan Peninsula

Mandalay

Lashio

Burma Road

BURMA

Irrawaddy

Sittang

Bay of Bengal

Tharrawaddy

Rangoon

THAILAND (SIAM)

100 miles
150 km

Burma and India

Kohima. This offensive had been partly prompted by the first and most famous of General Orde Wingate's Chindit operations, in which 3000 men crossed the Chindwin river, a north-western tributary of the Irrawaddy, in February 1943 and spent four months of incredible hardship on foot in the jungles behind the Japanese lines. Almost one-third of them had died before the remainder made their way out and back to India in the monsoon. The Japanese took note that the Chindwin could be crossed, and that hardy soldiers could move and fight in the worst terrain if they were efficiently supplied by air drops; and they decided to pre-empt any Allied attempt to repeat the exercise on a much larger scale, and to go for broke themselves. If they could reach and take Imphal and Kohima, the towns which blocked their path forward into Assam, before the onset of the monsoon in March–April 1944, the torrential rains would prevent effective counter-attacks by the 14th Army. The Japanese could then gather themselves to cut the main road and railway links with the Allied air supply route over the Himalayas to China – and could continue their advance into India, if the omens seemed auspicious.

John Hamilton was with 1 Gambia Battalion, part of 81 West African Division, when it pushed east into the Kaladan Valley, in the heart of the Arakan peninsula, in January 1944. The West Africans had the task of blocking off a possible route north and westwards across the mountains from the Kaladan, by which the Japanese might advance to take the 14th Army by surprise. Instead, it was the Japanese who got the surprise when 20,000 men emerged without warning in the Kaladan Valley. Their guns and jeeps had been transported to the Kaladan along the 'West African Way', a track seventy-five miles long, cut out of the jungle with machetes and surfaced with logs, that entered the valley at Satpaung after crossing six steep mountain ranges. Meanwhile, the African and European infantrymen of the Division had cut their way to the Kaladan across the jungle-covered mountains further south. These Arakanese jungles were not wheeled-transport territory, as John Hamilton describes:

A bamboo is very much like an enormous piece of grass. You've got a hard, solid, ivory-white root at the bottom, which grows sideways; then you've got the hollow stem. Our kind of bamboo grew in single stems, so close together that to go between them you've got to go sideways. If you're wearing a pack on your back, that's liable to snag on the stem. And of course they're not planted in neat rows, so that you've got to be zigzagging all the time, as well as continually side-stepping. Exhausting! And completely baffling. I mean, I've done that along a hilltop and thought I'd gone about three times as far as I had. Being on a hilltop, too, is no advantage, because you can't see through the bamboo.

These are very steep hills – almost one in one – and the ridges are knife-edge ridges, and the chaungs or creek valleys between them are just as narrow – only just wide enough to take a stream perhaps three or four feet wide. The hillside comes straight down, there's the bed of the chaung and then the opposite slope going straight up. The bed of the chaung is slabs of sandstone, all higgledy-piggledy, and water just deep enough so you can't lift your feet out of it, so you're sort of ploughing through the water all the time. Of course your boots and socks are sopping wet, and every now and then you stub your boot on one of these slabs that's sticking up a bit.

If, in addition, you try and negotiate this sort of path at night when the moon is not up and you can't even see the man in front of you – until you bump into him – it's the nearest thing to Stygian blackness and utter frustration that you can imagine.

Our bit of the Arakan jungle was so deserted. It was like desert in the sense that we practically never saw an animal, or even bird life. One or two people saw an elephant. Barking deer you heard, but never saw; monkeys you heard chattering, sometimes clattering through the bamboo, but you never saw them. There was a kind of lizard that produced a most remarkable cry, which one may politely render as 'Tuck-tou'. Other people rendered it otherwise...

One was rarely in a village. If you were it was usually empty. You hardly ever saw locals. And, of course, you hardly ever saw a Japanese – not even when there was stuff flying around. What you could *not* see, taking it all round, was more remarkable than what you could, by a long chalk.

The jungle may have seemed devoid of animal residents, but there were plenty of other forms of life to interest the soldiers of the 81st West African Division – among whom was Aziz Brimah, the Muslim chief's son from Accra, now serving with 5 Battalion, Gold Coast Regiment. Brimah was soon to earn the nickname 'Lawrence' for his coolness under fire. But some residents of the Arakanese jungle got under even this man's skin. 'There was something we called tiger leech. It's very small, very thin. If it gets to your body it will suck your blood and get bigger and bigger. So we used a cigarette end or a match on the under of that thing; it will take its fangs out. But if you don't do that, but just pull it off, the fangs will stay within your body and it will go bad – very bad.'

Kofi Genfi was in this second Arakan offensive too, with 7 Battalion,

Gold Coast Regiment; at first in the Kaladan and later – after an epic westward march of forty miles in four days over terrain such as John Hamilton describes – on the Kalapanzin river nearer the coast. Genfi experienced the jungles during the start of the monsoon in April, when several inches of rain would fall in a few hours.

To be in the Burma jungle is the hell. The climate there was so hot. In certain places the sweat would soak through your shirt – we were served with salt and water to drink. After walking about fifteen miles, very soaked and very tired, immediately you reach HQ position you have to do digging. I give my allowance of rum and cigarettes to the others, so they will do my digging for me!

Mosquitoes were a big problem – malaria mosquitoes. During this campaign we slept in the open and you could see the mosquitoes everywhere. If you are not lucky there will be heavy rain, and then you will sleep in the rain like a frog . . . and sometimes frogs will drop at you, when it is raining. The monsoon rains – oh, dear, dear, dear! It rains: it rains. You are soaked; you don't undress. You dry off when the rain stops. For three weeks you are not taking off your top dress, you are not taking off your shoe . . . oh! Woe betide you when you take off your shoe! The foot will be very white, as a pig's trotter. And – it – will – *stink!* . . . up to a mile away! Oh, dear, dear, dear!

This kind of country was difficult enough to survive in, let alone to fight over. There was no such thing as a soldier who felt at home in the Burmese jungle, according to John Hamilton; everyone, friend and foe alike, struggled to get around and do their jobs.

Some people seemed to believe that everybody who lives in West Africa lives in the jungle – absolutely not true. And even if people live in the jungle, they don't spend their time penetrating it. So jungle is difficult terrain for *anyone* to fight in.

Once the Japanese were well dug in, in bunkers with plenty on top of them, they were very difficult indeed to get at. A 3.7 howitzer, the largest gun we had, is ineffective because the shell just explodes with no penetration; and a plane had to get a direct hit on a bunker, which they didn't do because they couldn't see them. Dense bamboo, you see; it's like a lace curtain. If you're inside it you can see out, but if you're outside you can't see in. I can remember a Japanese party opening fire with a machine-gun on a hillside where we'd done some very hasty digging-in, and it was obvious in spite of the spoil lying around that they couldn't see our position, because their fire was all going over our heads. And by the same token, it was quite hopeless to try and pinpoint exactly where they were firing from.

These rarely seen enemies, the Japanese, were respected by the Commonwealth soldiers for their skill and subtlety in jungle warfare and their suicidal bravery, while at the same time they were despised – and feared – for their ruthlessness and for the cruelty they showed to the Burmese civilians. Some of the soldiers came across mutilated villagers; Danny Misra of the Rajputana Rifles, for example, found some who had had their tongues cut out so that they could not reveal where the Japanese were. These atrocity stories spread like wildfire, along with the first vague rumours of what was happening in the Japanese prisoner-of-war camps. The Japanese quickly became demonised, so that all Japanese soldiers were invested with the potential for bestial cruelty that some of them certainly displayed. No one wanted to become a prisoner of the Japanese; and on the comparatively rare occasions when the boot was on the other foot, Japanese captives were sometimes killed out of hand. The Burmese jungle was probably the Second World War's cruellest theatre.

Aziz Brimah:

The Japanese put leaves all over their bodies and they crawl gradually, as if they were trees or grass. We'd been trained and lectured as to all these tricks. If there's two trees near together they can fix a machine-gun to each one and tie a rope to each trigger, then lie in the middle. If he see you coming, he'd pull this rope: *kak-ak-ak-ak-ak*! Then that one: *kak-ak-ak-ak-ak*! Then he'll release a mortar bomb: *bam-bam-bam*! You'll think there are so many people, but it may be just one or two.

We found they were torturing our prisoners. They dig a hole and put honey all over the body, and leave in the sun like that. For the ants. You see? At first we were catching them as prisoners, but it was no use bringing prisoners. We had an Intelligence Section to interview them, but the Japanese never give out any information. They are so stone-headed people. When we found the sort of thing they were doing we don't spare them any longer. We shot them – we chopped their heads off. We don't allow our officers to see. We just eliminate them.

As for the fighting itself – John Mumo of the 11th East African Division tells laconically of what a man originally recruited in Kenya for the medical corps might find himself doing *in extremis*:

We had a very bad battle with the Japanese on the border between India and Burma. My job in this battle was just to shoot, to fire my rifle. It was a .303, with a bolt action. I killed a lot of Japanese. That didn't worry me – if I hadn't killed them they would have killed me. They were quite fierce. I certainly didn't want to be captured – who would accept that? We knew they didn't take prisoners, but just killed them.

I was wounded in that battle, here on my right leg – you see the scar behind my knee? It was a flesh wound and didn't penetrate to the bone. They attacked from behind. We weren't in trenches, but lying out in the open. As the sergeant-major I had just risen up to give the men their orders when I was hit. It felt exactly as if a sharp knife had been drawn across my leg. I put a field dressing on the wound; then I went on fighting.

One effect of the fearsome reputation of the Japanese was to make inexperienced troops nervously trigger-happy, especially in the already nerve-racking environment of the deep jungle at night. The Ugandan soldiers of 4 Battalion, King's African Rifles – thanks to the realistic battle inoculation ordered for them by their CO Derek Watson – were cool enough to hold their fire when Japanese 'jitter parties' came screeching and banging around at night, trying to provoke them into firing off precious ammunition and giving away their positions. But for the men of 25 Indian Division the first brush with the enemy proved too much, as Krishen Tewari – promoted captain, and a very new arrival in the Burma jungle – recalls:

On our first day of battle in Arakan I think the Japanese had come to know that the troops had been changed in front of them. That night they sent us a jitter party, as they used to call them. Two or three Japs must have crawled up, thrown some crackers and crawled away back to their bunkers. Our chaps, at night, in the dark, thought the crackers were a massive attack and they opened up on their fixed lines. The next company, in the dark, heard the noise and they also let go on their machine-guns. And the next battalion, same thing. The whole Brigade was firing – it was massive!

So we were all awake. I was manning the exchange, with a number of trunk calls going on, and the Brigadier was woken up and he was talking to the General. Immediately, the Divisional artillery fire was called for – *intense* firing! It died down after about two hours and at first light the General himself came from Divisional Headquarters to check up on the replenishment needed. There was no ammunition left with anybody. We had fired off the entire first line.

Between the Kalapanzin River and the western coast of the Arakan rises the Mayu Range, a crucial defensive line. In February 1944, 25 Indian Division was sent there to take over from 5 Indian Division. Their job was to hold up the Japanese advance through the Arakan and to try to secure the heights of the Mayu Range. One feature especially, Hill 551, overlooked a section of the Buthidaung–Maungdaw road between two tunnels. The Japanese were shelling Allied transport from the hill and needed to be dislodged – a task that 5 Indian Division had tried and failed to accomplish. Krishen Tewari watched as his own Division mounted a new attack.

> This was the first time I have seen an infantry assault on a hill feature. It was a Gurkha battalion; they were shouting their battle-cry of the Gurkhas, and they had their bared kukris in their hands, rifles slung across their shoulders and a bag of grenades. They assaulted this position and they threw the Japanese out. Beautiful sight – it is etched in my memory. You could see our troops running up the hill and those people trying to fire at them, and occasionally a Gurkha falling down also, hit by the bullet. You could see the heads of the Japanese through the slit of their fortification. A very charged atmosphere. The final assault on an objective is worth watching. It's something so beautiful, because people are falling and yet others are carrying on.

The beauty of the scene faded, though, when Tewari made his way up to the summit of Hill 551 after the assault: 'The stink was so appalling on that hillside. How those people could have held that hill feature with that stink of rotting bodies, Japanese and Indian from the earlier assaults ... They were just lying there unburied, undisposed of. And it's a *horrible* stink – and yet, people have to do their duty. It's part of the game. I picked up a bayonet from a Japanese who had been badly broken up. I just wanted a memento; I was not bothered about the state of his body.'

The respect – perhaps adulation would not be too strong a term – accorded to the Gurkhas, those splendidly tough and warlike Nepalese allies of the British, was a source of irritation to John Hamilton of 1 Gambia Battalion:

> General Slim thought the world of Gurkhas. Everybody thought Johnny Gurkha was a wonderful chap, a wonderful soldier. But they knew nothing about the West Africans, so they discounted them. They thought we were a bit of a Fred Karno's Army, that we could be put somewhere nobody else would particularly want to be; and if it was a bit jungly, that was all right, because we could survive in the jungle. But the West African Division was thought of as purely defensive. Nobody thought of using us positively. I believe that we could have taken Myohaung, the bottleneck for all the Japanese supplies and movements in and out of North Arakan, in February 1944, if anyone had thought we could do it.

The fact is that Slim and the other 'sepoy' generals thought well of Indian troops, but they did not think much of the West Africans. I'm afraid that the carriers and the soldiers of the West African forces remain the unremembered men of the Forgotten Army. At the time – unlike with the Indians – there was no political imperative to keep the African troops happy by rewarding them with decorations or showing them their efforts were appreciated.

When a Sikh havildar won a VC for his part in defending an Indian mountain battery's guns, while a Gold Coast private was awarded only the Military Medal for holding up a Japanese assault party for several hours with a Bren gun while badly wounded and on his own, a Gold Coast officer expressed the regiment's opinion in verse:

> The General wired Corps: 'There are bags of dead Japs;
> What about gongs to encourage the chaps?
> For most of them fought, though some of them ran,
> And they didn't half bash old Kaladan Sam.'

> Next day Corps replied: 'A VC you must pick,
> Say a dead Gurkha, or part-damaged Sikh,
> For the Africans, voteless, are not worth a damn;
> You might as well decorate Kaladan Sam.'

'Where the African does have the advantage in jungle,' says John Hamilton, 'the African peasant is used to living hard. He doesn't expect a spring mattress to sleep on, and he hasn't any fancy ideas about his food. He likes it and he likes enough of it, but he isn't a gourmet. He can live hard – harder than the Japanese – and manage extremely well. Also he does see and hear, almost without exception, far better than Europeans: far, far better.'

Some Africans in 81 WA Division were valued for another specifically non-European skill. The Division, operating in largely trackless, mountainous jungle, could only be supplied by air drops into jungle clearings, and the provisions could only be moved from one place to another on the heads of carriers. Aziz Brimah used to watch admiringly as these brave unarmed soldiers retrieved the parachuted supplies, often under mortar fire: 'At that time we don't have vehicles; you cannot take vehicles to the jungle. This jungle was rough and steep, with very high mountains and very thick trees. So we had what you call "Auxiliary Group" – some soldiers who were trained not to fight, but to carry anything that we have by head, on their head. These people were particularly employed to do that; it is the only solution, without it there is no other way.'

The European officers with the 81st did not carry their own packs. 'Instead,' John Hamilton says, 'we had what we called "boys", who in wartime were called "enlisted followers". They wore the same uniform and equipment as everybody else, but they weren't armed and their job was to be a batman, or personal servant. They carried our large packs, while we marched with our small pack or haversack. They were paid about a shilling a day – which was the same pay, incidentally, as the other African soldiers.'

There were some instances, however, in which the black-skinned soldier held an advantage over his white-skinned officer. The whites held the maps and gave the directions, so they were prime targets. Mutili Musoma, a Kenyan serving with 11 East African Division in northern Burma, says of the Japanese: 'They didn't happen to see an African before. Our units were going to fighting and we had a European as our leader. As soon as the Japanese could see it was Africans coming at them they keep waiting and let them pass – waiting for the European right at the back. The European was to be killed first – this was the way – because he gave the orders. So the Europeans would get a big can of boot polish and cover their faces with it, so the Japanese, they can't work out whether it is European or African.'

Given the structure of the British Army, and the comparative education levels of blacks and whites, the Europeans saw their role as providing leadership. 'We had to provide the know-how,' comments John Hamilton, 'the sort of "Where-do-we-go" and "How-do-we-do-it".' And the Mauritian, Etienne Marot of the King's African Rifles, concurs: 'In the KAR the white NCOs and the black NCOs were separate – a separate structure. With evolution, towards the end of the war, the black NCOs had developed; they were much better at dealing with their own men. But you needed a white cadre, there were no two ways about it.'

In the women's services, too, equality of rank between black and white was still only a twinkle in Whitehall's eye. Of FANY Headquarters in Nairobi Juanita Carberry remarks, 'I never saw a black woman in [officer's] uniform in those days. We had – what did they call them? – African orderlies. And in Signals we had Africans that came and took things from here to there, that sort of thing. But nobody on an equal footing, no.'

Kofi Genfi, Gold Coast:

When I enlisted, a black soldier in the Gold Coast Regiment was paid 1s. a day, excluding Sundays – 25s. a month. During the war a white NCO was paid, at the lowest, £10 a month. My wartime pay as an NCO was 30s. a month. We couldn't do anything about that. We were not actually paid in the jungle; when we were on leave in India we were given pocket money, but our pay itself was paid back here in the Gold Coast. At the end of the war I had about £50, for four years' service.

The British wartime NCOs, apart from the regulars, were not well educated and were poorly trained, we felt. But, for the fact they were white, they were made corporal or sergeant. You never saw a white private soldier – because he might have to take orders from a black NCO. There was segregation everywhere. In Chittagong the white NCOs and the black NCOs were having their own hospital and their own mess. Only very recently have the British come down from their pride. I would have liked the chance to become an officer. Whoever would not like to have been promoted!

We felt we had not been treated fairly over pay and promotion. That attitude brought about our fight for independence.

As demonstrated by Colonel Cole of the Colonial Office, during his patient proddings of the War Office over the Sergeant Anthony, Private George and Signalman St Elmo Smith promotion questions back in 1941–2, Whitehall was not blind to these inequalities. And indeed, when the dust had settled the matter had been raised again towards the end of 1942 in a specifically African context. A year earlier the military authorities in Africa had already seemed to be in favour of commissioning Africans, provided that they measured up to the job. But in 1942 General Giffard, GOC Military Forces in West Africa, had commented that 'Africans with suitable educational qualifications to carry the responsibilities of commissioned officers did not want to fight, and those that did want to fight did not reach the educational standards required of commissioned officers'[11] – rather a blanket statement. In a letter to the Colonial Office written in June 1942 General Platt, GOC Military Forces in East Africa, had noted that the increase in the number of British NCOs in the King's African Rifles on the outbreak of war had lessened the African NCOs' opportunity to command, and they had consequently lost some of their men's respect: 'Many African soldiers look to the white man to give the lead, and the farce is frequently seen of small parties going out, even on ordinary duties, accompanied by both a British and an African Serjeant.' He goes on to bewail the inexperience of many new British wartime NCOs, 'very few of whom have ever been out of the British Isles [or] had any experience of dealing with natives.' Platt felt that 'the East African is not yet fitted for commissioning as an officer, but the time will come when strong pressure will be brought to that end', and he recommended introducing African platoon commanders at Warrant Officer rank, at a decent salary of 105s. a month. 'It will give a well earned opportunity for advancement. It will be walking before attempting to run. It will restore to senior African soldiers their sense of responsibility and leadership, and their position. It will in time admit of a reduction in British personnel.'[12]

Senior KAR officers and East African colonial governors supported this sensible and far-sighted suggestion. The Colonial Office went further, seeing it as only a stepping stone to the granting of full commissions: 'It should not be regarded as a way out of granting commissions to Africans, and this should be made clear.'[13] However, General Giffard in a telegram of 9 August 1942 gives the whole notion a thumbs-down: 'The tribes from which the infantry are recruited in West Africa do not provide men with sufficient education to perform the duties of platoon commanders ... I do not intend to introduce the African Platoon Commanders into West African units.'[14]

Less than twenty-five years after General Giffard composed that telegram the last Union Jack would be hauled down in fully independent West Africa.

As for the attitude of white officers serving with black troops in Burma – Derek Watson of the King's African Rifles probably speaks for most of them: 'Some American asked me, "Weren't you frightened of soldiering with African troops?" I said, "Why?" He said, "Well, you captured their country. Were you not expecting to get a shot up the backside, or something?" I said, "Never entered my mind."'

Early in March, 81 West African Division had to withdraw from the Kaladan Valley, having first occupied the village of Kyauktaw and then being forced to yield it to the Japanese. Aziz Brimah, with 5 Battalion, Gold Coast Regiment, helped to cover the withdrawal; and John Hamilton, the last man out, recalls seeing the Japanese dancing round the top of Pagoda Hill near Kyauktaw in temporary triumph. By this time the main Japanese offensive in the north was well under way, and they were pressing forward to besiege Kohima and encircle Imphal, where the 14th Army was making its stand. These battles were to decide the fate of Burma and India. Of the total Japanese force of just over 80,000 men, 53,000 would be lost; and once again their beleaguered soldiers, cut off from all supplies, would have to resort to cannibalism before and during the Japanese retreat from June 1944 onwards. The 14th Army would suffer three times fewer casualties and would be able to launch forward its own decisive offensive with all of India's resources at its back. But the grim reality of war in Burma was to set a mark on every man who was there, and each would have to find his own way through this psychological jungle.

Victor Nunoo, Gold Coast: 'You see some people dead and you can't identify them. Maybe their head has been smashed, or maybe they have been dead for a week when you find them and they are decomposed. Only way you can identify them is to pick their Army discs and their papers. At the moment you are trying to pick a disc from a dead friend, you can't bear to touch him. You can't, but you have to. You become frightened – but you have to hold yourself up and keep your courage.'

Aziz Brimah: 'If you are in a war you forget everything. There was no time to pray. This jungle war was not a child's play – it was something very dangerous, I think unprecedented anywhere. You become a different person. You left behind every civilian attitude, every gentle attitude. You forgot ... everything. That is why, after the war, they did not let us come home straight away. They gave us two good months, with money, to go to any part of India. It was something to refresh us, to let us come back to a human being.'

John Mumo: 'Men are not really supposed to talk about those experiences – they are your secrets. When we left Kenya we were young men and our custom says that at that age, if you are not married, you are not supposed to touch a dead body. But when we went out to war we were compelled to do those things. We did not dare to talk about it, back home in the village: so those were our secrets.'

John Borketey, Gold Coast:

The first time I saw front-line action I was very, very frightened, because I was just a young soldier – I was twenty. I became very, very fearful. But I mastered it. We were told what would happen if we were prisoners-of-war. You would be taken by the enemy and killed or tortured. They will cut your meat into pieces: cut here, and here, and here.

I have killed very many Japanese. All the time you have to fight and then win firefight. Otherwise they will kill you. You can never feel tired at all. If you are tired, you are going to die.

I was having a small prayer book with me. A thing that I used to read day and night, for God to protect me. I used to put that in my haversack. God protect me from so many accidents. Once I was crossing a river, first in the line. The Japanese opened fire on us. Number 2, 3, 4 and 5 behind me were killed. But nothing touched me. God is my protector.

Aziz Brimah: 'This fight we took like a Jihad, a Holy Battle. So it was allowed to Muslims. If you don't fight – they will come to your home, and kill you!'

Victor Nunoo:

Some of our people had certain things – talismans – with them, to help them. Some bought them in India and took them into Burma with them. When you are wearing these talismans and you are shot at – off you go. You disappear.

We had two sergeant-majors. They were having these things. They can stretch their hands and gather their soldiers who are just around them, twenty–thirty people, and lift them up and move them to a different place altogether. Some of these people were in occult societies. The soldiers knew who had these powers and they liked to be in their company.

Some people went to the fetish before they left Ghana, and they took some things overseas with them. I did not, but I bought two in India. I don't know what was inside them – I didn't dare examine them! A friend took me to town and we met two ladies. They took us to an old man who was having these things. He said: 'You take this. You will always be a lucky man and you will never be hurt in any attack.'

Before we came back home I threw them away. But some people kept theirs. They should have discarded them, because these things were only to be used in war. But they didn't – and that's why some of them got mad later on.

At about the time that John Hamilton's Gambian soldiers were hacking their way out of the Arakan mountains into the Kaladan Valley, eighteen-year-old Frank O'Donnell was resting in the Italian coastal town of Ortona. Not that the teenage Canadian artilleryman was enjoying a winter seaside holiday on Italy's Adriatic coast. A lot had happened in Italy in the four months since O'Donnell had landed with 1 Canadian Division in the toe of the peninsula in September 1943. The Italian dictator, Benito Mussolini, had been daringly rescued from prison by German special forces and was now heading a puppet Government in northern Italy; but his country had ducked out of her Axis commitments and had prudently shifted allegiance to the Allied side. The German Army had occupied Rome and was entrenched behind a whole series of fortified lines stretching from the Tyrrhenian Sea on the Mediterranean coast of Italy to the Adriatic on the east of the peninsula. At New Year 1944 it was the Gustav Line that most concerned the Allies: a barrier stretching from Minturno, between Naples and Rome on the Mediterranean coast, across to just north of Ortona on the Adriatic. Behind this line the Germans – equal in strength to the Allies – had dug in for the winter. It was mountainous country, cold and inhospitable at this season, and the fighting as the Allies tried to break through the Gustav Line was savage, ridge-by-ridge, street-by-street combat.

The stench of rotting bodies became a keynote of the war for most soldiers, and for Frank O'Donnell it would be the thing he'd remember most clearly about moving up through the ruins of Ortona, a once-charming harbour town now broken and flattened. Fighting here had been so intense, so personal, that at times the Canadians would be occupying the ground floor of a house while the Germans were in possession the next floor up. Now 'you could only get through by a narrow strip which had been cleared; the roads were just rubble from the buildings that had fallen in. There wasn't anything that was untouched. I suppose it was a pretty town once.'

In early January 1944–5 Canadian Armoured Division came up to Ortona and passed 1 Canadian Division. They were going up for their baptism of fire, taking with them Joe Oldford from Cape Breton Island, now a company sergeant-major in the Cape Breton Highlanders, and Wilmer Nadjiwon of the Ojibwe Indians, a private with the Perth Regiment. Frank O'Donnell watched them go:

> I remember when we saw them pass us in their trucks, going up to put in their attack on the following day, they were laughing and singing. We were shouting at them, kinda mocking them: 'Poor silly buggers!' and stuff like that. 'You don't know what you're in for! You'll find out!' – and worse. We felt they shouldn't have been put in there; we felt they didn't know enough to protect themselves; we felt they were green. By that time we'd been in some kind of action for half a year, so we kinda knew the ropes.
>
> I met some of them later, in the hospital. A guy from the Perth Regiment, particularly, I recall. He'd been stitched with a machine-gun. And he said: 'We didn't have a clue.'

The attack, by 11 Brigade of 5 Canadian Division on 17 January, was an attempt to gain the high ground east of the River Arielli, in a coastal countryside largely flat but broken by river valleys. It was, in fact, a diversionary attack, feigning the start of an immense Allied push north through the eastern end of the Gustav Line. The intention was to tempt troops and armour away from the western end, where a landing at Anzio, between the Line and Rome, was to take place in four days' time. In view of the attack's secondary status, the Commander of the 8th Army had emphasised in his orders, 'Heavy casualties are *not* to be incurred.'

The Perths began the attack at 5.30 a.m. – entirely untried troops, assaulting well-defended positions across open ground like some re-enactment of the Battle of the Somme. It was a mess from the outset. They were shelled as soon as they started. There were muddles over communications, due to smoke and haze in the Arielli Valley and to breaks in the telephone lines caused by German mortar fire. A second attack in mid-afternoon failed and at dusk the Perths were withdrawn, having had three officers and forty-four men killed, sixty-two men wounded and twenty-nine taken prisoner.

Wilmer Nadjiwon:

We used a method of going in at daylight, and we got slaughtered. We lost a lot of people, our first day in. Broad daylight – you know, they could see you coming. They're up on a bank and you're coming across the flats – oh, they peppered us all right. I can't thank the British for that. I was anti-tank, on a five-pounder gun. I could see the infantry going ahead of us and being cut down. It didn't actually affect me as much as you'd think. I'd had a lot of talk back home on the reservation with the old soldiers from the First World War, about how they just piled up the bodies. So you expect it.

Shortly after noon the Cape Breton Highlanders started off to gain the ridge ahead of them. They had come close to their objective when the machine-gun crossfire began. The raw soldiers, seeing friends falling, took cover. But they could not use their radios effectively to communicate with their HQ because the aerials made their positions too conspicuous. As dark fell, they, too, were withdrawn from the shambles of an attack in which they had lost thirteen killed and thirty-three wounded.

Joe Oldford:

It was supposed to be a two-company attack and a flanking movement, but somewhere along the line somebody had changed the plans. And now, instead of coming in from both flanks, we were going four or five hundred yards straight up the centre; and there were the Germans on the ridge across, looking down at us. That was our baptism of fire, and we got a good 'un.

What they did – they were quite adept at it – they pinned you down with machine-gun fire and then hammered you with the mortars. We had one feller,

Macintyre – we thought he was dead. He lay out in a trench for four days and finally somebody saw him signalling with a piece of mirror he had in his pocket. His leg was off, up here. I still see him when we have a reunion each year. A good man.

About one-fifth of the inexperienced soldiers taking part in the attack had become casualties during the day. Altogether the two untried Canadian regiments had paid their butcher's bill to the tune of sixty men dead, ninety-five wounded and twenty-nine captured – all for absolutely nothing, to dangle a piece of bait that the Germans did not even sniff at.

Just as the men fighting in Burma had each to work out his own road to survival, so here in Italy the soldiers learned to face up to fear and the steady erosion of their stockpile of friends. When 5 Canadian Division, chastened by the toll at the Arielli diversion, switched from daylight to night attacks, Wilmer Nadjiwon found it easier at first:

> It was far better at night. You could yell and that made you feel better – making a noise. If you could yell and scream, you could feel sort of like a warrior.
>
> In fact, you're a very brave man there at the beginning. It's only after you come out and go back in – come out and go back in – that you begin to see that people are not around, that your friends are not around any more. Then it starts to affect you. You say, 'My number's in there somewhere. Just which one is it?' It gets to be, after a while, more difficult each time you go in. It's tougher: you're scareder. You still go, eh; but you haven't got the confidence that you had at the beginning.

CSM Joe Oldford, like many another, took his footing on the bedrock of Army discipline and Army orders:

> I would say that the training you went through is designed to harden you to battle incidents. With one action after another, you just get hardened. You don't *like* what you see, but you're told: 'You must continue, you must keep going, don't stop to help the wounded, that's what we have stretcher bearers for.' It's natural to want to stop and help, of course, and lots of times we did that. What can you do? There's bodies lying on the ground – you're going to help, if you can.
>
> You can criticise orders all you like, but you've got to go anyway. I may not like the orders I receive from my Company Commander; but I have to go, and I have to make sure that the men that are in the Company don't see any fear in my eyes. You don't like it, but you have to accept it.

Near the western or Mediterranean end of the Gustav Line the Liri Valley swung off north, carrying Route 6 to Rome, seventy-five miles away. At this point three rivers converged – Liri, Garigliano and Rapido – overlooked by the sixteenth-century buildings of the Benedictine monastery of Monte Cassino, which was spectacularly perched at the summit of a steep ridge. It was the strongest point of the Gustav Line, dominating the southerly route to Rome, and had been well fortified by the Germans who were positioned just outside the walls of the monastery itself. They did not use the monastery buildings for artillery observation, though many Allied soldiers who fought at Cassino are still convinced that they did. The fact remained that from January 1944 the monastery was the focus of four months of bitter assault-and-repulse fighting, as the Americans, New Zealanders, Canadians, British, Indians, Poles and Free French tried and failed to break through to the Liri Valley. For almost exactly the same length of time other British and American forces were penned up sixty miles north of the Gustav Line in a bridgehead at Anzio, having dithered long enough after their January landing there to allow the Germans to lock them in. It was an anxious time for the Allies; a time of steady, apparently fruitless loss among the wintry mountains around Cassino, whose monastery seemed to be an ever-open eye looking down on them.

After nearly two months of costly attacks the New Zealand General Bernard Freyberg requested, and the US 5th Army Commander General Mark Clark ordered, a bombing attack on the monastery, which was carried out on 15 February. The bombing achieved its aim and destroyed the historic building, but in the process created perfect machine-gun strongpoints for the defenders in the vaulted cellars under the rubble. Cassino village nearby was likewise destroyed. It would be another three months before the ruins of the monastery were finally taken, on 18 May, by Polish soldiers. Within a week the Gustav Line had been forced, and a break-out from the enclave at Anzio had begun. By 4 June the Americans were entering Rome.

Those who fought at Cassino would be left with ineradicable images of the monastery and its destruction.

Frank O'Donnell, Canada:

You could see the whole monastery from the south. We were looking up at it. It was huge – it had windows all along, several storeys of windows. It was white, and it looked as though it had been there for ever.

It was just another target. When you're firing, it's a sort of impersonal thing.

You don't see the result. You're not close enough to see somebody dying in front of you. It's not a man-to-man thing.

Tom Somerville, New Zealand: 'We were right under Cassino, firing on the castle on the hill. Cassino was perched right up on the edge of a very steep-sided ridge. With glasses you could see people moving around inside the monastery. When we came to fire on it – well, we were only too glad to see such a strongpoint pushed off that ridge. But we made a mess of it; only made it easier for the Germans to hide in the rubble.'

Nila Kantan, India:

I was doing a porter's job – no vehicles could go where we were. On our shoulders we carried all the things up the hill. The gradient was 1 in 3; almost on all fours we had to go.

I was watching from this hill all the bombers going in and unloading their bombs there. Then, soon after that raid, 1400 guns blasted at that hill. American super-heavy guns, I think. I was sitting in a jeep half a mile from the guns, and the jeep went up and down. The monastery was completely ruined.

Tom Somerville: 'Freyberg was all for bombing Cassino because of the loss of life trying to storm it: units wiped clean out, you know? We had a full view of the whole thing. We saw these great flights go over and drop their bombs. When they started it was an overcast sort of a day, and after a while the sky was covered with little travelling ripples; it must have been the vibrations. Ripples right across all the clouds, like ripples on water.'

Paul Gobine, Seychelles:

Oh God, that was atrocities, really. Five hundred planes, bombing Cassino town. When they finish, then others come. They reduce that place to nothing. Only one thing stand up; that was a sign, Hotel de Rosa. And a crucifix. Everything – no monastery, no town, no nothing at all. All gone.

Vesuvius, the volcano near Pompeii – it erupted. And the ash come as far as Cassino. Then my boys said, 'Well, this is God sending a curse on us.'

Wilmer Nadjiwon, Canada:

When the Polacks went in, all you could see was smoke. Nothing but guns firing – big guns, big guns, big guns, eh. Oh God – just roll, roll, roll ... We were amazed at the speed of their machine-guns. They had one gun there that could do 1350 rounds a minute. Our fastest one, I think, was the Bren gun, which did 650. In places where they had a gun pit we saw heaps of machine-gun shell cases five feet high.

Tom Somerville, New Zealand

Above – in the British War Cemetery in Alexandria, beside the grave of his brother Prid who died of wounds on 17 July 1942 in Alexandria British War Hospital.

Above – at the summit of the Great Pyramid, Egypt, 1941.

Right – after Anzac Day parade, 1997.

Above Off-duty in Britain: 'Dusky' Sinyinde, a South African balloon operator, amuses RAF colleagues with a tap dance.

Below West Indian ATS volunteers are entertained to tea and biscuits at the residence of the Earl of Harewood

During the V1 flying bomb campaign over London and south-east England in 1944/5, death and destruction could descend without warning at any time.

Above A woman stepping off a bus in central London turns in shock as a V1 explodes near Drury Lane.

February 1942: Newly captured prisoners-of-war sweep the streets of Singapore at the orders of the Japanese, while Malay civilians observe this ritual humiliation of their former colonial masters.

Above Allied prisoners-of-war at Fallingbostel camp in Germany show their delight at liberation, April 1945.

Below Scenes like this, at Belsen, were to haunt the minds of many servicemen who uncovered the terrible secrets of the concentration camps during the final days of the war.

Above Krishen Tewari, India (left), at Kuala Lumpur in 1945. Beside him is Salim Yazdani of the Punjab Regiment. These two friends, one Hindu and the other Muslim, were to be separated when Yazdani went to Pakistan after the partition of India in 1947.

Above Krishen Tewari today, at Auroville in south-east India.

Right Balwant Singh Bahia (India) as a young soldier before his service in Burma.

Below Balwant Singh Bahia today, at home in the West Midlands in Britain.

Four African veterans of the Burma campaign;

Al-Haji Abdul Aziz Brimah (above left) and Nana Kofi Genfi II (above right) of Gold Coast (now Ghana).

John Mumo (left) and Mutili Musoma (right) of Kenya.

VE Day in London, 8 May 1945. 'Boy, we had a ball. Oh Lord, what can I say? It was a wild and hectic time.

When we went through, everything was down – you could hardly get through with the rubble.

Nila Kantan:

I still can't forget the Cassino ruins. There was nothing but rubble. The bodies were still trapped, stinking – I had to cover my nose as I passed through. I saw legs there, blown off the stomach. I have never seen such a number of dead bodies in any battle. I counted more than 800 – then I gave it up. They were just there in the rubble, covered with a blanket. I felt very sorry. I didn't know where they were born, how they came there, whether they were enemy or our own troops – they were all mingled together. So many New Zealanders, British, Germans, Indians ... Seeing that, I felt there should never be a war again. I abhor war. I hate war.

In Cassino there happened another thing. The Germans used to put booby traps here and there. I was sitting watching one small child playing with her parents. She picked something up and threw – and both her parents were killed. That remarkably struck me. That child, that innocent child. She doesn't know what it is; just picked it up and threw it, and both her parents were killed. Then I thought: 'This war – it's abominable.'

When I started, I wanted to see all these places, all these new things. When I saw war in the desert, it was different kind of war. I didn't understand about war then. But when I saw the bodies in the ruins of Cassino, then it changed my mind. I asked: 'What for man is fighting man, and killing?' After the war I used to feel it so often; the scene used to come to my mind. Even now, as I talk to you, I can see the whole scene before me in my mental eye. But time heals everything, gradually.

The year 1944, like its two predecessors, would prove a bad one for the Australian Signal Corps officer, Rod Wells, in Borneo. After discovering the prisoners' radio and Wells's secret diary in Sandakan camp, and after they had finished torturing him, his Japanese captors had dumped him – along with his friend and co-conspirator Captain Lionel Matthews – in jail at Kuching. 'I wasn't too bad; I was down to about five stone from ten and a half stone. A pretty fat guy!' On the night of 29 February, Matthews and Wells were taken out of their cell.

They gave us each a banana; well, that was a bad omen. Next morning we were taken into the church hall at Kuching and tried. No charge, no defending officer. We were given the verdict. Recommended sentence: capital punishment.

We were taken back to court next day; the court had reconvened to confirm the sentence. 'Matthews – capital punishment. Wells – twelve years' solitary confinement and penal servitude.' Lionel and I parted company with a shake of the hand and a few personal messages to his wife in Adelaide. Then he was taken out and shot.

Rod Wells was taken to Kuching wharf and, in a bizarre piece of theatre, nailed up in a crate, in which he was swung by crane into the hold of a ship. There he was let out and the ship set sail. Two days later they landed in Singapore – where Wells had been captured two years before – and the Australian was taken to the notorious Outram Road Jail, a Victorian colonial prison that had been condemned as unfit for human habitation by the British before the war.

On entering Outram Road Jail I found the most terrible sights of dejected people with absolutely no will to live, just slowly walking around. From the back you could see their reproductive organs hanging down between their legs – there was just no flesh on them. It made sitting very hard. The hip bone would be pressing into bare skin. But you just had to sit and put up with the pain.

Everything was done to order. No talking was allowed. When no order was given, you were silent and just stayed in the same position you were in when the last order was given. At nine o'clock at night you were sent back to your cell. There was a light on all night inside the cell, so that there was not a second of the twenty-four hours you were in darkness. And this went on, for me, for twenty-three months, including my period in Kuching. Twenty-three months in solitary.

We worked at picking strands of hemp out of old ropes, to make new ones. The strands were too tough to break with your hands; you had to follow them to find out where they started. If you left any of those knots untouched you got a belt across the back with a sword in its scabbard. And as an added incentive, if you didn't do a hundred of these lengths of rope in a day by picking out about 200 lengths of hemp from each – you got no rice that day.

Meals were roughly five ounces of cooked rice and a bit of stewy water with a bit of weed in it, green grassy stuff. Tea – that was like a hundred-to-one whisky and water, pale discoloured stuff that was always cold when you got to it.

The little pair of shorts you had on had your number on it. 641, that was me. You had to learn that number in Japanese pretty quick, because that was your name and address and everything else. I lost all identity. I was no longer a POW – I was a criminal; just a number. That was the worst thing of the lot. Just a number.

The volunteers of the Trinidad and Tobago contingent of 1 Battalion, the Caribbean Regiment, were continuing with their training. Beresford Martin from Tobago had good reason to remember his battle inoculation under live fire, at jungle training school over in Trinidad. 'When I got down flat, I saw a little rising in front of me a good way off, maybe thirty feet. I crawled to it. When I got there I found it was a biting ants' nest. The shots were falling right in that nest, so I could not pass it. I put my steel helmet down on the ground in front of me, so that if a bullet hits that it will glide off. I couldn't raise my head from the nest; and the ants sting me all over my neck. Yes! When I got up from there all my neck was in blood. Well – a bite is better than a bullet.'

There is a good chance that the machine-gun that pinned down Martin in his ants' nest was wielded by Carlton Best from Port of Spain, by now a training sergeant. 'I was allowed 2 per cent casualties,' Best says. 'If I killed two in every hundred I'd be all right; if I killed three, I'd be having a lot of questions to answer.' In April, Best and the other overseas service volunteers left the Caribbean for training camp in the United States, where the boot was on the other foot: 'When we got to Fort Eustace camp in Virginia I was on the receiving end. We had to crawl up trenches under machine-gun fire at night, under tracer bullets. I came out of the trench, turned on my back and watched those lovely red tracer bullets, criss-crossing. Oh, they were pretty ... they were pretty!'

Fortress Britain was a-bulge by June 1944, bottom-heavy with men and the materials of war. Everyone knew that the long-awaited invasion of Occupied Europe was coming. The Germans certainly knew it, and knew that it would happen somewhere along the northern coast of France. They felt the most likely place for a seaborne assault would be in the Pas de Calais, the closest point to Britain. But the beaches of Normandy had been settled by the Allies as the invasion point well over a year before 'Operation Overlord' took place. The beaches were suitable for the swift landing of scores of thousands of men, the area was relatively lightly defended and it was within the radius in which a fighter based in Britain could offer air cover.

A massive deception took place in the months before 'Operation Over-lord'. Bogus movements of men and materials were not too carefully disguised; genuine ones were scrupulously hidden. The camps full of waiting men and dumps full of war materials were dispersed all over the southern half of England, as were the thousands of vessels needed to carry them to Normandy. Misinformation was freely available. Hard facts were rigorously censored. The *Luftwaffe* was only able to operate reconnaissance flights over Kent, so their cameras were fed with images of tanks, landing craft, gliders and dumps all over that county – all dummies. It was an unsettling, exciting time in the south of England for the young Commonwealth servicemen and women gathering there. Raymond Walker, the Cape Breton Island RCNVR sailor who had helped put his fellow Canadians ashore at Dieppe in 1942, returned from leave in Canada in January 1944 and was now waiting, with a hundred thousand other youngsters, for the green light on 'Overlord'. 'We were waiting for the invasion somewhere down on the southern coast of England – and we had one hell of a time down there. Oh, God! We met up with a lot of Canadian soldiers stationed around there, including one of the fellows from Cape Breton – his people ran the funeral halls in Sydney. He said, "Come on; a barrel of beer fell off a NAAFI truck and we've got her back there," he said, "and they're gonna tap her." Did we ever get loaded that night? – oh, good God! Great times, eh?'

There were plenty of American soldiers in the south of England at the same time; but the Canadians did not have much time for them, according to Ray Walker: 'The Americans – now, we didn't get along too well with them. They put on a show, you know; they figured they were better than anybody else, which they weren't. When we first went over to England, there was no Americans. Then they started landing over there; well, the price of everything just jumped sky high. They'd go ashore and they'd spend all their pay in one night. They spoiled things for the rest of us, you know? Between you and me – they're a bunch of bullshitters!'

Reg Burt, the Tottenham-born Canadian gunner who had been in England on anti-aircraft duty since 1940, was about to get his first taste of action overseas. Burt and his colleagues had come a long way since their first night in action, when they discovered they had left their Bofors gun's breech block back in the depot. Now they were highly skilled light artillerymen, selected to knock out pillboxes and provide air cover for the Régiment de la Chaudière and the Queen's Own Rifles of Canada during these two regiments' landings. Even in the tight security of the military compound, the young gunners found ways to amuse themselves as they waited: 'We went to the Hards at Gosport, where we were kept in a guarded compound. You couldn't go out at all. We were issued French money, called "occupation money"; so quite a few of us got over the fence and went to this little pub up the street. We had no English money, so we just gave the bartender our occupation money. He took it! They clamped down, though, after a few more tried it.'

'Operation Overlord' was to be carried out under the overall control of the US General Eisenhower, Supreme Commander of the Allied Expeditionary Force (as the invasion army was called) and directed on the ground by the Field Commander, General Montgomery. The plan was to land five divisions on the first day of the invasion, with 60,000 men in the first wave. Such an enormous number of men arriving so quickly was thought to be a necessity. The German commanders were considered capable of rushing reinforcements to Normandy from all over France and overpowering any smaller force. The AEF was to establish its bridgehead quickly, with the help of paratroop landings to secure strategic points, and a massive naval and aerial bombardment of coastal defences before the main assault. The force was to secure its perimeter and fight off German attacks, while more men and materials poured into the bridgehead from the giant Mulberry artificial harbours that would be towed across the Channel in pieces and assembled off Arromanches and Port-en-Bessin.

With 'Operation Goodwood' the British and Canadians would secure the town of Caen, seen as a gateway that would open the road to Paris; while the Americans would swing right and break out to capture the port of Cherbourg on the tip of the north-jutting Cotentin peninsula. PLUTO (Pipe Line Under The Ocean) would supply the necessary fuel at long range for the eventual break-out from the bridgehead, which would start a general Allied drive across northern France towards the Low Countries and Germany.

Five groups of beaches in the Bay of the Seine to the east of the peninsula were chosen and code-named for the landings. Reading from the west, they were Utah and Omaha which the Americans would assault, and Gold, Juno and Sword where the British and Canadians would land. The Chaudières and the Queen's Own Rifles were earmarked for the Juno beaches, north-east of Caen. And so it was for Juno that Reg Burt set out from Gosport on D Day, 6 June 1944. 'On the morning of D Day the mood was apprehensive, I guess, which naturally you would be. I was sick, to tell you the truth. On the barge they gave us a grab-all pill – and a brown paper bag as back-up, you know. Of course we were quite busy, too, getting the guns and trucks on. Bombers! They just filled the sky. You could hardly put a finger in between them. I don't know how many thousands there were – but there must have been a hell of a lot, I know that.'

Raymond Walker of the RCN was on his way to the Juno beaches too, to help land the Régiment de la Chaudière from his ship, *Prince David*: 'The weather wasn't good. The weather, in fact, was real bad; there was an awful swell, eh. As far as landing ... gee whizz, the place was bombarded! They had monitors, they had battleships that were firing quite a while before we got there. They had these LCTs – Landing Craft [Tanks] – that had been made into rocket ships. They tell me the steel deck would be red after they'd fired those. You'd see a whack of 'em going in. And the Air Force had bombed the defences too.'

Alec Dennis, in the RN destroyer *Savage* off Le Havre, was out on the eastern edge of all the activity and found D Day 'a complete, 100 per cent anticlimax.' Even so, he could not help but be impressed by what he was witnessing: 'You never saw such an armada in your life. Landing craft, minesweepers, bombarding destroyers and cruisers and battleships and monitors – the whole bloody lot. And then this wonderful organisation of Mulberries and all that stuff being towed across. It was really quite ... probably the most remarkable sight one's ever seen.'

Prince David arrived off the Juno beaches at about 7.30 a.m. Raymond Walker and the Chaudières set off for the shore in their landing barge on a rising tide, which covered an offshore reef and some cunning obstructions placed there by the defenders. 'A lot of the smaller landing craft hit these X-shaped things like fence posts under the water,' says Walker. 'There was a mine on each one; the barges would hit them going in, get the bottom tore out. The fellers got out, up to their necks in water; some of them drowned. The barge right next to us was hit – a man had to jump over and I guess the poor feller couldn't swim. He was an English feller, Royal Navy. He was down there hollering for help, and no one could help him. So he drowned right there in front of us.'

Reg Burt made his landfall a little later in the morning, arriving to find the assault well under way. Amphibious tanks had been supposed to spearhead the Juno landings, bu ʾie troops had preceded them instead and had run into strong Germaı resistance from emplacements overlooking the beaches:

As we got near Juno we could hear a lot of shells landing. We had a visit from an Me 109 that ran up the coast – he took quite a chance. Some guns fired upon him; we didn't. We were too busy trying to get in. We had what they called a wet landing. Our guns and trucks were all greased up for going in the water. And I guess we went in in about seven foot of water, which was quite a ways from the shore. The guys hung on to the gun – it was a self-propelled gun – and went in on the side of it. So when we got on shore, of course, we were all wet. I brought up again, I'm afraid. I wasn't a brave man by any means.

It seems quite likely that Raymond Walker and Reg Burt were in fact on the same beach at the same time; for the RCN sailor found himself making an unplanned landing along with the Chaudières:

Our barge was damaged and we couldn't get back to the *Prince David*; so we had to stay there on the beach after we'd put the guys ashore. There was a cliff there, not very high; if you stood up you could see over the top of it, but of course you couldn't stick your head up because of snipers and small-arms fire. And an amazing thing – we'd been there hardly any time, and in the middle of all this fire the Salvation Army was right there on the beach...

I wasn't at all prepared to be on the beach. I never had a rifle or a side-arm or anything. Eventually we got on an LST and they took us back to *Prince David*.

There was a funny thing happened while we were on the beach. One of the larger landing craft went aground and a whole load of pusser's rum came ashore in those stone jars with the wicker around them. Some of the fellers got a hold of that, and we all got into that and felt pretty good. A feller that was with us – Rumdum we used to call him, because when he got drunk he wouldn't stagger but couldn't talk – coming back, he got up on to *Prince David*'s deck and the Captain said, 'Take that poor man to the sickbay, he's shell-shocked.' He wasn't shell-shocked – he was drunk as a lord!

As soon as Raymond Walker got back on board *Prince David* they headed out to sea. Walker would be back in England before nightfall. But for Reg Burt the urgent necessity was to press on inland as soon as possible, to get away from the enemy fire.

As soon as we got the gun clear of the water we took off all the grease and whatnot else and got it ready for action right there on the beach. Both sides of us there were people landing on the beach and a beachmaster directing everyone. We listened to him all right, because he probably knew a hell of a lot more than we did. We had a big railway gun firing on us, and snipers. So we didn't stay on the beach very long – we started inland just as quickly as we could.

243

One of the worst problems was these damn snipers that were firing on us. It wasn't only Germans either. There were some French people too – civilians. One girl was caught with a rifle; she must have been seventeen or eighteen. The Chauds got hold of her. There was no arrest or trial or anything like that. She didn't live very long, I'll tell you.

Geraldine Turcotte of the Royal Canadian Air Force was half-way across the Atlantic in the troopship *Andes* when the news of D–Day came through: 'We had to get out of our bunks at five o'clock in the morning and get down on our knees. Oh, yes! Everybody in the whole ship! It came over the Tannoy: "Everybody! Out of your bunks and on your knees! The boys have landed!" – I can still hear it. Yes – yes, indeed.'

And the New Zealander, Jack Brown, heard of the landings from his prison camp guards in Leipzig: 'They said to us, "Oh, you'll never succeed. You'll never get on there." And we said, "Oh, you silly bastards..."'

Back in England, Sheila Parkinson had been moved to an American camp at Bushey Park, in charge of a hundred FANY drivers who were to go out to France as soon as possible after the D–Day landings.

Now these girls had been brought up and led lives where they had learned to call a spade a spade. They'd all been dug up from county families, and they considered themselves to be entirely adequate to anything. They'd been hand-picked by their previous owners and 'Post & Promoted' to me: that was the term for getting rid of anyone who didn't quite toe the line. They'd been brought up in families where you gave as well as received; service, therefore, was part of their make-up. *And* they had been used to getting their own way. They were quite splendid.

The FANYs were going to France to deliver a fleet of big caravans and Daimler cars to Supreme Headquarters, Allied Expeditionary Force (SHAEF), which was based in the old palace of the Sun King at Versailles. Sheila Parkinson got the girls and the vehicles down to Southampton Docks and found the US Liberty ship that was to take them across the Channel. She would need all her powers of persuasion and sense of humour during the next few days.

The crew of this ship had gone into Southampton to get drunk. The dockers were about to go on strike. So I said to them, 'Look, just get us into the ship and then you can go on strike.' So they did. They found us some camp beds, down in the hold. I said to the Military Police, 'Please come and sit on top until the crew come back.' They said, 'We can't do that – we can only operate ashore.' I said, *'Please* do – think if it was your sister.' So they did. When the crew came back, drunk, there were whoops of delight when they heard what they'd got on board.

It was a very rough crossing, so many of the girls were seasick. And the crews of those Liberty ships ... The Captain was large and fat and rather repulsive, and he insisted that he was supposed to look after people and that I was to share his cabin with him. Well, of course, the girls were all standing around giggling; they thought this was just wonderful. I managed to persuade him that I wouldn't be much fun and he'd be better off having the bed to himself ...

Anyway, we got across to Omaha Beach. A lot of these Liberty ships had been standing off with their cargoes, which they hadn't been able to unload. So I got the cook to throw a party and the electrician to put up lights, and we'd got enough musicians among our FANYs to have a small band. I said, 'We'll have carefully chosen invitations, only for people who are going to be helpful – that's people with DUKWs, people who can do this and that to get us ashore.' It was a *much* sought-after invitation. They all climbed up the ship's side and came in, and we had a hilarious, delightful party, and I said: 'One day's grace, and then – appear! Because we want everything on land.' Which they did.

Then began one of those strange wartime journeys during which everything seemed edged with hallucinatory clarity and imbued with almost unbearable intensity:

We were the first women anyone had seen there. The whole country of Normandy was devastated by bombing, ours and the Germans'. The French women were living in basements in these blitzed towns and villages we went through. The lilacs were in bloom, and they all came out from these dug-outs under the ground and broke off these boughs of lilac – I can still see it, I'm weeping as I think of it now – and they said, 'Lilac, lilac.' So we had lilac all over everything ... It was very moving, it really was.

We went on – eleven days without a bath or even taking our clothes off. We got to a tiny village and everybody was so tired from sitting that the girls just lay down to sleep, head to toe, in a fleet of undertaker's hearses. A delightful governess came with one gladioli as a welcome ...

So finally we arrived in front of the palace at Versailles, and drew ourselves up, covered with mud, and said, 'Here we are.' And some sprig of the Army appeared, and all he said was: 'You're a day late.'

The Canadians and British had been badly held up at Caen, the fiercely defended Normandy town they had hoped to take on D Day itself. The 21st Panzer Division was garrisoned in Caen; soon reinforced, they held off their opponents for over a month. In the broad swing of events this did not matter too much, as it concentrated German troops and armour on this section of the Allied bridgehead, the east, and offered the Americans a weaker defence to push through in the western sector when they launched their break-out late in July. By 20 August they had reached Falaise, twenty miles south of Caen, and joined up there with the Canadians to form a united wall behind which 50,000 German troops and two Panzer divisions of heavy armour were trapped and captured – though many more had got away before the 'Falaise Pocket' could have its top sewn up.

The fighting for Caen was markedly bitter and bloody; and Reg Burt was stuck there in the thick of things for the best part of two months. When the way was finally clear for him to go through the town he noticed what so many other soldiers observed about a newly captured town. 'Caen was in ruins – and it smelled a lot of dead, of course. It's a smell you never forget; I can't describe it. One of the things, too, is those little ticky maggots that get into the flesh – we used to call them tickers. You can actually hear them, ticking away, eating the flesh of the bodies.'

One of the features of the battle for Caen had been the massively destructive effect of the bombing carried out by the Allied air forces. Bomb-aiming techniques had been improving as the war progressed, but no bomb-aimer could yet guarantee that what he hit was what he had been supposed to hit. Some servicemen saw the funny side of friendly fire. 'I guess, during the whole war,' says Frank O'Donnell, 'I was bombed by the Italians, by the Germans, by the Americans, by the British and by the Canadians – and the closest anyone ever came to me was the Canadians.' And Charles Bell of New Zealand remembers, 'We used to say: when the German bombers come over, the English duck; when the English bombers come over, the Germans duck; and when the Yank bombers come over, every bastard ducks!'

But it was not a laughing matter when the bombs were accurately placed and actually hit home. Reg Burt was the victim of a mistaken bombing attack by Allied planes, an experience that shook him to the very core:

Well ... I had a bad experience. Just between Falaise and Caen. Lancasters and Halifaxes bombed us in broad daylight. We were just on the edge of a quarry. The Queen's Own were just in front of us, about half a mile away. The first two or three waves came over us and bombed the Germans; then somebody five miles to the rear supposedly put up a flare, a yellow flare which indicated, 'Bomb from here on.' So the bombing came right through us.

Our sergeant told us not to man the guns, just get in the holes, which we did. Hell, you can't fire at your own planes. They even machine-gunned us, they were so low. Well, I got buried with some other guys. You know, Lancasters carry very heavy bombs. One landed not too far away from us and it caved in the dug-out. I got out; one guy died. We tried to get him out, but he was dead by the time we did. And all this time the bombing was still going on. There was the 12th Field and the 13th Field down in the quarry – they really took a pasting. You saw guys burning, you know, from the bombs.

They sent me back to Caen. I couldn't talk, couldn't hear. I was there for four or five days; then I went back to the unit when they were in Falaise. But I was never right from then on. You know – it takes a long time to get over it.

Nerves in England, too, were being frayed around this time by the opening of the Germans' V1 campaign. The pilotless V1 flying bombs, or 'doodle-bugs', launched from sites along the French coast that were still beyond the Allies' front line, came crashing down at random on London and the south-east of England, causing hundreds of deaths and thousands of wounds. The first one fell on London on 13 June 1944, the same day as Geraldine Turcotte arrived in the city. The tension of waiting for the flying bombs' motors to cut out and the bombs themselves to fall – it was impossible to predict exactly where – was hard for the highly strung Canadian, who was working in the Administration section of the RCAF, located in the famous Knightsbridge store, Harrods:

I was a nervous wreck – I couldn't get used to them. When they took us from the place we were staying on the first night back to Headquarters, the taxi-driver says, 'It was a pilotless plane! It was a pilotless plane!' And he kept repeating that all the way. He was stunned. Oh, they were terrible. They – were – terrible! My God! I can still see them going through the sky, with the big red bellows bit behind. You'd say, 'Keep going – keep going – keep going ... don't stop! ... don't stop!' – 'cause you knew if they stopped overhead, you'd be stopped too.

There was one really bad doodlebug episode. Had I been at the bus stand, as I normally was to get to work on time ... but my hair was curly and I'd washed it, and I couldn't get the comb through it, so I was late leaving. I was in my room, and my room just went right up like that and came back down again. And I let one scream out of me! Of course everybody came running. My window was open and all you could hear was falling glass – I'll always remember that. And then, down at the end of the street, was ... an awful mess. Boy, oh boy.

So, you know – it was food for thought. It took me a while to get over seeing that. But you didn't let on. It was ... within you.

There were several voluntary organisations that made it their business to show hospitality to the young servicemen and women from overseas, and try to give them some relief from the tension of wartime dangers and difficulties. One that Geraldine Turcotte remembers with affection is the Lady Cadogan Club:

Oh, they were fabulous with us. All you had to do was get your officer to phone them and say, 'So-and-so would like to go to a castle for a weekend,' or just go anywhere. The English people were just fabulous – they really took care of you. Oh, my! – they couldn't do enough for you.

This one lady, her name was Lady Gowan and her husband had been in the Army – she lived in this huge hotel – she wrote to me and she wanted me to go for dinner. I was petrified! I didn't want to go. Well, she was offended. She phoned my officer and she said, 'What have I done, that I should deserve this?' So my officer said, 'You're going to have to go. You shine up your buttons and your shoes, and go.' I went! Lo and behold, when I got there the door was opened by a footman, and oh! the whole works. She came trailing across the hall, with a long gown on. I was just shaking in my boots. Anyway, we go in and there is this officer with braid up to his elbows – do you know who it was? Bomber Harris! Can you imagine? He was marvellous. He made me parade around with my uniform. He liked the hat, the little hat we had. And he said, 'Why can't *we* have those?' And it wasn't very long afterwards that they had them, the RAF girls. So I had my effect!

Sometimes the girls were invited, not just for their own sweet sakes, but to help with entertaining young servicemen who were convalescing from wounds. It could be a harrowing duty: 'Oh, some of them were sights – my God! But you couldn't ever let on that it was abhorrent; you daren't let them know. One night we went to a Hallowe'en party across the Lambeth Bridge and they'd asked some of the lads from Basingstoke – the unit for facial burns. My God, I didn't know any different. And I said, "Why have they got such frightful Hallowe'en masks on – such terrible false faces?" And someone said to me: "They're not false faces – they're *their* faces."'

The last year of the war saw the Allied bombing campaign finally begin to have the long-hoped-for effect. Now that Pathfinders were pinpointing targets, navigational and bomb-aiming equipment and techniques were better, and the Luftwaffe was becoming a spent force, the German economy could be seriously damaged. And, while the Lancaster remained the RAF's preferred heavy workhorse, the twin-engined Mosquito light bomber had become the speedy thoroughbred of the Royal Air Force.

Two weeks after D Day the Jamaican airman, John Ebanks, embarked on his first operational flight as navigator in a Mosquito with 571 Pathfinder Squadron based fifty miles north of London at Oakington in Cambridgeshire. As with the Canadian air-gunner, Charlie Hobbs (now into his second year as a prisoner-of-war in Germany), a plane crash had messed up Ebanks's chances of qualifying as a pilot. Having gained 100 per cent in his maths and flying tests, the twenty-four-year-old Jamaican was on course to become a competent operational navigator. But that did not stop him experiencing those universal first-night nerves:

I felt very excited, very nervous. Up to that stage I was a good boy – the youngest licensed lay preacher in the Anglican Church of Jamaica, in fact – and I said a prayer before take-off and before coming back. That first trip we got to Hamburg, flying at 30,000 feet, and bombed; but the bomb release had iced up and the bomb didn't go. You can imagine how disappointed we felt!

The Mosquito – well, we were the fastest small bomber in the air at that time. We could go, normal air speed, 300 mph. At 30,000 feet you can have winds of 200 mph; so with a good tail wind I have been to Dusseldorf in one hour. Of course it took nearly four hours to come back against that wind. People say the body of the Mosquito was made of cardboard, but it was plywood. I don't think our ground crews ever got the credit they deserved, because you'd come back at three o'clock in the morning after getting shot up, and you'd look at the plane and think: 'How the hell did we get back in this? It's like a sieve!' But by seven o'clock that morning it would be like a new plane.

By this stage of the air war pinpoint bombing could be accomplished very accurately by a highly trained Mosquito crew; but John Ebanks draws a distinction between marking industrial targets away from urban centres, and the kind of work the Pathfinders were expected to do over the cities themselves:

When we went to a target like a machine factory, the Pathfinders were supposed to go over and drop a flare on it – within yards, you know. Pinpoint the target. When we went to Berlin we didn't have any specific target. Just drop it into the middle of the city. When we go to Cologne, same thing. Our job – this is what we were told, anyway – was to keep the inhabitants of Berlin awake all night, so they couldn't do much work next day. That was why we called this type of operation the Milk Run. Twenty of us would go in at eight o'clock at night. Another twenty would go in at eleven o'clock. Every time the planes came over the city the people would have to go to the shelters. So they never get sleep. We know it was effective, because a German soldier was killed on the Russian front and they found on him a letter from his mother in Berlin saying, 'My God, we can't get any rest on account of these bloody English bombers coming over.'

A month after the Americans entered Rome the German C-in-C of the South-West Army in Italy, Field Marshal Albert Kesselring, was pulling back up the Italian peninsula. At various points his forces stopped to make a stand and hold up the Allies' advance – the Americans and Free French on the Mediterranean coast, the 8th Army along the Adriatic. Around this time the men from Trinidad and Tobago, after their battle training in the United States, landed in Italy with the 1st Battalion, the Caribbean Regiment. The Tobagonian Vernon Alexander, like the Seychelles Islander Paul Gobine a year before, quickly realised the advantages of learning pidgin Italian: 'Naples was like I read in a book at school. Italians, they were hostile people – very hostile. But after a time, when we got to know the language, we'd say in Italian, "*Buon giorno*, good day. How are you? Where are you going? *E possibile*, is it possible I can come with you, *Signorina?*" And they would say, "*Si, si, molte possibile*, plenty possible!" '

The Caribbean Regiment was destined never to catch up with the front line, now right in the north of Italy. In spite of all their battle training the West Indians were withdrawn to Egypt before the year was out – to protect them from the unaccustomed rigours of a snowy northern winter, they were told. This was a bitter disappointment to Carlton Best: 'If we had fought ... if we had fought, I would have been able to show you a VC. That's what I would be presenting to you. I didn't want anything else but a VC. I didn't want all the other medals. The Victoria Cross, that was what I wanted – a posthumous one!'

The Canadians, however, were right in the thick of it, up against the Gothic Line. This, like the Gustav Line, was a cross-peninsular fortified line, running from just south of Rimini on the Adriatic coast to Massa, about forty miles north of Leghorn on the Mediterranean. The Gothic Line itself was to prove a nut less tough to crack than the Gustav Line had been. An 8th Army assault in the last days of August 1944 broke through near the Adriatic end; by early September the US 5th Army was also through, in the centre of the line. When severe winter weather closed down the offensive towards the end of October, the Allies had fought their way almost to the edge of the great shallow Po Valley that stretches across the top of the Italian peninsula.

In early August Frank O'Donnell, advancing from the Gustav Line with the 5th Army, was in an observation post near Florence. Here he had the novel experience of watching Italian soldiers going in to attack their erstwhile German colleagues:

> The Italians – they were something else. I'll tell you this: one of the Italian guys got caught by the Germans, and they sent him back to us stark naked – to show their contempt, I imagine.
>
> Well, there they were – on our side! We were in a big farmhouse, and the Italian officer put on a huge pot of vino over the fire in the house to make what they called grappa, while his men went out on patrol. He kissed every soldier on both cheeks before they went and he did the same thing when they came back.
>
> Then they were replaced by the Loyal Edmonton Regiment, and the contrast was really something. The Captain of the Loyal Eddies had a couple of his men marched in on some charge. There was no charge sheet or nothing; he just said to him: 'You haul ass, you bastards! Back you go,' he says, 'and if you do it again I'll deal with you – personally.' That was his words – 'Haul ass, you bastards!' There was no kissing on both cheeks with him!

Wilmer Nadjiwon of the Perth Regiment and Joe Oldford of the Cape Breton Highlanders were taking part in the 8th Army's stop-go, gruelling, hard-fought advance up the mountainous eastern side of Italy. The Perths and the Cape Bretons shared many assaults and very many deaths during these summer and autumn months of 1944. Since the débâcle on the Arielli river in January, says Wilmer Nadjiwon, some lessons had been learned about frontal assaults in daylight. Now the object was to steal through the enemy lines by night, so as to be able to surprise him from behind at dawn:

> At night you can go pretty close to him and just sneak your gun past him on the road. It's not too dark, anyway; you can read a newspaper by night in a

battle, with no trouble at all. Then, in the morning, you're behind him. His guns don't traverse, so he can't aim at you. The guys used to take their Bren guns and shoot down into his position, and he'd quit. It was good. We had a bit of luck that way. The only daylight fighting we'd do is when he's on the run and we'd have to catch up to him. But as soon as he stopped, we'd wait till dark and go in again.

At about this time, on and around the Gothic Line, CSM Joe Oldford was at the sharp end of the offensive. His actions here, and later on in Holland, would win him a Distinguished Conduct Medal. Oldford did not tell anyone – even his children – about his DCM for more than forty years. 'I kept all my wartime experiences bottled up,' he says, 'to my sorrow. But most veterans who were through action are the same. They feel it sounds like they're bragging if they tell a story, when actually they're not. I'd rather not talk about things like that, for fear of being misunderstood. And yet – I know I should have talked to my kids about it.'

One of these actions took place at Montecchio, on the Gothic Line. The Cape Bretons and Perths were ordered to capture a number of strongpoints on the Monte Luro heights, spurs of high ground that overlooked the town of Montecchio. The Germans had prepared the area meticulously to give them every defensive advantage. Houses and trees were cleared away to open unobstructed lines of fire. Minefields were sown by the River Foglia, and anti-tank ditches dug. Machine-gun posts, barbed wire and pillboxes were dotted across the slope up which the assault would be made. Anti-tank guns, tanks and flamethrowers had been well dug in. At 5.30 p.m., in broad daylight, Joe Oldford's B Company started off through this carefully planned death-trap.

On 30 August 1944 [reads the DCM citation] CSM Oldford was with B Company, leading a daylight assault across the River Foglia in the initial action against the Gothic Line. Flat ground offered no cover, and the assault troops came under extremely heavy and accurate fire from enemy weapons of all types. The leading Company suffered very heavy casualties. Every movement was observed from the enemy positions on the high ground which was the Company's objective. In the face of this intense fire, and faced with almost certain death, CSM Oldford dashed forward across 300 yards of open ground to reach the forward platoons. These platoons had suffered many casualties, and had been scattered by the intense enemy fire. With great coolness CSM Oldford re-organised the remnants, and for five hours held the position. CSM Oldford's courage and leadership relieved a very serious situation.

Joe Oldford:

Montecchio was in mountainous country; grape vines and olive orchards. There was very little else, because the Germans had cleaned out the cattle and the farmyards. Intelligence and scout patrols had gone all over the terrain, walked all over ... nothing there. A few days later we received orders to go in and occupy this Hill 120 – there was nothing there, they said.

My Company was the lead company. We got across the highway and up Hill 120 – two platoons, one left and one right; one in reserve. We got to the crest of the hill and all hell broke loose. Machine-gun fire. What the Germans had done – behind the back slope of the hill they had dug in, into the hill. They had 300 men in there, a hospital, beds, everything. Unless you got over the top of the hill and searched around, you'd never know it was there.

As long as there's mortar fire and machine-gun fire on you, then you're pinned down. You have to find what cover you can. There's no way you can run anywhere. You're working uphill, too. It was a hard way up, because the Germans had the advantage all the way. There was a house on the crest of the hill and they were in part of that, covering the windows and doors. It was a hard go.

We never did have full company strength in those attacks. A company is what? A hundred and twenty-eight men? If you had sixty-six or seventy you were lucky. There was so much action we were losing people all the time, and you never got the reinforcements you needed. I think I had about eighty-six men going in on that attack, and when we had to pull out I had about thirty-three men left. However ... that is the way of war.

Even if soldiers under fire did find a bullet-riddled building in which to take cover, they had to be constantly on the alert for booby-traps. Joe Oldford's men on the Gothic Line had to learn to be wary of anything out of the ordinary.

The Germans would leave something that's designed to catch your curiosity, and if you picked it up – you're gone. And they were very, very ingenious. This platoon officer took his men into a house and he said, 'Don't touch anything.' There was a watch on the table, attached to a wire. He said to his men, 'You get outside and get cover. I'll be out in a little while.' He took the watch, very carefully, and he backed out. There was a slit trench very conveniently dug right by the door. So he got down in the slit trench, took the watch and gave its wire a yank. Didn't blow the house up – he blew the slit trench up, and himself with it. Oh, they were uncanny – they were uncanny, the way they could second-guess you.

Two months before the Cape Breton Highlanders went in to assault Hill 120, and 5000 miles to the east of Montecchio, another epic battle for a hilltop took place. The scene was Lone Tree Hill, on the Burmese–Indian border. A medal for bravery and cool leadership was won here too; a Military Cross, to be worn on the tunic of Danny Misra of the Rajputana Rifles.

By 23 June 1944 the main Japanese offensive in Burma had ground to a halt, with appalling losses sustained. It had all started so well in February, with the diversionary attack in the Arakan peninsula into which British, Indian and African troops had all been drawn; then the main push westwards across the Indian border, right up to the towns of Kohima and Imphal. But here the Japanese had found General Sir William Slim's 14th Army established among the hills, forewarned by accurate intelligence of their plans to encircle both settlements. However, the Japanese thrust was so quick that by the end of March prospects were looking grim for the defenders. Encirclement was the key to the battle. By 5 April Kohima, to the north, was completely surrounded. In a deadly two-month siege fighting was often hand-to-hand; during the famous battles centred on the District Commissioner's tennis court, grenades were lobbed from Japanese to Allied trenches and vice versa, as close as tennis balls had been lobbed by the DC and his guests before the war. But Slim kept the beleaguered garrison supplied from the air and by June the siege had been lifted.

At Imphal, about sixty miles to the south, reinforcements were able to arrive by air, and although at times the front lines were as close and the fighting as vicious as at Kohima, the defenders of Imphal were able to deal with the numerous infiltrations behind their lines carried out by the Japanese. In July the offensive was reversed and the Japanese were withdrawing through the jungly mountains of northern Burma, with US General 'Vinegar Joe' Stilwell's forces of Americans and Chinese coming down on them from the north and the 14th Army pushing them from the west. It was the first serious set-back they had had in Burma, the prelude to eventual defeat.

Lone Tree Hill is a jungle-covered height near Shenam to the south-east of Imphal. Danny Misra gives a superb description of what happened there between 23 and 26 June, events that were typical of many such incidents during the sieges of Imphal and Kohima:

The Japanese had outflanked us on the Tamu Road – a small force of infantry, with a howitzer on an elephant. They brought it up on to Lone Tree Hill, which overlooked the entire area. They were so pleased to see us below that they fired a shot which landed in our Headquarters.

Everyone was very worked up. What has gone wrong? How can this shot have come from behind us? Immediately a message came through to say that these troops must be winkled out from this Lone Tree Hill. The CO said to me, 'I'll take two companies to deal with them; you take charge of the rear.' I pleaded with him, saying I didn't want to be LOB – Left Out of Battle. He said, 'No, no, no.' I said, 'Let's toss for it.' So we tossed a coin, and I won. Next minute I was off, with the two companies – about 200 men.

It was getting dark and I did not know exactly where the enemy was. We came across a dead Jap. 'Must be very near it,' I said. Then I saw the hill. We attacked straight away, a frontal attack. Speed was of the utmost importance, because they were digging in and reinforcements were coming. They realised they had got a very valuable position.

We got to within thirty yards of the objective and then were grenaded back. We had flesh casualties, nothing lethal. I realised it wasn't on. I withdrew and took up a different position, sent a message that the first attack had failed. We waited all night, watching, heckling them – trying to provoke them to open fire, to know where their machine-gun is.

Morning came; time for another attack. To ask for artillery support would be useless – we were too close to the enemy. But I knew that under air attack the Japanese would withdraw, then rush back as soon as the planes had gone. So I asked the Air Force liaison officer for an air strike from north to south. 'You strafe, you bomb, you create merry hell,' I told him. 'But don't go away after the first strike. Turn round and make dummy runs, and we'll rush in while the Japanese are still withdrawn.'

The Lord helped us. We got to the top: no firing, nothing. Immediately I told my men, 'Spread out and put your LMGs [light machine-guns] in front, facing the enemy.' After ten minutes the planes flew away and the Japanese returned, unsuspecting, chatting away and laughing, the officers with their gloves on and bare swords. We opened up at thirty yards, and I saw with my own eyes the enemy dropping like flies. They then thought it wise to withdraw. I said, 'I shall expect a counter-attack at about 0700 when it is dark.' Believe it or not, it came at that time. Everything opened up – again they withdrew. I knew that in the early morning would come their final counter-attack. So it happened.

This one was hand-to-hand fighting. I was there – I saw it. At such a time you feel both detachment and absolute hatred. I am not a man who could kill anyone, not even a fly; but at that moment your one aim in life is to kill him.

I felt myself change – I become a demon. I swear, I scream. The Muslims shout their battle-cry; the Rajputs cry, '*Jai Mata*! Victory to the Mother!' and the Jats shout the war cry of Hanuman the monkey-god. The Japanese, too – they were shouting '*Banzai!*' and wielding their samurai swords ... a medieval sight.

After the struggle they withdrew completely and I knew that we had won. I thanked the Lord; it was a tremendous feeling of relief and joy. Having reached such an extreme state of hatred, you can't hate any more. You become detached again. You see the dead enemy, and they seem like so many partridges you have shot. But we feel very sad when we see our own men. There is a feeling of loss. You remember each person and what they were like.

There in the jungle we did our utmost to perform the different religious last rites for the dead. While we were organising funerals, a message came from the CO – 'Well done, Danny! I've had a signal from General Slim to say "It was called Lone Tree Hill, but hereafter it will be known as Rajputana Hill".'

With the Japanese in retreat from the border area, the 14th Army geared itself for a monsoon offensive in southern Burma. This was to be the start of the greatest – and, ultimately, the victorious – push eastwards and southwards, and it began in torrential rain, which quickly turned every jungle track into a river of slippery mud. In these conditions Derek Watson took his 4th Battalion of the King's African Rifles into Death Valley.

The Kabaw Valley (*Kabaw* meaning 'death') had earned its local name because of the malaria, scrub-typhus and other jungle diseases it harboured. It lay just across the Burmese border, running south and west to the town of Kalewa on the River Chindwin, the objective of this advance by 11 East African Division. Derek Watson's 2000-strong column – code-named WATCOL – set off down the Kabaw Valley on 12 September. The first mile took two days to complete, with the askaris having to cut and lay logs to form a track, so that the mules carrying supplies and guns could avoid the mud which would otherwise have swallowed them up to their bellies. There were flooded chaungs across the route which had to be crossed, high north-south ridges on every side, sheer cliffs on their right, steep bamboo slopes on their left, and incessant rain. Soon the whole force was on air supply, the packages dropped into clearings hacked by the men out of the wet, muddy jungle. This was not exactly a picnic. On the way they kept coming across signs of the Japanese retreat. 'When we got down the valley a bit,' Watson remembers, 'we found two houses full of dead Japs, or dead and dying. And we just ... where the hell did we get the petrol from? ... we just burned the whole bloody thing. Smell was *appalling.*'

Sometimes the Japanese were very much alive. Mutili Musoma from Machakos in Kenya, serving with 302 Field Regiment, recalls their cunning and their stubborn bravery:

> The enemies were trained to make a sound like an animal, like those baboons. *Wooo-ooo-ooh*! And you can't make out whether it's someone. Then soon, if you are not careful or aware, you will only hear one shot – you're dead. There were a lot of bamboos and the Japanese were hiding under that bush. Like that, one man can struggle you more than twenty people. No one can go round the place where he is. He can kill more than thirty or forty.
>
> The Japanese was hard trained. He can't accept to surrender. When he sees that he's unable to manage anything more, he simply burns his rifle and ammunitions; and after that, he accept you to kill him. But he can't accept to be arrested. If he refused to go and try to resist, we simply took out the panga and killed him. Cut his head off. I killed many with the panga.

A fortnight after setting off, WATCOL came to Leik Hill, a high knife-edge ridge above the track where the Japanese were well dug in inside bunkers. What followed was 4 KAR's most ferocious battle of the war, with attack and counter-attack in thick jungle, on a track so bad that Watson could hardly find a piece of level ground to site the howitzers of his mountain battery.

> It was a bloody great hill [says Watson]. The Japs had a bunker set back from the top, and we got into this – the Japs had left the position – and pinched an officer's haversack, which we brought back. Inside was rice paper done on two rolls of wood – you rolled it out, a great long thing – and it had the whole of the Japanese Army layout before they attacked Kohima. The Japs must have wanted it back, because directly after that there were jitter parties out, coming round our position yelling and screaming. However, they didn't get it: we handed it in.

On 10 October Watson's men attacked the fortified hilltop, but were repulsed. 'I sent a signal back saying we'd failed to take it, and they said, "Oh, you've got to withdraw." I said, "I refuse to withdraw, because I've got wounded and I really haven't got enough mules to put them on. So I suggest the rest of the brigade comes up."' They did come up, and over two days, 22–3 October, 4 KAR finally captured the Japanese positions one by one – 'They were all down gullies. You couldn't see anything, you know: pitch bloody dark' – culminating by rushing the bunker on the top of Leik Hill and silencing its defenders with a 'beehive' explosive. There could be no artillery support for the attackers, given the conditions; it was a case of running forward into fire. Derek Watson's force lost nineteen dead and 102 wounded. On the ridge, after the battle, twenty-three Japanese bodies were counted.

It was Burmese jungle fighting epitomised: bitter, prolonged, nerve-racking and deadly, in miserable conditions, carried out by men who were already exhausted and falling victim to sickness of one form or another – particularly the whites, according to the Gold Coast soldier John Borketey: 'Europeans suffered from malaria, dysentery and pneumonia. If they drank from the water, within two–three days you would see them on a stretcher being carried to the airlift to India. But we Africans could drink that water; we didn't suffer at all.'

Derek Watson was one of the sufferers. Shortly after the battle at Leik Hill he was invalided out of the Kabaw Valley and back to India. 'I'd had amoebic dysentery on me for a month. It was so bloody painful; it felt as if something had got hold of your balls and was squeezing them all the time.'

Soldiering in the Far East was not entirely concerned with pain, disease, death and the jungle. Every few months the men, if lucky, could hope to be taken back across the border for some rest and relaxation in one of the great Indian cities. The Gold Coast Regiment sergeant, Kofi Genfi, always a bit of a ladies' man, got to know the pleasures of Calcutta, Madras and Karachi during his service. It is Madras that he remembers with most affection.

Oh, the Indians were very kind to me. In Madras I went to dance – I am a ballroom champion dancer. I sat down, but I couldn't get a partner. I was shy. I didn't know how to engage a lady.

A man came and said: 'Do you want to dance?' He could see I was shy, a soldier in army dress. He said, 'Come, come.' He gave me his wife. And luckily enough, she was a dancer. We started to dance, and they all stopped and looked at me as if I was giving a demonstration. At the end, there was applause. Then every lady wants to dance with me! Oh, yes ... I remember that day.

In northern France the Allied Expeditionary Force was continuing to forge eastwards from Normandy. General de Gaulle entered Paris on 25 August. By the beginning of September both American and British forces had crossed the Seine; within a couple of days they were in Belgium. Brussels was liberated on 3 September. There were some difficulties during this headlong gallop. Supply lines were stretched – the desert war problem – because some vital Channel ports were still in German hands and much of the material needed had to come via Mulberry and PLUTO back in Normandy. And there was a conflict of opinion about the weight and direction of the continuing push into Germany – Montgomery believed that it could be done with a narrow but massively powerful northern thrust focused through Holland; the Americans preferred a more diffused front with greater weight in the south along the French–German border. Once Montgomery was into Belgium he persuaded the Supreme Commander, General Eisenhower, to allow airborne landings ahead of the Allied advance, to seize key bridges in Holland across the rivers Waal and Meuse, across some canals and across the River Rhine at Arnhem. These were essential points to possess in such flat, easily flooded terrain.

'Operation Market-Garden' went well – two-thirds of it. Starting on 17 September, the American 101st Airborne Division captured canal bridges north of Eindhoven; by 21 September the American 82nd Airborne Division, helped by British tanks, had secured bridges across the Meuse and the Waal about twenty-five miles north-east, around Nijmegen. But disaster struck the most northerly of the three airborne landings, at Arnhem, where the 1st British Airborne Division had intended to take a railway bridge and a road bridge over the Rhine. Faulty planning meant that the first landings here took place several miles outside Arnhem, imposing delays. Back luck dictated that a strong Panzer division was unexpectedly present in the town. Some reinforcements, hampered by the weather, arrived late. The railway bridge was blown up as the Allies reached it. The timetable began to lag as things went wrong, so that in spite of great bravery and individual initiative on the part of the paratroopers, their opponents' hand was always strengthening as theirs weakened. By 26 September the remnants of the 9000-strong division had slipped away south across the Rhine, leaving more than 6500 men dead or captured in Arnhem.

Among these last was Ronald Henriques, the Jamaican paratrooper who had taken part in the Sicilian landings over a year before. Henriques, carrying a bazooka, had boarded his plane in England to fly to Arnhem with just one instruction left echoing in his mind: to kill Germans.

We left the coast of England early in the morning; must have been around five or six o'clock. When we dropped, a few of the lads hurt themselves in bad landings. I got down all right, got my 'chute off and we started marching up into Arnhem. On the way we smashed into a German officer in a car – must have been a big boy – and his driver, and we slaughtered them. We just left it one side and went up past the bridge. A lot of bodies, a lot of deaths were there – a tremendous amount.

We had to get across that river in these rubber boats. It was a rough time crossing that river; we were under fire all the time. But you know, it's not easy to kill people who are moving and floating. When we got across the river we did a lot of machine-gun work. We had to get behind these big trees, to get a little protection. We'd move from one spot to another, going forward, and eventually open fire at around twenty-five to thirty yards. We don't let any unit come closer to us than that, so it's almost hand-to-hand fighting.

As with many others faced with the stark reality of kill or be killed, Henriques found himself surprisingly calm and matter-of-fact in these desperate hours.

When you see your friends being killed around you, you don't feel anything. You've just got to grit your teeth and take it. You're in a war; there's no way of feeling sorry for anybody. You just keep on going. Afterward, you feel differently. Like when I was in prisoner-of-war camp and saw this sergeant, a very nice fellow who'd helped me with a lot of things – completely blind. A shell must have burst right in front of him. I'll say this – war is a crazy thing, isn't it? We don't need a war, do we? I didn't hate the Germans. Of course you have feelings when you have to kill a man; but when you're going through action, nothing seems to matter. You've just got to go forward and do what you've been trained to do.

Anyway – we were getting very hungry and were short of food. Then big food bags were dropped to us. We were pretty pleased to see them.

Throughout the 'Market-Garden' operation the paratroops were kept supplied by small unarmed DC3 cargo planes, flying through strong anti-aircraft fire. Ronald Henriques took part in several dangerous dashes across open ground to retrieve the precious supplies; and a fellow Jamaican, E. K. Powell, was one of those who helped deliver the goods from above. Powell, still in his teens, was a trainee flight engineer with Bomber Command. Convalescing in Wiltshire after a bout of pleurisy, he'd volunteered to help with the 'Market-Garden' drop, never dreaming that his little adventure might backfire on him.

We flew there in broad daylight. The DC3s were very, very slow and very, very stable. We were dropping weapons and food. There was a terrific lot of flak around, a lot of fire from the ground. The port engine went on fire – we could see it burning. I suppose what we expected, frankly, was that the pilot would not continue; he would turn around, because the Allied lines were just across the road. But he said, 'Those fellers down there need the food. Let us continue.' It was his duty to the men on the ground. So we just kept throwing out these parcels. Some were parachuted; some we saw bouncing.

Then – I do not know exactly whether the other engine was hit, but the pilot said, 'Abandon aircraft.' So we all parachuted out; but he continued the flight. I don't know why in the hell he would do that, because I'm sure he could have got out.

We could see the plane from our parachutes, falling in a shallow dive, blazing like hell. I suppose he just lost control. But we were fine. We landed among the Americans and they took us back to England.

For Ronald Henriques, down on the ground in Arnhem, there would be no lucky escape:

Well, we were crossing a field and a machine-gunner got on to us. I got hit in my leg, here, and somewhere along on the other side I got a ricochet – that wasn't much, but this one was bad. The Germans came up. One fellow wanted to shoot me, but there was a big strapping fellow there who said 'No'. He spoke to me in German, but I didn't understand him. They took me into the place where their doctors were and they took the bullet out of my leg with a magnet – I'd never seen anything like it.

I felt kind of annoyed with myself. I'd got pretty far, and I'd have liked to have gone on: to have put *them* in the bag. But anyway they put us on railway trucks, and they took us off into Germany.

Arnhem was the greatest experience I ever had ... not that I'd like to go back.

The soldiers in the great advance found mixed receptions in the towns which they entered. Back in the men's home countries the images shown in magazines and on the newsreels were of ecstatic locals garlanding their liberators. The mood among both soldiers and civilians was sometimes less euphoric, as Sam Meltzer found as he moved east with the RASC:

Some of the French weren't happy with our chaps. There was quite a lot of animosity back and forth. The soldiers were told: 'You can't treat every woman like a prostitute.' Certainly when we got to Belgium, though, they ran out with their bottles of wine. And when we crossed the River Meuse, chocolate and free cigarettes won the day with the locals.

We liberated Limbourg. The people were a little bit on the pro-German side, being so near the border. Our chaps resented being sent to Limbourg, I think. The Americans had already taken Paris, where everyone had asked, '*Où est les Anglais?*' And then of course the Canadians got a few plum jobs – Amsterdam was one of them. And we got Limbourg.

Meanwhile, back across the French border, Sheila Parkinson of FANY was supervising her 100 drivers around the SHAEF Headquarters in Versailles. Here she had a good opportunity to compare the entirely contrasting characters of two of the chief architects of the Allied drive to Germany – the diplomatic General Eisenhower and the brusquely single-minded General Montgomery.

Eisenhower was a good co-ordinator and totally civil – a proper soldier. He should never have gone into politics, because politics are cynical; and soldiers, on the whole, aren't. He liked to know how the FANYs were getting on and so on. A warm man. Whereas Monty was cold; he was: 'Tell me these three things, and go!'

I saw him addressing the men. He always made sure he was high up, on the back of a lorry or whatever. The rain was pouring down, and these men stood around and muttered and muttered and muttered. Then Monty appeared. He spoke to them in the most ungraphic language, but he told them exactly what was happening, as he saw it. They all listened to him and they all said at the end, 'Well, it'll be all right if *he's* about.' He had an amazing rapport with men – it was a soldier talking to soldiers, in language which soldiers would understand. But he had no time for women at all.

After a time the cracks began to show. People noticed it first in sleeplessness, or in outbursts of temper, or in a strange difficulty in doing what should by now have been second nature. Sometimes it was fear slipping off the leash; sometimes it was guilt at causing death; more often than not it was simply the tension and strain of war, draining the resilience of these fit and well-trained young men and women. Some of them had been coping with it, or ignoring it, or hiding from it, for five years now.

Pierre Austin, Royal Australian Navy:

I think one reaches the stage where you're beginning to think, in the back of your mind, 'I'm still here – but for how long?' It wore you down, in the end. I first realised this when I found myself very reluctant to go below at night. I was lying there one night in the middle watch and suddenly felt: 'No – I want to get up top!' You're still in your early twenties; you've never felt this sort of thing before. You think: 'What? . . . Good God – I'm scared! I'm waiting for the Big Bang.'

You couldn't talk about it to anyone. You might refer to it obliquely, to a friend, but you wouldn't come out with it directly. If you once admitted it – then you'd fall apart. I think we realised that, without being able to articulate it.

Joe Oldford, Cape Breton Highlanders:

Show me a man under those conditions who wasn't frightened, and I'll show you a liar – or a fool. I mean that. Talking to kids in school, I say to them, 'You want to ask me anything, go ahead. But don't ask me one question: whether I ever killed anybody. Because I don't want to know that myself.' They say, 'Were you ever scared?' I say, 'Yes, I was scared all the time. And anybody that ever said he wasn't scared was a fool, a liar, or he wasn't there.'

Geraldine Turcotte, Royal Canadian Air Force:

No way did I go to an air-raid shelter. Never did – never did! I said, 'If I'm going to get it, I'm going to get it in my bed.' But they'd find me behind the door in the morning, with the mattress wrapped round me. They'd find me at work, leaning up against the wall, asleep. So finally they said, 'You're going to have to go up to Scotland, to get away from this. Or – you'll have to go back home.' And I said, 'There's no way I'm going back home – not now!' So I went up to Scotland. And I couldn't sleep there, because it was too quiet!

Frank O'Donnell, Royal Canadian Artillery:

When you speak about fear – there are different types of fear. Fear of losing part of your body, or one of your senses; of being blown into oblivion; of someone consciously doing you harm, person to person; of stumbling on to something, ergo your own fault. Fear that you won't show up well, of letting the side down, of losing control of yourself. Fear in retrospect – that's when it grabs you, *after* the event.

You have to bounce back if you do temporarily lose control; otherwise you'd be lost. And in action, anyway, you never believe it does have your name on it. That's your protection. If you lose that . . .

Nervous talk could be quite contagious. Attitudes, rumours, general feelings can easily be passed from one man to another. A unit can become pretty helpless, pretty quickly. I think everybody understood that a frightened man had to be discouraged from running away – not because he's going to haul ass, but because he might encourage *you* to. You'd rather do without someone like that: you'd rather go it alone.

John Ebanks, Royal Air Force:

The tension was always there. Over Berlin one night, I remember seeing two Mosquitoes going down, shot down by ack-ack. And you could see them, as they were going down, burst into flames. Now that really gave me a jolt, you know.

Another night – and this is something I can thank my pilot Doddy for – we had come back from a Berlin trip; it must have been about our twelfth or thirteenth trip. Doddy and I shared the same room. He asked what is worrying me. I said to him: 'Doddy, I wonder how many innocent people we killed in Berlin tonight.' This was the only time I ever saw him get angry or cross. He said, 'Now you stop that damn nonsense. I'm telling you something, now. You see a lot of people in the asylum, in the mental wards – that's how they started. You are not supposed to worry about whether you kill anybody or not. You're sent on a job; you do it, and you come back and you forget it. That's our business.' He really was sharp with me. And I took his advice. It could have got to you, if you didn't have somebody like that to say: 'Now you stop your damn nonsense.'

Pierre Austin of the Royal Australian Navy had been waiting with growing apprehension for the Big Bang to happen; and in late October, in the Leyte Gulf on the eastern edge of the Philippine Islands, it did. *Australia* was one of the ships taking part in what would turn out to be the biggest naval action of all time, following American landings in the Philippines. The Japanese Navy came down on the landing force and its escorting ships, looking to decoy the latter away before moving in to destroy the former. The Allied fleet was indeed lured away, in pursuit of Japanese aircraft carriers which looked like threatening the landings (they were in fact only lightly loaded with aircraft); and the Japanese ships were able to get at the US landing force. However, they failed to press home their advantage and eventually withdrew after what amounted to a costly defeat. Nearly 11,000 Japanese sailors and flyers had died in the five days of the battle, during which kamikaze or suicide planes were deployed for the first time. *Aus-*

tralia, with Pierre Austin on board, was one ship to receive a direct kamikaze hit.

> Suicide planes were attacking us. At this late stage of the war, after all one had
> survived, the feeling was: 'Not now – please, not now!' We knew it was going
> to be our war; we were going to win, no two ways about that.
>
> With a suicide aircraft, you're wanting to blow it out of the sky, if you can.
> But even if it's hit, its course is such that its momentum will carry it into the
> ship if you're not lucky. It's no good killing the pilot – the aircraft is there, it's
> coming. Literally, you either have to blow it out of the sky, or ... It's almost, I
> would imagine, an extension of hand-to-hand fighting: the nearest that a
> sailor gets to that. It's a very personal form of attack.
>
> I received some burns, from our friends coming on board ... That was the
> end of my sea-going, in effect.

It was a single-engined Val dive-bomber that did the damage, crashing
into *Australia*'s foremast early in the morning. The Val was firing as it
came in, and released a shrapnel bomb before it struck the ship. The air
defence positions, the director control tower and the bridge were engulfed
in petrol fires and shattered by exploding cannon shells. The captain and
navigator of *Australia* were killed, the commodore badly wounded, thirty
officers and men were killed or died of their wounds, and sixty-four officers
and men – among them Pierre Austin – were wounded, most of them with
burns. Austin ended up in hospital back in Australia; it would be several
years before the painful skin grafts and other rebuilding operations were
complete, and – as Austin himself puts it – 'made him pretty' again.

The Caribbean island of Trinidad provided numbers of men for the merchant service, and also crew members for various craft of the auxiliary
naval services. When HM tug *Busy* left the West Indies in late 1944 as
escort to a convoy bound for Scotland via the Cape and Italy, she had
among her crew one Trinidadian teenager with a thirst for adventure and
a good time. Cue the cruise of Signalman Winston Seales of the Trinidad
Royal Naval Volunteer Reserve:

> Brazil! Well, I was so young, all I can tell you is that I was looking for girls –
> seriously! First time I see a Spanish girl, I go crazy. They had a red light district
> that they took us to, and that's where all the night-life goes on. These females
> are not permitted to go out of that area, and they have a licence on them ...
> Welcome to Brazil!

We came to Capetown. I didn't enjoy it very much. I had a very humiliating experience in Capetown. I went to the naval postal agency to collect the ship's mail and messages. The bloke said to me, 'Yeah, we got some mails for you, sure. You from HMS *Busy*?' So he pushed a book in front of me and says: 'Can you write?' I said 'What do you mean, can I write? I don't understand what you're saying – if I can *write*?' The next man to me heard this and he told him, 'Of course he can write – he's a signalman!' I was very embarrassed. Then the man apologised; he took me for one of the Africans.

The police would move you on if they see you talking to the Africans. They didn't want us to do that at all. They seemed to claim that we were too advanced and they were too backward; we most likely would impart some of our knowledge to them and open their ideas. I insisted I must talk to them – they're my people. The police didn't want to hear that. They took me down and locked me up in the police station. Lieutenant Campbell, the captain of the *Busy*, came and said, 'You can't lock this man up.' – 'Oh, sorry, Sir, sorry, Sir!' So I was quickly let out.

Then I was sneaked into some sort of political meeting and had to tell them what life was like in Trinidad. They were very interested. But I had to be sneaked in and sneaked out again at the end.

I got into a fight at Agadir, in French Morocco. We went in the Country Club and they didn't want to serve us. We sat there at the table; we ring the bell and so on, but nobody came. A chap came up to us and told us that we are not allowed there. Our Leading Seaman, a chap by the name of Gibbs, was a Barbadian – he started throwing things about, and wrecking the place and whatnot; and we joined in.

At Naples the Italians were very starved and poor. You'll go into the town and by the time you get back to the ship you'll have no shirt. They'd buy it off you. They had the money, but they had no goods. My business in Naples was making money, because there was the opportunity there. I was visualising that we were going to England, and you were getting 14,000 lire in exchange for £1. So my business was to hustle any amount of pounds I can get to take to England, by selling all the things I had bought up on my way here – lipsticks and toiletries from South America, which I'd bought to take home. The Italians were giving 5000 lire for one lipstick; so I'd sell it, at such fabulous prices. I had a lovely little electric iron I'd bought to take home for some little girl I had there – I sold it!

By the time I left Naples and got to Portsmouth, I had something like £50 to spend.

*

Towards the end of 1944 some of the servicemen were already on their way home. Gordon Fry, the South African gunner who had been captured at Tobruk two years before and had escaped from his Italian prisoner-of-war camp in 1943, left Switzerland when the US 7th Army came north after landing in August in the south of France. By November, Fry was back in Capetown and beginning three months of POW leave. His black fellow countryman, Frank Sexwale, having lost his appetite for service along with his right to carry arms, was also on his way out of the war; he would embrace a politically influenced future in South Africa. The New Zealanders, Jim Tait and Tom Somerville, having each put in four years' overseas service, had been recalled and were on their way back to Wellington.

For most, though, the year ended with many hundreds of miles still separating them from their homes and families. Bob Taunt of the Australian 2/2 Battalion, having survived his encounters with the Germans in Greece and Crete, and with the Germans and Italians in the Western Desert, was facing the Japanese in the rain forests of Papua New Guinea as he entered his fourth year on active service. The battalion had taken over from US troops around Aitape, to the west of Wewak on the island's northern coast, a very swampy, jungly area where the Japanese seemed able to live off the local food gardens, strike suddenly and melt away as they pleased. They were still ensconced in bunkers on the peaks; but there was a feeling among the Australians of 2/2 Battalion that the Japanese would only fight if actively provoked at this stage of the war – and why prod the hornets' nest unnecessarily? Nevertheless, as Bob Taunt recalls, an offensive spirit had to be maintained, even in the most unpromising situation:

We had to go out in the jungle on patrol. We were killing twenty, thirty, forty a day; but it was difficult, because we were attacking and they were defending, and they wouldn't give up or anything like that. They'd dig a little slit trench and stop in there, and you couldn't get them out. You'd have to throw a grenade in on them, or give 'em the flame-thrower.

At one time the whole 2/2 Battalion was engaged – six or seven hundred men – but only one platoon of about thirty-five men was doing the actual fighting and the rest of us were just passing their ammunition to them. There was only room for a platoon at a time to fight on those razor-back ridges. And the guns couldn't fire accurately; if you missed the exact target, the rounds just went over and down into the valley beyond. At one time, in fact, we signallers deliberately brought the fire down on ourselves. We sent the infantry 300 yards back down the track, while we ranged the guns in on ourselves. They hit the trees above us with treebursts, to give us an idea of where their range was, and we sent them back directions.

At night, sometimes, we were so close to the Japs that we couldn't speak to send messages back by radio-telephony. We had to use morse code. I think the worst thing of all for the infantry blokes was at night, when the Japs used to infiltrate with knives or bayonets on long bamboo poles. Some of the blokes had very bad nerves, you know? One bloke said to me: 'I'm all right during the day, Bob – but Jeez, at night I'm bloody ratshit!'

Back at home, meanwhile, families had been waiting for news of their loved ones. Not all letters that were sent from the war zones arrived safely at their destination; and those that did could have unlooked-for effects, like the one that Nila Kantan sent back to his family in Tamil Nadu:

One of my letters was not delivered. It was sent instead to a Dead Letter Office they used to have in the Post Office. All those undelivered letters went to there. My letter reached that office and they put a seal on it: Dead Letter Office. Then somehow or other it was again delivered.

My father was away. My stepmother asked some fellow who lived opposite my house, 'What is this that has just come?' He saw the seal: Dead Letter Office – 'He is dead!' he said to her. They all started weeping. Then, when my father came, he asked, 'What is this all about?' – 'Oh, he's dead!' – 'Let me see the letter,' he said. Then he started laughing: 'Who said he is dead? Call that fellow! I have something to say to him!'

Mahinder Singh Pujji, shot down over the desert in his Kittyhawk fighter shortly before El Alamein, had spent much of 1943 and 1944 fighting an unpleasant domestic war, strafing insurgent Pathan tribesmen in the hills of India's North-West Frontier. Now he was serving with the Indian Air Force in Burma, promoted to acting squadron leader and CO of No. 4 Squadron, able to take the controls of one of his beloved Hurricanes and fly all the missions he could against the retreating Japanese in the Arakan peninsula. This was, essentially, a mass slaughter, which continued for the best part of nine months after the 14th Army launched its third Arakan offensive at the end of 1944. Wherever the Japanese could be found – the remnants of the diseased and starving Imphal and Kohima survivors, or fresher troops – they were killed, a policy in theory made easier to stomach by knowledge of Japanese atrocities, but in fact still hard to square with a normally operating conscience.

'I wanted to fly maximum hours possible,' says the flying-crazy Pujji. 'So I put my name down on every flight. There I started killing Japanese. I killed a lot of Japanese soldiers in Burma. That troubles me now. I think: what a bad man I was. I went out of my way to locate them, find them and kill them. What had they done to me? I feel very bad about it.'

In the Burmese jungle Pujji came up against the INA, the Indian National Army of defectors – many of them erstwhile prisoners-of-war – who had sided with the Japanese. INA members, under their radical Indian leader Subhas Chandra Bose, believed that they would gain independence for India – not to mention an instant alleviation of pain and hunger – by supporting the invaders of their country. And the Japanese used the INA as bait against more loyal Indians:

> The INA used to come near our lines at night and call out to us with loud-speakers: 'Come along, come along this side, there's no point fighting, you're not going to live if you do. You're only killing yourselves.' Two of my own pilots joined them – they had been shot down in the south of Burma. They spoke on loudspeakers: 'Mr Pujji! I've got a senior rank and I'm having a wonderful time! Why don't you come over? I've spoken to the people here about you and they would love to have you. You'll be a commanding officer!' and so on – something like that. I never replied; you only laughed. It was more or less a joke for us.
>
> What we thought was: if the INA succeeds, instead of the British it will be the Japanese domination in India. We knew that the Japanese were very cruel. We had an impression that they will be far worse than the British, if at all there was a change of ruler. That was the feeling we had. And, as an educated person, I was aware that I was fighting for the British. The majority of the Indian population was uneducated; they didn't even know what was happening – it was only the educated ones who have a voice, who have something to say about independence. Congress didn't want to co-operate with the British, but at the same time they didn't want to go in with Subhas Chandra Bose and the Japanese. They didn't want to *fight* the British – after all, Mahatma Gandhi was against violence.

In Cairo, at Christmas 1944, Carlton Best was also making some thoughtful comparisons between his lot and others'. The Trinidadian was a good athlete and had been chosen to represent United Services as a relay runner in a sports competition. Once again, it was the situation of the non-white South Africans that made a big impression:

> I was staying in the same hotel as a South African fellow – Vincent de Gama was his name, a high jumper. He was a Cape Coloured man. I was the same complexion as him, but I noticed that for all I tried to talk to him, he wouldn't talk to me. So the last day of the sports I walked up to his room, and sat on his bed and said, 'How come I'm trying to chat with you and you're not talking to me? I want to know how you're getting along – you might want to know where I come from and how *I'm* getting along. I'm from the Caribbean, from the West Indies.'
>
> He said why he didn't want to talk to me was because a fellow his complexion was not supposed to talk to a man of my skin. Oh, God, I nearly died! I said, 'My God, you're in a bad way! If they divide you up in different shades of colour, not skill, however can you all get together to oppose these people who are running your country? You're in a bad way, a real bad way.'

There were occasions when the ordinary men and women who had volunteered for wartime service, caught in the whirlpool of action and struggling to avoid being sucked down, could find themselves party to terrible events. The vortex could suddenly quicken and darken; normal checks and restraints could disappear, the thin veneer of civilised behaviour strip itself away. Then people could act in ways that in peacetime, back in their usual frame of mind, they would never have dreamed they might behave. Some of these incidents became public knowledge; but at that time, in the days before television brought every unit's deeds into every living-room, most did not. Mostly the only judge and jury on the case were the participants themselves. They will have to live with their private judgements on their own actions for the rest of their lives.

> There was this house that our platoon was defending at a crossroad in Italy. A Tiger tank comes along the road; these really were something, with the big eighty-eight-millimetre gun and all that armour. One of our chaps got down in a ditch with his Piat anti-tank gun and fired two shots – and these damn things just bounced off this tank. So another chap ran around and jumped on the tank, and he hammered on the roof. The German inside must have thought that it was another German, I suppose, because he opened the hatch up and this guy threw a hand grenade in. This thing went off – *boomp* – inside and the tank careered off, back up the road in reverse, till he veered off into a ditch. The other tankies didn't like that, and they eventually got the house back.

There was a bit of trouble about that house. In fact there was a group of about fifteen prisoners in there and the platoon commander didn't believe in letting a group like that go loose. Because of these tanks – because they were going to take the house, there was no doubt about that, and our Piat gun was useless – well, the prisoners all got shot and stacked up around the doors like sandbags, for barricades. I just want to say that I, personally, never ever shot any prisoners.

At the time, only we and the Germans knew about it. The Germans knew about it because they got back into the house and found the weapons stacked, so they knew the dead men had been prisoners. After that the Germans sent these pamphlets over. They said they'd met us before in North Africa, they'd met us at Cassino and other places, and we'd been gentlemen before this – but now they were not going to take any more prisoners, because we hadn't.

But we just about wiped that division out, anyway, in the next big action we had.

*

Burmese villagers – they are very mild and very backward. Some are almost naked, with a small loincloth. They were in league with the Japanese. We killed many of them. Japanese would leave arms dumps; Burmese would carry bullets for them in baskets and cover them with food. We found them one day. We shot them. It was a sort of returning to them what they would do to you. One of the platoonists would shoot them.

But we didn't shoot women and children. If we see a Japanese body and we had the chance, we would dig and bury him. That's the reason why we won the war – because the Allies were very kind, but the Germans and Japanese and Italians were very wicked. They were doing bad things, and God will not be happy with those who do that. Yes!

It was a bizarre image that summed up the fighting in Italy in 1944 for the Canadian teenager Frank O'Donnell: a piece of grotesquerie, glimpsed on the road to Rome:

About twenty yards off the road there was a German guy in a field. I think he must have been an officer, because he had lots of silver on his uniform. He was standing upright and he was in a pose like a statue, with one arm up, as though he was throwing something. Stiff, and dead, and standing in that field. We passed him in the truck, and no one had the guts to go over and give him a push. So we just left him standing there: absolutely upright, and totally stone dead.

SEVEN

Full Tide: 1945

*We had won the victory. You had music here, dancing there,
all in the roads and so on – people having a ball. Crazy
people . . . cra-a-zy people!*   Winston Seales, Trinidad

*To be free was just unbelievable. You just kept . . . looking
for your guards. It's a very hard feeling to describe, liberation.
I was a very, very lost person . . .*   Jack Brown, New Zealand

In Burma, the new year was less than a week old when soldiers of 25
Indian Division landed unopposed on Akyab Island to take over the
port at the mouth of the Kaladan River. The third Arakan offensive had
got under way the month before, and now the Allies' 14th Army had started
an unstoppable eastward momentum which would lead to the recapture
of Rangoon on 3 May. Krishen Tewari's landing on Akyab was unorthodox:

Somebody advised me that when you have to land, you'd better not wear your
shoes and forget about your hat – you just go in shoeless and hatless. I was
taken in by this joke at my expense. When I landed I wished I'd worn the
shoes, because the beach was quite rough. Anyway, I went to see the forward
troops, and by the time I came back to the beach the Brigadier's launch had
gone. I had to hitchhike, in bare feet, back to Brigade Headquarters. I'll never
forget that – how I got left behind with no hat and no shoes!

Admiral Lord Louis Mountbatten, Supreme Commander South-East

Asia, had been in the saddle since August 1943 – a magnetic figure, attracting as much criticism for his autocratic high-handedness and burning ambition as admiration for his energy, resourcefulness and drive to get things done. With the fighting men he had General Montgomery's directness, allied to a quick sense of humour. Peter d'Cunha of the Royal Indian Navy, relaxing in harbour at Akyab after the landings, was caught napping by the great man:

> One fine evening about seven o'clock I was on a small patrol boat in the creek, sitting at the wireless set, very much engrossed in listening to English music broadcasting on Radio Ceylon. I had my earphones on and was leaning back with my legs cocked on the table – I never expected that anyone would come there. All of a sudden I got the shock of my life. Somebody removed the earphones from my head. I was thinking, 'Could it be some enemy?' I turned round and looked. All I could see was gold stripes, going straight up. It was nobody else but Lord Mountbatten. He asked me my name and I told him. He said, 'You seem to be very fond of English music.' Then he just put back the earphones on my head, and he said: 'Enjoy yourself; but be a little bit alert. You never know who's coming!'

Krishen Tewari had his shoes and hat on when he made his next landing, on 22 February, with 51 Brigade of 25 Indian Division, on the beaches just south of Kangaw to the east of Akyab. This landing was a different affair from the Akyab caper. Japanese shellfire on to the beaches was heavy and accurate, and the beaches themselves were muddy and steep, leading into deep tidal chaungs that ran inland among mangrove swamps. Kangaw village had to be captured in order to block off the coastal roads and tracks by which the Japanese might escape from the advancing Allies. Under cover of their own naval bombardment the Indians landed behind a wave of British Royal Marine Commandos. After a week they had secured Kangaw. Losses were heavy on both sides – the Royal Marines lost sixty-six men and had 259 wounded during Japanese counter-attacks, and the defenders themselves probably lost more than 300. The memory of one of the British marines is lodged in Krishen Tewari's mind:

> We were landing from LCAs, and we came under intense shellfire when we went across on to the beach where the commandos had landed. On a landing the idea is to get safe inland, away from the beach, so you dash as fast as you can. If a shell lands in front of you, you might duck and swerve left or right, but you keep running like mad until you get to the place where you are going

to dig in – a couple of hundred yards, perhaps. The speed carries you through: nobody thinks about dying or being wounded at such a time.

Commandos were not supposed to dig in. Too defensive: their whole tactic was offensive, offensive, offensive. While I was running past, a number of commandos were lying dead on the beach. There was a chap lying with his face up, facing the sky, and I thought, 'He's also dead.' Then he shouted, 'Hi, buddy!' So I momentarily stopped. And he made one of those classic remarks, which still rings in my head: 'If this be life – roll on, death!'

Kenyan interlude ... Derek Watson had been posted from Burma back to Nairobi after his tribulations in the Kabaw Valley with 4 KAR. But a desk-wallah's job among stay-at-home soldiers was the last thing likely to appeal to him:

There were so many regular soldiers in this bloody office in Nairobi, you know, running Balls For Burma – 'but don't bloody well send me anywhere near Burma' – it made me absolutely sick. I think one was probably slightly queer, too, having been in the jungle for a long time. I know my wife tried to make me go to dances, and I tried to drink myself into form, and that's hopeless.

Seeing all these people enjoying themselves, it made you feel: 'Well, what the bloody hell have I been doing this for, all this time, when these people have been sitting back here doing absolutely damn-all?'

Over in the UK the Royal Canadian Navy stoker Raymond Walker, following his experiences with pusser's rum on the D-Day beaches, had got himself into trouble with the naval authorities:

Well, I managed to miss my boat in Cardiff and got sent to the glasshouse in Scotland for fourteen days. I think I was the only Canadian there; there was a lot of English fellers that had jumped ship. It wasn't bad, you know. You turned to; you had PT. There was an old feller there with a monocle on and a swagger stick, a Navy feller – oh, good God Almighty, he hollered and squealed! They put us through gun drill – well, you know how good I'd be at gun drill, being a stoker. Hundred-pound projectiles, eh – oh, my God!

What you got for breakfast in the morning: you got porridge. No sugar or nothing with it, just salt. Scottish style, eh? – stick to your ribs. Dinner time: I don't know what the hell it was, but it was all chewed up anyway. Then on Sunday you didn't get any meat, because you didn't turn to or do any PT.

I only served seven days of my sentence, so it wasn't too bad. Of course, there was no smoking in there; so when the shore patrol came to pick you up and take you back to your ship they gave you a cigarette as soon as you got outside – just in case you were dying for one!

After his release Walker found himself serving on motor torpedo boats based at Ostend, harrying German supply shipping in the English Channel. These were night encounters, like the ones that the South African MTB Officer, Bob Gaunt, had grown used to – high-speed interceptions at forty knots and more, firing back and forth, deafening noise and blinding light, hair's-breadth decisions made under great pressure. In these early months of 1945 the Royal Navy's Alec Dennis – now in command of his own destroyer, HMS *Valorous* – was experiencing the other end of torpedo attacks as he shielded East Coast convoys from German E-boats operating out of Dutch ports. The war was certainly not over yet.

American, Polish and Commonwealth bomber crews were still flying day and night operations over Germany and what remained of Occupied Europe, pounding industrial targets, troop and tank concentrations, transport systems, rocket-launch sites, dockyards – and cities. Almost 4000 tons of bombs were dropped on the south-east German city of Dresden on the night of 13–14 February 1945, creating a firestorm that devastated the city and killed upwards of 135,000 people. No one could claim this to be a strategic target.

None of those who had flown in Bomber Command's aircraft in the early and middle stages of the war was still on operations. They were either posted as administrators or instructors or senior station staff, or dishonourably discharged due to 'lack of moral fibre', or in hospitals or prisoner-of-war camps, or dead. The New Zealand pilot, Paul Radomski, was instructing commandos in small-arms techniques; the Canadian air-gunner, Charlie Hobbs, was enduring his second year as a prisoner-of-war; the Jamaican bomb-aimer, Dudley Thompson, was a liaison officer between the RAF and the Colonial Office; his fellow Jamaican, Mosquito navigator John Ebanks, had been awarded the Distinguished Flying Medal after completing fifty operations, but had been turned down for further offensive flying duties – the incidence of casualties from air fatigue among second-tour crews was too great for him to be risked.

A third Jamaican, E. K. Powell, having survived bailing out of a burning DC3 while helping out with the 'Market-Garden' air drop, was still on operational duties as a flight engineer on Lancaster bombers. There was a tremendous amount for a young man to learn, and you needed a cool head to concentrate:

You're busy; believe me, you'd be surprised at how busy you are. For instance, the altimeter – you have to find out what height you are, to start with. Various gauges – somebody would shout about fuel supply which seemed to be cut off to the port outer, or the starboard inner. The navigator's telling the pilot what course is coming up. Then of course the Leader would be calling you up, telling you when to go through with your run over the target. Everybody's shouting at one another, and you have to listen to this through your earphones. The man that everyone gave credit to was the feller in the tail – the rear-gunner. He'd be out there all on his own, trying to get someone to listen. You learn to pick your way through all this. And with everyone getting excited you will be using plenty of swear-words – though at my age I wasn't expected to know them, anyway.

It was a lot of responsibility for a teenager, to be in charge of the lives of others; but believe me, you had a lot of training. The memory you have at seventeen, eighteen, nineteen you never get again. I would know every damn circuit in the plane. I could tell you each cable colour, where it went and just exactly what it did. And yet the war was finished before I was old enough to vote.

Down on the ground in England, Geraldine Turcotte of the RCAF, having returned to London from her recuperation break in Scotland, stumbled across another side to the war – one hidden from most of the civilians who saw in their newspapers, and on the cinema newsreels, stories about the Allied armies' victorious advance across northern Europe towards Germany:

They did an operation on my sinuses at No. 24 General Hospital at Watford. I could hear this moaning at night, and I'd say to the nurses, 'What do I hear? I hear somebody moaning.' They'd say, 'No, it's the wind – the wind.' The first thing I did when I got up was to go out and look in the hallways. There were cots everywhere, with wounded soldiers that they were bringing home from overseas, wounded from the fighting in Europe.

I waited three times to have the surgery on my face, because the doctor would get drunk. And no wonder – he'd been looking after them all night long and was slated to see to me at eight o'clock in the morning.

Not many saw that side of the war. And we weren't allowed to try and comfort them – I guess they were in very bad shape, those that were brought in there. Oh, it was sad ... really sad.

In northern Italy the Allies and the Germans had been facing each other south of the Po Valley all through a fierce winter. The Allies had lost a large part of their strength when seven divisions were withdrawn shortly before June 1944 to help in the invasion of France, and with the Germans in a purely defensive role Italy had become something of a side-show to the thunderous events taking place further north. However, every skirmish remained a matter of life and death to those caught up in it.

The New Zealand infantryman, Charles Bell, in northern Italy with the Maori Battalion he had so passionately wanted to join, quickly learned the combat skills necessary for a front-line soldier involved in house-to-house, village-to-village fighting. But scrappy, confused situations often arose, in which quick thinking on the spot was the only skill required.

In the north of Italy they had stop banks, for flood protection, built all over the place. They had railway lines on them and a lot of canals. They were ideally suited for defence, and the Germans had had time to prepare them.

One day a chap in the artillery told me he wanted to 'take a stroll up the sharp end'. So I took him up to the stop banks on the front line. I went up the side of one stop bank – and there on the other side was a platoon of Germans. They were saddling stuff on to horses; they didn't expect anybody there.

I saw a figure in the window of a house, pulled my Luger out – I'd 'liberated' it from a dead German – and took a pot-shot at him. He disappeared. Then I ducked back and said to the artilleryman, 'Let's pull back to the far side of our bank and we'll call for a stonk' – which was all the guns anywhere within range shooting on one spot. On the way back I fell in a stream. I was trapped underwater with the lanyard of my Luger hooked round a branch, drowning. I broke the lanyard off and got out.

We got over our stop bank. Then a little Honey tank – a Kiwi machine with a two-pounder gun – saw us, and from way across the field it opened up on us with its Browning. Two Spandaus dug into the German bank were having a go at us too, by this time. So I told the artilleryman to go and tell the Honey tank to stop shooting at us, and to put a stonk on the far side of the German bank and catch their platoon. He didn't want to go, but I told him I'd keep the Germans off him. So he made his rush and I fired off a couple of shots; then I lay back on the bank and emptied the water out of my gumboots. I waited for a while, and then I heard the artillery going *boom-boom-boom* in the background, then *wheee-wheee-whooosh* – the stonk going in, right on to that platoon.

I waited till it was over – then I just got up and walked out of it.

In March the Germans in Italy lost their clever and stubborn Commander, Field Marshal Albert Kesselring, when Hitler ordered him home to shore up the collapsing defences of Germany. His replacement, General von Vietinghoff, was refused permission to make a tactical withdrawal by Hitler. In April the Allies began their final advance and drove their opponents across the River Po. Seeing that the position was hopeless, Vietinghoff asked for an armistice. On 2 May it came into effect. Nearly a million German soldiers surrendered in northern Italy, and the long-drawn-out Italian campaign was over. A week earlier, Italian partisans had captured Benito Mussolini in German disguise. On 28 April they shot him and his mistress, and hung their bodies upside down from meat-hooks on the Piazzale Loreto in Milan for the citizens to jeer at and photograph.

In northern Europe there had been a winter halt for the Allies too; not just a halt, but a December counter-offensive by the Germans, through the forests of the Ardennes in Luxembourg and southern Belgium, which all but threw the Allies back on their heels. The plan had been for two Panzer armies to drive north-west to retake Antwerp on the Belgian coast – a port which the Allies had possessed since September, but which they had only just reopened for supplies, thanks to German possession of vantage points on both banks of the Scheldt estuary between Antwerp and the sea. One of the Panzer armies would pierce through the Ardennes; the other, further north, would sweep across the Meuse at Liège. The British and Canadians in Holland would be split from the Americans in Belgium and Luxembourg; their supply lines would be neatly snipped at source. It was a fantastically bold late throw of the dice by Hitler, committing all his armoured resources in one ultimate effort. The Battle of the Bulge did produce a great bulging salient fifty miles deep, like a bubble blown outwards to bursting point. But the Allies first held, then pushed back the Panzers. By the end of January 1945 the bubble had been deflated and was once more flat against the western border of Germany. The Allies were free to continue their advance. They crossed the Rhine in March and, by 18 April, had encircled and forced the capitulation of all the troops in Ruhr, Germany's industrial heartland.

The Russians, meanwhile – keen to reach and take Berlin first – had been advancing even faster than the western Allies. Post-war Russian domination of eastern Europe (particularly Poland), and the east-west partition of Germany, had already been agreed between America, Russia and Britain – or, more accurately, between Franklin Roosevelt, Josef Stalin and Winston Churchill – during their tripartite conferences at Teheran in November 1943 and at Yalta in the Crimea in February 1945. The arrangement was the only way to keep the Russians firmly on board the Allied ship of many nations, and it at least settled the vexatious question of the future of those unfortunate, much-fought-over countries to the east of Germany and Italy – and, by the way, the immediate destiny of Greece, whose communist insurgents looked likely to overthrow the pro-British government. Stalin promised to withhold Russian influence there, if he could apply it in the more northerly Balkan states of Romania, Bulgaria and Hungary. Churchill had agreed to this. The political map of Europe for the next half-century had been quickly and effectively sketched by the three most influential men on earth.

Down at the sharp end, these last few months of the war in Europe were a strange time for many of the young servicemen and women involved in the great Allied drive east. Everyone knew that the struggle was as good as over. Yet death, or the threat of death, looked as close as ever. The horror and poignancy of war seemed ever more present, the deeper they pressed into the Low Countries. It was as if the extraordinary adventure that was coming to an end was determined to stamp itself indelibly on their inner eyes and ears, to stake a permanent claim on their futures.

Frank O'Donnell:

We were just setting up a gun position, somewhere near the Dutch border, and that evening a whole bunch of Germans came out of the woods where they'd been hiding, unbeknownst to us, and started to attack the guns. We were firing on those guys through open sights. Several of them got right into our gun positions. One of our guys actually strangled a German, right beside his gun. It was some kind of an evening. Next morning some British tanks came up with flame-throwers. One of them lobbed what they called a petard into a house in which some Germans had ensconced themselves. The house just – blew apart.

Reg Burt:

We picked up two guys that had been in the infantry, and they had been dead quite some time. We'd moved into this position in the afternoon and we hadn't eaten for quite a while. But first we had to bury them. One of the guys let out a lot of gas; his leg came off...

So we got them buried; then we opened up the can of mutton and veal that we had. On top of the meat it's this bluey-grey colour; and when you stuck the knife in, gas escaped ... well, I didn't eat.

Frank O'Donnell:

Later I passed a trench by the side of the road where a bunch of Germans had been caught by one of the flame-throwers and incinerated. War, to a large degree, is *smell*. The sense of smell I don't think has ever been properly described by those who write about war. It's a difficult thing to do. You could *taste* the smell; you could almost *see* it. It permeated your whole body. And the smell wasn't just of death, it was an amalgam of things. The smell'd be of brick dust, it'd be of gunpowder, it'd be of burnt wood, of dead animals that had been lying in a field and would suddenly explode, because the bellies'd be distended, and they'd let go with a smell that – you just can't describe.

Reg Burt: 'Have you ever had tulip stew? Well, I have. We had a gun pit near a farmhouse and they gave us some. The tulip stew – you couldn't even tell that it *was* tulips. I guess they put in seasoning, or something; it tasted a bit like cabbage. Tulips were literally all they had to eat.'

Frank O'Donnell: 'I don't think we liked the Dutch very much. We saw that they were treating their own very badly. You could see the girls with their hair cut off; they were marching them through the streets. They were making their own concentration camps for collaborators.'

Sam Meltzer:

We were the first to enter Nordhausen concentration camp. The Polish guards were still there. The camp was all sprawling huts, like prefabs. There was the main extermination block in the centre. A very big square. Barbed wire. A gateway and guard towers. All out in the countryside.

They had been burning before we got there, so the camp smelled like hell. People were coming to us crying. I can distinctly remember, after we'd fed them and made some of the local people help clean up the mess, the poor buggers of guards being sent back to Poland. Then we had the very sticky position of policing the place, because the concentration camp victims were going into the village and beating up the Germans.

I think, by this time, you felt you'd seen it all, you know? You'd lost a lot of friends. I can remember feeling anger about the people who had done that sort of thing, yeah. But there was actually a lot of mixed emotions there, especially when you had to control these people who were victims. No doubt they looked on us as the villains.

Reg Burt: 'I don't think I've spoken about the war since that time. If my grandchildren ask me about the war – you know, "What did you do?" – I'd tell them the funny things. As far as they're concerned, no one killed each other. My wife thinks I went out dancing every night...

Just before the end of the war, Sheila Parkinson found herself parted from her FANY drivers at SHAEF Headquarters in France and posted to General Montgomery's 21st Army Group Headquarters at Bad Oeynhausen in north-eastern Germany. She was sent to take over L Company of ATS, girls from the tough streets around Scotland Road in Liverpool, who had been manning anti-aircraft guns. They had just staged a mutiny. Sheila Parkinson had to overcome their mistrust of her 'snobbish' FANY background and learn to understand them: 'girls who always went to bed in their vests; girls who were scrupulously clean but never took a bath because there wasn't a bath at home; girls who didn't understand the laundry system. I said, "Now, a couple of your sergeants are going to have a bath and then it's your turn." Well – the language! Luckily I couldn't understand half of it. The floor was *awash* with water. I told them, "You've all got 'L' on your sleeves – L for Love! You're going to get dressed in your best clothes, and go out and make an impression on the land."'

Most of the ATS girls were more innocent than their demeanour and language suggested, and some of them made rather too good an impression on a land full of eager young soldiers. Sheila Parkinson had to do a fair bit of 'hedging and ditching', as she calls it:

> Perfectly natural thing – the men were enchanted. There were some girls who said, 'No, no,'; so they filled them with this Bols – colourless, but far from innocuous – put it in their orange juice. Some of the girls came to see me and said they knew nothing until they found themselves highly pregnant. And I said, 'Bad luck – you had no *fun* out of it.'
>
> One dear little thing, about nineteen years old – I said, 'Would you like me to write to your mother and explain about this extraordinary thing that's landed on you?' And she said, 'Oh, no, don't worry about that – Mum'll just be glad she didn't let the pram go.' Mum was going to absorb that child; it was clearly part of their way of living. That seemed a reasonable attitude in my view of things: that these children – only young girls, after all – would be sent back home pregnant and their families would accept them.

Civilians in the liberated towns and villages may have given the oncoming Allies a mixed reception, but there was one group of unwilling residents of central Europe who were unequivocal in their joy. The roads of Europe were in spate now, rivers of human beings flooding west, away from the advancing Russians, hoping to cross over into the Allied-occupied territories. Ten million Germans alone came west at this time and more than two million died trying to do so. In among this tide of frightened, misery-stricken people were thin eddies of Allied prisoners-of-war, herded this way and that by the guards who had taken them out of their camps and now did not know whether to treat them as prisoners, or as hostages, or as passports to the west.

They had all been able to hear the guns for weeks before their camp gates were finally opened. After that, each man had his own extraordinary tale to tell. Ronald Henriques, the Jamaican paratrooper incarcerated since being taken prisoner at Arnhem in September 1944, remembers the indifference of his guards towards the end, and how he vomited up the first meal he ate as a free man. For Thomas Hunter in Stalag VIIIB, a captive since the Dieppe raid of August 1942, approaching freedom was signalled by the waggling wings of British aircraft as they flew over the camp, and by his guards who would fetch a map and show the POWs which towns had just fallen to the Allies. It was the baths and the clean clothes that he most enjoyed when he and his friends were turned over to the Americans. When Hunter returned at last to his unit they asked him if he was prepared to go out to the Far East to liberate Hong Kong. His response was to the point: 'No friggin' way!'

The *arbeitskommando* of POWs clearing air-raid damage and burying bomb victims around Leipzig had had a particularly tough time of it. Jack Brown, the New Zealand shepherd turned infantryman, had been captured in a Greek mountain cave in May 1942 after a year on the run. By April 1945 he had been in the bag for almost three years. Now, unmistakably, there were signs and portents:

You knew things were getting grim, as far as the Jerries were concerned, when their attitude changed. They took a different stance. I think they had the idea that we were thinking, 'When things are finished we're going to put in a report on you.' So they tried to be friendly – hoping that, if they'd given you a belt in the arse with a rifle butt, you might overlook it.

Then you could hear the *boom! boom!* of the guns. Ah! That sounds good, eh? Something's going on, boy! They packed us up, got us out on to the road and for about a week they marched us round in circles. So a few of us got sick of that and decided about three o'clock one morning that we were going to bugger off. The guards weren't interested – they just let us walk off. We walked all day, through the German lines, keeping in file. The Germans took no notice. There was devastation all around: bomb holes, shell holes. We marched towards the guns – only way to go.

All of a sudden we see a couple of jeeps coming towards us. Bloody Americans. Oh boy, oh boy! We'd walked right through no man's land without a damn thing happening to us. They pulled up smartly. They were a front-line group and they just couldn't believe we were Englanders. 'Keep walking, keep walking, boys, you're right; you're in safe land now.' So we kept walking, right into the Yankee lines. Oh, the relief . . .

They bumped us up into this airbase they had. The first thing I saw was this big black feller walking along, swinging his arms, and he had this big white loaf of bread in his hand. And I thought: 'Oh, God – what I'd give for that bloody loaf of bread!'

Tail-gunner Charlie Hobbs of the Royal Canadian Air Force, a prisoner since the crash of his Lancaster in Occupied France in April 1943, was in an Air Force POW camp at Fallingbostel near Hanover. From the hut windows he had seen RAF bombers illuminated by searchlights during night bombing raids, and USAF planes flying overhead in enormous formations by day. Reports came in thick and fast on the prisoners' radio; the Russians had crossed the eastern German border, the Americans were over the Rhine, the Canadians were through Holland. Just before the end, Hobbs and his fellow prisoners were bundled out on to the roads:

They weren't really taking us anywhere, they were just marching us. They'd tell us to turn left or right and the whole column would do it. If the Russians pushed one way, they'd bring us the other way. If the British pushed this way, they'd send us that way. This went on for a month. We were starving; they weren't feeding us. We stole what we could, but they had dogs on these columns, you know. We got strafed by our own fighters, too – killed many of us. So it wasn't a very happy time.

I talked to my buddy Cam, who couldn't run because he'd had part of his foot shot off. I said, 'Cam, this isn't for me. Do you think you can get away?' He said, 'No, I couldn't get out of it quick enough.' So I gave him all the food we had and waited until I got the opportunity to skip out of the column, and I took off and headed into the trees at the side of the road. I didn't stop. It took me five days, heading west, steering by the stars. Slept in the daytime, travelled at night. Eventually I was spotted by a German farmer's boys. The farmer told me to come down to the house and he gave me some milk, which I hadn't had for years. Then he said, 'I'll lead you to the British lines.' He was just a simple farmer, but I felt at least he was human.

So I walked into a British bivouac. I thought the guy was going to shoot me. I was too tired to feel much. They fed me food that I hadn't seen in years –

white bread! Bacon and eggs! Lord, the camp cook really went out of his way. Then he takes me out to his ammunition carrier and opens up all the trays, and every one of the trays has nothing but French wine in it. I don't know where they carried their ammunition. He hands me this bottle – to hell with my blooming breakfast! Of course, I couldn't handle that. Just too much for me. I didn't throw up, but it might have been better if I had!

By 25 April 1945 Berlin was completely surrounded by Russian troops. On 26 April they assaulted the centre of the city. On 29 April Adolf Hitler married his mistress, Eva Braun. Next day, at 2.25 p.m., the Red Flag was flown from the shell-scarred ruin of the Reichstag. An hour later, Hitler and Eva Braun killed themselves with poison. Their associates burned their bodies, as the Russian soldiers fought their way from floor to floor of the Reichstag. On 2 May, at three o'clock in the afternoon, the guns fell silent, with Berlin heaped with rubble and the Third Reich lying in ruins. A general ceasefire was declared on 5 May. In Rheims, two days later on 7 May, General Alfred Jodl signed an unconditional German surrender. The war in Europe was over.

In Britain, 8 May 1945 was declared to be Victory in Europe or VE Day ...
    Peter Cayley, Royal Canadian Navy:

It was a lovely morning. We'd been escorting a convoy round Land's End and were just going into Falmouth to fuel. About 11.30, Churchill's speech came on. This was the first time the bridge loudspeaker had not been tuned to the sonar. It was rather impressive, because he was talking about the ships at sea, and at that moment the mist lifted and there was the coast of England ahead. Then the bo'sun's mate came on the bridge with a pannikin, to splice the mainbrace and said: 'Sir – you may have some rum.'

Raymond Walker, Royal Canadian Navy: 'We were in Yarmouth. We spliced the mainbrace – yeah, we spliced her twice that time, and then we went ashore that night and spliced her some more!'
    Bob Gaunt (South Africa), Royal Navy:

We'd been sweeping oyster mines, not a particularly nice job. Then we were sent to bring a German flak ship in to Dover. Most of our crew were from London – Cockneys. We got an order saying no one could be given leave to go to London, because there'd be too many people there, too much traffic.
    We had a young seaman on board whose sister was getting married that day

in London, so we said 'Go'. As he was hurrying to get dressed, he took a packet of twenty cigarettes off the mess table. He'd got another packet in his pocket with two cigarettes in; so the naval patrol and the dockyard police picked him up and put him in jail – for attempting to smuggle cigarettes. So he never got to the wedding.

Paul Gobine, Seychelles Pioneer Corps: 'King George VI, the Queen, Princess Elizabeth in her uniform, Princess Margaret – they stood on the balcony at Buckingham Palace. Churchill came out – thanks God that day he didn't have his cigar in his hand. Instead, he was waving. People were crying; and I was crying. All people from my mob were shouting: "Princess Lillibet! Lillibet! Lillibet! It's our Princess!" – you know?'

Geraldine Turcotte, Royal Canadian Air Force: 'I was down there at Buckingham Palace on VE Day. Oh, that was something else! You know, when we went downtown in London we always wore our civvies. But that day we wore our uniforms. We were shined right up and – oh yes, real dapper. So anyways, we got down there and the two princesses were among the crowd. I could have just reached out and touched them. And I can still hear the lady-in-waiting saying to Margaret: "Now, behave like young ladies." She says back: "I'll have you know I'm a Princess!" '

Winston Seales, Trinidad Royal Naval Volunteer Reserve:

Boy, we had a ball. Oh Lord, what can I say? All over the place – a-a-all over! You were given a bed, man, free of charge, no problem at all. You had no worry about eating, drinking, smoking. People would pick you up and want to take you here, there and everywhere. It was a wild and hectic time.

I think we had about two days of it. I didn't sleep at all. It was a wild party. You came out of the Union Jack Club in the morning, you crossed into Hyde Park, and from there – it was all a mess! You didn't know where to go next, what to do next. Someone says, 'Let's go and have a beer.' Everybody becomes one happy family. That was so surprising and so nice: everyone became unified. We had won the victory. You had music here, dancing there, all in the roads and so on – people having a ball. Crazy people ... cra-a-azy people!

It was a shame, says Peter Cayley, that things couldn't have been like that on the other side of the water: 'On VE Day the good burghers of Halifax in Nova Scotia decided it'd be a good idea to close all places of entertainment – including the liquor stores. This is hard to believe, but it's true. Canadian sailors never liked Halifax anyway – too prim and proper, and there weren't enough facilities for sailors. So they ran amok and sacked the liquor stores and got the liquor, and there were ... disgraceful scenes.'

Other 'disgraceful scenes' were being enacted elsewhere in Europe, as one 'soldier of the Commonwealth' makes clear:

> I'd done a mine course and it paid off. This bank ... accidentally got blown up, let's say – the vault, you know? – and out came all this money. Banca d'España cheques and Hungarian bank bonds in denominations of 100,000. Now the Banca d'España cheques were negotiable. When we got to Trieste, there was this, er, large house that all these females were in, you see. So we got into this house for a bit of R & R. After being there a couple of hours I came out and was supposed to hand over about 80 lire to the lady at the desk down below. I think the smallest note I had on me was something like 250,000. I can still see this lady throwing up her hands at the sight of it and going: '*Mama mia!*' I could have bought the whole building, let alone paid for my entertainment. '*Mama mia!*' – I can hear her now.

In the ruins of Berlin, Private Sam Meltzer's long war came to an end. He had gone over to France with the BEF on the outbreak of war and come back again via Dunkirk in the darkest days of 1940. He had been in the North African desert, behind the lines in Arab disguise, and had been repatriated from Sicily after suffering bad napalm burns. He had landed on the Normandy beaches shortly after D Day and had seen the worst of war during the Allied advance through the Low Countries. Now, in a Berlin already divided up between America, Britain, France and Russia, Meltzer received an invitation from the Russians to visit their camp at Spandau. 'We were asked to leave our arms at the gate, and we went and had a big supper. What an uncouth bunch of buggers they were: all Mongolian types. I can quite distinctly remember a little Italian fellow, a slave labourer, coming up and slipping me a note that said: "Help. Get me out." Very little we could do – we were their guests.'

In the Berlin of 1945 the spoils of war were all to the victors: 'In Berlin we saw German soldiers; they were trickling back from the Russian front, with their frostbitten feet all covered with newspapers. The worst thing for them was seeing the girls associating with British soldiers. One fellow said to me: "For six years I fought you as a soldier. Now the German girls have capitulated to you without a fight." Very bitter. The girls wouldn't look at them. *We* had the chocolates and the cigarettes...'

Among these nonchalant young victors there was a growing mood of discontent with the leadership that had carried the British through those six years of war. The coalition National Government was on its last legs and people wanted a change. On 5 July the British electorate voted to replace Winston Churchill with Clement Attlee at the head of a Labour government. The voters were by now scattered across the world, and it took three weeks to collect and count their ballot papers. In *The Second World War* Churchill describes how he woke early on 26 July, the day the election results were to be declared, 'with a sharp stab of almost physical pain. A hitherto subconscious conviction that we were beaten broke forth and dominated my mind. All the pressure of great events, on and against which I had mentally so long maintained my "flying speed", would cease and I should fall. The power to shape the future would be denied me. The knowledge and experience I had gathered, the authority and goodwill I had gained in so many countries, would vanish. I was discontented at the prospect...'

Churchill might have seen the foreshadow of his defeat a few days earlier, written in the demeanour of Sam Meltzer and his fellow soldiers when the Prime Minister and the man who was to replace him drove through Berlin on their way to a conference in Potsdam. 'When we were on parade in the Wilhelmstrasse,' Meltzer recalls, 'Clement Attlee came down in a car with Winston Churchill. The Germans all looked to see who it was; the British soldiers turned their backs. It was something they'd learned from Gandhi during the civil disobedience in India. They turned their backs on that car. Churchill wasn't popular, as witness the fact that he wasn't re-elected. It was the mood of that time.'

When the fighting ended in Europe there were still plenty of outposts where no Allied presence had yet been positioned to take over from the defeated Germans. A few days after the German surrender Alec Dennis of the Royal Navy took *Valorous* up to Kristiansand in Norway. Dennis had come a long way since the spring of 1940 when, as a sub-lieutenant in the *Griffin*, he had helped evacuate British and French soldiers from Namsos. Now he was returning as Captain of his own destroyer, in order to land one Lord Teynham to take charge there.

Teynham was a naughty man. He went into the town and came back with some very pretty girls. Had 'em all down in my cabin, and we were drinking away. Suddenly Teynham says: 'Oh, by the way, the German delegation's coming on board at two o'clock, to surrender.' This was half-past one, and the place was full of drink and pretty girls! Of course, the Germans came right on time. Kept 'em waiting on the quarterdeck while we all got ready; then we finally had the surrender.

There were about seventeen U-boats there, a division of soldiers and something like 12,000 Russian prisoners-of-war. The Russians were a problem. None of them wanted to go back home – but they had to. Some of them shot themselves, or drank themselves to death, to avoid it. It was really rather shocking. They didn't get much of a welcome from Stalin, I imagine. All the time you were thinking, 'Thank God we're what we are, and not among this lot.'

A party of SAS chaps had arrived on the airfield just before us; they'd just liberated Belsen and they didn't like Germans at all. They were very rough with them. Told them all to clear off out of Kristiansand, then set up a road block five miles out of town: 'Everybody out!' Took all their loot – cameras, binoculars, fur coats, champagne. 'Right, on your way!' They knew how to deal with these jokers. The SAS were extremely brave men, there's no doubt at all about that – and also extremely wild. We had various parties with them that ended with their sentries shooting up at us, and dropping sandbags on the Brigadier-General's jeep. Oh, dear! Letting it all out, you know.

The liberated prisoners-of-war had been flown back to England for a period of convalescence and recovery. Thomas Hunter, in hospital, was urged to eat six small meals a day; it would take a year for his stomach to recover from its prolonged ordeal. Jack Brown was taken down to Margate, the seaside resort on the Kent coast, where the once self-reliant, self-sufficient New Zealander now faced up to unforeseen difficulties:

To be free was just unbelievable. You just kept ... looking for your guards. It's a very hard feeling to describe, liberation. I was a very, very lost person when I was not with my little group of fellow prisoners. I found that very hard, to come back to reality again. To think for yourself – that's a hard thing to come back to. Luckily I did have some of that group from the camp; that was the helpful part there, we were still a group.

I had a heck of a job to get back on the food again, too. They gave us roast meals and so on, but we just couldn't handle it. The smell of it was beautiful, but it was too rich. And of course we got crook when we ate it. We couldn't drink very much either – our stomachs just weren't geared for it, eh. A couple of drinks, and you were half silly.

There remained, of course, the problem of the Japanese.

The signing of the unconditional surrender by the Germans, though a severe blow to the already reeling Japanese, did not push them into capitulation. They had been defeated in Burma two months before Berlin fell. By May they had fallen back through the Philippines, the Marianas, the Carolines and the Solomons. They had lost control of eastern New Guinea. The Americans had taken Iwo Jima at a cost of 6000 deaths (the Japanese defenders lost 21,000 dead) and were on their way to securing Okinawa (Japanese dead here would total a mind-boggling 110,000). Iwo Jima and Okinawa were two islands on the approaches to Japan from the South Pacific, where bombers and reconnaissance planes could be based for operations against the Japanese Home Islands themselves. The Japanese Navy and Air Force had been virtually annulled as potential threats to the Allied advance on Japan. The Japanese cities were being bombed from low level by the USAF, with effects easily as terrible as those wrought on Germany. Over a million tons of Japanese merchant shipping was sunk between April and August by Allied mines and naval action. The Japanese empire was swiftly strangling and bleeding to death. Defeat for the Japanese already looked certain, though everyone feared the terrible slaughter on both sides that would inevitably follow what now looked inescapable – a full-scale Allied invasion of Japan.

However, the Japanese still held some of the Marshall Islands, some of the Carolines and some of the Marianas out in the Pacific. They held all eastern China and the Chinese seaboard. New Ireland and Bougainville to the east of New Guinea were theirs. And they were still in control of the great arc of mainland and islands that included Siam, French Indo-China, Sumatra, Java, western New Guinea, the Celebes, Borneo, Malaya – and Singapore.

I took a gamble on my life [says Rod Wells] because I knew I wouldn't survive any longer in Outram Road Jail. I'd been in solitary there for well over a year. I was getting weaker and weaker; I could feel my heartbeat getting slower, down to about twenty-five beats a minute.

We were being used to dig foxholes for a last Japanese stand against the invasion they knew was coming. If an Outram Road POW got really sick he was transferred back to the hospital in Changi. I felt I'd got nothing to lose. So I just toppled over and lay there. The guard came up and kicked me in the ribs. Then they dragged me out of the hole and left me in the sun for the rest of the afternoon. I kept absolutely still. At night they took me back to the cell and left the cell door open – put my food just at the door's edge, with a Jap sitting just out of sight waiting for me to come and get the rice.

One guard came up and said, 'Eat your rice. No rice, no Changi.' But I just said, 'No, I'm too sick.' So they took the rice away. This went on for two days. Boy, it was a temptation just to grab that rice and sock it down! They said, 'Do you want a doctor?' I couldn't believe my ears! I said, 'No, too sick' – 'You want water?' – 'No, no.' There was no bravery attached to it – it was just pure self-preservation. It was the last road; no other road to go down, except the end.

At last I heard them chattering and hear these magic words: 'Yappety-yappety-yappety-yappety ... Changi ... yappety-yappety-yap.'

They took me on a stretcher and put me on a truck. And the minute we drove out of the gates and the big chain door came down – there was a guard on me who wasn't Kempei Tai, but just an ordinary soldier – he passed a cigarette to me. I just said, 'Thank you very much' and he smiled and lit it for me. And that was the first semblance of any civility I had ever had out of the Japanese.

> *Here come the Aussies, to capture Tarakan,*
> *It's just the kick-off, we're heading for Japan;*
> *If you could see the grim-faced men,*
> *And their mates the RAN,*
> *And backed up by the Air Force –*
> *We'll capture Tarakan.*
> Marching song of 2/48 Battalion

In May 1945 Les Rowe landed on Tarakan with 2/48 Battalion. Since surviving the decimation of the battalion during ten days of front-line fighting at El Alamein, Rowe had learned all about jungle combat in Papua New Guinea. Back in the desert he had relied on older, harder, more experienced comrades to help him through. 'Now, though, it was a different battalion. We'd lost almost all the men we started with. Now you'd got young people looking to *you*, asking *you* what it's going to be like.'

Tarakan was a small, swampy island off the north-eastern coast of Borneo, its interior a mass of razor-back clay ridges blanketed in rain forest. Nearly 2000 Japanese were hidden around the island in the usual well-camouflaged bunkers. Snipers had concealed themselves up trees and down gullies. The highways were efficiently booby-trapped. Tarakan was a small but tough nut to crack. The Australian ships and planes gave the island a four-day pounding before the soldiers went in to land on the muddy beaches at 8 a.m. on 1 May.

The RAN ship we were landing from had been working with the Americans, landing their troops, and the crew couldn't get over the difference. They said, 'With the Americans, you can't get them to put their heads up; with the Australians, you can't get them to put their heads *down!*' Some of the Americans had had to be chased out of the barges, with a pistol waved around and all that sort of stuff. With us, they just dropped the rope and the Australians were in the water, gone. They'd formed this impression that we were lackadaisical, didn't bother to wear our tin helmets, slouched around. But that all changed when the business started.

The Americans, by this time, had fought their way into the northern Pacific, leaving behind – some Australians felt – a nasty mess that the Aussies were going to have to mop up at considerable cost to themselves. 'Mopping up' was a mild enough term for what, in practice, amounted to a wholesale slaughter of the Japanese wherever they were found. That figure from the US capture of Okinawa is worth repeating – the dug-in Japanese defenders lost *110,000 dead* on that one fifty-mile-long island, nine times as many as the exposed attacking forces. The Australians knew that those entrenched on Tarakan would not surrender. But 2/48 were very well supported at this victorious stage of the war:

Tarakan was a terrific show. You still had this World War One rifle, but by now you felt you were on the winning side. You'd got all these ships with you, you'd got the Air Force. In the desert, even three miles behind the front line, there was never a time when you could say you were safe. You never knew when something was going to come in from above. But in the jungle, even if the fighting was only 200 yards away, you could more or less say you were as safe as in a brick house – unless you were actually at the point where it was taking place.

At night, though, the Japanese could be out there twenty yards away and you wouldn't know they were there. Oh, they were shocking at night. They'd come round with shells with a lighted mosquito coil for a fuse and they'd throw a few of those in amongst you. In some cases they had bayonets tied on long sticks. Yes – very bad.

It took two months to secure Tarakan. The 1800-strong Japanese garrison lost 923 men in the first phase of the assault; withdrawing in June, they lost another hundred; in mopping-up operations in August another 225 were killed. Two hundred and twenty-two prisoners were taken. About 300 were unaccounted for, some of them still in hiding and potentially deadly. This, in microcosm, was what happened to almost all Japanese garrisons. In a hundred similar islands, as their overblown instant empire imploded, the dire tragedy was rerun during these middle months of 1945.

There was a room in Changi [says Rod Wells] where chaps would wait to be brought news from the radio operator down the corridor. At about two o'clock one morning I found all these chaps sitting round, puffing cigarettes they'd been saving for ages. 'Come and join us,' they said. 'Someone's got a bottle of sake.' I said, 'Forget that – it won't do you any good.' He said, 'It's over, you know.' I said, 'What's over?' He said, 'The war.' I said, 'Ah, don't be stupid.' He said, 'They've dropped a bomb, a big bomb.'

On 6 August 1945 the US B-29 bomber *Enola Gay* dropped an atomic bomb on the city of Hiroshima in south-west Japan.

'We were in Tharrawaddy,' says Balwant Singh Bahia of REME, 'on the main road north of Rangoon, on 6 August. We were working and these two sergeants – one white man, one Indian – with us in the signal lorry. About one o'clock he told us the news, because they passed it over the wireless. He says, "Oh, war finish! War finish! They have dropped atom bomb on Japan." I said, "What's that one?" He says, "I come back one minute." Oh! They opened up small beer bottles, you know.'

Two days later Russia declared war on Japan and invaded Manchuria. The day after that, 9 August, a second atomic bomb was dropped, this one on Nagasaki. By this time, in conventional bombing raids, 50 per cent of Tokyo had been destroyed by fire; 56 per cent of Kobe; 44 per cent of Yokohama. On 10 August Japanese troops were ordered to cease fighting – an order that not all of them obeyed. On 14 August Japan agreed to an unconditional surrender. The fifteenth was proclaimed VJ or Victory over Japan Day.

On 16 August, the following day, the Japanese in Hong Kong agreed to surrender. George Barron of the Royal Rifles of Canada, who had been incarcerated in Shampshui Po prisoner-of-war camp since Christmas 1941, remembers the scene when US Admiral William Halsey arrived off Hong Kong with his 3rd Fleet:

The very ship that had brought us to Hong Kong, the *Prince Robert* – it was there. There was British ships, American ships, Australian and New Zealand and Dutch ships in this enormous convoy; there were over 300 ships in it, the biggest convoy that ever sailed in the Pacific. But they let the Canadian ship come in first, because there were Canadians in the camp.

Then they brought in the commandos, the British and Australian commandos, and they cleared the island of all the Japanese. I had a friend in that operation, an Australian Navy man, and he said, 'George, there wasn't one Jap left alive in Hong Kong. We killed every bloody one of them.'

They came into the camp, and brought in chocolate bars and cigarettes and one thing and another. The guards had walked off by then, of course – they'd heard what was coming.

They took us off from Hong Kong. I went on a British hospital ship that took us to Manila and I was in the hospital there for about a month. I was happy to be free, of course; happy to be out of that camp. But I didn't feel too good. I had TB on both lungs and severe malnutrition, as well as all the tropical diseases. The doctors in Manila – I heard them say to each other: 'Oh, this'll take ten years off these men's lives.' So I joked with them, saying, 'Oh, yeah? Well, I'm going to live to be 100, anyway!' And I'm eighty-seven now, so I haven't done too bad.

Across the South China Sea in Changi camp, Singapore, the news of the atomic bomb detonations in Japan had thrown Rod Wells and his fellow prisoners, by now so accustomed to pessimism, into a painful flutter of expectation. It was the changed attitude of his Japanese guards that revolted the Australian, even as it tormented him with the prospect of an end to the nightmare:

The second day after hearing the news I went out to wash at the wash bucket. There was a Japanese squad taking the guard over. I thought, 'God, how much longer am I going to have to bow my head to these bastards?' But as I was about to fold my hands and bow, this one guy gave the order 'Eyes Right' and he saluted me as he went by. Then I knew. Within half an hour they were running round the camp: 'Would you like cigarette? Would you like water? Anything you want?' I just ignored them, though that wasn't what I felt like doing to them.

Then a plane flew over and dropped leaflets to us, saying that next morning a commander and four medical orderlies would arrive by air. So the whole of Changi was up at four o'clock, waiting. Just before sunrise this lone plane flew over and dropped out some white parachutes – a medical officer, a commander and these four medical orderlies; then ten or fifteen black parachutes with forty-four-gallon drums packed with all sorts of exotic things – food, medical supplies, cigarettes. And these characters landed. They were all Englishmen from South-East Asia Command, from Colombo – and there they were, great strapping big blokes.

There was a lieutenant with this big pistol with six rounds in the chambers. We said, 'The Japs won't like that; you'll get into a lot of trouble.' We were still in that psychological mood, you know. 'Cheer up,' he said, 'you can tell them what you like, hit them over the head with a hammer, anything. Don't mess around – just give them orders. Treat them like scum, that's all they are.'

The dropping of the atomic bombs undoubtedly saved an enormous number of lives. Jim Tait of the Royal New Zealand Navy was due to go to the Pacific; Alec Dennis of the Royal Navy, likewise. Etienne Marot, the Mauritian serving with the King's African Rifles, had embarked at Mombasa and was on his way to Burma when the Japanese formally signed the instrument of surrender on 2 September 1945 on the US battleship *Missouri* in Tokyo Bay. These three, at any rate, were to take no further active part in the war – which, officially, was now at an end.

However, the Supreme Commander South-East Asia, Admiral Lord Louis Mountbatten, was well aware that Malaya was one of the territories still in Japanese hands. A landing would have to be made – unopposed, everyone hoped – so as to get Allied troops in on the ground as soon as possible. 'Operation Zipper', which took place on 9 September – a week after the Japanese surrender in Malaya – would certainly have led to great loss of life and military embarrassment for the Allies, had the defenders been minded to oppose it; for the landing beaches at Morib, south of the Malayan capital of Kuala Lumpur, having been stated by Intelligence to be of firm sand, turned out to be of deep, sticky mud. Sand bars offshore upset some of the landing craft; others grounded on unseen runnels that crossed the beach.

Krishen Tewari of 51 Brigade, 25 Indian Division, was selected to take part in this misadventure:

The first time I saw the Malaya map, with a big arrow pointing to the beaches where we were going to land, the heart missed a few beats. Then the Colonel turned round and said, 'Krishen, your Brigade is going to do the assault landing.' So my heart missed a few more beats!

We were on the high seas when the surrender was announced, but we were told to carry out the assault landing anyway. If the war had not finished, our attack would have been a bit of a fiasco. We were supposed to drive from the landing ship in a DUKW, an amphibious three-ton lorry, on to the beach. That DUKW drowned; it got stuck in the marshy beach of Morib. We had no choice: the Brigadier, Reggie Hilton, was the first one to jump in. And he disappeared under water, because he was as short as I am. So I had to jump in also. Soaked! The Brigadier's jeep also got drowned. The Signals jeep had arrived, so the Brigadier turned round: 'KK! Aren't you going to drive me?' – 'Yes, Sir!' – it was such a privilege.

Another of those strange, vivid, highly charged wartime episodes followed:

We drive down the road towards Kuala Lumpur. We go through civilian crowds and they're all waving to the victorious army, and the girls – ah, the girls ... The Brigadier shouts: 'Stop! Stop!' and he's getting kissed by the girls. So after a while he says, 'KK! Now *you* sit and get kissed, and *I'll* drive!' But I said, 'No, Sir, the victorious Commander must be driven, not drive.'

Now some Australian general had given an Order of the Day that every Japanese officer and Other Rank would salute every Allied soldier, irrespective of his rank. 'However,' he said, 'to show our contempt for the way you've treated our prisoners, a Japanese soldier's salute will not be returned.' So we came to where Japanese troops were lined up on one side of the road, and they gave a salute to the Brigadier. And he just ignored the salute. I asked him, 'Do you want me to stop?' And he said, 'No – leave the bastards alone.'

Balwant Singh Bahia was embarrassed to receive the same treatment when he encountered the defeated Japanese:

From Rangoon our Division went to Indo-China, to collect gun and arms from Japanese in Saigon. All Japanese officer salute us there. We say, 'Don't salute us, because we are same soldiers like you.' He say, 'No, our King say salute to everyone. We don't know if you are officer or you are soldier, but we salute.'

And in the morning they are told to clean our vehicles.

Phil Rhoden, by now a lieutenant-colonel in command of the Australian 2/14 Battalion, was another who had an odd, other-worldly end to his Far East war. All through the South-East Asia Command area there was a pressing need, after the Japanese surrender, to disarm and round up Japanese forces, to reach the POW camps and free the prisoners as quickly as possible, to maintain the rule of law and to put some kind of civil administration in place of the now dismantled Japanese military rule. The obvious candidates for the task were the various Allied battalions, regiments and brigades still scattered around the region, none of them over-keen to postpone their homegoing.

In October, 2/14 Battalion were sent to the Celebes, an island cluster between Borneo and New Guinea, centred on a large island shaped like some fabulous sea creature with outflung tentacles. The Celebes had been part of the Dutch Empire, but the Japanese during their tenure of nearly four years had encouraged the local people to throw off these colonial shackles. Now the Free Indonesia Movement had political clout and was not going to co-operate with the islands' former masters. Administration had therefore all but broken down. The 'Heighos' were local guerrillas, trained by the Japanese, who could be expected to cause trouble. There were 23,000 Japanese on the islands, outnumbering the native population three to one. There were Dutch women and children, ex-internees, to be looked after. There was a raft of local princelings and dignitaries who had to be kept sweet, or the islands would not function day to day. And the soldiers of 2/14, not surprisingly, wanted badly to go home. It was, as Phil Rhoden mildly puts it, an exciting time.

Well, we were sent to the seaport of Parepare, a hundred miles north of Macassar, and we didn't get home until February 1946. At Parepare we had two roles – one was to get the country back on its feet, because the Dutch had been chucked out by the Japs. We had to get some of the Dutch staff working again. And the second role was to incarcerate the Japanese 2nd Army. It was one of the most exciting times, a complete change from what we'd been doing during the war. I was like a local Governor, with immense powers.

We used to have a conference for the Dutch East Indies people every morning. One day I asked one official if he'd been out to a certain agricultural area. He said, 'No, my car has broken down' – of course, he was driving round in a tremendous Buick which he'd pinched off the Japs. I said, 'Well, take a Battalion jeep.' – 'Oh, no, Colonel, I could not be seen in a jeep! It is only small. Think of my "face"! I must go in a big car.'

I said: 'Get into that jeep, and go.' And he went.

About the time that Phil Rhoden was taking up his duties in the Celebes, Sheila Parkinson was attending a trial in Germany. The defendants were Josef Kramer, the 'Beast of Belsen', and a number of ex-guards at the concentration camp. Kramer had had experience at Auschwitz and as *Kommandant* at Birkenau, before he was transferred to Belsen in November 1944. From then on, tens of thousands of prisoners were dumped in Belsen with no food, water or attention of any kind. Disease and starvation stalked the camp. Some inmates resorted to cannibalism. Those who liberated Belsen on 12 April 1945 found 10,000 unburied corpses piled all over the camp and in its huts. Thousands more lay in mass graves. Huts built to accommodate 100 inmates were crammed with ten times that number. People dying of disease and starvation shared their bunks with the dead. There was no sanitation of any kind; inmates too weak to go outside, as most were, relieved themselves where they lay. The compounds were packed – one, where typhus was raging, held 8000 men; another held 23,000 women. The only source of water was a single tank in which dead bodies were floating; prisoners were drinking from this.

Josef Kramer was *Kommandant* at Belsen when the horrified Allied troops discovered the camp in this condition. Photographs of Kramer and the camp guards, taken at the time of the trial, show them looking like Neanderthalers, pinch-mouthed and moronic – an extraordinary gallery of cruelty. Sheila Parkinson sat in on their trial for the three days that Josef Kramer was in the witness box.

> They had these rows and rows of camp warders down one side. Very few of them were German. They were long-term asylum cases, to look at them – mental cases.
>
> You know, there are different sorts of cruelty, aren't there? When I was there it was Kramer who was being examined. He was being questioned in English; the English was turned into German; he replied in German; and the German was turned back into English. So every question was very, very slow and very dreadful.
>
> At one point his wife said she wanted to give evidence. She loved that man, and she talked about the prisoners who made up the camp orchestra and how he loved music. And everything she said dropped him further into the mire. There's a terrible cruelty about doing this – not physically, but mentally, so slowly and over such a long time. It was truly awful.
>
> Q   Did you ever go into Belsen camp?
> A (Mrs Rosina Kramer)   One Sunday afternoon. I went into the place where they were weaving and my husband told me with great pride about the beautiful orchestra which was playing. He wanted to show me that.[15]

> He looked so ordinary. There was something hypnotic about the Nazi indoctrination. And those rows and rows of guards staring moronically into space, looking as if they'd been picked out of a lunatic asylum to do that job.
>
> I think my main horror was the implacable rectitude of the questions ... and that man's wife trying to help her husband and all she was doing was sealing his fate. I was just appalled for everyone concerned in that – one of the things one will never forget.

And so, sooner or later, they made their way back home...

Jim Tait, RNZNVR: 'They just gave you a little chit to say you were placed on the reserve list. There were no thanks for your service. You just finished.'

Aziz Brimah, Gold Coast Regiment: 'My family brought a white horse to the parade ground to fetch me. My father and I rode on this horse up to our house, with thousands and thousands of people playing along the way, on all sorts of drums.'

Raymond Walker, RCN: 'There was only about two phones in this area at that time, so I couldn't let my wife know. I just got off the train, got a taxi and walked in the house. It was in the afternoon, coming on evening. And there she was, with her sister, just getting ready to go out to Bingo.'

Geraldine Turcotte, RCAF: 'When I came home they took my picture, with my mother and my teddy bear mascot that I'd had all through the war. And that's when my mother took my hat off, and she says, "I thought so!" I said, "What do you mean?" And she says: "Your hair's gone white." '

PART THREE

AFTERMATH

EIGHT

Reckoning

You can't just come home after a war is over, take off your khaki, put on your civilian clothes and walk out as if nothing has happened.   Joe Oldford, Canada

Some of them, the lucky ones, slipped smoothly enough into the post-war world. It was easiest for those who stayed on in the services and continued to live within that well-ordered framework. Most of the Commonwealth servicemen and women, though, were hostilities-only volunteers. Some found their old jobs waiting for them when they came back home; some resumed their studies where they had left off. Others got fixed up with a new educational course or a fresh job without too much difficulty, or returned to the family farm or business or plot of land. A few entered the twilight world of the long-stay hospital patient. Most simply went home to their parents or wives or husbands, and got on with the business of picking up the threads of their lives again.

They wanted to settle down, to have some money in their pockets. The procreating instinct, suppressed during the war, now came chirping out and demanded to be attended to. Years of communal living made the prospect of nest-building irresistible, and for many ex-servicemen and

women there were favourable interest rates, cut-price mortgages, rehabili-
tation grants, subsidised furnishings.

A prospective employer, looking at these men and women, would have
rated them high in confidence and self-esteem. They were still young,
many of them barely into their twenties, but they had grown old in
responsibility. They had brought their bomber crews safely back from fifty
trips over the Ruhr, or stormed sniper-infested Italian towns, or calmly
worked on through air raids. They had steered several hundred fellow men
unharmed between Arctic icebergs, U-boat torpedoes and cruisers' shells;
they had stayed awake through the night to rearm fighters at Biggin Hill,
or to track submarines in the North Atlantic, or load ammunition trucks
in the Western Desert, or mend telephone cables under fire in a pitch-
black Burmese jungle. Most of them could think on their feet, carry out
orders efficiently and stay unflustered under pressure. There was no reason
to suppose that they would not bring these admirable qualities to bear
just as successfully on their civilian working lives.

As for their personal lives – success there was more problematical. But
initially they had a surge of goodwill to surf on. Most of their friends and
families were delighted to see them safely back; most were proud of them
and wanted to show it. There were congratulations, kisses, parties, love-
makings, back-slappings, photographs, weddings, welcome-homes. Then,
after a few weeks or months, they were expected to simmer down and get
on with life. After all, the war was over; it was time to put all that behind
them, and get back to the real world.

For many of the servicemen and women, though, the real world was
the one they had left behind them. The experience that they had been
through was so vivid, yet wholly untransmissible. It was, and would always
be, a part of them; for many of them the most intense passage of their
lives. Yet unlike any other experience, it had absolutely no relevance to
ordinary, everyday life. Many could not hook their wartime and peacetime
selves together. Their families did not want them to keep hanging around
with their ex-service comrades; yet these were the only ones who could
understand what they had been through, the things they had seen and
done, the things others had done to them or to their fellows.

It was not just the horrors and terrors that they withheld from their
friends and families – the way a once-beautiful town smells and looks
when you march through it after a siege, or the sound of a Japanese jitter
party under the trees at night, or what you feel when you have sent an
enemy pilot down in flames, or the expression on the face of a drowning

man as you pull up the scrambling nets and leave him behind in the water. It was also indelible messages from other cultures: the way a white South African private bawls at a black South African sergeant, the slow-burning words of Mahatma Gandhi in a Madras cinema, the fury of an Indonesian communist guerrilla against his colonial masters. It could be as simple as lilacs in Normandy lanes, or a captured Italian cigar in Tobruk, or a bowl of tulip stew among flooded Dutch polders, or the stink of a Desert Rose, or the laughter of girls in a Trieste whorehouse. They had carried these things back home in their heads, but there was no way on earth they could present them to the people there, as they could hand out the silk stockings and electric irons and chocolate that they carried in their kitbags.

For some, this post-war alienation showed itself in a general inability to settle down. Phil Rhoden had had a highly successful war by anyone's standards, rising to command 2/14 Battalion with the rank of lieutenant-colonel, seeing active service in the Middle East and the Far East, confidently controlling events and leading men in a number of important actions. Now he was back in his law practice in Melbourne, resuming a high-powered solicitor's career. Yet he says, 'I found it very difficult to settle down. My wife tells me even now that I was impossible to live with. I was jumpy, and dreamy ... waking up at night thinking about the war ... and I was impatient and so on. It took me a long while to settle down. I think it stemmed from those experiences in New Guinea. I used to think about it a lot. It had its mark upon me.'

Jim Tait, having begun the war as an RNZNVR ordinary seaman and ended it as a lieutenant, was back on his dental course at university in New Zealand. He, too, found it 'difficult to go from being a first-lieutenant in a submarine and a Big Man, to suddenly sit down with chaps who were five or six years younger than me and be a humble student again. There were majors and wing-commanders doing the same thing and some couldn't hack it.'

Peter Cayley of the Royal Canadian Navy remembers 'getting a very vivid feeling of: What am I going to do now? What's it all about? I'd grown up, really, in the wartime Navy, when everyone had the same objective – to win the war. Now, suddenly, here was a situation: How are we going to get on with life without this great big aim? There was a distinct void, for a while.'

For Tom Somerville, home in New Zealand after his long artillery service in the North African desert and in Italy, it was ordinary life that felt unreal:

'It seemed to me as if the bottom had fallen out of everything; as if what had been our life for four years, the people you'd been living with for four years ... as if, suddenly, everything had changed.'

Tom Somerville's younger brother, Ted, had served among the Pacific islands with the Royal New Zealand Air Force during the latter stages of the war. He likens the effect of wartime service overseas to 'being broken into three pieces, or three people, that could never be made whole or made back into one again. You became these three entirely different people: the man who one was before the war, the man who fought overseas, and the man who came back. One knew who the first two were; but the third man had to reinvent himself. You just couldn't get back to being the person that everyone at home was expecting you to be, the person they had known before you went away. You didn't even know who you were now.'

Joe Oldford of the Cape Breton Highlanders, who had been decorated for his bravery and leadership in Italy, reinforces the point: 'You can't just come home after a war is over, take off your khaki, put on your civilian clothes and walk out as if nothing has happened. You can't ever get back to the man you were – I don't think so, anyway.'

Or as Mbithi Muinde, a Kenyan sergeant who served in Burma with the 11th East African Division, succinctly puts it: 'If I was to strike you with my walking stick now, you would remember it, wouldn't you? That was how the war was struck into our minds.'

Some of the returned servicemen and women had to cope with physical changes. Geraldine Turcotte's fiery red hair had turned white after a year under flying-bomb and rocket attack in London. Ex-prisoners-of-war such as George Barron and Thomas Hunter had stomach problems or bone disorders as a consequence of malnutrition. Almost all the gunners experienced hearing loss and for some of them tinnitus became a life-long affliction – a buzzing noise for Etienne Marot of Mauritius, a ringing sound for the Canadian, Wilmer Nadjiwon of the Cape Croker Indians. Bomber pilots had spinal pain from the long hours of sitting hunched over heavy controls that had to be wrestled around by brute force. Facial tics and speech impediments showed how some people's nerves had been over-strained for years. And there were manifestations of nervous exhaustion that went beyond the physical.

John Borketey, Gold Coast: 'After the war, it comes back at first. It used to trouble me. In my dreams I would see the Japanese come to attack me, and I would shout. My father would come in and say, "What is happening?

Have no fear – all these are things you have faced before." In 1951 I went to the Reverend Minister to pray for me and they stopped troubling me.'

Frank O'Donnell, Canada: 'Delayed reaction certainly can bother you. When I came home I was a little difficult to live with for a while. Sometimes I didn't want to sleep on a bed. I preferred the floor. You're safer down there, less of a target. It becomes second nature – look for the low ground. I knew it was kinda dumb, but it was more comforting.'

Wilmer Nadjiwon, Canada: 'After the war it's hard to cope. Takes a long time to wind down – years and years and years. You wake up with jerks, see people at night that you know are dead. Battle is not a good place to be, you know? I've seen, as far as I could see either way, Germans laying in an anti-tank ditch which our artillery had got to. They were just laying, laying, laying . . . hard to cope with, that kind of sight.'

Victor Nunoo, Gold Coast:

Many people came back and they were not normal – from the experiences they had had. I know a friend who was desperate all the time. Every time we were drinking or went out together, he starts shouting as if he's getting mad or something. He pictures the whole operation in his head.

I myself had a small problem afterwards, marching back home: each time I sat down, I would get these pictures. But after a time they disappeared. When we got back we had a welcome – everyone shouting and singing, and happy to see us. When we saw that, it helped to put bad things out of our minds.

The shouting and the singing could only go on for so long; after that, families and friends expected to reap a dividend of normality. This, for those ex-servicemen and women who were trying to cope with a state of mind that had yet to be labelled 'post-traumatic stress disorder', was the biggest hurdle of all. They could learn to wear a mask with the general public, but their families saw them when the masks came off, when anger and frustration were given expression. Some succeeded in pushing the stopper into the bottle and kept it there, to their long-term psychological detriment. Others let their pain out in toxic drips. Many wives and relations felt they would never surmount these obstacles to a return to everyday life. Many did not.

The ex-POWs had to struggle particularly hard to get back on an even keel. Jack Brown, the once-confident, self-reliant New Zealand shepherd, went through the whole gamut of emotional problems, and those close to him were dragged along as well.

All the servicemen were expected to just come back and pick up life where they left off. Well, it wasn't on – it wasn't to be, with that sort of experience behind them. It's not that people didn't treat you well: the difficult part was that you couldn't really talk to people, because they didn't really understand what you were talking about. They had a job to understand what had happened to a person, because you couldn't really explain yourself. You would flare up for no reason. People who knew me were probably wondering what the hell they'd done wrong. Of course, they hadn't done anything wrong. They knew the person who went away – but what they could never know was what had made the change in me.

For a start, you had to get back into talking generalities, find something to chit-chat about, unless you were talking to your own group of ex-POWs. So you didn't talk, you didn't say much. And I think, if we could have had a little bit of help there, a bit of encouragement to talk things out, it would have gone a long, long way. Unfortunately we got no counselling, and that's something I could have done with.

Jack Brown's problems, exacerbated by shell-shock from a near-miss bomb blast during his imprisonment in Leipzig, worsened to the point where his mother persuaded him to go into hospital for a course of electro-convulsive therapy, in those days a pretty crude, make-or-break treatment. Brown believes it worked and saved him from long-term psychiatric illness. But an even more effective remedy was embarking on a good solid marriage:

I had a very understanding wife: I was one of the lucky ones. They put up with a hell of a lot, you know – I didn't realise then, though I do now. We were very, very moody people when we came back. Your nerves had shattered you; it's something you had to learn to live around. Some of the wives couldn't hack it. Those of us who had wives who could – we were damn lucky. Mind you, starting a family was the best thing that happened to me, because I had something else to think about. Didn't have time to worry about my own troubles then!

There were difficulties for many home-comers in relating to other people – casual acquaintances or strangers – who had not been overseas. Some Gold Coast men, according to Kofi Genfi, found that the changes they had gone through made them unacceptable in their own culture:

People found that we had changed; in character, in habits. We became callous. If I am to dwell on character – we became unfeeling, because of the things we had seen. If someone got wounded and blood was coming, it was not horrible to you.

Most people here categorised us as madmen. Some who returned, when they got drunk, they tried to harass the people in their village. The villagers would even run away from them. It didn't happen to me: education gives very high culture. Ninety per cent of us were illiterate, though, and it was usually the uneducated men who behaved in this way.

In the social world of Canada it was the indifference of those who had stayed at home that irked Peter Cayley of the RCN: 'I think a number of people had the same feeling: we felt that we'd been doing something very worthwhile. But when you went in among a group of people in Toronto or Ottawa they'd say, "Oh, how interesting!" – but in fact you could see that they couldn't wait to get on to discuss their pinochle hand or whatever. People were not basically too interested in other people's adventures abroad.'

Frank O'Donnell, still only nineteen when the war ended but carrying a heavy load of grim memories, points to censorship of letters written from the battle zones as a prime cause of lack of understanding back home among largely untravelled people with little or no experience of foreign cultures.

Soldiers were taught, in the Service, that in their letters home they were to put on a cheerful face. And if they didn't the letter wouldn't pass the censor. You know, there was no such thing as defeatism allowed in those letters: the black pencil went over it. There was no such thing as actual descriptions of what went on all around. Now I got some letters from my brother which were graphic about his experiences; but that was inter-Service mail, so it wasn't subject to the censorship.

So that when you got home, perhaps that self-censoring feeling was ingrained. And people here didn't have a clue about the effects of all these experiences – even about the effects of the travel, the social experiences. Canadians didn't know as much about Europe, about the outside world, as they do now. We were like men from a new planet to them.

Then of course you got the selfish ones who were sorry the war was over, because they'd lost their war jobs. Plus there had been rationing, of a minor nature – and we actually heard some complaints about the rationing! There were still shortages – you couldn't buy a car for a while, you know – and we'd hear people complaining about that ... You'd just turn away. You didn't want to get into that kind of an argument.

If there was shoulder-shrugging and yawn-stifling at the war experiences of Frank O'Donnell and Peleg Cayley, there was open hostility for Frank Sexwale of South Africa's Native Military Corps when he returned home.

Our own people, in general, didn't like the idea of us having taken part in the war. When we came back we had very few friends. People said: 'You went to fight for our oppressors. What did you fight for? You were given assegais and knobkerries against the might of Rommel. You were fighting to maintain your own oppression.' We were in a minority; we couldn't talk to anyone. You remember that we had those terrible Pass Laws at that time; and if you were stopped by a policeman and you told him you had been a soldier he'd say, 'What? Kaffir soldat?' He wouldn't believe that a black man could have been a soldier.

I well remember J. C. Smuts coming to our base camp in Egypt and saying to us: 'The South Africa you are going back to will not be the same South Africa that you left.' But it was the *status quo*, or even worse.

For non-white men and women, encountering racial disadvantage again on their return home proved a bitter disappointment – even for those like Wilmer Nadjiwon of the Canadian Ojibwe Indians, who had been forewarned by First World War veterans of how things were likely to be:

A lot of soldiers that we fought right beside would hardly recognise you after the war. They were taken right over by their white community. There was the odd one who'd come over and visit you on the reserve, but it wasn't the general rule.

There'd been no such things as racism in the war – it was just, you know: 'Here's another soldier.' So it struck you when you encountered it again back home. I remember going into a bar and ordering a drink, and the barman said to me: 'Show me your permit.' Well ... let's put it that I wasn't very nice after that, to him or his bar. I couldn't believe I could be standing there, having served my country, and be refused a drink – be back in that same old racial-prejudice situation.

I remember very well: there were so many from the reserve who had gone to war that we wanted our own Canadian Indian Legion. The Canadian Legion allowed us to form a Legion, gave us a charter – but no right to sell beer, or even to drink beer at banquets. So I never joined. I just said, 'To hell with it – you can keep your goddamn Legion.'

Now if you allowed it today, you'd still be treated and feel like a second-class citizen. But I don't allow it.

The close companionship and mutual dependence of the wartime service unit – the bomber or fighter squadron, the infantry platoon or company, the ship's crew, the supply unit, the POW camp hut-mates – compared unfavourably, the South African Bob Gaunt found, with the way that working and social groups operated in peacetime.

You always think that your crew is the best, the finest guys, the most wonderful crowd you ever knew. I mean, these chaps went through so much and never once grumbled about anything. Able seamen, ordinary seamen, signallers, telegraphists – to me that *was* the Navy, the lower deck. My problem was that in peacetime I would compare people to the wonderful guys I'd sailed with in wartime, and found myself thinking that they in no way measured up to them. You thought: 'My God, what a lot of whingers' and things like that. This was quite wrong, of course: utterly unfair. But this is what war does to one.

For these reasons many of the returned ex-servicemen and women, feeling cut off from meaningful communication with either families or acquaintances, got into the habit of fobbing them off with a funny story, or a dismissive phrase or two. 'Talking about the war' became a mutually agreed no-go area, which enquirers learned not to approach for fear of a brusque rebuff, or to avoid the frustration of meeting yet another deflective comment.

Tom Somerville: 'I didn't want to talk about it to people. The kids used to ask me and I just used to make a joke of it. I didn't want to tell them the raw side of anything.'

Jack Brown: 'You didn't talk about it because people really didn't understand. A mass grave full of broken bodies of men, women and children is a very hard thing to visualise. How could you visualise a thing like that if you hadn't seen it for yourself?'

Ted Somerville:

You'd left behind that man who did those things in the islands, or in Egypt. Often loved ones couldn't understand you, why you didn't want to talk about it. Even with your friends who'd been through the same thing as you, you'd often not mention the war. I'd seen Japanese atrocities on the natives of the islands – fingers chopped off, noses sliced off, tongues cut out – just for fun, some of it, for no reason. Oh, they were really appalling sights.

Many people found it very difficult. A lot of marriages didn't survive; a lot of those that did were unhappy.

And when the ex-servicemen and women did talk about the war, it was generally to the only people they could be sure would understand them, would know that they were not bragging or shooting a line or exaggerating. No need to lay out in painful or boring detail the underlying circumstances, the geography, the strategic situation; no need to introduce a cast of characters, or explain just why brave men freeze at the sight of an eighty-eight-millimetre gun, or why men and women can carry a heavy load of guilt because they have survived and their friends have not. A single word – 'Murmansk', or 'Cassino', or 'Cologne' – would suffice to set the scene in all its colours for those who had been there.

John Mumo, Kenya: 'Only those who were with you in the fighting would know how many enemies you had killed and that you were a hero because of killing several people. But not back at home: no one would consider you a hero there. That is why many askaris spend so much time talking and reminiscing with each other.'

Frank O'Donnell:

You don't want to describe some of the worst parts of it – and even if you could, what purpose would it serve? Do war stories really deter anybody, or do they encourage them? I think how many of these war stories start is with a short episode coming back into your mind. You want to share it. But for those who hadn't been there you need to give it a beginning, a middle and an end. So it becomes 'another war story'.

But if you're talking to another veteran you only have to mention a place-name, a scene. He knows exactly what you mean. You don't have to describe it in any more detail.

By contrast with all of this, there were other ex-servicemen and women who did not find it so hard nor so painful to close the book of their war and to shelve it. Alec Dennis of the Royal Navy thinks he was hardly changed in any way by his extraordinarily vivid and varied wartime experiences. 'It was really rather water off a duck's back, in my case. I was in a profession and I was very glad to have pursued it to the utmost; and I wasn't going to go ashore while I could continue at sea, where I thought I ought to be. It was part of the game – it was what you were there for. I didn't want to be anywhere else. It really never bothered me, seeing so many very unpleasant things. No sleepless nights, or anything like that. However, even now, if I smell the smell of oil fuel, or hear chaps shouting in the water – it comes straight back.'

John Mumo, the Kenyan sergeant-major who served in the medical corps with 11 East African Division in Burma, is of the same opinion: 'To me it didn't have such an impact. I was able to fit back in my family, carry on with my life. I could talk freely to my children about what had happened to me. The only lasting effect of the war has been my wound – sometimes it hurts when the weather is bad.'

Pierre Austin of the Royal Australian Navy, badly burned in a kamikaze attack during the Battle of Leyte Gulf in 1944, had better cause than most to sink into a slough of despond as he undertook a very slow and painful struggle back to good health. But instead, he found himself able to think positively:

> Generally I had a satisfactory level of compensatory help after the war. They paid for my degree course; the pension is tiny, but – I'm functioning! This might sound a bit silly; but you know how people get counselled and heaven knows what, nowadays? Well, when I got back, they said, 'Oh, you're back, are you? Got a lot of catching up to do, haven't you?' And you got on with it and did just that. I didn't want counselling – but that's just me, you know? There's nothing buried to bring out. You're here – life's to be lived – get on with it! That's all there is to it, really.
>
> A tremendous help to me, I suppose, was my wife's family. Now, *they'd* suffered. They were from Pomerania – lost everything. And their attitude was: 'What the hell? So we've lost the war and our possessions. We're going to get on with it; we'll get on our feet and, if we work hard enough, we'll make a go of it.' That was an inspiration to me.

And Sheila Parkinson of FANY, returning to a bomb-battered London from Germany, was able to compare her wartime lot favourably with the lives of the women on the Home Front: 'What those women back in Britain had been going through! Collecting salad bottles from rubbish dumps and cleaning them for reuse by the factories; getting scratched to ribbons picking hips and haws to make rose-hip syrup for children. They'd lived – oh, such an appalling life, and never ever complained; and I thought about the comfortable life I'd been leading, always eating good food and so on, and felt very embarrassed.'

What the ex-servicemen and women expected by way of grants, pensions, resettlement land and funds, gratuities, concessions, or any other practical assistance in the business of settling down after the war, depended entirely on the Commonwealth country from which they had originated. Few, if any, thought that service with the Crown entitled them to a jackpot payout; most believed that they would be 'seen right' in recognition of the sacrifices they had all made in greater or lesser degree. Some were properly assisted. Others were left unsatisfied, their disillusion compounded by changes in government that shifted responsibility from the British to the newly independent states.

Paul Radomski, the Polish New Zealand bomber pilot, remembers taking advantage of a housing loan of up to £1500, repayable over forty years at 3 per cent, and a repayable loan of £100 for furniture. Many New Zealand employers had held the volunteers' jobs open for them; and land for sheep farming was made available to those who wanted a fresh start. Raymond Walker of the Royal Canadian Navy, returning to Sydney Mines in Cape Breton Island, went on sixty days' leave at full pay; then he received a government gratuity of several thousand dollars, two suits of clothes, furniture, free dental work and the offer of further education. He opted to use some of his gratuity to fund himself on a course in interior decorating; it stood him in good stead a few years hence after various jobs away from Cape Breton had come to nothing. The ex-Japanese prisoner-of-war George Barron, in hospital back in Canada with complaints that ranged from two broken hips and TB on both lungs to fractured wrists and eye and throat problems, was on a 100 per cent pension from the date of his discharge in January 1946. All his war pay had been saved back home as well, and interest paid on it, with POW pay on top of that; so that, although broken in physical health (though not in spirit), he was not in financial difficulties. Wilmer Nadjiwon, the Cape Croker Indian, received $2300 like every soldier, 'but whites were allowed to borrow up to $10,000. There was no housing available, so I bought a house from my father with my $2300.'

Servicemen from the Caribbean islands had a wide variety of opinions about their treatment after the war. The Jamaican bomb-carrier, Dudley Thompson – soon to make a brilliant career for himself as a lawyer and administrator – worked on resettlement for ex-servicemen in the island. 'Everybody would be given a suit of clothes, and we offered educational courses here or in the UK, during which the families would get the same allotment as when the person was in the services. Another provision was settlement on the land, which we encouraged and pushed. Each ex-serviceman who applied would get five acres of land and provision to have a bit of a small house. Tradesmen could be given a cash grant to buy a new set of tools; not very much, but enough to give them a start. Personally I believe we should have done much more for education; however, we ex-servicemen had had an exposure to the outside world which helped us, all of us, very much.' Keith Levy, another ex-RAF Jamaican, points to the courses the returnees had taken in the UK as a bonus for their home islands: 'There were mechanics, there were electricians; there were lawyers, there were doctors; there were draughtsmen – every branch you can think of, men came back from England trained as such. Name the job, and you had men equipped to do it. It had a great impact on Jamaica, the return of the men of the Royal Air Force.'

In Trinidad, the cocoa giant Cadbury handed one of its estates in the Maracas Valley to the colonial government for division among ex-servicemen. Carlton Best, back home from Italy and Egypt, applied for a block of four and a half acres there, occupied it in 1947 and worked it up from a wild state into productivity as a smallholding. He continues to live there today, on the same lease as when he took it over, still hoping for the land to be legally made over to him. As for Tobago, a conversation between three of its ex-servicemen of the Caribbean Regiment shows how they feel:

Beresford Martin: If I had to rely on what I got from the Army, I'd be a dead man now. The finance they gave me couldn't even feed a little baby for three months.

Vernon Alexander: I was given, I think, three months' pay. Before the end of the third month that pay was finished – I had seven children. So that money was rotten and forgotten before three months, and since then I haven't received anything.

Beresford Martin: There was a land settlement, but the land was at Louis D'Or, too far from the place where I live. It was out of the way for me; I couldn't accept it. For men who offered their lives, I think the ex-servicemen should have been treated better.

Vernon Alexander: Now the responsibility should be the Trinidad and Tobago Government.

Beresford Martin: I wouldn't accept that. We were fighting for the British.

Edwin George: When I was demobbed, I received an envelope with $3.

Beresford Martin: I did not receive any recompense in financial terms. We became like dogs on the street.

Vernon Alexander: However, I feel proud of these medals that I'm wearing. They are like feathers around my cap.

For Indian ex-servicemen, study fees and payment towards accommodation while studying were on offer from the Dominion Government, and ex-servicemen in search of a job tended to be looked on favourably. But the situation of the Anglo-Indians (descendants of mixed marriages in India) deteriorated after Indian independence in 1947, when these Christian ex-servicemen's entitlement to a state pension slipped through the religious and cultural net. They were deemed to have been 'serving the Raj'. Provision for most of India's wartime 'hostilities-only' veterans, in fact, was sketchy and inadequate, regardless of their race or creed. The same was true, by and large, for black Africans not in the regular armed services. 'In the jungle we were not being paid,' says Kofi Genfi of the Gold Coast Regiment, 'it was all paid back here in Ghana. So I had about £50 saved, for four years' service. We were not offered land. Some were offered rooms in an ex-soldiers' housing estate.' Aziz Brimah from the capital, Accra, agrees: 'The pension here was lousy. You did not go to the war for reward; but when your counterparts in Britain, in New Zealand, in Australia, are given all sorts of things – well, you naturally feel you must be taken care of too. A bullet doesn't know any colour, you know. If British officers or African soldiers were hit by the bullet – same effect!' Victor Nunoo of the Gold Coast Regiment, paid a shilling a day while fighting in the Burmese jungle, returned to Africa to find that his family had managed to save only a little of what had been sent home to them to add to his £26 gratuity.

Frank Sexwale of South Africa had sent 75 per cent of his pay back home to his parents in Northern Transvaal, but they had spent it all to keep going while their son and chief bread-winner was away at the war. That was a common problem in cultures where the family finances relied so heavily on the young, fit and educated. When Sexwale was demobbed, he says,

No arrangement was made for my welfare or my people's welfare. Our people were just demobilised. No arrangement was made for their training; there was no compensation, nothing at all. What we found: the white people had a subsistence from the government; give them some money, according to the rank they held during the war, until they found a job. Coloured people were just like us; they didn't get a subsistence. There was an allowance for children during the time you're not working. You were given about £6 – that included a pair of trousers – and a bicycle if you had a job. The bicycle was to help you pull yourself up, pull yourself together, to get you to work – if you had work. Personally I did not even get a bicycle, because I was not employed. They said to me, 'Well, you have no job – you don't need a bicycle.'

On his return to South Africa, Bob Gaunt worked on resettlement of ex-servicemen.

Whites were offered a plot of land [he says] and a government grant. Those who'd matriculated could go to university free, but those who'd joined up straight from Standard 8 didn't get that. It caused a lot of resentment. But no one was demobbed until they'd got a job. For the blacks and Coloureds that certainly was not the case. For them it was: 'Off you go! Thank you very much!' The Coloureds did get treated slightly better than the blacks, however, because the Afrikaner looked at the Coloureds a bit differently. He recognised that, somewhere back along the line, he had kinship ties with them.

The Cape Coloured sergeant, Charles Adams, had been sending money home to his mother and found a helpful sum waiting for him. On discharge he was given money for clothing and a gratuity because of his rank; he also accepted the free bicycle, because he had fixed up a job in an engineering firm after rejecting the offer of work as a ganger on the railroad. 'That was not a job,' he says scornfully. 'It used to be all whites before the war; that was a special job for whites only. But after the war all the whites became foremen.'

During the war, 186,218 white male enlisted volunteers served with South African forces, and £10,019,844 was made available for their resettlement through the Financial Assistance Scheme – an average of about £54 a head. For the 24,975 white female volunteers there was £133,566, which amounted to around £5 for each person. For the 45,015 members of the Cape Corps £70,964 was allotted: £1.15s. per man. For the 77,239 volunteers with the Native Military Corps, the South African government found £5795 – about 1s.6d. for each volunteer.

As the servicemen and women of the British Commonwealth, handsomely settled or not, began to build new lives for themselves and to look to the future, so did the countries they had returned to. After such convulsive upheavals things were never going to be the same again. If anyone, before the war, had doubted the ascendancy in world importance of America and Russia, and the relative decline in influence of the British Empire–Commonwealth, they could hardly do so now, with the Cold War freezing the eagle and the bear into monolithic counter-postures that over-shadowed the limping of the poor old shabby, decent, bankrupt imperial lion. During their years of service the ex-soldiers, sailors and airmen of more than forty countries had seen too much, been exposed to too many new influences, to be satisfied with an unquestioning return to colonial rule. The fiascos at Singapore and Hong Kong had shown just how powerless the mother country was to defend her dependants in the modern world. Regard for Britain was still high among most war veterans: 'pluck', 'guts', 'determination', 'decency' were concepts associated with the British character that the war had actually reinforced. But the only way to go now, it was acknowledged in London and in capital towns and cities from Accra to Suva, was out from under. Somehow this Empire of the owners and the owned was going to have to transmogrify into a Commonwealth that would truly be a free association of sovereign independent states. If Britain could retain the respect and affection of the other members after the metamorphosis, that would be a major achievement in itself.

India was the first to go, 'awakening to life and freedom', as Jawaharlal Nehru put it, at midnight on 14–15 August 1947. The newly free countries of India and Pakistan, divided to accommodate the desire of the Muslims for their own homeland, were born in blood. Frightful massacres took place as millions of people, freely leaving or brutally driven out of one or the other country, moved east and west across the Punjab. The straws had been in the wind since mutinies early in 1946 by units of the Indian Navy, incensed by a range of grievances which included the old pay and promotion colour divide and, more importantly, accusations of insensitive and insulting behaviour on the part of British officers. It did not take many such sparks to set fire to the ready tinder of discontent, and plenty of ex-servicemen had wartime memories of such wrongs to draw on. The Muslim League's Direct Action Day in August 1946 turned into mob violence between Muslims and Hindus in Calcutta, during which several thousand people were murdered. India's last Viceroy, Lord Louis Mountbatten, was appointed in February 1947, and oversaw the partition of the country and the dawn of independence. He has been blamed for rushing the measures through, and increasing the pressure and panic that led to the slaughter in the Punjab. His recommendation that the timetable for independence should be accelerated was seen as having undermined the work of the Radcliffe Commission, which was looking at the fine detail of post-partition boundaries. However, Mountbatten was keenly aware of the racial, religious and political tensions that were threatening to tear the Indian armed services apart – services that would have to be relied upon to hold together and act effectively in the all too likely event of a breakdown of law and order.

Immediately after Independence Day the killings started, and continued for three months. By the time they had flickered out, towards the end of 1947, over half a million Indians and Pakistanis lay dead. Millions more had been dispossessed, raped, beaten, stripped of all they had, forced across borders they did not want to cross.

Balwant Singh Bahia remembers hiding in the REME workshop toilet to escape being sent to Lahore, in newly created Pakistan. Nila Kantan, who had been accepted into a parachute battalion, was in Quetta, north of Karachi, on 15 August 1947: 'We all toasted for Pakistan, and the Pakistanis toasted for the success of India – it was so good. Then, after two or three days, the great Quetta killings started.' He recalls hundreds of people clinging like ants to the carriages, cattle trucks and engines of the refugee trains. Danny Misra of the Rajputana Rifles tells of a Muslim baby being thrown alive into a burning house, a Sikh youth being ritually butchered like Halal meat by a mob and other unspeakable acts, beyond anything he had witnessed in Burma: 'Horrible, horrible things ... men descended below the level of beasts. We should all hang our heads in shame at what we did.' Krishen Tewari, as Adjutant of the Signals Training Centre in Jabalpur, had met some of the 1946 mutineers and endured long lectures from them on the evils of serving the British. At Independence he was in Delhi, with responsibility for dividing the Indian Army Signals Corps assets between India and Pakistan. 'I've seen the horrors of Partition,' he says, 'so I know that in the name of religion anything terrible can be done.' Danny Misra and Krishen Tewari would both attain the rank of major-general and see service in many post-war conflicts – Tewari, in fact, was to become a prisoner-of-war of the Chinese in 1962, during their Tibetan border war with India. Yet neither can cite anything more terrible in all their experience than the trains packed with dead bodies that would pull into Amritsar, Rawalpindi and other Indian and Pakistani cities, nor anything more futile and sad than the loss of good Muslim friends who became sealed off from them on the 'other side'.

In 1948 white South Africa elected a hard-line white supremacist government. Within ten years everyone in South Africa had been rigidly classified according to race, and the Coloured community had been disenfranchised. Charles Adams felt bitter about this, but since the Coloureds tended not to bind together to fight for their rights as did the blacks, he did not feel there was much that he could do about it.

In 1959 the Promotion of Bantu Self-Government Act became law. It would promote the 'self-government' of the eight Bantustans or black homelands set up to ensure separate development – in other words, apartheid – of blacks and whites. On 8 March the following year the black community's forum, the African National Congress, was banned, two weeks before sixty-nine blacks were shot dead by panicky white policemen at a rally in Sharpeville. In 1961 the South African Government proclaimed the country a republic. Refused a renewal of South Africa's Commonwealth membership because of the government's apartheid policies, the Prime Minister, Dr Hendrik Verwoerd, announced that the country would leave anyway. In 1964 Nelson Mandela and his activist associates were sentenced to life in jail for sabotage. White South Africa was building a laager for itself and digging its own grave as it did so. And it was about now that Frank Sexwale, who was working in a hospital in Johannesburg, became active in the ANC. 'I was living in Soweto at the time. I had to be very cautious. If the Government finds that you are in politics you will lose your job, and you don't want to bite the hand that feeds you. I registered myself in the ANC under a false name and I became active in politics. I had to be very, very careful. It was a case of going underground; I would go to meetings at night, where you would find policemen taking notes.'

On 11 June 1976 the Soweto riots began. Police opened fire on protesting students; after four days nearly 200 had died and there had been wide-spread destruction. For Frank Sexwale's family it was only one point on a continuum of revolutionary activity: 'Oh, my children were very much involved. They were in the forefront. My eldest son, his brother, their two sisters and this one they called Tokyo. He got that name at school, where he used to play karate – but we only knew him as Tokyo when he came back from military training in the Soviet Union.'

The war veteran's son returned to South Africa in 1977, slipping across the Swaziland border heavily armed and rigorously trained, with the intention of sparking a black uprising. Tokyo Sexwale and two colleagues were arrested, but escaped from the police van after blowing it up with a grenade. On the last night of 1977 Frank Sexwale was woken at home in the early hours, handcuffed and taken to the police station, to find his son there. Tokyo had just been recaptured.

I found my son handcuffed. I felt terrible. Tears started rolling from my eyes. I could not even talk. But he – he lifted his handcuffs and said, 'Power to the people.'

His case came on in 1978. I was in court every day of his trial. He was sentenced to eighteen years on Robben Island, where Nelson Mandela and the others were. When he got there he wrote me a letter. He said he is sorry they did not pass the death sentence, he is so determined to fight.

Tokyo is nowadays the Premier of Gauteng in the Transvaal. But it is only now that I can feel proud of him. I could not feel proud of him then, a man who was in so much trouble. The whole family felt terrible. But he had my moral support, he had the support of the whole family. We knew it was the struggle.

It took the South African blacks five post-war decades to achieve what they wanted in the way of self-government. In the Gold Coast, by contrast, the returned ex-servicemen had a rapid and decisive effect on the future of their country. The British were proud of their handling of the Africanis-ation of the Gold Coast military and administrative echelons. Sergeant Seth Kobla Anthony had been the first African soldier to get a commission; in the same year, 1942, the first two Gold Coast men were appointed to the administration of the colony. Most of the Gold Coast's population had been enfranchised during the war, and by 1946 the country's legis-lative council was the first among Britain's African colonies to have a black majority. However, out of well over 500 senior administrative posts, fewer than 100 were yet occupied by Africans. The charismatic young politician, Kwame Nkrumah, coming back to the Gold Coast in 1947 after ten years' studying in the USA, turned a growing mood of impatience to his advantage as he became a focus for independence agitation.

On 28 February 1948, the temperature in the Gold Coast abruptly changed during a rally by ex-servicemen in Accra. Since their return from Burma they had been petitioning the colonial government for proper pensions and for adequate health care. 'They kept promising, promising, promising,' says Victor Nunoo, 'but they didn't do it. So we decided to march on Osu Castle, the government building.' The trouble that followed was, according to Nunoo, fuelled by the ex-soldiers' wartime reactions:

> We marched from the parade ground towards the Castle. This police officer, Imray,* came with armed Gold Coast police. He said: 'Go back.' We said, 'No, we want to go to the Castle.' We kept on advancing. This Imray snatched a gun from a policeman and cocked it. Then he fired. Two men in front of me were killed. We started to run. Then he shot again and killed another man, a private. We had no weapons, not even cudgels or sticks.
>
> When this incident occurred it aroused everybody's anger. People became

* Superintendent Colin Imray.

wild. We couldn't get Imray – he ran. So we went back. As we were going towards the Assembly House, every white man we saw, we had to stop him, beat him, burn his car. When we entered the town, any white man's store, we had to break it, loot it. I took part in this myself. We became furious. It turned us back into reliving our experience in Burma – that war type of madness.

Shops belonging to Europeans and Asians were looted and burned in several towns. Prisoners were freed from Accra's central jail. The riots lasted for the next two days, spread 100 miles inland, and claimed twenty-nine lives. 'Nkrumah calmed us down,' says Victor Nunoo. 'He called us back to the parade ground again. He told us that we must tell our friends in the rest of the country to stop, or the Colonial Governor would suppress us. And he told us that he could help us to get what we wanted. After this, I became a political man.'

By 1951 Kwame Nkrumah's Convention People's Party had been voted into power. In 1952 Nkrumah became Prime Minister and on 6 March 1957 realised his ambition when the British colony of the Gold Coast became Ghana, the Empire–Commonwealth's first independent black African nation. 'The British were reluctant to let go,' comments Kofi Genfi, 'but the forces on them were too great. We tried to make them unhappy. They were very badly abused in the Press. We were attacking them and abusing them. So there was no comfort for them to stay.'

In the Caribbean things were moving too. Jamaica had had universal suffrage and a wholly elected Lower House of Parliament since 1944. In 1957, as Ghana gained full independence, the Commonwealth's Caribbean islands formed the West Indian Federation. Mutual support was the idea, but it soon became clear that the islands – some large and rich, others small and poor – were never going to be equal partners. In 1962 Jamaica struck out and became independent, the same year as Trinidad and Tobago. 'We had everything properly in place,' Carlton Best says of the Trinidadian handover. 'It's hard for new countries to leave the mother country and find their own resources. Better to plan it carefully than to rush into it. There comes a time when the mother country herself wants to throw you off her back, because she has more pressing problems at home. We had to try and change our viewpoint a little, to focus on our independence. But we didn't want to achieve it by violence. A Ghanaian told me: "We were looking to you, as leaders of the black race – waiting for you to overthrow the Colonial Government any minute." I said to him that was disgusting to any Caribbean.'

In 1960 the British Prime Minister, Harold Macmillan, made his famous 'wind of change' speech to a white audience in Capetown.

In the twentieth century [Macmillan told them] and especially since the end of the war ... we have seen the awakening of national consciousness in peoples who have lived for centuries in dependence on some other power.

Fifteen years ago this movement spread through Asia. Many countries there, of different races and civilisations, pressed their claims to an independent national life. Today the same thing is happening in Africa ... In different places it may take different forms, but it is happening everywhere.

The wind of change is blowing through the continent.

It was a wind of change that was eventually to blow all the white settler communities of Africa into a corner. Northern and Southern Rhodesia, along with Nyasaland, had formed a Central African Federation in 1953 that lasted for ten years. When Southern Rhodesia made a Unilateral Declaration of Independence in 1965 a white settlers' rebellion began which it would take an embarrassed British government fourteen years to solve. And even then, independence for a renamed Zimbabwe would only arrive thanks to bush fighters from next-door Mozambique adding their weight to Rhodesia's own fighters for black majority rule – among whom was Zimbabwe's first Prime Minister, Robert Mugabe.

In Kenya the whites had all the most productive farmland and a pleasantly privileged way of life they were keen to safeguard. In the 1930s they had tried to establish an East African Dominion, comprising Kenya, Tanganyika and Uganda; the postage stamps had come into being, but the white Dominion had not. In the early years of the war they had banned the Kikuyu Central Association, the black Kenyans' political front. After the war they jailed the Kenyan nationalist leader, Jomo Kenyatta, for his activities in support of the Mau Mau. These were the KCA's much more direct and violent successors with whom, between 1952 and 1956, the whites were embroiled in a vicious bush war. Independence came in 1964; and the first Prime Minister of independent Kenya was Jomo Kenyatta.

The Mau Mau Emergency in Kenya was just one of many such emergencies – 'brush-fire wars', they have been aptly styled – faced by Britain over the quarter-century that followed the Second World War, as she tried to prepare her colonies for a viable independence. Most of these emergencies were 'East of Suez'; either in sticky corners of the world such as Palestine and Cyprus, where British troops found themselves caught between opposing factions who would kill them to get at each other, or in spots such as the Suez Canal Zone and Aden, where their hearts did not warm to the job of sacrificing themselves to maintain a presence among people with whom they felt precious few ties. Or they were fighting insurgents such as the communist Chinese in Malaya, or guerrillas like the Mau Mau in Kenya, at whose hands the majority of the local native people were also suffering.

Many of the Commonwealth's Second World War veterans helped the old lion to deliver these final defensive paw-strokes. John Ebanks, the Mosquito navigator from Jamaica who had been awarded the DFM for his fifty operations over Germany, postponed his law studies to serve for three years in Malaya. Sergeant John Mumo fought the Mau Mau in his native Kenya, and thought them 'very poorly armed, with mostly traditional weapons of arrows, spears and home-made guns'. The South African, Robert Gaunt, having taken out a British passport to enable him to continue serving in the Royal Navy, led three lines of landing craft into Suez in HMS *Diamond* during the ill-conceived Anglo-French invasion of 1956 (Gaunt was also to see the sharp and extremely secret end of the Cold War while working in Naval Intelligence.) The Seychelles Islander, Paul Gobine, has a highly exciting story of escaping from a hostile group of Arabs in the Canal Zone, after a faulty pistol had let him down – 'No effective fire! When I brought the revolver to test at the ammunition expert, there is one hundredth of an inch preventing that firing pin from firing.'

Etienne Marot of the Royal Pioneer Corps of Mauritius served in Palestine during the Arab–Jewish partition of 1946–7, and in the Canal Zone of Egypt in the early 1950s. He went to Germany for three years, then back to England where he supervised the clearing of unexploded ordnance on Ministry of Defence ranges. In 1964 he was posted to Aden, a British Crown Colony on a hot, dry peninsula at the southernmost tip of Saudi Arabia where the Egyptian leader Colonel Nasser had been fomenting and encouraging the Yemenis to revolt against their 'colonial oppressors'. It was a vicious, hole-in-corner war that lasted three years, a war of grenade attacks, sniper shots, terrorist bombs and secret murders, during which the Army lost ninety men killed and over 500 wounded. British civilians, including the families of the servicemen, were seen as fair game. In 1964, when the trouble started, there were thirty-six terrorist incidents, mostly perpetrated by the NLF or National Liberation Front. During 1967, the last year of British occupation, there were almost 3000. On 29 November 1967 the last soldier withdrew, Southern Yemen became independent on the stroke of midnight, and the final paw-print of the lion was erased from the Middle Eastern dust. Etienne Marot's account of what it was like in Aden stands as an epitaph for all those brush-fire wars.

I stayed two years in Aden. That was horrible. It was – pardon the military language – the arsehole of the world, the worst posting I ever had. Ah! horrible, horrible. And so hot!

You did not know your enemy. But at least we had only one enemy. The Adenee is a mixture of blood from the ports: he is a true bastard. What is worst in the world has been deposited in that harbour.

I had four children, and you never knew from one day to another what would happen. My son, Christopher, came out of the officers' beach one day carrying a little parcel wrapped up in a waterproof wrapping. He brought it to me and said, 'Dad, look what I've found in the sea.' There was a bomb disposal officer there. He said 'God!' He grabbed it and ran; then he threw it, and it exploded on impact.

Our laundry was done by a sort of dhobi there; he would bring the laundry on the verandah, and my wife would stand about twenty yards from him and make him peel it one by one. Because if you took that basket inside, there might be a bomb in it.

I was at a dinner party – I was Mess President at the time, and we were invited by the RAF to their mess. Three of us went. Dinner took place on a huge patio outside the mess, because it was so hot. The tables were arranged in a U-shape. We were all in white mess kit.

We had soup. While the plates were being cleared an object landed on our table and ran down from right to left. It passed me and I recognised a grenade. I wasn't the only one. We threw ourselves and our chairs backwards on to the ground, flat on our backs. Within seconds it went – *baaa-oou*! Blew the table in half. One poor woman at our table, a nursing sister, unfortunately stood up and turned round before throwing herself down, and she got the shrapnels in her back. One of the officers I had detached to come with me got a shrapnel right through his mess kit, which blew up his elbow. Only that lady was badly hurt, but the amount of blood was fantastic. One officer got it through his ear and his white mess kit was just a lump of red.

I was very, very proud that night to be British. The Royal Air Force band stopped perhaps a minute ... perhaps I'm exaggerating ... forty-five seconds. Then they carried on. On the menu that night was Steak Rossini. It was served – an hour late, but it was served.

In the 1950s Britain – desperate to rebuild her war-shattered and debt-ridden economy – advertised in her colonies and former dependencies for workers to come over and settle. Tens of thousands of West Indians arrived from the Caribbean and shivered their way as best they could into the British way of life. Most thought they were already familiar with it. Ex-servicemen and women who had served in Britain during the war found it not too difficult to adjust, but Connie Macdonald – soon to be Connie Mark – had completed all her ten-year service in Jamaica. When she came to England in 1953 the well-brought-up, middle-class Methodist girl found the naked racial prejudice of the Londoners a real shock. Characteristically, her defence took the form of attack, as she confronted the 'just-rented-it-dear' landladies and 'so-sorry-but' employers with a good swingeing damn-your-eyes spirit:

Oh, there was a lot of prejudice. The only reason I got a job as a medical secretary was because I was bloody determined that I wasn't going to clean anybody's floors. I used to go for jobs and they would say, 'Oh, Madam, we're not quite sure how well you're educated.' And I'd say, 'Look, I'm British. I've had the same education as you've had.'

I'd go to an agency and the woman on the phone would say, 'I'm just waiting ... no, I'm sorry, I've got to hang up.' So I'd say, 'Just a minute, Madam – just tell them I'm coloured and ask them if they will work with me. Don't bother to go to the other office so you can ask them if they'd mind accepting a coloured person – just do it here in front of me.' Sometimes I'd get mad – I'm only human – or sometimes I'd take it. Depend if they caught me on me off-day or not.

The only people who would rent us rooms is our own black people. And they are the worst people to rent rooms from. They used to buy these big houses; one room's rent would pay for the house and all the rest were their profit. Whereas a white person would get a whole flat for £1.5s. we used to have to pay £3 or £4 for one room. So we were our own worst enemies.

Of course, in those days you didn't have the Commission for Racial Equality. So you would see: 'Room for Rent – No Irish, No Coloureds, No Children, No Dogs.' I remember I had a white friend I worked with, and I told her. She said, 'Oh no, Connie, people wouldn't do that.' I said, 'OK, you come and I'll show you.' We saw this room for rent. I went and knocked on the door and I said – as courteous as I can be courteous – I said, 'I see you have on the board a room for rent.' – 'Oh, my dear, I just rented it, but I've not had time to go to take the card out of the door.'

Now round the corner – this was in West Kensington – round the corner was my white friend. So she went and asked for the room, and the woman said to her, 'Oh, do please come in. Let me show you, to see if you like it.' So I come round the corner, man, and when she's coming out the house – strategic, it was like a film – before the door even closed I went up and I said to the woman: 'How is it, *Madam*, that you just told me the room was rented, and now you show it to my friend?' I said, 'I don't want the room. I just had to prove to my friend here how awful you white people are to us coloured people.' What could she say? She couldn't say anything.

Radical change rumbled and stirred throughout the British Commonwealth, even in the traditionally conservative and traditionalist white Dominions of Canada, Australia and New Zealand. In the 1970s Francophone and Francophile Quebec very nearly drifted free of the rest of the Federation of Canadian states. Many Australians and New Zealanders – particularly younger-generation Australians – were keen to see a loosening of constitutional ties with the Old Country. To the distress of a great number of war veterans, the establishment of an independent Republic of Australia became a topic vigorously debated across the country. The UK's 1973 entry into the European Economic Community seemed to signal not just the end of preferential trade agreements between the Dominions and Britain, but a kind of cold-shouldering personal rejection as well. The high-handed manner (as it seemed to Australians) in which the Governor General, Sir John Kerr, dismissed the Australian Prime Minister, Gough Whitlam, in 1975 and replaced him with the leader of the Opposition, didn't improve relations. And what stung most of all was the withdrawal of preferential treatment for Commonwealth passport holders – British passport holders, in effect – at Heathrow airport and other points of entry into the UK.

John Ebanks, Jamaica:

Churchill had promised us that as long as the British Empire lasted we would have free entry into England. And that wretched Labour Government came into power and they kept none of Churchill's promises. I had not renewed the English passport I took out in 1953, remembering what Churchill said and thinking it was unnecessary. When it expired, they would not renew it, the British authorities. They said, 'No, no, no, you are a Jamaican, you must get a Jamaican passport.' That annoyed me. A promise was reneged on.

Jim Tait, New Zealand:

I think my views changed once Britain joined the EEC. I can recall arriving in Heathrow from South Africa; there was our plane, and a Qantas plane came in and one from Canada. There might have been eight or nine hundred people trying to get through and there was the sign: 'Europeans straight through.' There were a lot of Aussies who'd had to join a very long queue, and there were these Germans and French saying 'Heh! Heh!' as they walked straight through. We had to stand for ages, while these French and Germans were giving us the two fingers as they went past. I wonder that some of those Aussies didn't jump that barrier to get at them, you know.

Paul Radomski, New Zealand: 'I was told to join the aliens' queue. I refused to go through it. The last time I came to England, to help her fight a war, there was no bloody aliens' queue!'

When the ex-servicemen and women of the Second World War contemplate the state of their own countries today their views tend to be sharp ones. Rod Wells thinks that a Republic of Australia would be no better than a banana republic and says he would emigrate if it happened. Bob Taunt, on the other hand, still feels betrayed by Churchill's attitude towards Australian troops: 'He reckoned we were deserting, that's my view; he wanted to keep our troops in the Middle East and prevent them going home to defend Australia. Well, that changed my mind. Before, I was very, very patriotic. Now, I think that a republic is the only way to go.' Les Rowe, survivor of El Alamein, New Guinea and Tarakan, wonders what the modern Australian identity really is. 'Nowadays the most common name in the phone book is not Smith or Jones, but a Vietnamese name – Nguyen – there's pages and pages of it. I can remember the hoo-hah that went on in the 1930s when the first Italian fruiterer opened a shop in Hampton. Oh, shocking! So if you scratch the surface of a modern Australian deep enough, you may find a Digger down there somewhere – but nowadays he'd be made up of many different sorts of people.'

White South African ex-servicemen like Gordon Fry of the Capetown Highlanders do not enjoy being blamed for the evils of apartheid; it was not the thinking soldier, Fry says, who voted the Afrikaner-dominated ultra-nationalist government into power after the war. But he is cautiously optimistic about the future of his country. Bob Gaunt, the Royal Navy torpedo-boat officer, now lives in England, but has kept close associations with South Africa and has made numerous visits back to his homeland. He thinks that casual visitors to the post-apartheid South Africa do not see the half of it.

The Western Province is where all the tourists go. So most outsiders' view of South Africa is really a view of the Cape, which is a very favoured province in many ways. In the other provinces things are very different. Because of 'affirmative action', blacks with little training are being appointed to experienced whites' jobs. Some feel they have 'arrived' – expensive hotels, private cars – while in towns like East London buses no longer run and there are taxi wars with shoot-outs in the main street. Big investors are beginning to think about pulling out; a recent World Bank survey showed South Africa as having the second-lowest productivity in the world, with one of the highest crime rates.

Going back to South Africa, I've been amazed to see in what luxury the whites live. In all my travels I've never seen such high standards of living. They have everything – but there's not an awful lot of cohesion, of working together. The blacks are not being helped by the experienced whites taking their 'packages' – that's a pay-off, with a really good pension and health care for life – and moving out into beautiful houses in white townships, shopping malls with everything. It's almost a laager mentality. Outside most of the main cities and towns there are these 'cluster homes' with enormous electric fences and high walls all round, being patrolled by private security. Thirty or forty homes in the compound, beautiful gardens, beautiful views. Panic buttons in the rooms; video cameras...

What the white ex-servicemen are saying is: Is this freedom? Is this what we fought a war for?

The Coloured community of South Africa feels squeezed once more, according to Charles Adams. But now it is blacks rather than whites who get the preferential treatment, while the country, Adams feels, is suffering: 'There's certain things in South Africa that's not right. Look at the amount of idleness, the murderers and rapists. And the amount of unemployment, particularly among Coloureds. If there's a vacancy for a job, they give it to a black first, before they give it to a Coloured or a white. Blacks bind together, but the Coloured community tends not to.' Like all the ex-servicemen, Adams has a warm regard for South Africa's President, Nelson Mandela, but thinks his white predecessor, F. W. de Klerk, should also be given credit as an architect of peace. 'I think Mandela made a lot of changes – but don't put de Klerk on one side. De Klerk was to South Africa what Gorbachev was to Russia, chopping down that Berlin Wall. De Klerk, when he became President, he said, "Do away with apartheid," just like that. So all the praise can't go just to Mandela.'

Frank Sexwale's view of ex-President de Klerk is more acerbic: 'He was forced to act as he did. He didn't do it of his own free will. He had to do it, like it or not.' But the ex-NMC man, after all the dust has settled, takes a balanced view:

White men – well, we take them as friends. We take them as brothers. It was never a question of 'the white man' – it was a question of a devilish government composed of white men. After all, many whites were opposed to what the government was doing. So our people have no hatred for the white man in general. It was not to do with hating the white man. All along, you have to identify the man that does wrong – and here, he just happened to be white.

For Bob Gaunt, the future of South Africa lies in reconciliation and racial co-operation, in combating the crime, unemployment and homelessness. No South African, he thinks, can afford to stand back from the struggle for that ultimate prize:

One has to say that what most of the whites of my generation say is: 'Yes, reconciliation. Fine. What's that mean? Black children in our schools? – Great. But we'll go on leading our own lives.' Happily, the younger generation don't share this view. I think it's going to be a very, very painful experience; but I think the blacks will realise that they can't do without the whites, and the whites will realise they can't do without the blacks.

Recently I went back to my old school, Selborne College in East London, and saw black boys and white boys rowing together and playing rugby together, playing in the orchestra, being prefects. I thought, 'This is great!' – that was my first reaction. Admittedly these were the sons of wealthy people; but they're growing up *together*, they're learning *together*, they're being young *together*. In the long run this will lead to nothing but good. It's a big, big hope. It's going to take time – but it will happen.

The small island states of the Commonwealth mostly claimed their independence during the 1960s and 1970s. The Seychelles became independent in 1976. Paul Gobine sees the role of the ex-servicemen as crucial in building the new country: 'We veterans brought the first wind of change in the Seychelles. At the time when we joined the Army it still was a very poor country. A man was lucky to get a job – he was earning about 5 rupees a month. Now many ministers, they are ex-servicemen. But now they have a pride, because their parents were illiterate and they are not. And some don't bother with the ex-servicemen any more.'

As for the ex-colonial countries of Africa – it is hard not to read a tale of woe in their fortunes since the heady independence days of the 1950s and 1960s. Ghana became independent in 1957, Nigeria in 1960, Sierra Leone and Tanganyika in 1961, Uganda in 1962. In 1963 it was Kenya's turn, along with the island of Zanzibar (which joined up with Tanganyika to become Tanzania). In 1964 Zambia (Western Rhodesia) and Malawi (Northern Rhodesia); in 1965 The Gambia – and, unilaterally, Southern Rhodesia; in 1966 Botswana (Bechuanaland) and Lesotho (Basutoland). Swaziland in 1968 completed the tally of African colonies which left the shelter of the mother country and immediately applied to forge a new relationship through free and voluntary membership of the Commonwealth. The litany of decline from a model of parliamentary democracy to virtual or actual dictatorships and one-party states; the grandiose schemes for super-highways, stadia, Pan-African Conference centres and other prestigious, money-gobbling projects while millions went hungry and infrastructures decayed; the growth of corruption, on a grand scale, once the reasonably impartial checks and balances of colonial rule had been removed – these form a continuous, depressing theme in the conversations of both the black and the white ex-servicemen and women of these countries.

Etienne Marot of Mauritius deplores the aftermath of colonial rule: 'Now all the colonies, large and small, are wanting more independence. But one looks around and one wonders – independence from what? Certainly not from poverty. They have gone down the drain, both in efficiency and in wealth. In the days of the colonial system, nobody died of hunger. Now – this is my view – they've all gone back to the Third World. Very much so. Hunger and lack of wealth is for all to see.'

Frank O'Donnell, now a lawyer in Toronto, addresses the question of why the British were successful at drawing together such a diverse collection of nations:

Britain had a reputation for being fair. The British could be counted upon, in the last analysis, to do the right thing. They were dependable and basically on the right side.

When the British first emigrated to the colonies they took their social mores with them. They knew what the law was from their forebears. The English had always had to deal with one another in their crowded island. And they brought that idea of social interaction with them to their colonies. A way of life. It was modified, because we have different ways of showing politeness, getting on with people, showing approval or disapproval. But the basis of it was still there. There was a civilisation that touched all of us.

By contrast, Dudley Thompson – Rhodes Scholar, High Commissioner in Nigeria, Queen's Counsel, Ex-Minister of State and Leader of Government Business in the Jamaican Senate, and ex-bomb-aimer in an RAF Lancaster – has no time at all for the colonial system:

> I would never say that people in Jamaica were better off under colonial rule. No, never, never – I think the colonial system is a bad system, a very bad system. The colonial system is just half a stage from slavery. It sounds strong, but it is true. We know what slavery is, what it stood for. To me, slavery was not so much abolished as transformed when it became colonialism. As a colonial, you had certain horizons and certain levels. Even in schools, the horizons for the children were lower – you could not pass above a certain stage. You still had a master-and-servant relationship. It put shackles on us. To harness the human mind is a wicked thing, it's an evil thing. So I have no respect at all, no admiration for colonialism.

Juanita Carberry, the Kenyan ex-FANY, who spent the best part of two decades at sea after the war in the Merchant Navy – 'You're shut up in a big iron box with some of the biggest bastards under the sun, and some of the finest people in the world' – lives in London nowadays. But her heart, first and always, is back in Kenya. To her, the colonial way was the only way: 'England was never home to me. This was – still is – a foreign country. Kenya is home. I was a colonial! I had trouble once with a British captain that I sailed with when I was in the Merchant Navy. He said, "I hate bloody foreigners." And I said, "Well, that should be OK, because in fact I am a British subject." So he said, "You're a bloody colonial." I said: "Yes, Sir – and I'm *bloody proud of it*!" '

When they come to hold up the mirror to Britain, the Commonwealth war veterans frame a rather blotched and foxed old dame. How they feel about her – once again – is how one feels about a parent whose feet of clay have suddenly become all too obvious. Exasperation, affection, disillusion, a sometimes grudging respect – but never indifference. Relationships with Britain still matter to this generation.

Pierre Austin, Australia:

> The thing that still impacts upon me, living in England as I do, is this concept

of class. It's there in Australia too, but far less marked. Over there, class is mobile, as it were.

I think Britain's slowly coming to grips with the notion that they're no longer a world power: not a great power. They're a respectable, middle-sized power that must make up its mind – is it in or out of Europe? I don't think they've a lot of choice and the sooner they get to grips with it the better.

By the way, you know how we tell in Australia if an aircraft's arrived from England, don't you? We can still hear the whining after the engines are switched off ... And that's the statement of a well-balanced Australian – a chip on both shoulders!

John Mumo, Kenya: 'Nothing changes in the way we feel about the British. We feel indebted to them, because they gave Kenya so much – in education, especially. And an idea of one God, which was important, as people beforehand had so many things that they worshipped as gods. The British streamlined that.'

Les Rowe, Australia: 'What I feel sometimes about the British, as our fathers used to say about the First World War, is that they used Australians as chopping blocks, for the real hard fighting. After the war, Churchill didn't come out to Australia to thank us, as Monty did. I don't think Churchill thought more of the Australians than we thought of him; and that goes for the British too. There's a quid pro quo there.'

Keith Levy, Jamaica: 'For the pre-war generation – and especially for the veterans who saw, as they think, England and the English exhibiting their best and most characteristic traits – the break has not yet been made. There's still a loyalty that you'll find here, and I think that's among the older folks. But how much account do the British take of that?'

Nila Kantan, India:

Do you think that India would have gained independence if there was no Second World War? I doubt it very much. The British realised that their imperial days were over and they have to give in. I think the war was a levelling-out. It changed the British character quite a lot. They were less snobbish afterwards.

I think – my own personal conclusion – that the British are, on the whole, very reasonable, very broad-minded. Whatever it is, I believe that Britain still has some respect for India, and so does India for Britain.

Kofi Genfi, Ghana: 'Only very recently the British came down from their pride. In 1964, when I went to Britain, on the bus an African would sit completely alone on the bench. No one would sit near you. But now, when I go to Britain, I see that British have married Africans and everything is mixed up.'

Edwin George, Tobago: 'We still look for leadership from Britain, even though we are independent. We're still members of the British Commonwealth and we're looking for them to set us an example. We're looking for Britain to be the Father of Nations – of the world. But now we're starting to think that you're weak. And that's wrong, you know?'

There are equally strong views on that paramount symbol of British tradition and British heritage, the Monarchy. For some, like the republican-minded Australian Bob Taunt, the whole idea of the Monarchy is 'a great stupidity, a load of baloney, bloody juvenile. I wouldn't go over the road to see them.'

Jim Tait, the quiet New Zealander, takes a measured and pragmatic view: 'I'm a monarchist at heart, in spite of being of Scottish descent. I like the idea of something just above presidential people or elected people. I recall talking to an American colonel towards the end of the war, round about the time that President Roosevelt died. They had to have compulsory church parades and were praying for Roosevelt. Obviously this man was a Republican, and he told me: "Every time we prayed I spat on the ground. No way was I going to pray for that bastard." That stuck in my mind.'

For others, their attachment to the British sovereign is a highly emotional affair. 'To me,' says the Seychellois, Paul Gobine, 'the Queen is a great things, you know? I like the Monarchy and I'll always return heartfelt thanks to the Royalty of England. Deep in my heart, the Queen of England will always be my Queen. Although the Seychelles is a republic now – you went to 90 per cent of the houses, you won't see a picture of the President. You'll see the pictures of Queen Victoria, King George V, King George VI and Queen Lillibet!' Geraldine Muter (née Turcotte), the Canadian of Northern Irish Protestant extraction, says with a laugh: 'If the Queen ever goes, you know who'll move in, don't you? The Pope! And then we'll all be finished!'

And Aziz Brimah, now himself Deputy Chief of Muslims, Yorubas and Nigerians in the Ghanaian capital, Accra, tells wavering Britons to stiffen their backbones and maintain their traditions:

I must be frank – I'm very proud of the British. We were brought up by the British, we were taught by the British. Recently I wrote to the Prime Minister, to the British Parliament, to the British Press and to the BBC. I said: 'Some of us who were brought up by the British, who feel British – we don't like what we're hearing about what's happening in Britain. Just because the Royal Family is having some problems now, some people would like to cancel the Monarchy.' I said: 'British is an ancient nation. And they stick to their principles. Most of these nations who have changed from Monarchy – I don't think British should follow that. The British people are one race, recognised all over the world. They have a history, they have a tradition. Every year people come to Britain to see this Monarchy, this tradition. Don't ever change your tradition!'

Views on the British Commonwealth itself also swing right across the spectrum. Some think it is finished as an institution, no longer capable of surviving because of new world economic groupings. With Britain looking, however reluctantly, towards Europe; Canada and the West Indies towards the United States; Australia and New Zealand towards the Pacific Rim – what can the Commonwealth possibly offer its members? Some think it is doomed by history; it took a world war to coalesce its people, but the present younger generation knows little and cares less about other member countries. 'Yet,' says Keith Levy of Jamaica, 'I've never seen such an outpouring from British people as I saw during those VJ Day celebrations in London in August 1995. Never before had the Commonwealth's role in the war been properly recognised; but it certainly was then.'

Some, by contrast, see it as a model for the future of the global village. Frank O'Donnell is an enthusiast for the values which he sees encapsulated in the Commonwealth: 'Consideration, fairness, dependability – these values can endure in places where at the moment they're not even recognised, such as the United Nations. The Americans seem to be trying to influence world events in much the same way as the British did in the nineteenth century, but they're too high-handed. In its better aspects – let's put it that way – I think the Commonwealth could be a great model. It's a Commonwealth of emigrants; it's probably the best hope for mankind, the kind of community that those emigrants engendered.'

There is no cup sweeter than the one you cannot drink from; and that was true for South Africa during her thirty-three-year exclusion from the Commonwealth. Ejected in 1961, she was not readmitted until 1994. The South African government may have said they did not care. But the exclusion deeply hurt many ordinary men and women – including some who had served, at least partly from idealistic motives, during the war. What the Commonwealth really means to those who support it can be gauged by what it meant when they had to gaze in from outside, like the Cape Coloured ex-soldier Charles Adams: 'Not being part of the

Commonwealth is like sitting at home and you don't join the club. With the Commonwealth you've got your British support. If anything happened in this country the Commonwealth would step in. The Australians and New Zealanders might feel that Britain can't be relied on any more, but they haven't yet gone through the mill that we've been through. I was one of the saddest men when we stepped out of the Commonwealth and one of the happiest men alive when we came back in.'

Bob Gaunt, talking to white South Africans on his return to his native land, found that the Commonwealth meant nothing to young people. 'But what surprised me was that people of my generation said they felt that the Commonwealth hasn't meant a thing since the war – not a thing, what with United Nations, Nato, lateral and bilateral trade agreements and so on. I'd expected, talking to old soldiers, that they'd say, "Oh yeah, the Commonwealth – great institution, great future." But they didn't. They said: "No, no; it doesn't mean anything."'

Over half a century has gone by since the men and women of the Commonwealth went off to serve in the Second World War. The courses of their lives have diverged one from another since the days when they all came under the same discipline, ate the same rations, grumbled over the same war service pay scales, shared the same extraordinary experiences and dangers, boredoms and jokes, fears and hopes. Some can now look back on lives that went well, on comradeships nurtured, families successfully raised, career ladders safely climbed. Others found life a struggle. There were unhappy marriages, periods of drifting between unsatisfactory jobs, drinking problems. Not all these could be attributed solely to the effect of wartime experiences. But many of the veterans found they needed help; either practical financial help, or medical help, or just an understanding ear to bend. Once more, the extent and quality of the help available depended largely on the country in which they happened to live.

Many could not rely on their own governmental organisations; after independence, the political paths that some countries took meant that basic health and welfare services were lacking. As each colonial country became independent in the post-war years the British government offered either to continue paying the pensions of veterans, or to hand over a lump sum to fund their future payment. Some newly formed governments opted for the cash. But not all honoured their agreements. Some spent the money. Others received it in the form of capital assets such as equipment, land or buildings, which were not – as was intended – realised, and the proceeds invested, for the benefit of veterans and their dependants.

War veterans felt they needed specialist help and support; and who more specialised, or better qualified to help, than they themselves? Already most Commonwealth countries possessed ex-services associations, set up after veterans returning home from the First World War faced a range of problems for which insufficient official help was available. In the 1940s these charitable institutions, most of them run voluntarily, some receiving support of varying quality from political or military sources, were swollen by an influx of returning servicemen and women. Some simply wanted a place to get together, to drink and socialise with fellow veterans. Others needed financial assistance, advice on their disability rights, help with finding and paying for medical or domestic equipment. Some of these felt strongly that they had been let down in terms of pension and gratuity. There was anecdotal evidence of injudicious statements by officers to soldiers while serving overseas – broad, general statements about the post-war conditions the men might hope for, which were taken as hard-and-fast assurances of specific financial help that could be counted on after the war. As an example, the Kenyan Armed Forces Old Comrades Association headquarters in Nairobi still sees askaris in their seventies and eighties turning up to find out when their 'promised money' is going to be paid over.

The Anglo-Indian ex-servicemen and women have tended to struggle, too – the Ex-Services Association of India, with offices in Bangalore, Bombay, Deccan and Madras, is the last bastion between some of its members and complete destitution. One man, living with his wife in his son's already crowded house, has to write a letter to the ESA each time he needs to pay for his medicines. Others receive their clothes as charitable hand-me-downs. There are no state pensions for those who served in wartime. In the Seychelles, Paul Gobine – now the Chairman of the Seychelles Ex-Servicemen's Association – is dedicated to getting redress for poorly supported veterans. 'Even the present Seychelles government,' he laments, 'they don't care about the soldier of the King. They don't bother about that. I have been on radio and television, even insulted the President. I don't give a damn, at my age; they can do what they want to me. My purpose in life now is to get them some recognition and help. I'll do it until the last drop of breath in my body. If there were not these people who gave their lives for King and Country, the politicians would not be there! There should be legislation compelling these people to recognise the ex-servicemen. They have been forgotten – completely forgotten, in their own country.'

In general, the associations in the old 'White Dominion' countries have proved highly effective as providers of practical and emotional support and as points of contact for the now ageing and sometimes lonely veterans. In some of the smaller Commonwealth countries, with only a diminishing handful of Second World War veterans, or in countries with dire social, financial and administrative difficulties, the welfare of the ex-servicemen and women is entirely in the hands of a very small number of very conscientious volunteers, many of ex-services background themselves. In some – like Ghana – the veterans have proved an influential group when sufficiently determined to band together and insist on their voice being heard. 'We formed the Veterans Association of Ghana,' says Victor Nunoo, 'and we started channelling our complaints. Now all wartime veterans get a pension from the Government – it is not enough, but it is something you can live on. If a veteran dies, the Association gives you a coffin and takes care of the burial expenses; and we have our own cemetery, free of charge. And the Association provides veterans with transport. I think the injustices are being put right, gradually.'

In Jamaica, says Keith Levy – Hon. Life Vice-President of the Jamaica Branch of the Royal Air Force Association – the Legion and RAFA work closely together, sharing a headquarters at Curphey Place in Kingston. They deal with literally thousands of letters a year asking for help – everything from a pair of new spectacles to medicine, clothing and house repairs. The administration and funding of the veterans' sheltered accommodation, Curphey Home, is just one of the calls on their energy – a commodity, Levy admits, that is diminishing as age creeps on every year. Another problem, right across the Commonwealth, is that ex-servicemen and women hate to ask for help; it hurts their pride.

A lot of mutual help and support is organised through the British Commonwealth Ex-Services League, founded by Earl Haig in 1921 and run from a modest London office by a tiny and dedicated staff. What they do not know about their fifty-four member organisations, in forty-eight countries around the world, is probably known only to the Lord. When local associations come up against requests or problems beyond their capacity to deal with, BCEL steps in with prompt help. In 1996, BCEL held its seventy-fifth anniversary conference in Capetown, South Africa. In the City Hall delegates heard the President of South Africa, Nelson Mandela, speak of the demons of racism and prejudice that had blinded the white governments of South Africa, of the spurning of the blacks' offer to fight Nazism as combatants, and of his pleasure at the South African Legion's recent acceptance of the black freedom fighters' organisation, UmKhonto We Sizwe – in which Mandela himself had been active – as a member; a development he saw as a step on the road to reconciliation. The BCEL men and women, of every shade of skin colour and political opinion, grinned and applauded in delight at the sight of the great man dancing and singing along with a Soweto schoolchildren's choir. Later, in a bus driving back to their hotel from a reception hosted by the Capetown Highlanders and Capetown Rifles, the delegates sang lustily and none too soberly. Men and women from Ghana, Jamaica, India, Australia, Canada, the Seychelles, The Gambia and Britain – all of them over seventy, arms around each other's shoulders, many with tears on their cheeks – roared the wartime songs into the soft Capetown night: 'Roll Out the Barrel', 'Bless 'Em All', 'I Belong to Glasgow', 'Maybe it's Because I'm a Londoner'.

Half a century has passed since they took off the khaki, or the light or dark blue, and walked out along the familiar yet alien ways of Civvy Street. For some, though, the war still lurks in the side alleys of their lives, sneaking out every now and then to surprise them. It may be a physical ambush. The Australian, Rod Wells, had a heart seizure out of the blue a few years ago: a sharp piece of bone, cracked over forty years before by two Japanese soldiers playing see-saw on his chest with a wooden plank, had calcified and was rubbing the left ventricle of his heart. Several operations and a lot of trouble followed. In Canada, George Barron also suffered long-term physical health damage as a result of his neglect by the Japanese in Shampshui Po POW camp: 'I had TB on both lungs. I still have a cavity on one lung, which could break at any time and drown me in my own blood. I've had fifteen operations since I came home. I've got two broken hips, a broken elbow – it's because of malnutrition, which weakened my system. My eyes have been bad too – but there's a whole bunch of guys who were in the camp who've got the same problems. The experience of war I had is on the shelf now; it's behind me. But the problems the war caused me, I've got. They're right here.'

More commonly, though, the veterans find themselves waylaid by phobias, anxieties, flashbacks and dreams. Jack Brown, as he recovered at home from being bombed by the RAF while in POW camp in Germany, gradually edged his way back into the stream of ordinary life again. Yet, fifty years on, Brown still cannot face flying and flinches if an aeroplane passes over his house. He has got used to waking up and finding himself under the bed if there has been a loud noise outside in the street. The Kenyan soldier, John Mumo, says that 'if he is surprised by a loud sound, like a tyre bursting, it triggers a memory immediately of being attacked by Stukas or by gunfire'. For Alec Dennis (now resident in Canada) the sound of men shouting in the water brings back the memory of a mined ship sinking off Harwich one cold October night in 1939. Paul Gobine of the Seychelles says: 'Some sad memories stay with me – oh, God! They bother me at times, even at home. My wife, sometimes she says, "Oh? You don't go to sleep?" I say, "It's OK. Later on, darling, I'll sleep." It comes then, you know? I feel it, you see. And you more feel it when you think of all those sacrifices you've done – you are forgotten heroes. When you have a duty to do, then you do it. But, recognise it or not, what you have done, God is there and sees.'

The Sikh airman, Mahinder Singh Pujji, in expressing his shame and regret at killing so many Japanese soldiers in Burma in 1945, would not find many ex-POWs to share his view. Surprisingly few ex-prisoners of the Japanese have allowed their experiences to consume them psychologically. But the continuing refusal of the Japanese government to make a formal apology and an offer of reparation on behalf of the whole Japanese nation has prolonged the distress and the gnawing anger of the ex-prisoners. Many veterans who fought the Japanese but were not taken prisoner share these ineradicable feelings of dislike and unease when faced with Japanese of their own generation. Phil Rhoden, now retired as a solicitor in Melbourne, remembers having to be restrained by his wife from barging one group off the pavement, and recounts his satisfaction at neatly landing a ball among a party of Japanese golfers standing on one of the greens at his golf club. And Pierre Austin recalls: 'I was taking an aeroplane flight quite recently. I got on and sat next to the window, and then two Japanese came and sat next to me. I had to get out of that seat. They were quite nice chaps, no doubt; but I had to get out.'

These are feelings, sufferings and memories that plenty of ex-servicemen and women have been unable to share with either friends or families. The veteran who dies, never having spoken about the war, is not a rare phenomenon. For many it is still only with their old comrades-in-arms, the people who were there, that they can truly relax and open up. Most of Jack Brown's ex-POW camp-mates have settled near each other and form a mutually supportive group in Auckland. 'We keep a good eye on each other,' he says. 'We're very much family – oh, yes. We're a comfort to each other. We've all had our bits of problems, but we've been very lucky to have wives who've put up with our ups and downs. I don't know, sometimes, how they do.' And Charlie Hobbs, the Canadian rear-gunner who spent two years in German POW camps, describes how he 'felt a great need to be with other POWs after the war. We didn't talk about our problems to anybody else – not problems, maybe, but ... situations. Cam and I are still in touch, fifty years later. Others wouldn't understand. We've had this happen time and time again, where people just don't understand, when you're talking to them. Their favourite question is, "What was it like?" How the hell do you answer that?'

Joe Oldford, Canada:

I'll put it this way. Every year we have a reunion of the Cape Breton Highlanders. We can sit down there and talk comfortably, because each of us knows where the other feller was and what he did, you know? Whereas if I were to go and have a beer in the Legion and I find a feller shooting off his mouth about what he did – you sort of move on and don't pay any attention, because the guy's talking nonsense; he's talking to be heard. If a man was there – why does he have to talk to anybody about it, just to get everyone listening to him?

Nila Kantan, India:

I don't talk about this sort of thing to anybody, because in India nobody is interested in World War Two. Only people who were there can appreciate, can understand what I talk about. But I come across very few – you would be surprised. In England you have the 8th Army Association, 14th Army Association, RASC Association, Africa Star Association. Here there is nothing like that.

When I came to England for the VJ celebrations in 1995 – on the Veterans' Day there were so many associations I could have joined! I was in all of those places. I have eight or nine medals from World War Two. I could have joined the Burma Star Association, Africa Star Association, Italy Star Association. The Cassino and Alamein Associations I could have joined; Tobruk, the Desert Rats; Greece I could have joined. But we have no such thing in India. Nobody bothers.

The reluctance of so many of the veterans to talk has left a whole generation more or less ignorant about what their parents did in the war and about what the war did to their parents. Phil Rhoden says it is his grandchildren, rather than his children, who cannot get enough of his experiences among the Pacific islands. 'I get fed up', says Connie Mark, 'with people telling me they didn't know there were black women in the British armed forces. It's just ignorance.'

Jamaican youths like to try out their streetwise politics on the ex-RAF veterans. From Flight-Lieutenant John Ebanks DFM they generally get a dusty answer: 'Some younger people jibe you now – "Oh, you went to fight for King and Country? You weren't fighting for Jamaica, it wasn't Jamaica's war." I say, "Don't be damn stupid. If we hadn't fought and won the war you'd all still be planting yams up in the hills." '

Nor does Keith Levy suffer young fools gladly:

Yesterday I was playing *Songs that Won the War* – Vera Lynn and 'There'll Always Be an England' – and I was singing it: 'There'll always be an England, and England shall be free ...' A couple of the youngsters said, 'Oh, here he goes, here he goes!' But you see – to them it doesn't matter.

Among the younger generation there would be a certain type who, when you say 'It's Battle of Britain Week – what are you going to give me?' would tell you: 'Man, I'm not giving you nothing. You went away to fight the white man's war.' But I find the answer easy: 'White man's war? You'd be speaking German today if we had not won!'

In the streets of Accra, according to Victor Nunoo, modern Ghanaian youth is rather more respectful. 'Up to this moment, when we are in town on parade in our uniforms, younger people come to see us. They know that we fought well, that we won the war. But they also know what we did to gain independence for Ghana. They say, "These are our fathers. These are our heroes. These are the people who brought us self-government." '

The veterans may not talk freely about their war to those who were not there; but there is, among most of them, a deep pride in what they did.

Nila Kantan, India: 'When I think of it now, I enjoyed those days. By God, how we spent all those days! It was very hazardous, really, in those far-off days. But now, when I think of it, it gives a great pleasure that we underwent all those difficulties. We were young; we could easily bear them.'

Frank O'Donnell, Canada: 'I meet people who have lived all their lives by the book, who've had a conventional education – who've never experienced what I've experienced. I feel sorry for them. I think: My God, where have you been? What have you seen? What have you done?'

Carlton Best, Trinidad: 'The day that they were sitting in the Legislative

Council considering disbanding the Trinidad and Tobago Regiment, one of the Members had about twenty men walking down St Vincent Street with placards saying they don't want no soldiers in Trinidad. I stood up there and watched them – and believe me, if my mother didn't give me a good religious training, I would have been one of the biggest bandits in Trinidad at that moment. When I saw these fellows demonstrating against soldiers and I think of what we all went through – it hurt, it hurt, it *hurt*.'

Reflecting on the vast reach and scope of the Second World War's effect upon the dozens of nations that make up the Commonwealth, the New Zealander Ted Somerville's image of a breaking into pieces looks ever more apt. The Dominions and colonies that were so closely bound to Britain in 1933, when Adolf Hitler became Chancellor of Germany, have gone their separate ways, impelled outwards by the metamorphic effects of the Second World War. All that links them to the mother country now is the loosest of voluntary organisations – still widely valued (the Republic of Cameroon and the former Portuguese colony of Mozambique both joined the Commonwealth in 1995), but nebulous, unpragmatic and elastic in a way that the old Empire builders and dwellers would scarcely have credited.

From where the veterans stand now, looking back down the long tunnel of time, their wartime experience seems – paradoxically – more brightly spotlit, sharper in significance, the further into the distance it recedes. They see now what they could not see before: the war's fracturing effect upon their long, unfolding lives. Most of them, by and large, came to terms with the post-war remaking of those lives. They would have liked the appreciation and understanding of their children, and of their con-temporaries who did not go to war. They would have liked to have returned to lands fit for heroes, or to take part in creating such lands, though heroes would be the last description most of them would choose for themselves. They would have preferred the war to have been over and done with when hostilities ended. But they learned that this war was not like that – if any war ever was. The best they could do was to do the best they could, a lesson the war taught each of them.

As for war itself: none glorifies it: 'War?' says Derek Watson, the British professional soldier of thirty years' service. 'I think it's terrible. Wanton destruction. A waste of bloody time.' Mutili Musoma, the Kenyan hos-tilities-only signaller, agrees: 'I give my children stories about the war. I tell them that war, it is not a good thing, actually. War is a very bad thing.

I have two sons with the Kenyan Army. And they are enjoying their chance. But I say to them: "War – this thing – if it comes, you will cry." '

Joe Oldford, the modest Company Sergeant-Major in Canada's Cape Breton Highlanders, brings it down to fundamentals:

You go back to a place you fought – say, five years after the war is over. The houses are all restored, the buildings are all restored, the roads are all rebuilt, the trees are all pruned and fixed and back growing, producing. But when you walk into the cemetery and see the stones there – then you realise that that's final. There's no way that those boys can be restored. That – is – final. Everything else can be brought back, but not those boys.

That is the futility of war.

Thomas Hunter of the Royal Regiment of Canada, sufferer and survivor of the Dieppe Raid of August 1942 and of three subsequent years in prisoner-of-war camp, speaks for hundreds of thousands for whom the war still plays in the theatre of dreams.

The dreams are there, especially in June. I don't know why in June, particularly – maybe all that heavy concentration of training, that fracas of marching and firing made a lasting impression. I have a stomach ache and throwing up around then, and the dreams. They wake you up in the middle of the night, startled. Different situations come to your mind – what was I doing there? Then you realise where you are: in your own bed. You get up, have a drink or a cup of tea, go back to sleep. They don't stay.

These things happen, they're in the back of your mind: periodically they come forward. In my waking life I never worry about it. It's over. Over, gone, done – it's finished. So ... just in dreams. Only in dreams.

'I don't think it damaged me,' says Tom Somerville, the New Zealand artilleryman. 'I always had my faith in the Lord. Put my problems there, and got some peace of mind.' For the lucky few, war provided a spiritual catalyst. Krishen Tewari, a major-general on his retirement from the Indian Army in 1972, became a devotee of the guru Sri Aurobindi and moved to the Auroville spiritual community outside Pondicherry, where he and his wife still live. 'The war experience', he says, 'was preparing me for this kind of life, made me convinced of a higher force at work. You don't have to worry; something else is controlling your destiny. If you surrender truly to that destiny it takes care of you. Our Mother has written that nations also have a soul of their own which dictates to them their destiny, if that soul is truly surrendered to the divine. She says quite clearly that India's soul is crying to spread the message to the rest of the world – to surrender to that force, forget materialism, go into the spiritual dimension. And I think, gradually, it's taking shape.'

In 1968 Nila Kantan left the Indian Army with the rank of captain. He had seen service in Eritrea and in the Egyptian desert at El Alamein. He had passed through Tobruk, fought his way to Tunisia and seen the Germans' desert army surrender there. He had been with the Allied advance up the Italian peninsula, attended the siege and destruction of the monastery and town of Monte Cassino, and served at many other Italian battles. He had been shipwrecked off Greece, and finished the war in South-East Asia fighting the Japanese in Java. He had witnessed the horrific mass killings during the partition of India and Pakistan, and later had served as a paratrooper in Indo-China in the 1950s. For almost thirty years this 'very lean, thin, puny' Indian from the banks of the Godavari river had gone to endless pains to put himself wherever trouble was brewing. Now the reluctant Brahmin beat his sword into a ploughshare, a very practical and literal ploughshare.

In the war I had very great experiences. I had most perilous moments in the sea, shipwrecked there. Sometimes I used to be very afraid during the battles. I did have fear – I cannot boast I was fearless or anything. I had all these experiences. And in a way it moulded me. I have seen what perils are, what real hardships are; I have seen how humanity can suffer.

I elected to live a primitive life among the poor. As far as possible I do some manual labour in the fields. I know the labourers' conditions. A farmer accused me: 'Oh, you are always on the side of the workers.' Yes, I am! I'm not a communist, but I have learned to know their hardships.

I have no ambition. I help poor boys in the Hosur area, and now I am educating a small girl, because poor girls are absolutely neglected in India. So – I am happy. I am not really an orthodox Hindu: my conception of God is something unimaginable. The gaining of *moksha* is not particularly important to me. *Moksha* means liberation – well, I am liberated, and I am quite happy.

Jack Brown, the New Zealand shepherd, could stand as the archetype of the British Commonwealth's white Dominion volunteers. Hardy, self-reliant, dependable, unfanciful, he had enlisted in the spring of 1940 readily enough – much as his father's generation had done a quarter of a century before – after a few beers at an upcountry agricultural show. He did it for no grand ethical motives, but because his friends were doing it;

because it was an opportunity to get away and see something new; because he thought maybe he should.

Brown hardly had time to settle into active service before the war picked him up and turned him inside out. Ambling into Taihape railway station that spring evening to pick up his enlistment papers, he could scarcely have foreseen the desperation of the retreat through Greece, the pain of his wound, the far greater pain of a year on the run and in hiding, the humiliation of capture, the frustration of prisoner-of-war camp, the psychological torment of Allied air raids and enforced work burying bomb victims in mass graves in Leipzig. The Kiwi shepherd could certainly never have imagined the struggle he would have to undertake – and would eventually win – to piece himself back together again after the war. Today, looking back over all that happened to him since that evening at Taihape more than fifty years ago, Jack Brown cannot see himself taking any other decision: 'As for whether I would do the same thing again ... yeah, I probably would. I wouldn't have been able to sit at home here and watch other blokes go. It might have been pride that made me go – possibly pride. But I couldn't have sat back and seen my mates go. Even though I know now that war is bloody stupidity, I still couldn't do that.'

The last word can rest with the first African colony to gain its independence from Britain after the Second World War. Kofi Genfi of the Gold Coast Regiment makes an epitaph for the imperial past, and a memorial for those who never came back home to play their part in building the future:

On the battlefield you see a friend lying dead, but you're pushing on. You have not the time to wish for him. You take his gun and bullets, and you go. Leaving him is not a small thing. As you climb the mountain, you are crying: 'Oh ... oh ... oh ...'

It is not a small thing.

ACKNOWLEDGEMENTS

During the two years I spent researching, travelling round the Commonwealth and writing this book, I received an enormous amount of help from sources all over the world.

First and foremost I would like to thank the ex-servicemen and women who so generously gave up their time to be interviewed:

Australia: Pierre Austin, Vernon Northwood, Phil Rhoden, Keith Rossi, Les Rowe, Desmond Sheen, Bob Taunt, Rod Wells.
Basutoland/Lesotho: Ernest Khomari.
Canada: George Barron, Edward Baker, Reg Burt, Peleg Cayley, Charlie Hobbs, Thomas Hunter, Paul Luciuk, Geraldine Muter (née Turcotte), Wilmer Nadjiwon, Glen Niven, Frank O'Donnell, Joe Oldford, David Thrasher, Raymond Walker.
Gold Coast/Ghana: John Borketey, Al-Haji Abdul Aziz Brimah, Nana Kofi Genfi II, Victor Nunoo, Benjamin Okai.
India: Balwant Singh Bahia, Noel Davis, Peter d'Cunha, Ronald Dunn, Maurice Fischer, Nila Kantan, Danny Misra, Mahinder Singh Pujji, Krishen Tewari, Karl Wheeler.
Jamaica: John Blair, John Ebanks, Ronald Henriques, Lloyd Johnson, Keith Levy, Connie Mark (née Macdonald), E. K. Powell, Dudley Thompson.
Kenya: Juanita Carberry, Mbithi Muinde, John Mumo, Morris Munyao, Mutili Musoma, Nzuki Nzivo.
Mauritius: Etienne Marot.
New Zealand: Charles Bell, Jack Brown, Kevin Forde, Paul Radomski, Ted Somerville, Tom Somerville, Jim Tait.
Seychelles: Paul Gobine.
South Africa: Charles Adams, Gordon Fry, Robert Gaunt, Frank Sexwale.
Trinidad: Michael Arneaud, Carlton Best, Vincent Mieux, Thomas Scoon, Winston Seales.
Tobago: Vernon Alexander, Edwin George, Beresford Martin.
United Kingdom: Joe Blencowe, Alec Dennis, John Hamilton, Sam Meltzer, Sheila Parkinson (née Kershaw), Derek Watson.

The opinions of a high-ranking or bemedalled officer may or may not be worthy of greater attention than those of an undecorated 'other rank'. In this book I wanted each contributor's story to carry as equal weight as possible. For that reason – unless the narrative has demanded otherwise – I have avoided referring to the ranks and decorations these men and women gained during their service. Some enjoyed long and tremendously distinguished service careers; others went through the war as 'hostilities-only' volunteers, never rising above the bottom rung of the promotion ladder.

Some of the men and women I talked to were practised interviewees. Others had never talked to anyone about their war. Each person made an invaluable contribution; without their input, this book would not exist.

My sincere thanks are also due, for their help and hospitality, to Bruce Ruxton of the Returned and Services League of Australia; Pat Herbert of the New Zealand Returned Services Association; Trevor Matcher of the Ex-Services Association of India and Commodore Lionel Jesudason of the Royal Indian Navy; Marizia Wazir of the Kenyan Armed Forces Old Comrades Association, Lieutenant-Colonel Charles Cooper of the Kenyan Legion and Colonel Jeremy Cumberlege; Harry Bent of the South African Legion; Hugh Greene, Duane Daly, Carl Boughner and Marlene Lambros of the Royal Canadian Legion and David Bookbinder of Veterans' Affairs, Canada; and Colonel Dan Prah of the Veterans' Association of Ghana.

For their help in putting me in touch with veterans in the UK I wish to thank Brigadier Malcolm Page, Lieutenant-Colonel Jeffrey Williams and K. H. 'Bunny' Nash; Wing-Commander N. P. W. Hancock of the Battle of Britain Fighter Association; Cal Heywood and Jim Gale of the Canadian Veterans' Association, UK; Rene Webb, N. Hawkins and Laurie Philpotts of the West Indies Ex-Servicemen's and Women's Association; and Decia Stephenson of FANY.

Roderick Suddaby (Keeper of the Department of Documents) and Christopher Dowling (Keeper of the Department of Museum Services) at the Imperial War Museum, Andrew Davidson at the Foreign and Commonwealth Library and Neil Cobbett at the Public Record Office made many knowledgeable suggestions for reading and research.

I certainly would not have known where to start this project, nor how to complete it, without the help, advice and enormous range of contacts made available to me by the London staff of the British Commonwealth Ex-Services League – Brigadier Mike Doyle, Lieutenant-Colonel Sam Pope, Iris Pearce and Bert Moore. These people and their colleagues, modestly at work behind the scenes, do an essential job superbly well.

I am grateful, as always, to Vivien Green of Richard Scott Simon; also to Ion Trewin and Rachel Leyshon for allowing me a very loose rein; and to Penny Grigg for her speedy typing.

Lastly I would like to thank my sisters Julia and Louisa for their hospitality; my wife Jane for all her support and encouragement and for working with me on this book; and my parents, Elizabeth and John Somerville – who both served in the Royal Navy during the war – for their many suggestions, for checking over my manuscript and for helping me in every possible way.

SELECT BIBLIOGRAPHY

General Histories of the Second World War

Arnold-Forster, Mark, *The World at War* (Mandarin, 1989)

Australia in the War of 1939–1945 (Australian War Memorial, Canberra)

Barnett, Correlli, *Engage the Enemy More Closely – The Royal Navy in the Second World War* (Hodder & Stoughton, 1991)

Butler, Sir James (ed.), *The History of the Second World War* (HMSO)

Churchill, Winston S., *The Second World War* (Cassell)

Clarke, Peter B., *West Africans at War – Colonial Propaganda and its Cultural Aftermath* (Ethnographica, London, 1986)

Deighton, Len, *Blood, Tears and Folly – An Objective Look at World War Two* (Pimlico, 1995)

Elliott, William Yandell and Hall, H. Duncan (eds), *The British Commonwealth at War* (Alfred A. Knopf, New York, 1943)

Fraser, David, *And We Shall Shock Them – The British Army in the Second World War* (Hodder & Stoughton, 1983)

Haunder, Milan, *India in Axis Strategy* (Klett-Cotta, German Historical Institute, London, 1981)

Keegan, John (ed.), *The Times Atlas of the Second World War* (Times Books, 1989)

Killingray, David and Rathbone, Richard (eds), *Africa and the Second World War* (Macmillan, 1986)

Lawlor, Sheila, *Churchill and the Politics of War* (Oxford University Press, 1994)

Martin, H. J. and Orpen Purnell, N., *South Africa at War* (Capetown, 1979)

Mervis, Joel, *South Africa in World War Two* (Times Media Ltd)

The Naval Service of Canada – its Official History (The King's Printer, Ottawa)

New Zealand in the Second World War (Historical Publications Branch, Department of Internal Affairs, Wellington)

Official History of the Canadian Army in the Second World War (Ministry of National Defence, Ottawa)

Official History of the Indian Armed Forces in the Second World War (Combined Inter-Services Historical Section, India & Pakistan)

Official History of the Royal Canadian Air Force: Vol. III – The Crucible of War 1939–1945 (University of Toronto Press)

Perry, F. W., *The Commonwealth Armies* (Manchester University Press, 1988)

Terraine, John, *The Right of the Line – The RAF in the European War 1939–1945* (Hodder & Stoughton, 1985)

More Specific Titles

Atkin, Ronald, *Dieppe 1942 – The Jubilee Disaster* (Macmillan, 1980)

Barker, A. J., *Eritrea 1941* (Faber, 1966)

Colvin, John, *Not Ordinary Men – The Battle of Kohima Re-assessed* (Leo Cooper, 1995)

Dickens, Capt. Peter, *Night Action* (Purnell, 1974)

Endacott, G. B., *Hong Kong Eclipse* (Oxford University Press, 1978)

Hobbs, Charlie, *Past Tense – Charlie's Story* (General Store Publishing House, Burnstown, Ontario, 1994)

Jackson, W. G. F., *The North African Campaign 1940–43* (Batsford, 1975)

Leasor, James, *Singapore* (Hodder & Stoughton, 1968)

Lomax, Eric, *The Railway Man* (Vintage, 1996)

Middlebrook, Martin, *Arnhem 1944 – The Airborne Battle* (Penguin, 1995)

Moorehead, Alan, *The Desert War* (Hamish Hamilton, 1965)

Pond, Hugh, *Sicily* (William Kimber, 1962)

Smurthwaite, David (ed.), *The Forgotten War – The British Army in the Far East 1941–1945* (National Army Museum, 1992)

Wall, Don, *Sandakan Under Nippon: The Last March* (D. Wall, Mona Vale, New South Wales, 1988)

Selected Unit Histories

Cody, J. F., *28 (Maori) Battalion* (Wellington, 1956 – part of *Official History of New Zealand in the Second World War*)

Glenn, John G., *Tobruk to Tarakan – The Story of the 2/48th Battalion, AIF (Rigby, Adelaide, 1960)*

Gray, Brian, *Basuto Soldiers in Hitler's War* (Masem-Basutoland Government, 1953)

Masel, Philip, *The Second 28th* (2/28 Battalion & 24th Anti-Tank Company Association, Perth, 1961)

Morrison, Alex and Slaney, Ted, *The Breed of Manly Men – The History of the Cape Breton Highlanders* (Canada, 1994)

Moyse-Bartlett, Lt-Col. H., *The King's African Rifles* (Gale & Polden, Aldershot, 1956)

Russell, W. B., *The Second Fourteenth Battalion* (Angus & Robertson, Sydney, 1948)

The History of the 2/2 Australian Infantry Battalion 1939–45 (2/2 Australian Infantry Battalion Association, 1977)

Other Helpful Titles
Attwell, Michael, *South Africa – Background to the Crisis* (Sidgwick & Jackson, 1986)
Carmichael, John, *African Eldorado – Ghana from Gold Coast to Independence* (Duckworth, 1993)
Dewar, Michael, *Brush Fire Wars – Campaigns of the British Army since 1945* (Robert Hale, 1984)
Elton, Lord, *Imperial Commonwealth* (Collins, 1945)
Fryer, Peter, *Black People in the British Empire* (Pluto, 1988)
Gourgey, Percy S., *The Indian Naval Revolt of 1946* (Orient Longman, 1996)
Holland, R. F., *Britain and the Commonwealth Alliance 1918–1939* (Macmillan, 1981)
Judd, Denis, *Empire – The British Imperial Experience from 1765 to the Present* (HarperCollins, 1996)
Lapping, Brian, *End of Empire* (Granada, 1985)
Mansbergh, Nicholas, *Problems of Wartime Co-operation and Post-War Change 1939–1952* (Oxford University Press, 1958)
Pocock, Tom, *East and West of Suez* (Bodley Head, 1986)
Rajan, Prof. M. S., *The Post-War Transformation of the Commonwealth* (Asia Publishing House, London, 1963)

Other Sources
Mohlamme, J. S., 'Soldiers Without Reward: Africans in South Africa's War' (Dept. of History, Vista University) – a paper read on 14.3.94 at the South African National Museum of Military History, Johannesburg
'Prejudice, Promises and Poverty: The Experience of Discharged and Demobilised Black South African Soldiers after the Second World War' (*South African Historical Journal*, Vol. 26, 1992)

CHAPTER NOTES

1 *The Desert War* by Alan Moorehead (Hamish Hamilton, 1965)
2 *The Second 28th* by Philip Masel (Perth, 1961)
3 Op. cit.
4 *Australia in the War of 1939–1945* (Australian War Memorial, Canberra, 1952)
5 *The Grand Alliance*, Vol. III of *The Second World War* by Winston S. Churchill (Cassell, 1950)
6 *The North African Campaign 1940–1943* by Sir William Jackson (Batsford, 1975)
7 This action features in *Night Action* by Captain Peter Dickens, DSO, DSC, RN
8 *The Hinge of Fate*, Vol. IV of *The Second World War* by Winston Churchill (Cassell, 1951)
9 Op. cit.
10 Lt-Col. Cole's correspondence and other documentation on these matters are in the Public Record Office at Kew in London, reference CO 820
11 *The Desert War*
12 Public Record Office, reference CO 820
13 Op. cit.
14 Op. cit.
15 Official transcript of the trial

INDEX

INDEX

World War I 17, 18–20, 23
Wright, Col 'Doc' 128–9, 130
Wryneck, sunk 78–9

xenophobia, British 97–9

Yalta Conference 1945 278
Yamashita, General 109

Yemen, South, independence 322–3
Yokohama, bombed 292
Yorktown, carrier 130

Zambia, independence 329
Zanzibar, independence in Tanzania 329
Zimbabwe 321
Zulus 13